Lecture Notes in Artificial Intelligence   8077

Subseries of Lecture Notes in Computer Science

Ingo J. Timm   Matthias Thimm (Eds.)

KI 2013: Advances in Artificial Intelligence

36th Annual German Conference on AI
Koblenz, Germany, September 16-20, 2013
Proceedings

 Springer

Volume Editors

Ingo J. Timm
University of Trier
Business Informatics I
54286 Trier, Germany
E-mail: ingo.timm@uni-trier.de

Matthias Thimm
University of Koblenz
Institute for Web Science and Technologies
56070 Koblenz, Germany
E-mail: thimm@uni-koblenz.de

ISSN 0302-9743   e-ISSN 1611-3349
ISBN 978-3-642-40941-7   e-ISBN 978-3-642-40942-4
DOI 10.1007/978-3-642-40942-4
Springer Heidelberg New York Dordrecht London

Library of Congress Control Number: 2013947742

CR Subject Classification (1998): I.2.4, I.2.6, I.2.10-11, H.3.3-4, I.6.3, H.5.2-3, H.5.5, F.4.1, F.1.1

LNCS Sublibrary: SL 7 – Artificial Intelligence

Typesetting: Camera-ready by author, data conversion by Scientific Publishing Services, Chennai, India

Printed on acid-free paper

Springer is part of Springer Science+Business Media (www.springer.com)

Preface

This volume contains the conference proceedings of the 36th Annual German Conference on Artificial Intelligence (KI 2013) held September 16-20, 2013, at University of Koblenz, Germany. Initiated by the German Workshop on AI (GWAI) in 1975, the annual German Conference on Artificial Intelligence is the premier forum for German research in artificial intelligence, and attracts numerous international guests, too. The conference traditionally brings together academic and industrial researchers from all areas of AI. The conference is organized by the Special Interest Group on Artificial Intelligence of the German Informatics Society (Fachbereich Künstliche Intelligenz der Gesellschaft für Informatik e.V.). Next to KI 2013, five co-located conferences took place, including the 43rd annual German conference on informatics (Informatik2013) and the 11th MATES 2013 (German Conference on Multi-Agent System Technologies), which is jointly held with the 4th JAWS (Joint Agent Workshops in Synergy). Together, this makes a perfect basis for interesting discussions and information exchange within the AI community and to the other communities.

Over the years, artificial intelligence has become a major field in computer science in Germany, involving numerous successful projects and applications. Its applications and methods have influenced many domains and research areas, like business informatics, logistics, eHumanities, finance, cognitive sciences, and medicine. These applications become feasible on the basis of sophisticated theoretical and methodological efforts and successes in the German AI community. Thus, the theme of KI 2013 is "From Research to Innovation and Practical Applications".

The review process was very selective. Out of 70 contributions submitted this year, the international Program Committee accepted 24 as full papers and 8 conditionally as short (poster) papers leading to an acceptance ratio of 46%. Each submission received at least three reviews and the members of the Program Committee invested considerable effort in the discussion of the submissions. The contributions cover a range of topics from agents, robotics, cognitive sciences, machine learning, swarm intelligence, planning, knowledge modeling, reasoning, and ontologies.

Together with MATES 2013, we were pleased to host four prominent invited speakers in the agent and AI community: "The Headaches of a Negotiation Support Agent" by Catholjin M. Jonker from TU Delft, "AI – Research and the Future of Automobiles" by Raúl Rojas from the Free University Berlin, and "Autonomous Systems Inspired by Biology" by Gerhard Weiss from Maastricht University.

In the first two days of the conference, five workshops with many additional presentations took place:

- Gabriele Kern-Isberner and Christoph Beierle organized the 4th Workshop on Dynamics of Knowledge and Belief
- Dirk Reichardt organized the 7th Workshop on Emotion and Computing – Current Research and Future Impact
- Joachim Baumeister and Grzegrz J. Nalepa organized the International Workshop on Knowledge Engineering and Software Engineering
- Stefan Edelkamp, Bernd Schattenberg and Jürgen Sauer organized the 27th Workshop on "Planen, Scheduling und Konfigurieren, Entwerfen"
- Marco Ragni, Michael Raschke and Frieder Stolzenburg organized the Workshop on Visual and Spatial Cognition

Additionally, together with the Informatik 2013, a doctoral mentoring program was offered at the beginning of the conference.

We would like to thank the authors and reviewers for their excellent work. Furthermore, we would like to thank Björn Pelzer, Ralf Schepers, Fabian Lorig, Ruth Ehrenstein, and Sarah Piller for their support in the organization of KI 2013. As chairs of the special interest group on AI (GI Fachbereich Künstliche Intelligenz), Antonio Krüger and Stefan Wölfl provided invaluable support in organizing KI 2013 – thank you. Last but not least, we thank the members of the KI 2013 Organizing Committee:

- Stefan Kirn
  (Industry Chair, University of Hohenheim)
- Andreas D. Lattner
  (Doctorial Consortium Chair, Goethe University Frankfurt)
- Jürgen Sauer
  (Tutorial Chair, University of Oldenburg)
- Ute Schmid
  (Workshop Chair, University of Bamberg)

July 2013   Ingo J. Timm
                                                      Matthias Thimm

Organization

General Chair

Ingo J. Timm   University of Trier, Germany

Local Chair

Matthias Thimm   University of Koblenz-Landau, Germany

Workshop Chair

Ute Schmid   University of Bamberg, Germany

Tutorial Chair

Jürgen Sauer   University of Oldenburg, Germany

Industry Chair

Stefan Kirn   University of Hohenheim, Germany

Doctoral Consortium Chair

Andreas D. Lattner   Goethe University Frankfurt, Germany

Program Committee

Klaus-Dieter Althoff	German Research Center for Artificial Intelligence (DFKI), Germany
Tamim Asfour	Karlsruhe Institute of Technology (KIT), Germany
Franz Baader	TU Dresden, Germany
Joscha Bach	Klayo AG, Berlin, Germany
Sven Behnke	University of Bonn, Germany
Ralph Bergmann	University of Trier, Germany
Philipp Cimiano	University of Bielefeld, Germany
Eliseo Clementini	University of L'Aquila, Italy
Cristobal Curio	Max Planck Institute for Biological Cybernetics, Germany

Kerstin Dautenhahn	University of Hertfordshire, UK
Frank Dylla	University of Bremen, Germany
Stefan Funke	University of Stuttgart, Germany
Johannes Fürnkranz	TU Darmstadt, Germany
Christopher W Geib	University of Edinburgh, UK
Birte Glimm	University of Ulm, Germany
Björn Gottfried	TZI, University of Bremen, Germany
Martin Günther	University of Osnabrück, Germany
Jens-Steffen Gutmann	Evolution Robotics / iRobot, USA
Malte Helmert	University of Basel, Switzerland
Otthein Herzog	TZI, University of Bremen, Germany
Gabriele Kern-Isberner	TU Dortmund, Germany
Stefan Kirn	University of Hohenheim, Germany
Thomas Kirste	University of Rostock, Germany
Alexander Kleiner	Linköping University, Sweden
Roman Kontchakov	Birkbeck College, UK
Oliver Kramer	University of Oldenburg, Germany
Ralf Krestel	Universtiy of California, Irvine, USA
Torsten Kroeger	Stanford University, USA
Kai-Uwe Kuehnberger	University of Osnabrück, Germany
Bogdan Kwolek	AGH University of Science and Technology, Poland
Gerhard Lakemeyer	RWTH Aachen University, Germany
Andreas Lattner	Goethe University Frankfurt, Germany
Volker Lohweg	inIT - Institute Industrial IT, Germany
Benedikt Löwe	Universiteit van Amsterdam, The Netherlands
Robert Mattmüller	University of Freiburg, Germany
Ralf Möller	TU Hamburg-Harburg, Germany
Marco Ragni	University of Freiburg, Germany
Jochen Renz	Australian National University, Australia
Benjamin Satzger	Microsoft, USA
Jürgen Sauer	University of Oldenburg, Germany
Bernd Schattenberg	University of Ulm, Germany
Malte Schilling	CITEC Bielefeld, Germany
Ute Schmid	University of Bamberg, Germany
Lutz Schröder	Friedrich-Alexander-Universität Erlangen-Nürnberg, Germany
René Schumann	HES-SO, Switzerland
Jan-Georg Smaus	Université de Toulouse, France
Daniel Sonntag	German Research Center for Artificial Intelligence (DFKI), Germany
Luciano Spinello	University of Freiburg, Germany
Steffen Staab	University of Koblenz-Landau, Germany
Heiner Stuckenschmidt	University of Mannheim, Germany
Matthias Thimm	University of Koblenz-Landau, Germany
Ingo J. Timm	University of Trier, Germany

Johanna Völker   University of Mannheim, Germany
Toby Walsh   NICTA and UNSW, Australia
Thomas Wiemann   University of Osnabrück, Germany
Stefan Wölfl   University of Freiburg, Germany
Diedrich Wolter   University of Bremen, Germany

Additional Reviewers

Holger Andreas   Denis Ponomaryov
Timothy Cerexhe   Marvin Schiller
Daniel Fleischhacker   Christoph Schwering
Johannes Knopp

Invited Talks

Autonomous Systems Inspired by Biology

Gerhard Weiss

Department of Knowledge Engineering
Maastricht University, 6211 LK Maastricht, The Netherlands
gerhard.weiss@maastrichtuniversity.nl

Abstract. We can currently see the rapid formation of an exciting multidisciplinary field focusing on the application of biological principles and mechanisms to develop autonomous systems – software agents and robots – that act highly flexible and robust in the face of environmental contingency and uncertainty. In this talk I will give an overview of various aspects of this field. The state of the art will be illustrated with divers examples of bio-inspired approaches to system adaptivity, functional and structural optimization, collective and swarm behavior, locomotion, sensor-motor control, and (co)evolution. A focus will be on representative work on biologically inspired autonomous systems done at the Swarmlab of Maastricht University, including recent research motivated by the behavior of social insects such as bees and ants.

About the Speaker

Gerhard Weiss is full professor of artificial intelligence and computer science and Head of the Department of Knowledge Engineering (DKE), Faculty of Humanities and Sciences, Maastricht University. Before joining Maastricht University in 2009, he was the Scientific Director of Software Competence Center Hagenberg GmbH, Austria, and Assistant Professor at the Department of Computer Science of Technical University Munich, Germany. He received his PhD (Dr. rer. nat.) in computer science from Technical University Munich and his Habilitation degree from Johannes-Kepler University Linz, Austria. His main interests are in the foundations and in practical applications of artificial intelligence, multi-agent technology, and autonomous and cooperative systems. He is editorial board member of several journals related to his research fields, and he has been in the program and steering committees of various international conferences and workshops. He was a Board member of the International Foundation for Autonomous Agents and Multi-agent Systems (IFAAMAS) and of two European networks of excellence (Agentlink and Exystence). Professor Weiss has served as a reviewer for several national, European and international research funding organizations and has been engaged as a scientific consultant and advisor for industry. See also http://www.weiss-gerhard.info.

AI – Research and the Future of Automobiles

Raúl Rojas

Department of Mathematics and Computer Science
Free University of Berlin, 14195 Berlin, Germany
Raul.Rojas@fu-berlin.de

Abstract. In this talk I will reflect on the development of autonomous cars during the last ten years, and also on the open research problems for the next decade. As we will see, accurate sensing is not a problem for mobile robots. Laser scanners and video cameras provide more than enough data for the purposes of safe navigation. However, making sense of this data is still a hard problem in some situations in real traffic. Humans are good at recognizing and predicting intentions and behavior – computers are still bad at this task. I will show videos of our experiments in the field driving in three countries and will speculate about the possible avenues of research for making robotic cars a reality.

About the Speaker

Raúl Rojas has been a full professor of Artificial Intelligence and Robotics since 1997 at Freie Universität Berlin. He received his PhD and venia legendi (habilitation) at this university. He studied mathematics and physics, as well as economics, in Mexico City. After the habilitation, he was appointed visiting professor in Viena and later professor of Artificial Intelligence at Martin-Luther-University Halle (1994-1997). Raúl Rojas' initial research was dedicated to the design and the construction of Prolog computers for Artificial Intelligence at GMD-FIRST. Today, he is working on a broad field of pattern recognition topics with special focus on neural networks and developing robots for various applications. With the FU-Fighters he won the world championship in RoboCup in 2004 and 2005. From 2006 on, he and his team have been developing autonomous vehicles, which were certified for city traffic in 2011. For his research on computer vision, Raúl Rojas received the Technology Transfer Award from the Technologiestiftung Berlin (Foundation for Innovation and Technology). He was appointed a member of the Mexican Academy of Sciences in 2011.

The Headaches of a Negotiation Support Agent

Catholijn M. Jonker

Department of Intelligent Systems
Delft University of Technology, 2628 CD Delft, The Netherlands
C.M.Jonker@tudelft.nl

Abstract. Negotiation is a complex process as it poses challenges to the negotiator on both the emotional plane as well as on the computational plane. Human negotiators are known to leave money on the table, have trouble getting a clear view of their own preferences and those of their negotiation partner, and sometimes find it difficult to deal with their own emotions and those of their negotiation partner. In this talk I will briefly outline the Pocket Negotiator project and it's prototype. I will show some solutions developed during the project and will discuss some of the open challenges. In terms of research fields, I combine Artificial Intelligence, Affective Computing, and Human Computer Interaction.

To find out more about the Pocket Negotiator project, please visit http://mmi.tudelft.nl/negotiation/index.php/Pocket_Negotiator

To try out the prototype, please use Chrome or FireFox to visit http://ii.tudelft.nl:8080/PocketNegotiator/index.jsp

About the Speaker

Catholijn Jonker (1967) is full professor of Man-Machine Interaction at the Faculty of Electrical Engineering, Mathematics and Computer Science of the Delft University of Technology. She studied computer science, and did her PhD studies at Utrecht University. After a post-doc position in Bern, Switzerland, she became assistant (later associate) professor at the Department of Artificial Intelligence of the Vrije Universiteit Amsterdam. From September 2004 until September 2006 she was a full professor of Artificial Intelligence / Cognitive Science at the Nijmegen Institute of Cognition and Information of the Radboud University Nijmegen. She chaired De Jonge Akademie (Young Academy) of the KNAW (The Royal Netherlands Society of Arts and Sciences) in 2005 and 2006, and she was a member of the same organization from 2005 to 2010. She is a board member of the National Network Female Professors (LNVH) in The Netherlands. Her publications address cognitive processes and concepts such as trust, negotiation, teamwork and the dynamics of individual agents and organizations. In Delft she works with an interdisciplinary team to create synergy between humans and technology by understanding, shaping and using fundamentals of intelligence and interaction. End 2007 her NWO-STW VICI project "Pocket Negotiator" was awarded. In this project she develops intelligent decision support systems for negotiation. See also http://ii.tudelft.nl/~catholijn.

Table of Contents

Using State-Based Planning Heuristics for Partial-Order Causal-Link Planning

Pascal Bercher, Thomas Geier, and Susanne Biundo

Institute of Artificial Intelligence,
Ulm University, D-89069 Ulm, Germany
firstName.lastName@uni-ulm.de

Abstract. We present a technique which allows partial-order causal-link (POCL) planning systems to use heuristics known from state-based planning to guide their search.

The technique encodes a given partially ordered partial plan as a new classical planning problem that yields the same set of solutions reachable from the given partial plan. As heuristic estimate of the given partial plan a state-based heuristic can be used estimating the goal distance of the initial state in the encoded problem. This technique also provides the first *admissible* heuristics for POCL planning, simply by using admissible heuristics from state-based planning. To show the potential of our technique, we conducted experiments where we compared two of the currently strongest heuristics from state-based planning with two of the currently best-informed heuristics from POCL planning.

1 Introduction

In most of today's classical planning approaches, problems are solved by informed (heuristic) progression search in the space of states. One reason for the success of this approach is the availability of highly informed heuristics performing a goal-distance estimate for a given state. In contrast, search nodes in plan-based search correspond to partially ordered partial plans; thus, the heuristics known from state-based planning are not directly applicable to plan-based search techniques.

One of the most important representatives of plan-based search is partial-order causal-link (POCL) planning [13,17]. POCL planning benefits from its least-commitment principle enforcing decisions during planning only if necessary. For instance, POCL planning can be done *lifted* thereby avoiding premature variable bindings. POCL planning has greater flexibility at plan execution time [14] and eases the integration for handling resource or temporal constraints and durative actions [20,3]. Its knowledge-rich plans furthermore enable the generation of formally sound plan explanations [19].

However, developing well-informed heuristics for POCL planning is a challenging task [21]; thus, heuristics are still rare. To address this shortcoming, we propose a technique which allows to use heuristics already known from state-based search in POCL planning, rather than developing *new* heuristics.

I.J. Timm and M. Thimm (Eds.): KI 2013, LNAI 8077, pp. 1–12, 2013.

This technique works by transforming a current search node, i.e., a partially ordered partial plan, into a new planning problem, into which the given partial plan is completely encoded, s.t. solutions for the new problem correspond to solutions reachable from the encoded search node. Then, we evaluate the heuristic estimate of the transformed problem's initial state using any heuristic known from state-based search, and use it as heuristic estimate of the search node. As it turns out, not every state-based heuristic works with our technique, but we obtained promising empirical results for some of them.

The remainder of the paper is structured as follows: the next section is devoted to the problem formalization. Section 3 introduces the proposed transformation. In Section 4, we discuss several issues and questions arising when using the technique in practice. In Section 5, we evaluate our approach by comparing our POCL planning system using four different heuristics: two of them are the currently best-informed heuristics known for POCL planning, whereas the other two use state-of-the-art heuristics known from state-based planning in combination with our problem encoding. Finally, Section 6 concludes the paper.

2   POCL Planning

A planning domain is a tuple $\mathcal{D} = \langle \mathcal{V}, \mathcal{A} \rangle$, where $\mathcal{V}$ is a finite set of boolean *state variables*, $\mathcal{S} = 2^{\mathcal{V}}$ is the set of *states*, and $\mathcal{A}$ is a finite set of *actions*, each having the form (pre, add, del), where $pre, add, del \subseteq \mathcal{V}$. An action is applicable in a state $s \in \mathcal{S}$ if its precondition pre holds in s, i.e., $pre \subseteq s$. Its application generates the state $(s \setminus del) \cup add$. The applicability and application of action sequences is defined as usual. A *planning problem* in STRIPS notation [5] is a tuple $\pi = \langle \mathcal{D}, s_{init}, g \rangle$ with $s_{init} \in \mathcal{S}$ being the *initial state* and $g \subseteq \mathcal{V}$ being the *goal description*. A *solution* to π is an applicable action sequence starting in s_{init} and generating a state $s \supseteq g$ that satisfies the goal condition.

POCL planning is a technique that solves planning problems via search in the space of partial plans. A *partial plan* is a tuple $(PS, \prec, CL)$. PS is a set of plan steps, each being a pair $l{:}a$ with an action $a \in \mathcal{A}$ and a unique label $l \in L$ with L being an infinite set of label symbols to differentiate multiple occurrences of the same action within a partial plan. The set $\prec \subset L \times L$ represents ordering constraints and induces a strict partial order on the plan steps in PS. CL is a set of causal links. A causal link $(l, v, l') \in L \times \mathcal{V} \times L$ testifies that the precondition $v \in \mathcal{V}$ of the plan step with label l' (called the *consumer*) is provided by the action with label l (called the *producer*). That is, if $l{:}(pre, add, del) \in PS$, $l'{:}(pre', add', del') \in PS$, and $(l, v, l') \in CL$, then $v \in add$ and $v \in pre'$. Furthermore, we demand $l \prec l'$ if $(l, v, l') \in CL$.

Now, π can be represented as a POCL planning problem $\langle \mathcal{D}, P_{init} \rangle$, where $P_{init} := (\{l_0{:}a_0, l_\infty{:}a_\infty\}, \{(l_0, l_\infty)\}, \emptyset)$ is the *initial partial plan*. The actions a_0 and a_∞ encode the initial state and goal description: a_0 has no precondition and s_{init} as add effect and a_∞ has g as precondition and no effects. A solution to such a problem is a partial plan P with no *flaws*. Flaws represent plan elements violating solution criteria. An *open precondition* flaw is a tuple $(v, l) \in \mathcal{V} \times L$

specifying that the precondition v of the plan step with label l is not yet protected by a causal link. A *causal threat* flaw is a tuple $(l, (l', v, l'')) \in L \times CL$ specifying that the plan step $l{:}(pre, add, del)$ with $v \in del$ may be ordered between the plan steps with label l' and l''. We say, the plan step with label l *threatens* the causal link (l', v, l''), since it might undo its protected condition v.

If a partial plan P has no flaws, every linearization of its plan steps respecting its ordering constraints is a solution to the planning problem in STRIPS notation. Hence, P is called a solution to the corresponding POCL problem.

POCL planning can be regarded as a refinement procedure [12], since it *refines* the initial partial plan P_{init} step-wise until a solution is generated. The algorithm works as follows [22]. First, a most-promising partial plan P is selected based on heuristics estimating the goal-distance or quality of P. Given such a partial plan P, a flaw selection function selects one of its flaws and resolves it. For that end, all *modifications* are applied, which are all possibilities to resolve the given flaw. A causal threat flaw $(l, (l', v, l'')) \in \mathcal{F}_{CausalThreat}$ can only be resolved by *promotion* or *demotion*. These modifications promote the plan step with label l before the one with label l', and demote it behind the one with label l'', respectively. An open precondition flaw $(v, l) \in \mathcal{F}_{OpenPrecondition}$ can only be resolved by inserting a causal link (l', v, l) which protects the open precondition v. This can be done either by using a plan step already present in the current partial plan, or by a new action from $\mathcal{A}$. The two-stage procedure of selecting a partial plan, calculating its flaws, and selecting and resolving a flaw is repeated until a partial plan P without flaws is generated. Hence, P is a solution to the POCL planning problem and returned.

3   Using State-Based Heuristics for POCL Planning

We encode a partially ordered partial plan into a new STRIPS planning problem. A similar encoding was already proposed by Ramírez and Geffner [18]. However, their encoding was used in the context of plan recognition for compiling observations away and it does not feature a partial order, causal links, nor did they state formal properties.

Given a planning problem in STRIPS notation $\pi = \langle \langle \mathcal{V}, \mathcal{A} \rangle, s_{init}, g \rangle$ and a partial plan $P = (PS, \prec, CL)$, let $enc_{plan}(P, \pi) = \langle \langle \mathcal{V}', \mathcal{A}' \rangle, s'_{init}, g' \rangle$ be the *encoding* of P and π with:

$$\mathcal{V}' := \mathcal{V} \cup \{l_-, l_+ \mid l{:}a \in PS, l \notin \{l_0, l_\infty\}\}$$
$$\mathcal{A}' := \mathcal{A} \cup \{enc_{planStep}(l{:}a, \prec) \mid l{:}a \in PS, l \notin \{l_0, l_\infty\}\}, \text{ with}$$
$$enc_{planStep}(l{:}(pre, add, del), \prec)$$
$$:= (pre \cup \{l_-\} \cup \{l'_+ \mid l' \prec l, l' \neq l_0\}, add \cup \{l_+\}, del \cup \{l_-\}),$$
$$s'_{init} := s_{init} \cup \{l_- \mid l{:}a \in PS, l \notin \{l_0, l_\infty\}\}$$
$$g' := g \cup \{l_+ \mid l{:}a \in PS, l \notin \{l_0, l_\infty\}\}$$

The resulting problem subsumes the original one and extends it in the following way: all plan steps in P become additional actions in $\mathcal{A}'$ (we do not encode the artificial start and end actions, since their purpose is already reflected by the initial state and goal description). For each plan step $l{:}a$, we introduce two indicator variables l_- and l_+ that encode that $l{:}a$ has not or has been executed. Initially, none of the actions representing the encoding of these plan steps are marked as executed and the (additional) goal is to execute all of them. Furthermore, these actions use the indicator variables to ensure that they can only be executed in an order consistent with the partial order of the partial plan.

Although the encoding can be done in linear time [1], the effort for evaluating heuristics might increase as search progresses, since the resulting problem is of larger size than the original one. We will discuss this issue in the next section.

For the sake of simplicity, the formally specified function enc_{plan} ignores causal links. Since causal links induce additional constraints on a partial plan (cf. Section 2), compiling them away, too, captures even more information. The compilation can be done as follows: let (l_1, v, l_2) be a causal link, $l_1{:}a_1$ and $l_2{:}a_2$ the two corresponding plan steps, and a'_1 and a'_2 their encodings within $\mathcal{A}'$. We need to ensure that no action with v as delete effect can be inserted between a'_1 and a'_2. To that end, we introduce a counter variable $count(v)$ which counts how many causal links with the protected condition v are "currently active".[1] To update that counter correctly, any (encoded) action producing a causal link with condition v has the precondition $count(v) = i$ and the effect $count(v) = i + 1$. Analogously, any (encoded) action consuming such a causal link has the precondition $count(v) = i$ and the effect $count(v) = i - 1$. Then, any (encoded and non-encoded) action having v in its delete list has the precondition $count(v) = 0$. Note that the original planning problem does not need to be changed for every partial plan, although we need to add the precondition $count(v) = 0$ to each action for which there is a causal link (l_1, v, l_2) in the current partial plan. We can process the domain only *once* by adding the precondition $count(v) = 0$ to any action for any state variable v in advance. Concerning the overall runtime for compiling away causal links, assume a' being a (compiled) action consuming n and providing m causal links. Then, $|CL|^{(n+m)}$ actions must be created to provide all possible combinations of the *count* variables, where CL is the set of causal links of the partial plan to be encoded. The compilation is therefore exponential in the maximal number of preconditions and effects of all actions. Hence, assuming the planning *domain* is given in advance, our compilation is *polynomial*. In practice, it is also polynomial if the domain is not given in advance, because the maximal number of preconditions and effects is usually bounded by a small constant and does not grow with the domain description.

Before we can state the central property of the transformed problem, we need some further definitions. Let $P = (PS, \prec, CL)$ be a partial plan. Then, $ref(P) := \{\langle PS', \prec', CL' \rangle \mid PS' \supseteq PS, \prec' \supseteq \prec, CL' \supseteq CL\}$ is called the set of all *refinements* of P, i.e., the set of all partial plans which can be derived from P

---

[1] For the sake of simplicity, we use functions to describe the counter. Since these functions are simple increment and decrement operations, converting them into the STRIPS formalism is possible in linear time w.r.t. their maximum value which is bound by the number of causal links in the given partial plan.

by adding plan elements. Let $sol(\pi)$ be the set of all *solution* plans of π. We call $sol(\pi, P) := sol(\pi) \cap ref(P)$ the set of all solutions of π refining P.

Now, we define mappings to transform partial plans derived from the planning problem $enc_{plan}(P, \pi)$ to partial plans from the original planning problem π.[2] The functions $dec_{planStep}(l{:}(pre, add, del), \mathcal{V}) := l{:}(pre \cap \mathcal{V}, add \cap \mathcal{V}, del \cap \mathcal{V})$ and $dec_{plan}(\langle PS, \prec, CL \rangle, \pi) := \langle \{dec_{planStep}(l{:}a, \mathcal{V}) \mid l{:}a \in PS\}, \prec, \{(l, v, l') \in CL \mid v \in \mathcal{V}\}\rangle$ are called the *decoding* of a plan step and a partial plan, respectively. Thus, given a partial plan P' from the planning problem $enc_{plan}(P, \pi)$, $dec_{plan}(P', \pi)$ eliminates the additional variables and causal links used by the encoding.

The following proposition states that every solution of the original planning problem, which is also a refinement of the given partial plan, does also exist as a solution for the encoded problem and, furthermore, the converse holds as well: every solution of the encoded problem can be decoded into a solution of the original one, which is a refinement of the given partial plan, too. Thus, the set of solutions of the transformed planning problem is identical to the set of solutions of the original problem, reachable from the current partial plan.

Proposition 1 *Let π be a planning problem and P a partial plan. It holds:*

- *if there is a partial plan P_{sol}, s.t. $P_{sol} \in sol(\pi, P)$, then there exists a partial plan P'_{sol} with $P'_{sol} \in sol(enc_{plan}(P, \pi))$ and $dec_{plan}(P'_{sol}, \pi) = P_{sol}$*
- *if there is a partial plan P'_{sol}, s.t. $P'_{sol} \in sol(enc_{plan}(P, \pi))$, then $dec_{plan}(P'_{sol}, \pi) \in sol(\pi, P)$*

Assuming the plan quality is based on action costs, we can use that proposition to find a heuristic function $h(\pi, P)$ that estimates the goal distance in π from the *partial plan* P by transforming π and P into the planning problem $\pi' = enc_{plan}(P, \pi)$ and setting $h(\pi, P) := \max\{h_{sb}(\pi', s'_{init}) - cost(P), 0\}$, where h_{sb} is any heuristic that takes a *state* as input. We need to subtract the action costs of P, since a heuristic estimate for P *excludes* the actions already present in P, whereas a heuristic estimate for s'_{init} should detect the necessity of inserting them and hence *includes* their cost as well. Taking the maximum of that value and zero is done in case the heuristic is overly positive and returns an estimated cost value lower than those of the actions already present in P.

Since, due to Proposition 1, the set of solutions of π is isomorphic to the solutions of π', even regarding action costs, using an admissible heuristic h_{sb} consequently makes $h(\pi, P)$ admissible, too. This is an interesting property of our approach, since there are no admissible POCL heuristics known to the literature.

Example. Let $\pi = \langle \langle \mathcal{V}, \mathcal{A} \rangle, s_{init}, g \rangle$ be a planning problem with $\mathcal{V} := \{a, b, c\}$, $\mathcal{A} := \{(\{b\}, \{a\}, \{b\}), (\{a\}, \{c\}, \{a\})\}$, $s_{init} := \{a, b\}$, and $g := \{a, c\}$. Let P be a partial plan which was obtained by a POCL algorithm as depicted below:

---

[2] For the sake of simplicity, our decoding assumes that no causal links were compiled away. Decoding the encoded causal links is straight-forward.

The arrows indicate causal links and A^1 and A^2 the actions of $\mathcal{A}$. P has only one open precondition: (a, l_∞), which encodes the last remaining goal condition.

The transformed problem, without compiling away causal links, is given by $enc_{plan}(P, \pi) = \langle \langle \mathcal{V}', \mathcal{A}' \rangle, s'_{init}, g' \rangle$ with:

$$\mathcal{V}' := \{a, b, c, l_+^1, l_-^1, l_+^2, l_-^2\}$$
$$\mathcal{A}' := \{(\{b\}, \{a\}, \{b\}\}), \qquad\qquad // A^1$$
$$(\{b, l_-^2\}, \{a, l_+^2\}, \{b, l_-^2\}), \qquad // enc(l^2{:}A^1)$$
$$(\{a\}, \{c\}, \{a\}), \qquad\qquad\qquad // A^2$$
$$(\{a, l_-^1, l_+^2\}, \{c, l_+^1\}, \{a, l_-^1\})\} \qquad // enc(l^1{:}A^2)$$
$$s'_{init} := \{a, b, l_-^1, l_-^2\}$$
$$g' := \{a, c, l_+^1, l_+^2\}$$

A heuristic estimate based on the transformed problem may incorporate the negative effects of $l^2{:}A^1$ and $l^1{:}A^2$ and has thus the potential to discover the partial plan/state to be invalid and thus prune the search space.

4   Discussion

Relaxation. Not every state-based heuristic is suited for our proposed approach. In order to determine how informed a chosen heuristic function is when used with our technique, one has to investigate the effect of the (heuristic-dependent) relaxation on the actions in $\mathcal{A}_{new} := \mathcal{A}' \setminus \mathcal{A}$. The actions in $\mathcal{A}_{new}$ (together with the additional goals) encode the planning progress so far, just like the current state does in state-based planning. Thus, relaxing them can have a strong impact on the resulting heuristic values. For instance, in our experiments, we noticed that the FF heuristic [10] always obtains the same estimates for the encoded problems of all search nodes making the heuristic blind.

Preprocessing. Some heuristics, like merge and shrink abstraction (M&S) [4,9], perform a preprocessing step before the actual search and make up for it when retrieving each single heuristic value. Since we obtain a new planning problem for each single partial plan, a naive approach using this kind of heuristics would also perform that preprocessing in every search node, which is obviously not beneficial (and no *pre*-processing). Thus, given a specific heuristic, one has to investigate whether certain preprocessing steps can be done only *once* and then updated per partial plan if necessary.

Runtime. Although the transformation itself can be done efficiently, the time of evaluating heuristics might increase with the size of the encoded problem. At first glance, this might seem a strange property, since one would expect the heuristic calculation time either to remain constant (as for abstraction heuristics [4,9]) or to *decrease* (as for the add or FF heuristics [6,10]), as a partial plan comes closer to a solution. However, since partial plans are complex structures and many interesting decision problems involving them are NP hard w.r.t. their size [15], it is not surprising that evaluating heuristic estimates becomes more expensive as partial plans grow in size.

Ground Planning. The presentation of the proposed transformation in the paper assumes a ground problem representation. However, the approach also works for lifted planning without alterations to the encoding function. In lifted planning [22], the given partial plan is only *partially* ground, i.e., some action parameters are bound to constants, and the remaining ones are either unconstrained, codesignated or non-codesignated. Using the same encoding process but ignoring these designation constraints already works as described, since the initial state of the resulting encoded planning problem is still ground and evaluating its heuristic estimate is thus possible without alterations. Encoding the designation constraints is also possible, but ignoring them is just a problem relaxation as is ignoring causal links.

5   Evaluation

We implemented the described encoding without compiling away causal links in our POCL planning system. We compare the performance of planning using the encoding with two state-of-the-art state-based heuristics against the currently best-informed POCL heuristics. We also show results for a state-based planner.

The used POCL planner is implemented in Java®. As search strategy, we use weighted A* with weight 2. That is, a partial plan p with minimal f value is selected, given by $f(p) := g(p) + 2 * h(p)$ with $g(p)$ being the cost of p and $h(p)$ being its heuristic estimate. In cases where several partial plans have the same f value, we break ties by selecting a partial plan with higher cost; remaining ties are broken by the *LIFO* strategy thereby preferring the newest partial plan. As flaw selection function, we use a sequence of two flaw selection strategies. The first strategy prefers newest flaws (where all flaws detected in the same plan are regarded equally new). On a tie, we then use the *Least Cost Flaw Repair* strategy [11], which selects a flaw for which there are the least number of modifications, thereby minimizing the branching factor. Remaining ties are broken by chance. We configured our system to plan ground, because our current implementation only supports a ground problem encoding.

As POCL heuristics, we selected the two currently best-informed heuristics: the *Relax Heuristic* [16] and the *Additive Heuristic for POCL planning* [22]. They are adaptations of the *FF heuristic* [10] and the *add heuristic* [6], respectively. Both heuristics identify the open preconditions of the current partial plan and estimate the action costs to achieve them based on delete relaxation using a planning graph [2]. These heuristics are implemented natively in our system.[3]

---

[3] Our implementation of the Relax Heuristic takes into account *all* action costs in a relaxed plan, whereas the original version assumes cost 0 for all actions already present. We used our variant for the experiments, since it solved more problems than the original version.

As state-based heuristics, we chose the *LM-Cut* heuristic [8], which is a landmark-based heuristic and an admissible approximation to h^+, and the *Merge and Shrink* (M&S) heuristic [4,9], which is an abstraction-based heuristic.

To evaluate heuristics from state-based planning, we chose to use an existing implementation. When planning using state-based heuristics, the POCL planner creates a domain and problem PDDL file for each search node encoding the corresponding partial plan, but ignoring causal links. We then use a modified version of the Fast Downward planning system [7] that exits after calculating the heuristic value for the initial state. While this approach saved us much implementation work, the obtained results are to be interpreted with care, since the process of calling another planning system in each search node is rather time-consuming: while the average runtime of the Add and Relax heuristics is at most 4 ms per search node over all evaluated problems, the LM-Cut heuristic has a mean runtime of 958 ms and a median of 225 ms. For the M&S heuristic[4], the mean is 7,500 ms and the median 542 ms. The very high runtimes of M&S are contributed to the fact that it performs a preprocessing step for every search node. Of course, in a native implementation of that heuristic in combination with our problem encoding, one would have to investigate whether an incremental preprocessing is possible as discussed in the last section.

Thus, the results using the state-based configurations are bound to be dominated by all others in terms of solved instances and runtime. Therefore, we focus our evaluation on the quality of the heuristics measured by the size of the produced search space in case a solution was found.

We evaluate on the non-temporal STRIPS problems taken from the International Planning Competitions (IPC) 1 to 5. Domains from the IPC 6 and 7 use action costs, which our system does not support. Missing domains from the IPC 1 to 5 use language features that cannot be handled either by our planner or by Fast Downward. From each domain we chose a number of instances consecutively, beginning with the smallest ones. The used domains and problems are given in Table 1; furthermore, the table contains the number of solved instances per domain by any of the four configurations. We also included results for the state-based planner Fast Downward. This planner, which is implemented in C++, clearly dominates our Java based POCL planner. For one problem, Fast Downward with M&S created 737 million nodes while our POCL planner created at most 2.9 million nodes, both for Add and Relax heuristic. Despite this discrepancy, the performance of the POCL planner using the Add heuristic surpasses Fast Downward using M&S in some domains.

The POCL planner was given 15 minutes of CPU time and 2GB of memory for each problem. For the configurations using the encoding, the call to Fast Downward also counts towards the time limit (including time spent generating the additional PDDL files), but not towards the memory limit. For the comparison with Fast Downward, we used a 15 minute wall time limit and no memory limit. All experiments were run on a 12 core Intel Xeon® with 2.4GHz.

---

[4] We chose f-preserving abstractions and 1500 abstract states. We chose a rather low number of abstract states to speed up the calculation time.

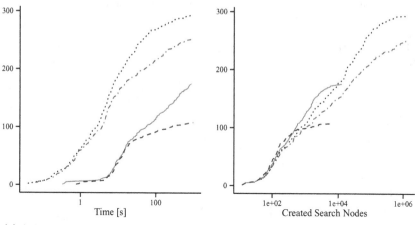

(a) Solved instances over CPU time.   (b) Solved instances over created nodes.

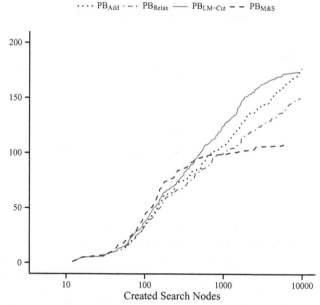

(c) Enlarged view of 1b; solved instances over created nodes.

Fig. 1. These plots show the number of solved instances on their y-axis, while the x-axis shows either CPU time or the number of created nodes. The configurations PB_{Add} and PB_{Relax} stand for POCL planning using the Add or the Relax heuristic, respectively. $PB_{LM\text{-}Cut}$ and $PB_{M\&S}$ denote POCL planning using the LM-Cut and the Merge and Shrink heuristic.

Table 1. This table gives the number of used problems per domain (n) and the number of solved instances per configuration and domain. The first configurations use our *plan-based* configurations and the right-most columns are the results of the *state-based* Fast Downward planner. All problems in the same block belong to the same IPC, from 1 to 5. A bold entry specifies the most number of solved instances among all configurations of the POCL planning system.

Domain	n	PB$_{Add}$	PB$_{Relax}$	PB$_{LM\text{-}Cut}$	PB$_{M\&S}$	SB$_{LM\text{-}Cut}$	SB$_{M\&S}$
grid	5	**0**	**0**	**0**	**0**	2	2
gripper	20	14	**20**	1	1	20	8
logistics	20	**16**	15	6	0	16	1
movie	30	**30**	**30**	**30**	**30**	30	30
mystery	20	8	**10**	5	5	13	13
mystery-prime	20	3	**4**	2	1	12	12
blocks	21	2	3	3	**5**	21	21
logistics	28	**28**	**28**	27	5	28	15
miconic	100	**100**	53	65	29	100	68
depot	22	**2**	**2**	1	1	11	7
driverlog	20	7	**9**	3	3	15	12
freecell	20	**0**	**0**	**0**	**0**	6	6
rover	20	**20**	19	9	5	18	8
zeno-travel	20	4	4	3	**5**	16	13
airport	20	**18**	15	6	5	20	18
pipesworld-noTankage	20	**8**	5	1	1	18	19
pipesworld-Tankage	20	**1**	**1**	**1**	**1**	11	14
satellite	20	**18**	**18**	4	3	15	7
pipesworld	20	**1**	**1**	**1**	**1**	11	14
rover	20	**0**	**0**	**0**	**0**	18	8
storage	20	7	**9**	5	5	17	15
tpp	20	**9**	8	5	5	9	7
total	526	296	254	178	111	427	318

Figure 1a shows the number of solved instances over the used CPU time. As we can observe the transformation-based heuristics are severely dominated by the natively implemented POCL heuristics, as we expected. Figures 1b and 1c show the size of the explored search space over the number of solved instances. This means that configurations with higher curves solve more problems using the same number of visited nodes. We can observe that both transformation-based heuristics act more informed than the existing POCL heuristics in the beginning. The transformation-based heuristic using LM-Cut remains above the best existing POCL heuristic (Add) for the complete range of problems it could solve. When using M&S the performance deteriorates for the more complex problems, which we attribute to the small number of abstract states. In fact, a reasonable number of abstract states should be chosen domain dependently [9]. It is also the case that many runs experienced time outs after having explored only a small number of nodes. This means that the true curves of the transformation-based heuristics are expected to lie higher than depicted.

In summary, we can state that the experiments offer a promising perspective on the usefulness of the proposed transformation-based heuristics. In particular the LM-Cut heuristic proved to act more informed than the currently best known POCL heuristic, in addition to being the first known admissible one. Since the calculation of LM-Cut does not rely on preprocessing, like the Merge and Shrink heuristic does, we are optimistic that a native implementation of LM-Cut for POCL planning will offer a significant performance boost for POCL planning.

6 Conclusion

We presented a technique which allows planners performing search in the space of plans to use standard classical planning heuristics known from state-based planning. This technique is based on a transformation which encodes a given partial plan by means of an altered planning problem, s.t. evaluating the goal distance for the given partial plan corresponds to evaluating the goal distance for the initial state of the new planning problem.

We evaluated our approach by running our POCL planning system with two of the currently best-informed heuristics for POCL planning and two state-of-the-art-heuristics from state-based planning based on the proposed transformation. Whereas the first two heuristics are natively implemented in our system, the latter two are obtained by running Fast Downward in each search node and extracting its heuristic estimate for the initial state. The empirical data shows that our encoding works well with the evaluated state-based heuristics. In fact, one of these heuristics is even more informed than the best evaluated POCL heuristic, as it creates smaller search spaces in order to find solutions.

In future work we want to implement the encoding of causal links and evaluate our technique using a native implementation of the (state-based) LM-cut heuristic. Furthermore, we want to investigate whether the LM-cut heuristic can be *directly* transferred to the POCL setting without the compilation.

Acknowledgements. This work is done within the Transregional Collaborative Research Centre SFB/ TRR 62 "Companion-Technology for Cognitive Technical Systems" funded by the German Research Foundation (DFG).

References

1. Bercher, P., Biundo, S.: Encoding partial plans for heuristic search. In: Proceedings of the 4th Workshop on Knowledge Engineering for Planning and Scheduling (KEPS 2013), pp. 11–15 (2013)
2. Blum, A.L., Furst, M.L.: Fast planning through planning graph analysis. Artificial Intelligence 90, 281–300 (1997)
3. Coles, A., Coles, A., Fox, M., Long, D.: Forward-chaining partial-order planning. In: Proceedings of the 20th International Conference on Automated Planning and Scheduling (ICAPS 2010), pp. 42–49. AAAI Press (2010)

4. Dräger, K., Finkbeiner, B., Podelski, A.: Directed model checking with distance-preserving abstractions. In: Valmari, A. (ed.) SPIN 2006. LNCS, vol. 3925, pp. 19–34. Springer, Heidelberg (2006)
5. Fikes, R.E., Nilsson, N.J.: STRIPS: A new approach to the application of theorem proving to problem solving. Artificial Intelligence 2, 189–208 (1971)
6. Haslum, P., Geffner, H.: Admissible heuristics for optimal planning. In: Proceedings of the 5th International Conference on Artificial Intelligence Planning Systems (AIPS 2000), pp. 140–149. AAAI Press (2000)
7. Helmert, M.: The fast downward planning system. Journal of Artificial Intelligence Research (JAIR) 26, 191–246 (2006)
8. Helmert, M., Domshlak, C.: Landmarks, critical paths and abstractions: Whats the difference anyway? In: Proceedings of the 19th International Conference on Automated Planning and Scheduling (ICAPS 2009), vol. 9, pp. 162–169 (2009)
9. Helmert, M., Haslum, P., Hoffmann, J.: Flexible abstraction heuristics for optimal sequential planning. In: Proceedings of the 17th International Conference on Automated Planning and Scheduling (ICAPS 2007), pp. 176–183 (2007)
10. Hoffmann, J., Nebel, B.: The FF planning system: Fast plan generation through heuristic search. Journal of Artificial Intelligence Research (JAIR) 14, 253–302 (2001)
11. Joslin, D., Pollack, M.E.: Least-cost flaw repair: A plan refinement strategy for partial-order planning. In: Proceedings of the 12th National Conference on Artificial Intelligence (AAAI 1994), pp. 1004–1009. AAAI Press (1994)
12. Kambhampati, S.: Refinement planning as a unifying framework for plan synthesis. AI Magazine 18(2), 67–98 (1997)
13. McAllester, D., Rosenblitt, D.: Systematic nonlinear planning. In: Proceedings of the Ninth National Conference on Artificial Intelligence (AAAI 1991), pp. 634–639. AAAI Press (1991)
14. Muise, C., McIlraith, S.A., Beck, J.C.: Monitoring the execution of partial-order plans via regression. In: Proceedings of the 22nd International Joint Conference on Artificial Intelligence (IJCAI 2011), pp. 1975–1982. AAAI Press (2011)
15. Nebel, B., Bäckström, C.: On the computational complexity of temporal projection, planning, and plan validation. Artificial Intelligence 66(1), 125–160 (1994)
16. Nguyen, X., Kambhampati, S.: Reviving partial order planning. In: Proceedings of the 17th International Joint Conference on Artificial Intelligence (IJCAI 2001), pp. 459–466. Morgan Kaufmann (2001)
17. Penberthy, J.S., Weld, D.S.: UCPOP: A sound, complete, partial order planner for ADL. In: Proceedings of the third International Conference on Knowledge Representation and Reasoning, pp. 103–114. Morgan Kaufmann (1992)
18. Ramírez, M., Geffner, H.: Plan recognition as planning. In: Boutilier, C. (ed.) Proceedings of the 21st International Joint Conference on Artificial Intelligence (IJCAI 2009), pp. 1778–1783. AAAI Press (July 2009)
19. Seegebarth, B., Müller, F., Schattenberg, B., Biundo, S.: Making hybrid plans more clear to human users – a formal approach for generating sound explanations. In: Proceedings of the 22nd International Conference on Automated Planning and Scheduling (ICAPS 2012), pp. 225–233. AAAI Press (June 2012)
20. Vidal, V., Geffner, H.: Branching and pruning: An optimal temporal POCL planner based on constraint programming. Artificial Intelligence 170(3), 298–335 (2006)
21. Weld, D.S.: Systematic nonlinear planning: A commentary. AI Magazine 32(1), 101–103 (2011)
22. Younes, H.L.S., Simmons, R.G.: VHPOP: Versatile heuristic partial order planner. Journal of Artificial Intelligence Research (JAIR) 20, 405–430 (2003)

Workflow Clustering Using Semantic Similarity Measures

Ralph Bergmann, Gilbert Müller, and Daniel Wittkowsky

University of Trier, Business Information Systems II
D-54286 Trier, Germany
bergmann@uni-trier.de
www.wi2.uni-trier.de

Abstract. The problem of clustering workflows is a relatively new research area of increasing importance as the number and size of workflow repositories is getting larger. It can be useful as a method to analyze the workflow assets accumulated in a repository in order to get an overview of its content and to ease navigation. In this paper, we investigate workflow clustering by adapting two traditional clustering algorithms (k-medoid and AGNES) for workflow clustering. Clustering is guided by a semantic similarity measure for workflows, originally developed in the context of case-based reasoning. Further, a case study is presented that evaluates the two algorithms on a repository containing cooking workflows automatically extracted from an Internet source.

1 Introduction

Cluster analysis is an established method that allows discovering the structure in collections of data by exploring similarities between data points. The goal of cluster analysis is to group data objects in such a way that data objects within a cluster are similar while data objects of different clusters are dissimilar to one another [6]. Cluster analysis has already been applied to different types of data, such as relational data, textual data, and even multi-media data.

In this paper, we address the problem of clustering workflows, which is a relatively new area of increasing importance [7,8,13,5]. Traditionally, workflows are "the automation of a business process, in whole or part, during which documents, information or tasks are passed from one participant to another for action, according to a set of procedural rules" [16]. Recently, more and more repositories are constructed by companies and organizations to capture their procedural knowledge as a starting point for reuse and optimization. For example, the myExperiment[1] virtual research environment enables the publication, search, and reuse of scientific workflows providing a repository of more than 2000 workflows. Recent efforts on workflow sharing supported by new standards for workflow representation will likely lead to repositories of larger scale. Further, research

---

[1] www.myexperiment.org

I.J. Timm and M. Thimm (Eds.): KI 2013, LNAI 8077, pp. 13–24, 2013.
© Springer-Verlag Berlin Heidelberg 2013

on methods for automatic workflow extraction from text [12] enables obtaining workflow repositories from how-to descriptions on the Internet. Also process mining [1,10,14] can infer process models (which are similar to workflows) by analyzing event logs, thus producing a large number of processes.

Clustering of workflows will likely become relevant as the size of workflow repositories increases. It can be useful to analyze the workflow assets accumulated in a repository in order to get an overview of its content and to ease navigation [7,8,13]. Identifying clusters of similar workflows could highlight the opportunity to unify similar workflows [5], thus reducing the number of workflows that must be supported in a company. Further, clustering might be used as an index structure for a workflow repository that can help to speed-up workflow retrieval [4]. Please note that workflow clustering [7,8,13,5] is significantly different from process mining [14,1,10] as process mining analyzes execution log data while workflow clustering analyzes the workflows themselves.

In this paper, we investigate workflow clustering by applying selected traditional clustering algorithms (in particular k-medoid and AGNES) to the clustering of workflows. The core of the application to workflows is the availability of an appropriate similarity measure for workflows, which replaces the traditional distance measure for n-dimensional data points. We propose to use a semantic similarity measure for workflows which we have developed and evaluated in our previous research as part of a similarity-based retrieval method [4]. This similarity measure can be configured according to a particular domain, based on an ontology of tasks and data items.

The next section presents our previous work on workflow representation and semantic workflow similarity. Then, section 3 describes our approach to workflow clustering before section 4 presents a case study investigating the proposed cluster algorithms to analyze a repository of 1729 cooking workflows. This paper ends with a conclusion and a description of potential future work.

2   Workflow Representation and Semantic Similarity

We now briefly describe our previous work on semantic workflow similarity [4], which is a cornerstone of the proposed clustering algorithms. We illustrate our approach by an example form the domain of cooking recipes. In this domain a cooking recipe is represented as a workflow describing the instructions for cooking a particular dish [12].

2.1   Representation of Semantic Workflows

Broadly speaking, workflows consist of a set of *activities* (also called *tasks*) combined with *control-flow structures* like sequences, parallel (AND split/join) or alternative (XOR split/join) branches, and loops. Tasks and control-flow structures form the *control-flow*. In addition, tasks exchange certain *products*, which can be of physical matter (such as ingredients for cooking tasks) or information. Tasks, products, and relationships between the two of them form the *data flow*.

Today, graph representations for workflows are widely used. In this paper we build upon the workflow representation using semantically labeled graphs [4], which is now briefly summarized. We represent a workflow as a directed graph $W = (N, E, S, T)$ where N is a set of nodes and $E \subseteq N \times N$ is a set of edges. Nodes and edges are annotated by a type from a set Ω and a semantic description from a set Σ. Type and semantic description are computed by the two mapping functions $T: N \cup E \to \Omega$ and $S: N \cup E \to \Sigma$, respectively. The set Ω consists of the types: *workflow node, data node, task node, control-flow node, control-flow edge, part-of edge* and *data-flow edge*. Each workflow W has exactly one workflow node. The task nodes and data nodes represent tasks and data items, respectively. The control-flow nodes stand for control-flow elements. The data-flow edge is used to describe the linking of the data items consumed and produced by the tasks. The control-flow edge is used to represent the control flow of the workflow, i.e., it links tasks with successor tasks or control-flow elements. The part-of edge represents a relation between the workflow node and all other nodes. Σ is a semantic meta data language that is used for the semantic annotation of nodes and edges. In our work we treat the semantic descriptions in an object-oriented fashion to allow the application of well-established similarity measures from case-based reasoning [2,3]. Figure 1 shows a simple fragment of a workflow graph from the cooking domain with the different kinds of nodes and edges. For some nodes semantic descriptions are sketched, specifying ingredients used (data nodes) and tasks performed (cooking steps). The semantic descriptions are based on a domain specific ontology of data items and tasks.

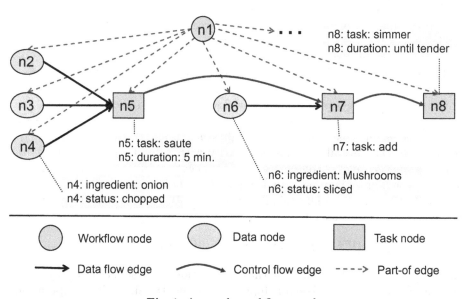

Fig. 1. A sample workflow graph

2.2   Semantic Similarity

The described graph representation of workflows enables modeling related semantic similarity measures which are well inline with experts assessment of workflow similarity [4]. The similarity measure for workflows allows comparing two complete workflows. Motivated by its use for similarity-based retrieval, one workflow is considered a query workflow $W_q = (N_q, E_q, S_q, T_q)$ and the second workflow is considered a case workflow $W_c = (N_c, E_c, S_c, T_c)$ from a repository. The similarity measure assesses how well the query workflow is covered by the case workflow. In particular, the similarity should be 1 if the query workflow is exactly included in the case workflow as a subgraph. Consequently, the proposed similarity measure is not symmetrical.

Our framework for modeling workflow similarity is based on a local similarity measure for semantic descriptions $sim_\Sigma : \Sigma^2 \to [0, 1]$ based on which node and edge similarity measures $sim_N : N_q \times Nc \to [0, 1]$ and $sim_E : E_q \times E_c \to [0, 1]$ can be easily defined. For example, the node similarity is defined as follows:

$$sim_N(n_q, n_c) = \begin{cases} sim_\Sigma(S_q(n_q), S_c(n_c)) & \text{if} \quad T_q(n_q) = T_c(n_c) \\ 0 & \text{otherwise} \end{cases}$$

Nodes with different types (e.g. a task node compared with a data node) are considered dissimilar; their similarity is always zero. The similarity of nodes of equal type is defined by the similarity of the semantic descriptions. In particular the taxonomical structure of the data and task ontology (ingredients and cooking steps ontology in the cooking recipe domain) is employed to derive a similarity value that reflects the closeness in the ontology as well as additional parameters such as the quantity of an ingredient used in a recipe. Due to the space limitations of this paper, we refer to [4] for more details and examples of how such local similarity measures look like.

The similarity $sim(W_q, W_c)$ is computed by means of a legal mapping $m :$ $N_q \cup E_q \to N_c \cup E_c$, which is a type-preserving, partial, injective mapping function of the nodes and edges of the query workflow to those of the case workflow. For each query node or edge x mapped by m, the similarity to the respective case node or edge $m(x)$ is computed through $sim_N(x, m(x))$ and $sim_E(x, m(x))$, respectively. The overall workflow similarity with respect to the mapping m, named $sim_m(W_q, W_c)$ is computed by an aggregation function (e.g. a weighted average) combining the previously computed similarity values.

Finally, the overall workflow similarity $sim(W_q, W_c)$ is determined by the best possible mapping of that kind, i.e.,

$$sim(W_q, W_c) = \max\{sim_m(W_q, W_c) \,|\, \text{legal map } m\}.$$

As a consequence of this definition, the computation of the similarity requires the systematic construction of such mappings m. While the similarity computation by exhaustive search guarantees to find the optimal match, it is computationally not feasible. Hence, we developed a memory-bounded A* search algorithm with an appropriate admissible heuristic to keep similarity computation feasible [4].

3   Workflow Clustering

We now describe our approach for using the described semantic similarity measure for clustering workflows. The goal of cluster analysis is to group data objects in such a way that data objects within a cluster are similar while data objects of different clusters are dissimilar. The following types of clustering algorithm can be distinguished: *Partitioning-based methods* structure the objects into k clusters based on centroids or representatives (algorithms k-means and k-medoid) while *hierarchical methods* build a tree of clusters in a top-down (e.g. algorithm DIANA) or bottom-up fashion (e.g. algorithm AGNES). *Density-based methods* (e.g. algorithm DBSCAN) identify regions with a high density separated by less dense regions to define clusters. *Conceptual clustering methods* (e.g. algorithms UNIMEM or COBWEB) do not only identify clusters, moreover they identify characteristic descriptions (a concept) for each cluster. As these methods handle the task of clustering differently, they also have different properties with regard to performance, calculation costs and requirements. For this reason there is no clear recommendation for a specific clustering method in general [6]. This leads to the problem of selecting a suitable method for a specific clustering scenario. Additionally, some methods need specific input parameters, e.g. the number of clusters k.

3.1   Selection of Clustering Method

To make use of the proposed semantic similarity measure, we selected clustering techniques that are capable of dealing with similarities. We decided to examine two clustering methods of different type. Hence, we selected AGNES as a hierarchical algorithm and k-medoid as a partitioning-based algorithm. Both algorithms are based on a distance/similarity computation between the data items. As both algorithms are well known [6], we now describe them only briefly.

k-medoid is a partitioning-based clustering method that separates the objects into a given number of k clusters. First, it randomly chooses k data objects, so-called medoids. The remaining data objects are then assigned to the closest medoid using a distance function $d(x, y)$ that assesses the distance of two data points. Then the total quality of the clustering is calculated. Traditionally, the quality of the clustering is calculated by summing the absolute value of the distance between the medoid and the data points belonging to the cluster. This initial clustering is iteratively improved. Therefore, for each medoid m and each non-medoid data point o a swap operation of m and o is performed and the resulting cluster quality is computed. The clustering representing the best possible is retained and the algorithm continues with the next swapping phase until the total quality of configuration does not improve anymore.

AGNES is an agglomerative hierarchical clustering method that starts with creating one cluster for each individual data point. Then the existing clusters are aggregated in a bottom-up fashion until a complete binary cluster tree is constructed. This aggregation process is performed iteratively. In each iteration a pair of clusters is selected and a new cluster is constructed by merging the data points of the two clusters. The two original clusters are linked as sub-clusters to the new cluster. The selection of the pair of clusters to be merged in each iteration is determined by the closeness of the clusters. Therefore, the set of unlinked clusters is searched for the closest pair of clusters. To assess the closeness of two clusters, several variants are established, called linkage criteria. They assess cluster closeness based on a measure of distance $d(x, y)$ of two data points. *Single linkage* defines cluster closeness as the minimum distance between the points of the two clusters, *complete linkage* uses the maximum distance, while *average linkage* computes the average distance.

3.2   Integrating Semantic Workflow Similarity

To apply k-medoid and AGNES for clustering workflows is quite straight forward. We assume that the given repository of workflows is represented as a set of workflow graphs as defined in section 2.1. This set is then clustered using the selected clustering algorithm. Hence, instead of n-dimensional data points the graphs are used. Further, the definition of distance $d(W_1, W_2)$ of two data points (here workflows) is replaced by the semantic similarity measure by $d(W_1, W_2) = 1 - sim(W_1, W_2)$. However, a difficulty with this approach arises because the distance functions used in the clustering algorithms are assumed to be symmetric $(d(x, y) = d(y, x))$ while the semantic similarity measure as defined in section 2.2 is asymmetric as it distinguishes a query from a case workflow. To address this problem, several approaches can be taken.

Modification of the Semantic Similarity Measure. The definition of the mapping function m and the aggregation function could be modified such that a bidirectional mapping is enforced. In addition, the local similarity measure sim_Σ must be restricted to symmetric measures only. While this approach is feasible in principle, it has the significant disadvantage that for applications that require both, retrieval and clustering, two different similarity measures must be modeled, which leads to additional effort.

Modification of the Clustering Algorithms. The clustering algorithms can be slightly modified in order to deal with the asymmetric nature of the similarity. As k-medoid always compares a medoid with a non-medoid data point, this comparison is already asymmetric. We can apply the semantic similarity measure such that the medoid becomes the query workflow and the data point becomes the case workflow. For AGNES the distance is used to compute the cluster close-ness according to the selected linkage criterion. To achieve a symmetric definition of cluster closeness based on the asymmetric semantic similarity measure, the linkage computation can me modified such that for each two workflows W_1 and W_2 the two similarity values $sim(W_1, W_2)$ and $sim(W_2, W_1)$ are considered.

Symmetrization of the Similarity Measure. Instead of modifying the semantic similarity computation or the clustering algorithm, the similarity measure itself can be symmetrized by aggregating the two similarity values $sim(W_1, W_2)$ and $sim(W_2, W_1)$ into a single value by a symmetric aggregation function α. Thus, the distance between two workflows W_1 and W_2 is computed as follows: $d(W_1, W_2) = 1 - \alpha(sim(W_1, W_2), sim(W_2, W_1))$. For α we consider three different options, namely: *min*, *max*, and *average*. Which option is selected has an impact on the similarity/distance. For example, consider two recipe workflows with a high similarity value in either direction. Thus, these recipes are very similar and contain almost the same cooking steps and ingredients, i.e. one may be used as a replacement of the other. Independent of the choice of α, the symmetric similarity value is high as well. However, if one recipe workflow is contained in the other recipe workflow (e.g. a bolognese sauce recipe in a recipe for spaghetti bolognese) the situation is different as one of the two similarity values is high while the other is low. Now, the overall symmetric similarity assessment differs strongly depending on α.

3.3 Performance Considerations

As the distance/similarity computation is quite frequently called within both clustering algorithms, the computational complexity of the semantic similarity measure involving the search algorithm for the optimal map m is a problem. We address this problem by caching, i.e., we perform the similarity computation in a pre-processing step before the clustering algorithm is started. Thus, a similarity matrix is pre-computed that stores the similarity value of each pair of workflows from the repository. As the individual similarity computations are independent from one another, they can be easily parallelized, taking advantage of multi-core CPUs. Additionally, we improved the performance of the clustering algorithms themselves. We focused on some of the computationally intensive calculation steps such as the estimating of the best swap operation in k-medoid and parallelized them as well.

4   Case Study: Clustering Cooking Workflows

The aim of this case study was to achieve a first evaluation of the proposed clustering approach on a specific workflow repository. Therefore, the approach was implemented, a repository was created, and a semantic similarity measure was defined. Then, the two proposed algorithms were tested using various variations of their parameters on the workflow repository. We aim at assessing whether the clustering algorithms are helpful to get an insight into the workflow data. As literature emphasizes both the importance and the difficulty of evaluation of clusterings [15], we focus on two purposive evaluations. In an internal evaluation we want to find out, how well the clustering results fulfill the usual requirements of homogeneity and heterogeneity. This evaluation is internal as it is based on indices derived from the clustering results themselves. An external evaluation is also performed to examine how well the clustering resembles a given human classification. In combination these evaluations should provide a better understanding of the clustering methods and the structure of the specific workflow repository.

4.1   Implementation and Repository Creation

We implemented the described clustering algorithms within the CAKE framework[2] [3] that already includes a process-oriented case-based reasoning component for similarity-based retrieval of workflows. The already implemented algorithms for similarity computation are used for clustering. For the domain of cooking recipes, a cooking ontology containing 208 ingredients and 225 cooking preparation steps was developed manually. A specific similarity measure for workflow similarity was defined according to the described framework. This includes the definition of local similarity measures sim_Σ as well as the definition of a weighting scheme. According to common practice in case-based reasoning, this similarity measure has been optimized manually for the retrieval of recipe workflows. We created a workflow repository containing 1729 workflows (on the average, 11 nodes per workflow) by automated workflow extraction [12]. The workflows have been extracted from `allrecipes.com` by applying a frame-based approach for information extraction using the SUNDANCE parser [11]. Each cooking workflow was automatically annotated by an appropriate semantic description formed by the ontology concepts. The quality of the resulting semantic workflows was ensured by manual postprocessing.

4.2   Internal Evaluation

For k-medoid clustering the number of clusters k is of high importance. Although it is not that essential for AGNES, it might be also useful to limit the number of clusters. Either the number of clusters can be used as a stopping criterion or an extract of a hierarchical clustering tree can be chosen [6]. In the following experiments we performed clustering with different values for the number of clusters k ranging from 2 to 100. Due to the fact that the results of k-medoid depend on the initial random selection of medoids, we repeated each run of k-medoid 5 times and selected the best clustering result. We applied the symmetrization approach for the similarity measure using all three variants: min, max, and $average$ and in addition the asymmetric variant of each algorithm. For AGNES we also varied the linkage approach to test all three variants.

For each clustering we determined three internal measures, namely cohesion, separation, and the silhouette coefficient. The cohesion of a single cluster is equivalent to the average similarity of all pairs of objects of the cluster. The total cluster cohesion measure is the weighted average of the cohesion of the individual clusters. The cohesion values range from 0 to 1, while a high value indicates highly homogenous clusters. The separation of two clusters is defined

---

[2] `cake.wi2.uni-trier.de`

as the average of all distances (1 - similarity) between all pairs of elements from both clusters. The total cluster separation measure, which ranges from 0 to 1, is the weighted average of the separation of all pairs of clusters. The silhouette coefficient [9] combines the idea of cohesion and separation into a single value ranging from -1 to 1.

Table 1. Cluster Results for k-Medoid

	Min Symmetr.	Mean Symmetr.	Max Symmetr.	Asymm. k-Medoid
Optimal k	2	2	3	2
Silhouette	0.16	0.15	0.07	0.06
Cohesion	0.22	0.29	0.36	0.28
Separation	0.82	0.75	0.67	0.74

Table 1 shows the results for the different variants of k-medoid. For each algorithm the results for the number of clusters k is shown which leads to the highest value of the silhouette coefficient. The best silhouette coefficients vary from 0.06 to 0.16, typically suggesting solutions with 2 - 3 clusters. While the silhouette coefficient enables evaluating how well a clustering result fulfills the goals of heterogeneity and homogeneity, it can be stated that even the best clustering results of these combinations don't reveal a strong cluster structure in the workflow repository. According to Kaufmann and Rousseeuw [9] a strong structure leads to silhouette values between 0.75 to 1. This interpretation is supported by cohesion and separation values. The clusters found by k-medoid are quite heterogenous due to high separation values ranging from 0.67 to 0.82 but not very homogenous as the cohesion values ranges from 0.22 to 0.36 only.

Table 2 shows the results for AGNES for each combination of algorithm and linkage (SL=single linkage, AL=average linkage, CL=complete linkage). For each combination the results for the number of clusters k is shown which leads to the highest value of the silhouette coefficient. The best silhouette coefficients vary from 0.05 to 0.22, which is in line with the results from k-medoid confirming that there is no strong structure in the workflow repository. Examining the other measures also confirms this interpretation. Cohesion varies from 0.20 to 0.39, hence homogeneity is very limited. Separation varies from 0.69 to 0.86 which means that there is quite a heterogeneity between different clusters.

Table 2. Cluster Results for AGNES

Algorithm	Min Symmetr.			Mean Symmetr.			Max Symmetr.			Asymm. AGNES		
Linkage	SL	AL	CL	SL	AL	CL	SL	AL	CL	SL	AL	CL
optimal k	2	3	2	4	23	2	2	9	2	3	2	2
Silhouette	0.21	0.22	0.16	0.11	0.16	0.05	0.09	0.16	0.06	0.05	0.18	0.13
Cohesion	0.23	0.20	0.20	0.29	0.35	0.27	0.35	0.39	0.34	0.29	0.27	0.27
Separation	0.82	0.86	0.86	0.73	0.75	0.76	0.68	0.69	0.70	0.74	0.77	0.76

4.3   External Evaluation

The goal of the external evaluation was to evaluate whether the clustering methods produce clusters of recipe workflows similar to the structure in a cookbook, i.e., a classification into salads, soups, etc. Because this classification information is not available in the current repository and because of the lack of structure identified in the internal evaluation, we decided to manually select and classify a small subset of recipe workflows. We defined 5 classes, namely salads, soups, cake, bread and pork and selected 25 recipes for each class. Then we applied the clustering methods for the selected workflows only. Due to space limitations we just present the results of k-medoid using the mean symmetrization approach, however the results for AGNES are quite comparable.

Table 3. Clustering results (3 classes)

		Classification		
		Cake	Salad	Soup
	1	20	0	0
Cluster	2	5	21	0
	3	0	4	25

Table 4. Clustering results (5 classes)

		Classification				
		Cake	Salad	Soup	Bread	Pork
	1	15	0	0	3	0
	2	2	14	1	1	7
Cluster	3	0	8	14	0	8
	4	8	2	0	21	3
	5	0	1	10	0	7

Table 4 shows the results of clustering 75 workflows belonging to the classes cake, salad, and soup. The results show that the found classification of the clustering algorithm matches well with the external classification. No soup recipe was classified wrong, while approx. 80% of the salad and cake recipes were classified correctly, leading to an overall classification accuracy of 88%. Table 3 shows the results of clustering all 125 workflows. It turns out that the classification structure is less well present. For example, the soup recipes, which were well classified in table 4, are nearly equally divided among two clusters. The pork recipes are spread among 4 clusters. The overall classification accuracy drops down to 56.8%.

To examine the clustering result more deeply we decided to determine the cohesion of each of the five classes and to compare them with the cohesion of the found five clusters (see table 5). Overall the cohesion of the classification is only 0.34 and is thus not very high. The class of soup and pork recipes have the lowest cohesion, which explains that they are not well clustered as shown in table 3. The overall cohesion that results from the clustering is even slightly higher than the cohesion of the manual classification of the recipes.

Finally, it can be concluded that clustering algorithms using the semantic similarity won't classify all recipes as one would expect in a cookbook. This is because the semantic similarity measure is based on the workflow structure and thus includes the preparation of the dishes. Contrary to this, the cookbook classification aims at the purpose or outcome of the recipes. However, two recipes

Table 5. Cohesion of classification and clusters

Classification						Clustering					
Cake	Salad	Soup	Bread	Pork	Average	1	2	3	4	5	Average
0.40	0.30	0.34	0.37	0.30	0.34	0.47	0.32	0.31	0.35	0.33	0.35

with different purpose could be prepared quite similarly (e.g. diced beef and beef salad). On the other hand, two recipes with the same purpose could be prepared quite differently (e.g. a tomato salad and a beef salad).

5   Conclusions, Related and Future Work

Workflow clustering is a new research topic, which is particularly important when the size and the availability of workflow repositories is further increasing. We have explored how the k-medoid and the AGNES algorithms can be adapted for workflow clustering based on a semantic similarity measure. Unlike previous work on workflow and process clustering [7,8,13,5] our approach enables to configure the semantic similarity measure in relation to a domain ontology of data and task items. Thereby it allows controlling the cluster algorithm such that the workflows are clustered according to the intended meaning of similarity. Thus, our approach is generic and can be applied to various domains by adapting the ontologies and similarity measures. As we have already applied our similarity measure to scientific workflows [4], we believe that our method could be considered an alternative to the work proposed by Silva et al. [13] specifically for this domain.

We have systematically applied the algorithms to analyze an automatically extracted set of cooking workflows, which is a workflow domain that has not yet been investigated by previous work on workflow clustering. The analysis revealed that there is only little cluster structure in the examined workflows, i.e., that the kind of preparation of the recipes varies a lot from recipe to recipe. The application of the algorithms to the analysis of a reduced set of workflows that have been manually classified according to five classes was only able to partially discover the given classification. However, it also discloses the fact that traditional classifications of recipes in a cookbook don't always resemble with the similarity of the preparation workflows.

Future work will include applying the presented methods on different data sets in different domains, e.g. for scientific workflows. The myExperiment platform could provide a good source of workflows for this purpose [13]. Further, we will investigate whether the cluster methods can be applied to derive an index structure for the repository that can be exploited to improve the performance of similarity-based workflow retrieval. Further, we aim at extending our approach to density-based clustering as proposed by Ekanayake et al. [5].

Acknowledgements. This work was funded by the German Research Foundation (DFG), project number BE 1373/3-1.

References

1. Van der Aalst, W.M.: Process mining. Springer, Heidelberg (2011)
2. Bergmann, R.: Experience Management. LNCS (LNAI), vol. 2432. Springer, Heidelberg (2002)
3. Bergmann, R., Freßmann, A., Maximini, K., Maximini, R., Sauer, T.: Case-based support for collaborative business. In: Roth-Berghofer, T.R., Göker, M.H., Güvenir, H.A. (eds.) ECCBR 2006. LNCS (LNAI), vol. 4106, pp. 519–533. Springer, Heidelberg (2006)
4. Bergmann, R., Gil, Y.: Similarity assessment and efficient retrieval of semantic workfows. Information Systems Journal (2012),
   `http://www.wi2.uni-trier.de/publications/2012_BergmannGilISJ.pdf`
5. Ekanayake, C.C., Dumas, M., García-Bañuelos, L., La Rosa, M., ter Hofstede, A.H.M.: Approximate clone detection in repositories of business process models. In: Barros, A., Gal, A., Kindler, E. (eds.) BPM 2012. LNCS, vol. 7481, pp. 302–318. Springer, Heidelberg (2012)
6. Han, J., Kamber, M.: Data Mining: Concepts and Techniques. Morgan Kaufmann (2006)
7. Jung, J.Y., Bae, J.: Workflow clustering method based on process similarity. In: Gavrilova, M.L., Gervasi, O., Kumar, V., Tan, C.J.K., Taniar, D., Laganá, A., Mun, Y., Choo, H. (eds.) ICCSA 2006. LNCS, vol. 3981, pp. 379–389. Springer, Heidelberg (2006)
8. Jung, J.Y., Bae, J., Liu, L.: Hierarchical clustering of business process models. International Journal of Innovative Computing, Information and Control 6(12 A) (2009)
9. Kaufman, L., Rousseeuw, P.J.: Finding Groups in Data - An Introduction to Cluster Analysis. John Wiley, New York (1990)
10. Montani, S., Leonardi, G.: Retrieval and clustering for business process monitoring: Results and improvements. In: Agudo, B.D., Watson, I. (eds.) ICCBR 2012. LNCS, vol. 7466, pp. 269–283. Springer, Heidelberg (2012)
11. Riloff, E., Phillips, W.: An introduction to the sundance and autolog systems. Tech. rep., School of Computing, University of Utah. (2004)
12. Schumacher, P., Minor, M., Walter, K., Bergmann, R.: Extraction of procedural knowledge from the web. In: WWW 2012 Workshop Proceedings. ACM (2012)
13. Silva, V., Chirigati, F., Maia, K., Ogasawara, E., de Oliveira, D., Braganholo, V., Murta, L., Mattoso, M.: Similarity-based workflow clustering. Journal of Computational Interdisciplinary Sciences 2(1), 23–35 (2011)
14. Song, M., Günther, C.W., van der Aalst, W.M.P.: Trace clustering in process mining. In: Ardagna, D., Mecella, M., Yang, J. (eds.) BPM 2008 Workshops. LNBIP, vol. 17, pp. 109–120. Springer, Heidelberg (2009)
15. Tan, P.N., Steinbach, M., Kumar, V.: Introduction to Data Mining. Addison-Wesley (2005)
16. Workflow Management Coalition: Workflow management coalition glossary & terminology (1999),
    `http://www.wfmc.org/standars/docs/TC-1011_term_glossary_v3.pdf`
    (last access on May 23, 2007)

Empathy and Its Modulation in a Virtual Human

Hana Boukricha[1], Ipke Wachsmuth[1], Maria Nella Carminati[2], and Pia Knoeferle[2]

[1] A.I. Group, Faculty of Technology, Bielefeld University, 33594 Bielefeld, Germany
{hboukric,ipke}@techfak.uni-bielefeld.de
[2] Cognitive Interaction Technology (CITEC), Bielefeld University, Morgenbreede 39,
Gebäudeteil H1, 33615 Bielefeld, Germany
mcarmina@techfak.uni-bielefeld.de, knoeferl@cit-ec.uni-bielefeld.de

Abstract. Endowing artificial agents with the ability to empathize is believed to enhance their social behavior and to make them more likable, trustworthy, and caring. Neuropsychological findings substantiate that empathy occurs to different degrees depending on several factors including, among others, a person's mood, personality, and social relationships with others. Although there is increasing interest in endowing artificial agents with affect, personality, and the ability to build social relationships, little attention has been devoted to the role of such factors in influencing their empathic behavior. In this paper, we present a computational model of empathy which allows a virtual human to exhibit different degrees of empathy. The presented model is based on psychological models of empathy and is applied and evaluated in the context of a conversational agent scenario.

1 Introduction

Research on empathic artificial agents corroborates the role of empathy in improving artificial agents' social behavior. For instance, it has been shown that empathic virtual humans can reduce stress levels during job interview tasks [17] and that empathic agents are perceived as more likable, trustworthy, and caring [7]. Furthermore, it has been found that empathic virtual humans can evoke empathy in children and can thus teach them to deal with bullying situations [16] and that a virtual human's empathic behavior also contributes to its ability to build and sustain long-term socio-emotional relationships with human partners [3]. However, it has been shown that in a competitive card game scenario, empathic emotions can increase arousal and induce stress in an interaction partner [1]. In line with neuropsychological findings [8] that humans empathize with each other to different degrees depending on their mood, personality, and social relationships with others, the modulation of a virtual human's empathic behavior through such factors would allow for a more adequate empathic behavior in the agent across different interaction scenarios. Although there is increasing interest in endowing artificial agents with affect, personality, and the ability to build social relationships, the role of such factors in influencing their empathic behavior has received little attention.

In this paper, we present a computational model of empathy which allows a virtual human to exhibit different degrees of empathy. Our model is shaped by psychological models of empathy and is based on three processing steps that are central to empathy [4]: First, the *Empathy Mechanism* by which an empathic emotion is produced. Second, the *Empathy Modulation* by which the empathic emotion is modulated. Third, the

I.J. Timm and M. Thimm (Eds.): KI 2013, LNAI 8077, pp. 25–36, 2013.

Expression of Empathy by which the virtual human's multimodal behavior is triggered through the modulated empathic emotion. The presented empathy model is applied and evaluated in the context of a conversational agent scenario involving the virtual humans MAX [12] and EMMA [6] and a human interaction partner. Within this scenario, our model is realized for EMMA and allows her to empathize with MAX's emotions during his interaction with the human partner.

The paper is structured as follows: In Section 2, we outline related work on existing empathic artificial agents. In Section 3, we present our approach to model empathy for a virtual human. In Section 4, we present the application scenario of the model as well as the results of an empirical evaluation of the empathic behavior generated by the model. Finally, in Section 5, we summarize the key contribution of our research.

2   Related Work

In previous research, much effort has gone in endowing virtual humans with the ability to empathize. McQuiggan et al. [13] propose an inductive framework for modeling parallel and reactive empathy. They called their framework *CARE* (Companion Assisted Reactive Empathizer) and based it on learning empirically informed models of empathy during human-agent social interactions. In a learning phase, users' situation data, such as their actions and intentions, users' affective states, bio-potential signals, and other characteristics such as their age and gender are gathered while they interact with virtual characters. The virtual characters respond to the user's situation with either parallel or reactive empathy. During interaction with the characters, users are able to evaluate their empathic responses using a 4 point Likert scale. Naive Bayes classifiers, decision trees, and support vector machines are used to learn models of empathy from 'good examples'. The induced models of empathy are used at runtime in a test phase to drive virtual characters' empathic responses. The evaluation of the characters' empathic behavior according to collected training and test data shows that the induced empathy models produce appropriate empathic behaviors.

Based on an empirical and theoretical approach, Ochs et al. [14] propose a computational model of empathic emotions. They analyzed human-machine dialog situations to identify the characteristics of dialog situations that may elicit users' emotions during human-machine interaction. The results of this empirical analysis were combined with a theoretical model of emotions to provide a model of empathic emotions. Once the user's potential emotion is determined, the agent's empathic emotion from the same type is triggered toward the user. They define a degree of empathy as a value that affects the base intensity of the empathic emotion depending on both the liking relationship between the user and the agent and the degree to which a user deserves or doesn't deserve his immediate situation (cf. [15]). The empathic behavior of the agent is empirically evaluated based on three conditions, a non-emotional condition, an empathic condition, and a non-congruent emotional condition where the agent expresses emotions that are opposite in their values of valence to the empathic emotions. The results show that the agent is perceived more positively in the empathic version and more negatively in the non-congruent emotional version.

Rodrigues et al. [18] propose a generic computational model of empathy. Their model is integrated into an existing affective agent architecture [9] and comprises an empathic appraisal component and an empathic response component. A perceived event by an agent that evokes an emotional cue in another agent is input to the empathic appraisal component together with the emotional cue. The emotional cue is input to an emotion recognition module and the event is input to a self-projection appraisal module. The outputs of both modules are combined to determine an empathic emotion as the output of the empathic appraisal. The empathic emotion is modulated by several factors (cf. [8]). Similarity is defined as the degree of congruence of the emotions provided by the self-projection appraisal and emotion recognition modules. Affective link is defined as the value of liking between the agents. The higher the average value of similarity and affective link, the higher the value of intensity of the empathic emotion. Mood is defined as the empathizing agent's mood which then affects the intensity of the empathic emotion as it affects that of other emotions (cf. [9]). Personality refers to the empathizing agent's resistance to feel particular emotions. Regarding the empathic response component, the empathic emotion generated by the empathic appraisal triggers a situation-appropriate action. The authors designed a small scenario with four synthetic characters to evaluate their model based on two conditions, an empathy condition and a no-empathy condition. The results show that the perceived values of empathy and affective link are significantly higher in the empathy condition and are thus in line with the theoretical assumptions underlying the model.

While significant advances have been made in modeling empathy for virtual humans, the modulation of the empathic emotion and the calculation of a degree of empathy have received little attention. Accordingly, we consider the modulation of an empathic emotion and the calculation of different degrees of empathy as a crucial aspect in further enhancing an artificial agent's social behavior. While in [18] and [14] only the intensity of an empathic emotion is modulated, we also modulate its related emotion category in our model. In this regard, we follow Hoffman's claim [11] that an empathic response need not be a close match to the affect experienced by the other, but can be any emotional reaction compatible with the other's situation. Furthermore, in previous research, evaluations have been based on either two conditions, *non-empathic* vs. *empathic* (e.g., [18]) or on three conditions, *non-empathic/emotional*, *empathic*, and *non-congruent empathic/emotional* (e.g., [14] and [1]). In contrast, we evaluated our model based on three different conditions that distinguished three different degrees of empathy, *neutral*, *medium*, and *maximum* empathy, thus allowing for a more fine-grained evaluation of the model and its underlying parameters.

3   A Computational Model of Empathy

The virtual humans MAX [12] and EMMA [6] have a cognitive architecture composed of an emotion simulation module [2] and a Belief-Desire-Intention (BDI) module [12]. The emotion simulation module comprises of a dynamics/mood component for the calculation of the course of emotions and moods over time and their mutual interaction, and of a Pleasure, Arousal, Dominance (PAD) space in which emotion categories are located and their intensity values can be calculated. The emotion simulation module outputs values of pleasure, arousal, and one of two possible values of dominance (dominant vs. submissive) as well as intensity values of emotion categories. Our computational model of empathy is integrated within the emotion simulation module. In the following, we briefly introduce the three processing steps underlying our model (cf. Section 1); (more details on parts of the model and on its theoretical foundation are available in previous work [4]).

3.1 Empathy Mechanism

In line with the Facial Action Coding System (FACS) [10], 44 Action Units (AUs) have been implemented for the virtual human EMMA's face. In an empirical study, a total of 3517 randomly generated facial expressions of EMMA were rated by 353 participants with Pleasure, Arousal, and Dominance (PAD) values. Based on these ratings, three dimensional regression planes of AUs' intensity values and PAD values were obtained and show the meaning of each AU in PAD space. By combining all planes of all AUs, a repertoire of facial expressions arranged in PAD space was reconstructed. Accordingly, based on her own AUs and their intensity functions (regression planes) in PAD space, EMMA maps a perceived facial expression to AUs with corresponding intensity values and subsequently infers its related emotional state as a PAD value. The inferred PAD value is represented by an additional reference point in EMMA's PAD emotion space. Its related emotion category and corresponding value of intensity can thus be inferred.

After detecting a fast and salient change in the other's emotional state which indicates the occurrence of an emotional event, an empathic emotion is elicited. That is, with respect to a predetermined short time interval T, the difference between inferred PAD values corresponding to the time-stamps t_{k-1} and t_k, with $t_k - t_{k-1} <= T$, is calculated as $|PAD_{t_k} - PAD_{t_{k-1}}|$. If this exceeds a saliency threshold $TH1$ or if $|PAD_{t_k}|$ exceeds a saliency threshold $TH2$, then the emotional state PAD_{t_k} and its related emotion category represent the empathic emotion. The threshold values can be interpreted as representing the virtual human's responsiveness to the other's situation (for more details on the empirical study and the *Empathy Mechanism* see [6] and [4]). Once an empathic emotion is elicited, the following processing step *Empathy Modulation* is triggered.

3.2 Empathy Modulation

The modulation of the empathic emotion is realized within PAD space of the virtual human's emotion simulation module. At each point in time an empathic emotion is elicited, the following equation is applied:

$$empEmo_{t,mod} = ownEmo_t +$$
$$(empEmo_t - ownEmo_t) \cdot (\sum_{i=1}^{n} p_{i,t} \cdot w_i)/(\sum_{i=1}^{n} w_i) \tag{1}$$

The value $empEmo_{t,mod}$ represents the modulated empathic emotion. The value $ownEmo_t$ represents the virtual human's own emotional state as the modulation factor *mood*. The value $empEmo_t$ represents the non-modulated empathic emotion resulting from *Empathy Mechanism*. The values $p_{i,t}$ represent modulation factors that can have values ranging in $[0, 1]$. The values w_i represent assigned values of weights for the modulation factors $p_{i,t}$ which also range in $[0, 1]$. Such modulation factors are, e.g, *liking* and *familiarity* which can be represented by values ranging in $[0, 1]$ from neither like nor dislike to maximum like and from non-familiar to most-familiar (cf. [15]). Note that, currently, negative values of $p_{i,t}$ are not considered in our model.

We define the degree of empathy as the degree of similarity between the modulated empathic emotion and the non-modulated one. Thus, the degree of empathy is represented by the distance between $empEmo_{t,mod}$ and $empEmo_t$ within PAD space (Fig. 1, left). That is, the closer $empEmo_{t,mod}$ to $empEmo_t$, the higher the degree of empathy. The less close $empEmo_{t,mod}$ to $empEmo_t$, the lower the degree of empathy.

Following [18], the more similar the virtual human's emotional state to the empathic emotion, the more sensitive the virtual human to the empathic emotion. The less similar its emotional state to the empathic emotion, the more resistant the virtual human to the empathic emotion. That is, the closer the virtual human's own emotional state $ownEmo_t$ to the empathic emotion $empEmo_t$ the higher the resulting degree of empathy. The less close the virtual human's own emotional state $ownEmo_t$ to the empathic emotion $empEmo_t$ the lower the resulting degree of empathy. Regarding the modulation factors $p_{i,t}$, the higher their value of weighted mean, the closer the modulated empathic emotion $empEmo_{t,mod}$ to the non-modulated empathic emotion $empEmo_t$ and the higher the degree of empathy. The lower their value of weighted mean, the less close the modulated empathic emotion $empEmo_{t,mod}$ to the non-modulated empathic emotion $empEmo_t$ and the lower the degree of empathy.

According to Hoffman [11], an empathic response to the other's emotion should be more appropriate to the other's situation than to one's own and need not be a close match to the affect experienced by the other, but can be any emotional reaction compatible with the other's situation. Further, according to the thesis of the dimensional theory [19], emotions are related to one another in a systematic manner and their relationships can be represented in a dimensional model. Accordingly, the modulated empathic emotion $empEmo_{t,mod}$ is facilitated only if it lies in an immediate neighborhood to the non-modulated empathic emotion $empEmo_t$. Hence, for each emotion category located within PAD space of the emotion simulation module, we defined a so called *empathy facilitation region* as a box surrounding the emotion category. For example, Fig. 3 shows the PA space of positive dominance of the emotion simulation module with the defined *empathy facilitation region* for the emotion category *annoyed*. As depicted in Fig. 3 (middle), the modulated empathic emotion $empEmo_{t,mod}$ has as related emotion category *concentrated* (neutral emotional state) and the non-modulated empathic emotion $empEmo_t$ has as related emotion category *annoyed*. Accordingly, once the modulated empathic emotion $empEmo_{t,mod}$ enters the *empathy facilitation region* defined for *annoyed*, it is facilitated or otherwise it is inhibited (e.g., Fig. 3, left). Within the *empathy facilitation region*, the modulated empathic emotion $empEmo_{t,mod}$ represents an empathic response that is compatible with the other's situation (cf. [11]). Thus, the virtual human is allowed to react with an emotion from a different emotion category (but compatible) with the other's emotion.

As mentioned earlier in this section, the degree of empathy is represented by the distance between $empEmo_{t,mod}$ and $empEmo_t$ within PAD space. Hence, once the modulated empathic emotion $empEmo_{t,mod}$ enters the *empathy facilitation region*, the degree of empathy is calculated and increases toward the non-modulated empathic emotion $empEmo_t$. Outside the empathy facilitation region, the degree of empathy is equal to 0 (Fig. 1, right). Within the empathy facilitation region, the degree of empathy is calculated by the following equation for each instance at time t a modulated empathic emotion $empEmo_{t,mod}$ is facilitated:

$$degEmp_t = (1 - \|\frac{empEmo_{t,mod} - empEmo_t}{maxDistBox}\|)^2 \tag{2}$$

The value $degEmp_t$ represents the calculated degree of empathy and ranges within $[0, 1]$. The value $maxDistBox$ represents the possible maximum distance between the values $empEmo_{t,mod}$ and $empEmo_t$ within the empathy facilitation region (Fig. 1, right). Note that the distances $\|empEmo_{t,mod} - empEmo_t\|$ and $maxDistBox$ are weighted distances in PAD space. That is, we defined values of weights for each dimension within PAD space. A polynomial function is chosen in order to get smooth values of the calculated degree of empathy. According to the dimensional theory [19], the pleasure dimension is the most agreed upon dimension, the arousal dimension is the second agreed upon dimension and the dominance dimension is the third and least agreed upon dimension. Thus, regarding the defined values of weight for each dimension within PAD space, we assigned a higher weight value to the pleasure dimension, a lower value to the arousal dimension, and a very low value to the dominance dimension.

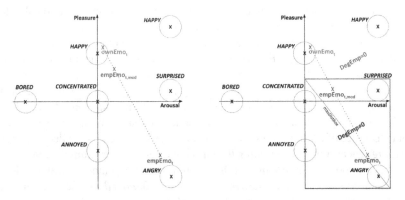

Fig. 1. The PA space of positive dominance of the emotion simulation module [2]. Left: $empEmo_{t,mod}$ as lying on the straight line spanned by $ownEmo_t$ and $empEmo_t$ (cf. (1)). Right: The *empathy facilitation region* defined for *angry* and the degree of empathy within PAD space.

As long as no further empathic emotion is elicited, the modulated empathic emotion represented within the virtual human's emotion module decays over time (cf. [2]). The decay function of the modulated empathic emotion is influenced by the degree of empathy, that is, the higher the calculated value of the degree of empathy, the slower the decay. The lower the value the faster the modulated empathic emotion decays. Once the modulated empathic emotion is facilitated, the next processing step *Expression of Empathy* is triggered.

3.3 Expression of Empathy

The modulated empathic emotion triggers EMMA's multimodal behavior as her expression of empathy. That is, EMMA's facial expression [6] and speech prosody [20] are modulated by the PAD value of her empathic emotion. The triggering of other modalities such as verbal utterances depends on the scenario's context.

4 Application and Evaluation

The empathy model is applied and evaluated in a conversational agent scenario where the virtual humans MAX and EMMA can engage in a multimodal small talk dialog with a human partner using speech, gestures, and facial behaviors [4] (Fig. 2, a). In this scenario, the emotions of both agents can be triggered positively or negatively by the human partner through, e.g., compliments or politically incorrect verbal utterances. During interaction, EMMA directs her attention to the speaking agent. When attending to MAX, EMMA's empathy process is triggered in response to MAX's facial expression of emotion. At each point in time, EMMA maps perceived values of MAX's facial muscles to her AUs and infers their related PAD value as MAX's perceived emotional state. Once an empathic emotion is elicited (cf. Section 3.1), it is modulated by EMMA's *mood* and her predefined values of *liking* and *familiarity* with MAX thus resulting in different degrees of empathy of EMMA with MAX (cf. Section 3.2). To investigate how the empathic behavior produced by our model is perceived by human participants, we conducted an empirical evaluation [5] of the model to test the following hypotheses, **H1**: EMMA's expression of empathy is perceivable by the participants, **H2**: EMMA's expressed degree of empathy is perceivable by the participants, **H3**: the human participants acknowledge different values of relationship between EMMA and MAX according to EMMA's expressed degree of empathy.

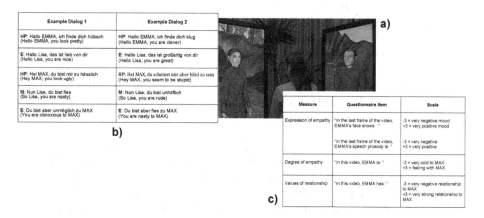

Fig. 2. a) MAX and EMMA displayed on two panels in the conversational agent scenario. **b)** Two example dialogs between Human Partner (HP), EMMA (E), and MAX (M). **c)** Schematic overview of the questionnaire. We used a 7-point Likert scale ranging from −3 to +3.

4.1 Design and Procedure

We designed 24 dialog interactions between EMMA, MAX, and a human partner (Lisa) (Fig. 2, b). At the beginning of each dialog interaction, the virtual humans are in a neutral emotional state. In each dialog interaction, Lisa begins by greeting EMMA and then praising her. Consequently, EMMA's positive emotional state *happy* is triggered. Simultaneously, EMMA greets Lisa and thanks her for being kind. Then Lisa greets MAX but proceeds to insult him. Thus, MAX's negative emotional state *angry* is triggered. Simultaneously, MAX responds with a negative verbal utterance such as "Lisa, you are horrible!". Meanwhile, EMMA empathizes with MAX to different degrees depending on her mood and her defined relationship to MAX. Note that MAX's facial expression of *anger* is interpreted by EMMA as showing the emotional state *annoyed* (cf. Section 3.1). Accordingly, the elicited empathic emotion $empEmo_t$ has as related emotion category *annoyed* (Fig. 3).

Each dialog interaction appeared in three conditions. To create the conditions we manipulated (within-subjects) the value of EMMA's and MAX's relationship, and accordingly EMMA's degree of empathy with MAX. EMMA was in the same positive mood because she was always first complimented by Lisa (this kept the modulation factor *mood* constant in all three conditions). We created the three conditions by manipulating the factor *liking*:

1. In a first condition (**neutral liking condition**, Fig. 3, left), EMMA's value of liking toward MAX is set to 0. This inhibits EMMA's modulated empathic emotion and her degree of empathy equals 0. Thus, EMMA continues in the positive emotional state *happy* triggered by Lisa's praise.
2. In a second condition (**medium liking condition**, Fig. 3, middle), EMMA's value of liking toward MAX is set to 0.5. This facilitates her modulated empathic emotion which has as its related emotion category *concentrated*. EMMA's degree of empathy equals 0.25, and she expresses the modulated empathic emotion. EMMA's values of degree of empathy and liking are higher than in the first condition.
3. In a third condition (**maximum liking condition**, Fig. 3, right), EMMA's value of liking toward MAX is set to 1. As a result, her modulated empathic emotion equals the non-modulated one (with the related emotion category *annoyed*). EMMA in this case expresses the non-modulated empathic emotion and her value of degree of empathy equals 1. EMMA's values of liking and degree of empathy are higher than in the other two conditions.

EMMA's facial expression and speech prosody expressed her degree of empathy. By contrast, the verbal utterance was identical in the three conditions. After MAX's response to Lisa, EMMA responded always with a negative verbal utterance (e.g., "You are nasty to MAX!", Fig. 2, b). Other behaviors of the virtual humans such as breathing, eye blinking, and conversational gestures were deactivated in all three conditions.

A total of 72 videos of the 24 dialog interactions in the three conditions were recorded. We constructed three experimental lists following a Latin Square design such that each dialog appeared in each list in only one condition. A total of 30 participants took part in the experiment, with each list assigned to 10 participants. The 24 videos contained in a list were presented in a random order to each corresponding participant. To test

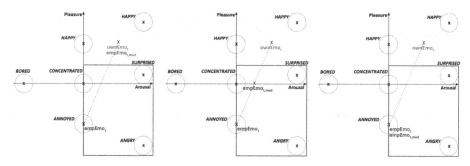

Fig. 3. The *empathy facilitation region* defined for *annoyed* represented as a box surrounding the emotion category. Left: neutral, middle: medium, right: maximum liking condition.

our three hypotheses, each participant was asked to complete a questionnaire after each presented video (Fig. 2, c).

4.2 Results

For the analyses of the data, we calculated the mean rating by condition for each of the four questionnaire items for participants and items (i.e. videos) separately. Next, we performed omnibus repeated measures one-way ANOVAs using participants and items as random effects. The results of the omnibus ANOVAs show a significant effect of condition for all four questionnaire items. To assess how the conditions differ from each other, we next performed a series of planned pairwise comparisons.

Expression of Empathy. The mean values show that EMMA's facial expression was rated as showing a positive mood in the neutral liking condition ($M = 0.883$), as showing a slightly negative mood in the medium liking condition ($M = -0.438$), and as showing a more negative mood in the maximum liking condition ($M = -1.554$) (Fig. 4). Regarding her speech prosody, the mean values show that it was rated as slightly positive in the neutral liking condition ($M = 0.521$), as slightly negative in the medium liking condition ($M = -0.550$), and as more negative in the maximum liking condition ($M = -1.592$) (Fig. 4). The pairwise comparisons show that the three conditions were rated as significantly different from each other for facial expression ($p < .001$) and speech prosody ($p < .001$).

Degree of Empathy. The mean values show that EMMA was rated as slightly feeling with MAX in the neutral liking condition ($M = 0.458$) and as progressively more feeling with MAX in the medium liking condition ($M = 0.992$) and the maximum liking condition ($M = 1.608$) respectively (Fig. 4). The pairwise comparisons show that the three conditions were rated as significantly different from each other ($p < .001$).

Values of Relationship. The mean values show that EMMA's value of relationship to MAX was rated as slightly positive in the neutral liking condition ($M = 0.325$), and as progressively more positive in the medium liking condition ($M = 0.888$) and the maximum liking condition ($M = 1.442$) respectively (Fig. 4). The pairwise comparisons show that the three conditions were rated as significantly different from each other ($p < .001$).

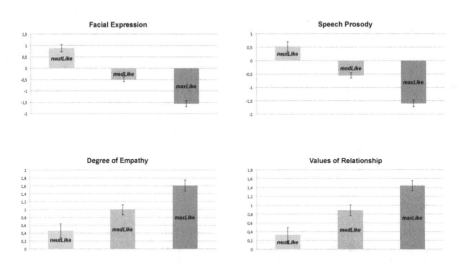

Fig. 4. Mean values and their standard errors for facial expression, speech prosody, degree of empathy, and values of relationship.

4.3 Discussion

The results show that EMMA's expression of empathy (facial expression and speech prosody) was appropriately recognized as positive in the neutral liking condition, and as progressively more negative in the medium and maximum liking conditions respectively. This confirms our first hypothesis **H1**, that EMMA's expression of empathy is perceivable by the participants, and suggests the appropriate modeling of her facial expressions and speech prosody.

The results show that EMMA's expressed degree of empathy with MAX was rated as significantly higher in the maximum liking condition than in the other two conditions, and as significantly higher in the medium liking condition than in the neutral liking condition. Hence, the results confirm our second hypothesis **H2**, that EMMA's expressed degree of empathy is perceivable by the participants. These results corroborate the theoretical assumption of our model that empathy occurs in a graded manner. The results confirmed moreover that both EMMA's facial expression and her speech prosody reliably indicate the three different empathy degrees. This corroborates our approach of modeling empathy not just as a binary function (emphatic vs. not emphatic) but rather in a graded manner that differentiates degrees of empathy.

Descriptively, Fig. 4 shows that the more EMMA's facial expression and speech prosody were rated as negative, the more EMMA was rated as empathic. That is, the more EMMA's expression of empathy was similar to MAX's expression of emotion, the more EMMA was perceived as empathic. This is in line with our definition of the degree of empathy as the degree of similarity between one's empathic emotion and the other's perceived emotion. That is, the more similar one's empathic emotion to the other's perceived emotion, the higher the degree of empathy.

Our analyses of the data showed that EMMA's different relationship values with MAX were perceived as such by the participants. The virtual humans' relationship was rated significantly higher in the maximum liking condition compared with the other two conditions, and also significantly higher in the medium than in the neutral liking condition. Overall, these results confirm hypothesis **H3**, which was that participants can perceive these subtle relationship differences that manifest through EMMA's speech prosody and facial expression. Descriptively, Fig. 4 shows that the higher they rated EMMA's expressed degree of empathy, the higher they rated EMMA's value of relationship to MAX. This is in line with our definition of the impact of relationship modulation factors in our model, e.g., *liking* or *familiarity*. That is, the higher the values of such modulation factors, the higher the similarity between the empathic emotion and the other's perceived emotion, the higher the degree of empathy. These findings further substantiate the theoretical assumption underlying our proposed model that empathy is modulated by several modulation factors such as the relationship between the empathizer and the observed other. Again, the results also show that both EMMA's facial expression and her speech prosody reliably indicate her different values of relationship to MAX thus providing further support for their appropriate modeling.

5   Conclusion

In this paper, we presented a computational model of empathy by which a virtual human can exhibit different degrees of empathy, an aspect that received little attention in previous research. In our model, regions of immediate neighborhood for each emotion category located in PAD space were defined. Accordingly, we defined the degree of empathy as the degree of similarity between a modulated empathic emotion and a non-modulated one within these defined regions. Hence, we exploited the assumed relationships between emotions in PAD space [19]. Note that the choice of the values of parameters in our model is a matter of design and evaluation. The findings of the empirical evaluation show that the virtual human EMMA is perceived as capable of exhibiting different degrees of empathy and values of relationship with MAX and thus warrants the conclusion that our model enhances a virtual human's social behavior.

Acknowledgments. This research is kindly supported by the Deutsche Forschungsgemeinschaft (DFG) in the Collaborative Research Center 673.

References

1. Becker, C., Prendinger, H., Ishizuka, M., Wachsmuth, I.: Evaluating affective feedback of the 3D agent Max in a competitive cards game. In: Tao, J., Tan, T., Picard, R.W. (eds.) ACII 2005. LNCS, vol. 3784, pp. 466–473. Springer, Heidelberg (2005)

2. Becker-Asano, C., Wachsmuth, I.: Affective computing with primary and secondary emotions in a virtual human. Autonomous Agents and Multi-Agent Systems 20(1), 32–49 (2010)
3. Bickmore, T., Picard, R.: Establishing and maintaining long-term human-computer relationships. ACM Transactions on Computer-Human Interaction (TOCHI) 12(2), 293–327 (2005)
4. Boukricha, H., Wachsmuth, I.: Empathy-based emotional alignment for a virtual human: A three-step approach. Künstl Intell. 25(3), 195–204 (2011)
5. Boukricha, H., Wachsmuth, I., Carminati, M., Knoeferle, P.: A computational model of empathy: Empirical evaluation. In: Affective Computing and Intelligent Interaction (ACII 2013), Geneva, Switzerland (in press, 2013)
6. Boukricha, H., Wachsmuth, I., Hofstätter, A., Grammer, K.: Pleasure-arousal-dominance driven facial expression simulation. In: 3rd International Conference on Affective Computing and Intelligent Interaction (ACII), Amsterdam, Netherlands, pp. 119–125. IEEE (2009)
7. Brave, S., Nass, C., Hutchinson, K.: Computers that care: investigating the effects of orientation of emotion exhibited by an embodied computer agent. International Journal of Human-Computer Studies 62, 162–178 (2005)
8. de Vignemont, F., Singer, T.: The empathic brain: how, when and why? Trends in Cognitive Sciences 10(10), 435–441 (2006)
9. Dias, J., Paiva, A.C.R.: Feeling and reasoning: A computational model for emotional characters. In: Bento, C., Cardoso, A., Dias, G. (eds.) EPIA 2005. LNCS (LNAI), vol. 3808, pp. 127–140. Springer, Heidelberg (2005)
10. Ekman, P., Friesen, W.V., Hager, J.C.: Facial Action Coding System: Investigator's Guide. Research Nexus, a subsidiary of Network Information Research Corporation, Salt Lake City UT, USA (2002)
11. Hoffman, M.L.: Empathy and Moral Development. Cambridge University Press (2000)
12. Lessmann, N., Kopp, S., Wachsmuth, I.: Situated interaction with a virtual human - perception, action, and cognition. In: Rickheit, G., Wachsmuth, I. (eds.) Situated Communication, pp. 287–323. Mouton de Gruyter, Berlin (2006)
13. McQuiggan, S., Robison, J., Phillips, R., Lester, J.: Modeling parallel and reactive empathy in virtual agents: An inductive approach. In: Padgham, L., Parkes, D.C., Mueller, J., Parsons, S. (eds.) Proc. of 7th Int. Conf. on Autonomous Agents and Multiagent Systems (AAMAS 2008), Estoril, Portugal, pp. 167–174 (2008)
14. Ochs, M., Sadek, D., Pelachaud, C.: A formal model of emotions for an empathic rational dialog agent. Autonomous Agents and Multi-Agent Systems 24(3), 410–440 (2012)
15. Ortony, A., Clore, G., Collins, A.: The Cognitive Structure of Emotions. Cambridge University Press (1988)
16. Paiva, A., Dias, J., Sobral, D., Aylett, R., Woods, S., Hall, L., Zoll, C.: Learning by feeling: Evoking empathy with synthetic characters. Applied Artificial Intelligence 19, 235–266 (2005)
17. Prendinger, H., Ishizuka, M.: The empathic companion: A character-based interface that adresses users' affective states. Applied Artificial Intelligence 19, 267–285 (2005)
18. Rodrigues, S.H., Mascarenhas, S., Dias, J., Paiva, A.: I can feel it too!: Emergent empathic reactions between synthetic characters. In: 3rd International Conference on Affective Computing and Intelligent Interaction (ACII), Amsterdam, Netherland. IEEE (2009)
19. Russell, J., Mehrabian, A.: Evidence for a three-factor theory of emotions. Journal of Research in Personality 11(3), 273–294 (1977)
20. Schröder, M., Trouvain, J.: The German text-to-speech system MARY: A tool for research, development and teaching. International Journal of Speech Technology 6(4), 365–377 (2003)

Cognitive Workload of Humans Using Artificial Intelligence Systems: Towards Objective Measurement Applying Eye-Tracking Technology

Ricardo Buettner

FOM University of Applied Sciences
Institute of Management & Information Systems
Hopfenstraße 4, 80335 Munich, Germany
ricardo.buettner@fom.de

Abstract. Replying to corresponding research calls I experimentally investigate whether a higher level of artificial intelligence support leads to a lower user cognitive workload. Applying eye-tracking technology I show how the user's cognitive workload can be measure more objectively by capturing eye movements and pupillary responses. Within a laboratory environment which adequately reflects a realistic working situation, the probands use two distinct systems with similar user interfaces but very different levels of artificial intelligence support. Recording and analyzing objective eye-tracking data (i.e. pupillary diameter mean, pupillary diameter deviation, number of gaze fixations and eye saccade speed of both left and right eyes) – all indicating cognitive workload – I found significant systematic cognitive workload differences between both test systems. My results indicated that a higher AI-support leads to lower user cognitive workload.

Keywords: artificial intelligence support, cognitive workload, pupillary diameter, eye movements, eye saccades, eye-tracking, argumentation-based negotiation, argumentation-generation.

1 Introduction

Towards programming the "global brain" [1] and realizing real collective intelligence [2], the vision of flexibly connecting billions of computational agents and humans is constantly recurring (e.g. [3]). Behind this vision lies the assumption that artificial intelligence (AI) supports humans in solving tasks and distributing the human/cognitive workload across the "global brain" [1–7] (fig. 1). It is human nature to "off-load cognitive work onto the environment" [7, p. 628, claim 3].[1] However, information systems (IS) scholars have traditionally investigated a user's cognitive workload and its derivatives[2] primarily based on

---

[1] Because of the limits of human's information-processing abilities (e.g., limits to the attention and working memory of the human brain), we tend to exploit the environment in order to reduce cognitive workload [7].

[2] Such as concentration, mental strain, mental stress, e.g. [8].

I.J. Timm and M. Thimm (Eds.): KI 2013, LNAI 8077, pp. 37–48, 2013.
© Springer-Verlag Berlin Heidelberg 2013

user-perceived/non-objective measures (e.g. MISQ: [9], JMIS: [10], DSS: [11], ISR [12]) or even discussed the need for user workload measurements without any measurement proposal (MISQ: [13]). Nevertheless, more and more IS scholars call for objective measurement techniques of user's cognitive workload and its derivatives (e.g. [14]) and a small group of IS researchers currently fosters the conducting of objective psychophysiological measures in IS research and recently formulated corresponding research calls (i.e. [15–17]).

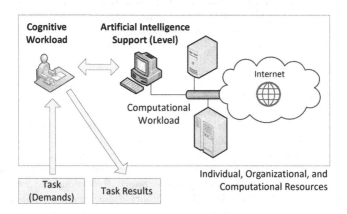

Fig. 1. Distributing human cognitive workload across the "global brain"

Replying to these research calls I show in this paper how the user's cognitive workload can be measured more objectively by capturing eye movements and pupillary responses via eye-tracking technology. Within a laboratory environment which adequately reflects a realistic working situation the probands had to use two distinct systems with similar user interfaces but very different levels of artificial intelligence support. In more detail I prototyped a test scenario derived from a typical real business environment in which extra-occupational MBA and bachelor students having professional working experience had to apply for jobs. The one system offers a chat function where the applicants had to situatively generate appropriate arguments on their own without any AI-support. The other system presented a set of AI-/system-generated arguments from which the users only had to select an appropriate argument. Recording and analyzing objective eye-tracking data (i.e. pupillary diameter mean, pupillary diameter deviation, number of gaze fixations and eye saccade speed of both left and right eyes) – all indicating cognitive workload – I found significant systematic cognitive workload differences between both systems.

Using this work I aim to contribute solutions to the current methodological problem of the objective measurement of user's cognitive workload when running AI systems (cf. [1, 3–6, 18–20]). In addition to these methodological contributions my results strongly emphasize the meaningfulness of the development of argumentation-based negotiation models using intelligent software agents (e.g. [21, 22]) from a human workload perspective.

The paper is organized as follows: After this introduction I firstly present in section 2 the state of the art concerning pupillary responses and eye movements as cognitive workload indicators in human psychophysiology and IS research. In section 3 I define the objectively measurable cognitive workload indicators, determine the hypotheses, and describe the test systems, the laboratory setting, as well as the sampling strategy. Next, in section 4 I present the objectively measured cognitive workload indicators and the results on the hypotheses evaluation. Results are then discussed in section 5. Finally, I discuss the contributions and limitations of my results and indicate future work in section 6.

2   Related Work

Despite the high level of interest in cognitive workload, there is still no universally accepted definition of this mental construct [8]. However, it is clear that cognitive workload results from mental processes when performing tasks – depending on the users's capabilities and the task demands, e.g. [23–25]. The corresponding user's cognitive workload measurement techniques can be roughly separated into two categories [8]: subjective self-assessment and rating scales (e.g. NASA TLX), and objective psychophysiological measures (e.g. pupillary responses). In the following two sections I concentrate on eye-related psychophysiological measures indicating cognitive workload and measurable by eye-tracking technology.

2.1   Pupillary Responses and Eye Movements as Cognitive Workload Indicators in Human Psychophysiology Research

The initial work on the relationship between cognitive workload and pupillary responses stems from Hess and Polt [24] and was published in 1964 in the Science journal. Hess and Polt [24] measured the cognitive workload of 5 probands by capturing the task-evoked pupillary diameter, but only based on simple multiplication tasks. Kahneman and Beatty [25] showed that the rate of the task-evoked pupillary diameter changes strongly in relation to task difficulty. Bradshaw [26] found the post-solution drop of the task-evoked pupillary diameter after finishing the task. Simpson [27] found that a subsequent indication of task completion causes a higher pupillary dilation during the preceding cognitive task. Based on testing 17 students, Kahneman, Beatty and Pollack [28] showed the stability of the correlation between cognitive workload and pupillary diameter for much more complex tasks (listening, calculating, talking) under different conditions. Following the fundamental investigations of Kahneman and colleagues [25, 28], the amount of user cognitive workload clearly corresponds with the pupillary dilation, e.g. [23, 26, 29].

Besides the diameter of the pupillary, some data from eye movements also indicate the user's cognitive workload level: Eye saccades are the rapid eye movements between points of fixation and often used for cognitive analysis [30, 31].

Information can only be perceived during fixations and not 75msec before saccades starting, during saccades, and 50msec after saccades. Since long fixations (>500 msec) indicate a deeper cognitive processing, cognitive workload is clearly positively correlated with the frequency of long fixations but negatively correlated with the saccade speed, e.g. [30, 32–34].

In general most of the psychophysiological work was based on pupillary-photographing technology, thus limited to measurements of well-seperated rudimental/basic tasks. But, IS usage is regularly very dynamic. However, very recently Wierda et al. [35] showed how eye-tracking technology can be used for high-temporal-resolution tracking of cognitive workload.

2.2 Pupillary Responses and Eye Movements as Cognitive Workload Indicators in IS Research

IS scholars have traditionally investigated user's cognitive workload and its derivatives [8] primarily based on user-perceived/non-objective measures (e.g. [9–12]) or even discussed the need for user workload measurements without any measurement proposal (e.g. [13]).[3] In the seldom case of using objective psychophysiological measures, IS research has mainly applied pupillary-based techniques indicating cognitive workload within the human-computer interaction domain, especially for adaption and personalization purposes (essential publications: [15, 37–43]).

When focusing on "AI-specific" work (in a very broad sense) in more detail, it can be summarized that determining the user's cognitive workload is often mentioned as a fundamental problem in human-machine systems (e.g. [18, 20]). The discourse on measuring the machine intelligence of human-machine cooperative systems (e.g. [6]) showed the need to quantify the cognitive workload of machine users and postulated the need for research on workload measures based on objective parameters such as behavioral signals, eye scanning movements, or physiological variables. Also the discussions about metrics for human-robot interaction emphasized the need for research into a more objective cognitive workload measurement technique (e.g. "At this point in time, there is a need to identify non-intrusive measures of workload..." [19, p. 38]). Accordingly a lot of trials and rudimentary/simple approaches on measuring the user's cognitive workload when using AI systems exist. For example, Pomplun and Sunkara [44] used the pupillary dilation as a cognitive workload indicator within a simple visual experiment asking users to find numbers in ascending order and read them out loud. Longo [45] sketched a very rudimentary framework for cognitive workload assessment using information technology. Cegarra and Chevalier [46] experimentally evaluated the cognitive workload of users solving a Sudoku puzzle

---

[3] Other IS-relevant disciplines show the same situation concerning user-perceived/non-objective cognitive workload measures. For example, Loft et al. [36] summarizes the state of the art concerning 22 existing models which predict cognitive workload in air traffic control. It is remarkable that all of 22 developed models were based on subjective workload ratings.

by capturing pupil diameter data from eye-tracking. Xu et al. [47] experimentally studied pupillary responses indicating cognitive workload when performing arithmetic tasks given by a computer under luminance changes.

However, it is noticeable that the "AI-specific" work on objective measuring the user's cognitive workload is very rudimentary (games, simple/trivial (arithmetic) tasks, non-evaluated frameworks, etc.). There is a research gap concerning empirical work on objective measuring the user's cognitive workload in laboratory experiments adequately reflecting realistic working/business situations. In line with this identified research gap more and more IS scholars call for objective measurement techniques of user's cognitive workload and its derivatives (e.g. [14]) and a small group of IS researchers currently fosters the conducting of objective psychophysiological measures in IS research and recently formulated corresponding research calls (i.e. [15–17]).

3   Methodology

I contribute to the AI-support – cognitive workload debate by investigating the research question *RQ: Does higher AI-support lead to lower user cognitive workload?* Since I aim to analyse the effect of different AI-support on the user's cognitive workload using objective workload indicatory from eye-tracking data, I choose an analysis-framework ensuring both a stable and repeatable test procedure as well as a test which adequately reflects a realistic working/business situation. That is why I analysed two systems A and B assisting users on job-interviews in a laboratory experiment with different AI-support. System A has a lower AI-support than system B. I used the following four cognitive workload indicators all captured from eye-tracking data:

1. **the pupillary diameter mean (PD_μ):** the tonic dilation measured by the time series mean of the pupillary diameter (e.g. [24, 28, 29, 48]),
2. **the pupillary diameter standard deviation (PD_σ):** the phaseal/dynamic aspect of pupillary dilation and reduction measured by the standard deviation (e.g. [23, 25]),
3. **the number of gaze fixation (GF):** the time-normalized number of gaze fixations > 500ms (e.g. [30, 32–34]),
4. **the saccade speed (SS):** the speed of saccades (e.g. [30, 32]).

Based on a consequent hypothesizing of each separate cognitive workload indicator I formulated four hypotheses. Since the pupillary diameter mean (PD_μ) as the tonic dilation is positively correlated with cognitive workload (e.g. [24, 28, 29, 48]), participants using the system A (which offers a lower AI-support) should show significant higher PD_μ values. Thus I hypothesize (H_1): *The pupillary diameter mean is significantly higher when using system A compared to system B* $(PD_\mu^A > PD_\mu^B)$.

In addition, the phaseal/dynamic aspect of pupillary dilation and reduction measured by the pupillary diameter standard deviation (PD_σ) also clearly indicates the cognitive workload level (e.g. [23, 25]). Thus I hypothesize (H_2):

The pupillary diameter standard deviation is significantly higher when using system A compared to system B $(PD_\sigma^A > PD_\sigma^B)$.

Since long fixations (>500 msec) indicate a deeper cognitive processing, cognitive workload is clearly positive correlated with the frequency of long fixations but negative correlated with the saccade speed, e.g. [30, 32–34]. Thus I hypothesize (H_3): The number of gaze fixations is significantly higher when using system A compared to system B $(GF^A > GF^B)$. and (H_4): The speed of eye saccades is significantly lower when using system A compared to system B $(SS^A < SS^B)$.

3.1 Description of Prototyped Systems with Different AI-support

To test my hypotheses, I prototyped two distinct e-recruiting systems A and B supporting online job-interviews before job-negotiation and -contracting. The systems offer a very different level of AI-support during the job-interview process. Since prior negotiation research identified argumentation-based models as very promising (e.g. [21, 22, 49]), I differentiated the AI-support level of the systems A and B by the automation-level of the argument-generation (user-generated versus system-generated) [50, 51]. That is why system A offers a chat function where the applicants can situatively generate appropriate arguments on their own without any AI-support (fig. 2). Therewith, in test system A, applicants were able to talk to the employer via an informal chat [52].

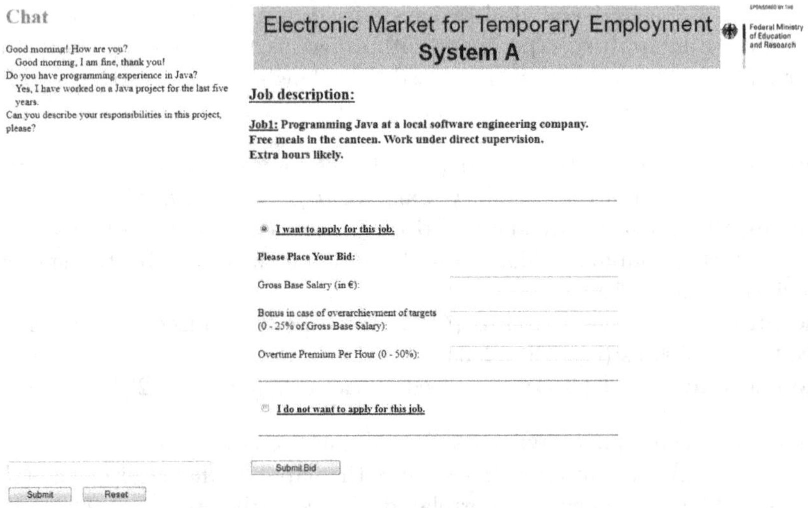

Fig. 2. System A offers a chat function where the applicants can situatively generate appropriate arguments on their own without any AI-support

In contrast to the low AI-support of system A, system B presents a set of AI-/system-generated arguments from which the users only had to select an appropriate argument (fig. 3, cf. [53]).

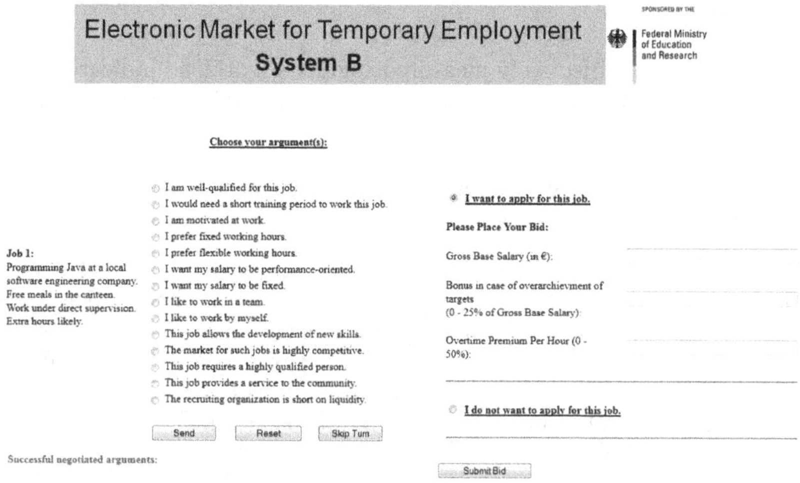

Fig. 3. System B presents a set of AI-/system-generated arguments from which the users only had to select an appropriate argument

To ensure a good level of functionality and usability, both prototypes were iteratively improved based on in-depth interview results from pre-test users. Since the pupillary response is primarily influenced by the luminance (e.g. [48]), the systems A and B have a very similar user interface (fig. 2 and fig. 3).

3.2   Laboratory Setting and Sampling Strategy

For this research, eye-tracking was performed using the binocular double Eyegaze Edge^{TM} System eye-tracker paired with a 19" LCD monitor (86 dpi) set at a resolution of 1280x1024, whereby the eye-tracker samples the position of participants' eyes and pupillary responses at the rate of 60Hz for each eye separately, cf. [54]. The eye-tracker was installed under the monitor and tracked the participant's eyes during the entire test cycle. As both the pupillary response in general [48] as well as the task-evoked response in particular [55] were primarily influenced by luminance, the lighting conditions were kept strictly constant.

Participants were recruited from a pool of extra-occupational MBA and bachelor students. All of them had professional working experience, making them suited to employment negotiations. To ensure that all participants understood the scenario and both systems, they were given introductions to the system and the computer interface. In a laboratory setting without any forms of disturbance, participants were asked to use both test systems A and B. During the experiment each participant had three job interviews on each system. A whole test cycle took about 20 to 30 minutes per participant resulting in 180,000 gaze data from eye-tracking.

4   Results

Table 1 presents the objectively measured cognitive workload indicators on system A and system B and the results of the evaluation of the four hypotheses.

Table 1. Results and hypotheses evaluation by test of significance (t-test, one-sided); System A offers a lower AI-support than system B

Hypo-thesis	Cognitive workload indicators (scale unit)			System A	B	Hypotheses evaluation (t-test)
H_1 : $PD_\mu^A > PD_\mu^B$	pupillary diameter mean (PD_μ, mm)	left eye		3.219	3.032	$p < 0.01$
		right eye		3.325	3.107	$p < 0.01$
H_2 : $PD_\sigma^A > PD_\sigma^B$	pupillary diameter deviation (PD_σ, mm)	left eye		0.223	0.144	$p < 0.01$
		right eye		0.271	0.136	$p < 0.05$
H_3 : $GF^A > GF^B$	no. of gaze fixations $> 500\text{ms}$ $(GF, \text{per sec})$			0.557	0.159	$p < 0.01$
H_4 : $SS^A < SS^B$	saccade speed $(SS, \text{m/sec})$			0.547	0.783	$p < 0.01$

5   Discussion

As shown in table 1, all four hypotheses were confirmed. It is surprising that all objectively measured cognitive workload indicators from pupillary responses and eye movement clearly showed a lower cognitive workload level of users on system B which offers a higher AI-support. Thus my results indicated that a higher AI-support actually leads to lower user cognitive workload (cf. research question RQ). In addition, my results strongly emphasize the meaningfulness of the development of argumentation-based negotiation models using intelligent software agents (e.g. [21,22]) from a human workload perspective. That is interesting because from user acceptance perspectives, users tend to prefer informal chat systems within negotiation processes. Furthermore, my results seems to be contrary to the IS-acceptance findings concerning the user-preference for informal chat systems within negotiation processes (e.g. [56,57]) – indicating a need for future research on the user workload – user acceptance relationship.

6   Conclusion

Replying to corresponding research calls, in this paper I showed how the user's cognitive workload can be measured more objectively by capturing eye movements and pupillary responses via eye-tracking technology. Within a laboratory environment adequately reflecting a realistic working situation the probands had to use two distinct systems with similar user interfaces but very different levels of artificial intelligence support. In more detail, I prototyped a test scenario derived from a typical real business environment in which extra-occupational MBA and bachelor students having professional working experience had to apply for jobs. The first system offered a chat function where the applicants had to situatively generate appropriate arguments on their own without any AI-support. The second system presented a set of AI-/system-generated arguments from which the users only had to select an appropriate argument. Recording and analyzing objective eye-tracking data (i.e. pupillary diameter mean, pupillary diameter deviation, number of gaze fixations and eye saccade speed of both left and right eyes) – all indicating cognitive workload – I found significant systematic cognitive workload differences between both systems. My results indicated that a higher AI-support leads to lower user cognitive workload. Through my results I contribute to the current methodological problem of objective measurement of a user's cognitive workload when running AI systems (cf. [1, 3–6, 18–20]). In addition to these methodological contributions my results strongly emphasize the meaningfulness of the development of argumentation-based negotiation models using intelligent software agents (e.g. [21, 22]) from a human workload perspective.

6.1   Limitations

My main limitation is rooted in the use of only four probands due to high laboratory costs for each test person. However, as shown in table 1 these four probands were sufficient for confirming all four hypotheses at a good significance level. Taking a look on the samples of other neuroscience/psychophysiological studies published in leading journals (such as [24]: Science, n=5; [25]: Science, n=5) or IS conferences (such as [58]: ICIS, n=6) four probands are an adequate amount. Furthermore, as indicated in section 1 I aimed to compare systems that had different levels of "AI-support". The definition of the notion of "AI-support" and consequently the measurement possibilities of this notion are not clear in AI-research. The use of the notion here in my work is worth discussing further, though it can said at least that I analyzed the cognitive workload when using "IT-enhanced decision support systems" with different levels of support. In addition, the systems have only been tested in a controlled laboratory experiment and not in the real-world. Hence, there are limitations concerning the generalization of the results based on the laboratory method.

6.2   Future Work

In order to deepen our understanding of the AI-support – cognitive workload debate future work should: (a) systematically extend the experiments on other AI-systems in order to re-test the hypotheses, (b) distinguish between "positive" workload (stimulating cognitive abilities) and "negative" workload inducing stress [9], (c) broaden the objective measurements from eye-tracking data to other physiological signals such as electroencephalogram, or electrodermal-activity, and (d) compare the objective measured cognitive workload indicators with perceived indicators. In addition, as discussed in section 5, my results indicated a need for future research on the user workload – user acceptance relationship.

Acknowledgments. I would like to thank the three anonymous reviewers who have provided helpful comments on the refinement of the paper. This research is partly funded by the German Federal Ministry of Education and Research (BMBF) under contracts 17103X10 and 03FH055PX2.

References

1. Bernstein, A., Klein, M., Malone, T.W.: Programming the Global Brain. CACM 55(5), 41–43 (2012)
2. Malone, T.W., Laubacher, R., Dellarocas, C.: The Collective Intelligence Genome. MIT Sloan Management Review 51(3), 21–31 (2010)
3. Davis, J., Lin, H.: Web 3.0 and Crowdservicing. In: AMCIS 2011 Proc. (2011)
4. Davis, R., Smith, R.G.: Negotiation as a Metaphor for Distributed Problem Solving. AI 20(1), 63–109 (1983)
5. Carneiro, D., Novais, P., Andrade, F., Zeleznikow, J., Neves, J.: Online dispute resolution: an artificial intelligence perspective. Artif. Intell. Rev. (2012) (in Press)
6. Park, H.J., Kim, B.K., Lim, K.Y.: Measuring the machine intelligence quotient (MIQ) of human-machine cooperative systems. IEEE TSMC, Part A 31(2), 89–96 (2001)
7. Wilson, M.: Six views of embodied cognition. Psychonomic Bulletin & Review 9(4), 625–636 (2002)
8. Cain, B.: A Review of the Mental Workload Literature. Report, NATO (2007)
9. Ayyagari, R., Grover, V., Purvis, R.: Technostress: Technological Antecedents and Implications. MISQ 35(4), 831–858 (2011)
10. Tarafdar, M., Tu, Q., Ragu-Nathan, T.S.: Impact of Technostress on End-User Satisfaction and Performance. JMIS 27(3), 303–334 (2010)
11. Gupta, A., Li, H., Sharda, R.: Should I send this message? Understanding the impact of interruptions, social hierarchy and perceived task complexity on user performance and perceived workload. DSS 55(1), 135–145 (2013)
12. Ragu-Nathan, T.S., Tarafdar, M., Ragu-Nathan, B.S., Tu, Q.: The Consequences of Technostress for End Users in Organizations: Conceptual Development and Empirical Validation. ISR 19(4), 417–433 (2008)
13. Wastell, D.G.: Learning Dysfunctions in Information Systems Development: Overcoming the Social Defenses With Transitional Objects. MISQ 23(4), 581–600 (1999)
14. Sun, Y., Lim, K.H., Peng, J.Z.: Solving the Distinctiveness - Blindness Debate: A Unified Model for Understanding Banner Processing. JAIS 14(2), 49–71 (2013)
15. Ren, P., Barreto, A., Gao, Y., Adjouadi, M.: Affective Assessment by Digital Processing of the Pupil Diameter. IEEE TAC 4(1), 2–14 (2013)
16. Dimoka, A.: What Does the Brain Tell Us About Trust and Distrust? Evidence from a Functional Neuroimaging Study. MISQ 34(2), 373–396 (2010)
17. Dimoka, A., Pavlou, P.A., Davis, F.D.: NeuroIS: The Potential of Cognitive Neuroscience for Information Systems Research. ISR 22(4), 687–702 (2011)
18. Stassen, H.G., Johannsen, G., Moray, N.: Internal representation, internal model, human performance model and mental workload. Automatica 26(4), 811–820 (1990)

19. Steinfeld, A., Fong, T., Kaber, D., Lewis, M., Scholtz, J., Schultz, A., Goodrich, M.: Common Metrics for Human-Robot Interaction. In: HRI 2006 Proc., pp. 33–40 (2006)
20. Johannsen, G., Levis, A.H., Stassen, H.G.: Theoretical Problems in Man-machine Systems and Their Experimental Validation. Automatica 30(2), 217–231 (1992)
21. Lopes, F., Wooldridge, M., Novais, A.Q.: Negotiation among autonomous computational agents: principles, analysis and challenges. Artif. Intell. Rev. 29(1), 1–44 (2008)
22. Amgoud, L., Vesic, S.: A formal analysis of the role of argumentation in negotiation dialogues. J. Logic Comput. 22(5), 957–978 (2012)
23. Beatty, J.: Task-evoked pupillary responses, processing load, and the structure of processing resources. Psychol. Bull. 91(2), 276–292 (1982)
24. Hess, E.H., Polt, J.M.: Pupil Size in Relation to Mental Activity during Simple Problem-Solving. Science 143(3611), 1190–1192 (1964)
25. Kahneman, D., Beatty, J.: Pupil Diameter and Load on Memory. Science 154(3756), 1583–1585 (1966)
26. Bradshaw, J.: Pupil Size as a Measure of Arousal during Information Processing. Nature 216(5114), 515–516 (1967)
27. Simpson, H.M.: Effects of a Task-Relevant Response on Pupil Size. Psychophysiology 6(2), 115–121 (1969)
28. Kahneman, D., Beatty, J., Pollack, I.: Perceptual Deficit during a Mental Task. Science 157(3785), 218–219 (1967)
29. Beatty, J., Wagoner, B.L.: Pupillometric signs of brain activation vary with level of cognitive processing. Science 199(4334), 1216–1218 (1978)
30. Rayner, K.: Eye movements in reading and information processing: 20 years of research. Psychol. Bull. 124(3), 372–422 (1998)
31. Leigh, R.J., Kennard, C.: Using saccades as a research tool in the clinical neurosciences. Brain 127(3), 460–477 (2004)
32. Van Orden, K.F., Limbert, W., Makeig, S., Jung, T.P.: Eye Activity Correlates of Workload during a Visuospatial Memory Task. Hum. Factors 43(1), 111–121 (2001)
33. Just, M., Carpenter, P.: Eye fixations and cognitive processes. Cognit. Psychol. 8(4), 441–480 (1976)
34. Just, M.A., Carpenter, P.A.: A theory of reading: From eye fixations to comprehension. Psychol. Rev. 87(4), 329–354 (1980)
35. Wierda, S.M., van Rijn, H., Taatgen, N.A., Martens, S.: Pupil dilation deconvolution reveals the dynamics of attention at high temporal resolution. PNAS 109(22), 8456–8460 (2012)
36. Loft, S., Sanderson, P., Neal, A., Mooij, M.: Modeling and Predicting Mental Workload in En Route Air Traffic Control: Critical Review and Broader Implications. Hum. Factors 49(3), 376–399 (2007)
37. Bailey, B.P., Iqbal, S.T.: Understanding Changes in Mental Workload during Execution of Goal-Directed Tasks and Its Application for Interruption Management. ACM TOCHI 14(4), 21:1–21:28 (2008)
38. Baltaci, S., Gokcay, D.: Negative Sentiment in Scenarios Elicit Pupil Dilation Response: An Auditory Study. In: ICMI 2012 Proc., pp. 529–532 (2012)
39. Iqbal, S.T., Adamczyk, P.D., Zheng, X.S., Bailey, B.P.: Towards an Index of Opportunity: Understanding Changes in Mental Workload during Task Execution. In: CHI 2005 Proc., pp. 311–320 (2005)
40. Wang, W., Li, Z., Wang, Y., Chen, F.: Indexing cognitive workload based on pupillary response under luminance and emotional changes. In: IUI 2013 Proc., pp. 247–256 (2013)

41. Bee, N., Prendinger, H., Nakasone, A., André, E., Ishizuka, M.: AutoSelect: What You Want Is What You Get: Real-Time Processing of Visual Attention and Affect. In: André, E., Dybkjær, L., Minker, W., Neumann, H., Weber, M. (eds.) PIT 2006. LNCS (LNAI), vol. 4021, pp. 40–52. Springer, Heidelberg (2006)
42. Ren, P., Barreto, A., Gao, Y., Adjouadi, M.: Affective Assessment of Computer Users Based on Processing the Pupil Diameter Signal. In: 2011 IEEE Eng. Med. Biol. Soc. Proc., pp. 2594–2597 (2011)
43. Zhai, J., Barreto, A.: Stress Detection in Computer Users Based on Digital Signal Processing of Noninvasive Physiological Variables. In: IEEE EMBS 2006 Proc., pp. 1355–1358 (2006)
44. Pomplun, M., Sunkara, S.: Pupil Dilation as an Indicator of Cognitive Workload in Human-Computer Interaction. In: HCII 2003 Proc., pp. 542–546 (2003)
45. Longo, L.: Human-Computer Interaction and Human Mental Workload: Assessing Cognitive Engagement in the World Wide Web. In: Campos, P., Graham, N., Jorge, J., Nunes, N., Palanque, P., Winckler, M. (eds.) INTERACT 2011, Part IV. LNCS, vol. 6949, pp. 402–405. Springer, Heidelberg (2011)
46. Cegarra, J., Chevalier, A.: The use of Tholos software for combining measures of mental workload: Toward theoretical and methodological improvements. Behav. Res. Methods 40(4), 988–1000 (2008)
47. Xu, J., Wang, Y., Chen, F., Choi, E.: Pupillary Response Based Cognitive Workload Measurement under Luminance Changes. In: Campos, P., Graham, N., Jorge, J., Nunes, N., Palanque, P., Winckler, M. (eds.) INTERACT 2011, Part II. LNCS, vol. 6947, pp. 178–185. Springer, Heidelberg (2011)
48. Steinhauer, S.R., Siegle, G.J., Condray, R., Pless, M.: Sympathetic and parasympathetic innervation of pupillary dilation during sustained processing. Int. J. Psychophysiol. 52(1), 77–86 (2004)
49. McBurney, P., Eijk, R.M.V., Parsons, S., Amgoud, L.: A Dialogue Game Protocol for Agent Purchase Negotiations. JAAMAS 7(3), 235–273 (2003)
50. Buettner, R.: The State of the Art in Automated Negotiation Models of the Behavior and Information Perspective. ITSSA 1(4), 351–356 (2006)
51. Buettner, R.: A Classification Structure for Automated Negotiations. In: IEEE/WIC/ACM WI-IAT 2006 Proc., pp. 523–530 (2006)
52. Buettner, R., Landes, J.: Web Service-based Applications for Electronic Labor Markets: A Multi-dimensional Price VCG Auction with Individual Utilities. In: ICIW 2012 Proc., pp. 168–177 (2012)
53. Landes, J., Buettner, R.: Argumentation–Based Negotiation? Negotiation–Based Argumentation! In: Huemer, C., Lops, P. (eds.) EC-Web 2012. LNBIP, vol. 123, pp. 149–162. Springer, Heidelberg (2012)
54. Eckhardt, A., Maier, C., Buettner, R.: The Influence of Pressure to Perform and Experience on Changing Perceptions and User Performance: A Multi-Method Experimental Analysis. In: ICIS 2012 Proc. (2012)
55. Steinhauer, S.R., Condray, R., Kasparek, A.: Cognitive modulation of midbrain function: task-induced reduction of the pupillary light reflex. Int. J. Psychophysiol. 39(1), 21–30 (2000)
56. Gettinger, J., Koeszegi, S.T., Schoop, M.: Shall we dance? - The effect of information presentations on negotiation processes and outcomes. DSS 53, 161–174 (2012)
57. Schoop, M., Köhne, F., Staskiewicz, D.: An Integrated Decision and Communication Perspective on Electronic Negotiation Support Systems - Challenges and Solutions. Journal of Decision Systems 13(4), 375–398 (2004)
58. Dimoka, A., Davis, F.D.: Where Does TAM Reside in the Brain? The Neural Mechanisms Underlying Technology Adoption. In: ICIS 2008 Proc., Paper 169 (2008)

Computing Role-Depth Bounded Generalizations in the Description Logic $\mathcal{ELOR}$

Andreas Ecke[1,*], Rafael Peñaloza[1,2,**], and Anni-Yasmin Turhan[1,***]

[1] Institute for Theoretical Computer Science,
Technische Universität Dresden
[2] Center for Advancing Electronics Dresden
{ecke,penaloza,turhan}@tcs.inf.tu-dresden.de

Abstract. Description Logics (DLs) are a family of knowledge representation formalisms, that provides the theoretical basis for the standard web ontology language OWL. Generalization services like the least common subsumer (lcs) and the most specific concept (msc) are the basis of several ontology design methods, and form the core of similarity measures. For the DL $\mathcal{ELOR}$, which covers most of the OWL 2 EL profile, the lcs and msc need not exist in general, but they always exist if restricted to a given role-depth. We present algorithms that compute these role-depth bounded generalizations. Our method is easy to implement, as it is based on the polynomial-time completion algorithm for $\mathcal{ELOR}$.

1 Introduction

Description logics (DLs) are knowledge representation formalisms with formal and well-understood semantics [4]. They supply the foundation for the web ontology language OWL 2 standardized by the W3C [22]. Since then, DLs became more widely used for the representation of knowledge from several domains.

Each DL offers a set of concept constructors by which complex concepts can be built. These concepts describe categories from the application domain at hand. A DL knowledge base consists of two parts: the TBox captures the terminological knowledge about categories and relations, and the ABox captures the assertional knowledge, i.e., individual facts, from the application domain. Prominent inferences are *subsumption*, which determines subconcept relationships and *instance checking*, which tests for a given individual and a concept whether the individual belongs to the concept.

The lightweight DL $\mathcal{EL}$ offers limited expressivity but allows for polynomial time reasoning [3]. These good computational properties are maintained by several extensions of $\mathcal{EL}$—most prominently by $\mathcal{EL}^{++}$, the DL underlying the OWL 2 EL profile [16], which allows for the use of nominals, i.e., singleton concepts, when building complex concept descriptions. The reasoning algorithms

---

* Supported by DFG Graduiertenkolleg 1763 (QuantLA).
** Partially supported by DFG within the Cluster of Excellence 'cfAED'
*** Partially supported by the German Research Foundation (DFG) in the Collaborative Research Center 912 "Highly Adaptive Energy-Efficient Computing".

I.J. Timm and M. Thimm (Eds.): KI 2013, LNAI 8077, pp. 49–60, 2013.
© Springer-Verlag Berlin Heidelberg 2013

for (fragments of) $\mathcal{EL}^{++}$ have been implemented in highly optimized reasoner systems such as jCEL [15] and ELK [11]. It is worth pointing out that the initial reasoning algorithm for extending $\mathcal{EL}$ by nominals [3] turned out to be incomplete, but a complete method has been recently devised in [12].

In this paper we describe methods for computing generalizations in the $\mathcal{EL}$-family by the help of the standard reasoning algorithms. We consider the following two inferences: The *least common subsumer* (lcs), which computes for a given set of concepts a new concept that subsumes the input concepts and is the least one w.r.t. subsumption; and the *most specific concept* which provides a concept which has a given individual as an instance and is the least one w.r.t. subsumption. Both inferences have been employed for several applications. Most prominently the lcs and the msc can be employed in the 'bottom-up approach' for generating TBoxes [5], where modellers can generate a new concept from picking a set of ABox individuals that instantiate the desired concept and then generalizing this set into a single concept automatically—first by applying the msc to each of the selected individuals and then generalizing the obtained concepts by applying the lcs. Other applications of the lcs and the msc include similarity measures [8,6,14], which are the core of ontology matching algorithms and more (see [7,17,9]). In particular for large bio-medical ontologies the lcs can be used effectively to support construction and maintenance. Many of these bio-medical ontologies, notably SNOMED CT [20] and the FMA Ontology [19], are written in the $\mathcal{EL}$-family of lightweight DLs.

It is known that for concepts captured by a general TBox or even just a cyclic TBox, the lcs does not need to exist [1], since cycles cannot be captured in an $\mathcal{EL}$-concept. Therefore, an approximation of the lcs has been introduced in [17], that limits the maximal nesting of quantifiers of the resulting concept descriptions. These so-called role-depth bounded lcs (k-lcs), can be computed for $\mathcal{EL}$ and for $\mathcal{EL}$ extended by role inclusions using completion sets produced by the subsumption algorithm [17,10]. In this paper, we describe a subsumption algorithm for the DL $\mathcal{ELOR}$—building on the one for $\mathcal{ELO}$ ($\mathcal{EL}$ extended by nominals) from [12]. Our algorithm is given in terms of the completion algorithm in order to extend the methods for the k-lcs to $\mathcal{ELOR}$.

Recently, necessary and sufficient conditions for the existence of the lcs w.r.t. general $\mathcal{EL}$-TBoxes [23] and $\mathcal{ELR}$-TBoxes [21] have been devised. By the use of these conditions the bound k for which the role-depth bounded lcs and the exact lcs coincide can be determined, if the lcs exists; i.e., if such k is finite.

Similarly to the lcs, the msc does not need to exist, if the ABox contains cycles [13]. To obtain an approximate solution, the role-depth of the resulting concept can be limited as suggested in [13]. A computation algorithm for the role-depth bounded msc has been proposed for $\mathcal{EL}$ in [18]. If nominals are allowed, the computation of the msc is trivial, since the msc of an individual a is simply the nominal that contains a (i.e., $\{a\}$). Thus, we consider the computation of the role-depth bounded msc in $\mathcal{EL}$ w.r.t. an $\mathcal{ELOR}$ knowledge base.

In this paper we introduce the basic notions of DL and the reasoning services considered in the next section. In Section 3 we give a completion-based

Table 1. Concept constructors, TBox axioms and ABox assertions for $\mathcal{ELOR}$

	Syntax	Semantics
concept name	$A \ (A \in N_C)$	$A^{\mathcal{I}} \subseteq \Delta^{\mathcal{I}}$
top concept	$\top$	$\Delta^{\mathcal{I}}$
nominal	$\{a\} \ (a \in N_I)$	$\{a\}^{\mathcal{I}} = \{a^{\mathcal{I}}\}$
conjunction	$C \sqcap D$	$(C \sqcap D)^{\mathcal{I}} = C^{\mathcal{I}} \cap D^{\mathcal{I}}$
existential restriction	$\exists r.C \ (r \in N_R)$	$(\exists r.C)^{\mathcal{I}} = \{d \in \Delta^{\mathcal{I}} \mid \exists e.(d,e) \in r^{\mathcal{I}} \wedge e \in C^{\mathcal{I}}\}$
GCI	$C \sqsubseteq D$	$C^{\mathcal{I}} \subseteq D^{\mathcal{I}}$
RIA	$r_1 \circ \cdots \circ r_n \sqsubseteq s$	$r_1^{\mathcal{I}} \circ \cdots \circ r_n^{\mathcal{I}} \subseteq s^{\mathcal{I}}$
Concept assertion	$C(a)$	$a^{\mathcal{I}} \in C^{\mathcal{I}}$
Role assertion	$r(a,b)$	$(a^{\mathcal{I}}, b^{\mathcal{I}}) \in r^{\mathcal{I}}$

classification algorithm for $\mathcal{ELOR}$, which serves as a basis for the computation algorithms of the role-depth bounded lcs and msc presented subsequently. The paper ends with conclusions and future work.[1]

2   Preliminaries

$\mathcal{ELOR}$-*concepts* are built from mutually disjoint sets N_C of *concept names*, N_R of *role names* and N_I of *individual names* using the syntax rule:

$$C, D ::= \top \mid A \mid \{a\} \mid C \sqcap D \mid \exists r.C,$$

where $A \in N_C$, $r \in N_R$ and $a \in N_I$. The individuals appearing in concepts are also called *nominals*. The sub-logic of $\mathcal{ELOR}$ that does not allow for individuals in concepts is called $\mathcal{ELR}$.

As usual, the semantics of $\mathcal{ELOR}$-concepts is defined through interpretations. An *interpretation* $\mathcal{I} = (\Delta^{\mathcal{I}}, \cdot^{\mathcal{I}})$ consists of an *interpretation domain* $\Delta^{\mathcal{I}}$ and an *interpretation function* $\cdot^{\mathcal{I}}$ that maps concept names A to subsets $A^{\mathcal{I}} \subseteq \Delta^{\mathcal{I}}$ and role names to binary relations on the domain $\Delta^{\mathcal{I}}$. This function is extended to complex concepts as shown in the upper part of Table 1.

Concepts can be used to model notions from the application domain in the TBox. Given two concepts C and D, a *general concept inclusion axiom* (GCI) is of the form $C \sqsubseteq D$. We use $C \equiv D$ as an abbreviation for $C \sqsubseteq D$ and $D \sqsubseteq C$. Given the roles $r_1, \ldots, r_n$ and s, a *role inclusion axiom* (RIA) is an expression of the form $r_1 \circ \cdots \circ r_n \sqsubseteq s$. An $\mathcal{ELOR}$-TBox is a finite set of GCIs and RIAs. An interpretation is a *model* for a TBox $\mathcal{T}$ if it satisfies all GCIs and RIAs in $\mathcal{T}$, as shown in the middle part of Table 1. An $\mathcal{EL}$-TBox is an $\mathcal{ELR}$-TBox (i.e., without the nominal constructor) that does not contain any RIAs.

Knowledge about individual facts of the application domain can be captured by assertions. Let $a, b \in N_I$, $r \in N_R$ and C a concept, then $C(a)$ is a *concept*

---

[1] Because of space constraints, some proofs are deferred to an appendix to be found at **http://lat.inf.tu-dresden.de/research/papers.html**.

assertion and $r(a, b)$ a *role assertion*. An *ABox* $\mathcal{A}$ is a finite set of (concept or role) assertions. An interpretation is a *model* of an ABox $\mathcal{A}$ if it satisfies all concept and role assertions in $\mathcal{A}$, as shown in the lower part of Table 1.

A *knowledge base* (KB) $\mathcal{K} = (\mathcal{T}, \mathcal{A})$ consists of a TBox $\mathcal{T}$ and an ABox $\mathcal{A}$. An interpretation is a model of $\mathcal{K} = (\mathcal{T}, \mathcal{A})$ if it is a *model* of both $\mathcal{T}$ and $\mathcal{A}$. With $\mathsf{Sig}(\mathcal{T})$ we denote the *signature* of a TBox $\mathcal{T}$, i.e. the set of all concept names, role names, and individual names that appear in $\mathcal{T}$. By $\mathsf{Sig}(\mathcal{A})$ and $\mathsf{Sig}(\mathcal{K})$ we denote the analogous notions for ABoxes and KBs, respectively.

Important reasoning tasks considered for DLs are *subsumption* and *instance checking*. A concept C *is subsumed by* a concept D w.r.t. a TBox $\mathcal{T}$ (denoted $C \sqsubseteq_{\mathcal{T}} D$) if $C^{\mathcal{I}} \subseteq D^{\mathcal{I}}$ holds in all models $\mathcal{I}$ of $\mathcal{T}$. A concept C is *equivalent* to a concept D w.r.t. a TBox $\mathcal{T}$ (denoted $C \equiv_{\mathcal{T}} D$) if $C \sqsubseteq_{\mathcal{T}} D$ and $D \sqsubseteq_{\mathcal{T}} C$ hold. The reasoning service *classification* of a TBox $\mathcal{T}$ computes all subsumption relationships between the named concepts occurring in $\mathcal{T}$. A reasoning service dealing with a whole KB is *instance checking*. An individual a *is an instance of* a given concept C w.r.t. $\mathcal{K}$ (denoted $\mathcal{K} \models C(a)$) if $a^{\mathcal{I}} \in C^{\mathcal{I}}$ holds in all models $\mathcal{I}$ of $\mathcal{K}$. *ABox realization* computes, for every concept name in $\mathcal{K}$, the set of individuals from the ABox that belong to that concept. These reasoning problems can all be decided for $\mathcal{ELOR}$, and hence also in $\mathcal{EL}$, in polynomial time [3].

There are two central inferences discussed in this paper that compute generalizations. The first is called the *least common subsumer* (lcs); it computes, for two given concepts, a (possibly complex) concept that subsumes both input concepts and that is the least concept with this property w.r.t. subsumption. The second is called the *most specific concept* (msc), which computes for a given individual a the least concept w.r.t. subsumption that has a as an instance w.r.t. $\mathcal{K}$.

The lcs does not need to exist if computed w.r.t. general $\mathcal{EL}$-TBoxes, i.e., TBoxes that use complex concepts in the left-hand sides of GCIs, or even just cyclic TBoxes [2]. The reason is that the resulting concept cannot capture cycles. Thus, we follow here the idea from [17] and compute only approximations of the lcs and of the msc by limiting the nesting of quantifiers of the resulting concept.

The *role depth* $(rd(C))$ of a concept C denotes the maximal nesting depth of the existential quantifier in C. Sometimes it is convenient to write the resulting concept in a different DL than the one the inputs concepts are written in. Thus we distinguish a 'source DL' $\mathcal{L}_s$ and a 'target DL' $\mathcal{L}_t$. With these notions at hand, we can define the first generalization inference.

Definition 1 (lcs, role-depth bounded lcs). *The* least common subsumer *of two $\mathcal{L}_s$-concepts C_1, C_2 w.r.t. an $\mathcal{L}_s$-TBox $\mathcal{T}$ (written: $lcs_{\mathcal{T}}(C_1, C_2)$) is the $\mathcal{L}_t$-concept description D s.t.:*

1. *$C_1 \sqsubseteq_{\mathcal{T}} D$ and $C_2 \sqsubseteq_{\mathcal{T}} D$, and*
2. *for all $\mathcal{L}_t$-concepts E, $C_1 \sqsubseteq_{\mathcal{T}} E$ and $C_2 \sqsubseteq_{\mathcal{T}} E$ implies $D \sqsubseteq_{\mathcal{T}} E$.*

Let $k \in \mathbf{N}$. If the concept D has a role-depth up to k and Condition 2 holds for all such E with role-depth up to k, then D is the role-depth bounded lcs *(k-$lcs_{\mathcal{T}}(C_1, C_2)$) of C_1 and C_2 w.r.t. $\mathcal{T}$ and k.*

The role-depth bounded lcs is unique up to equivalence, thus we speak of *the k-lcs*. In contrast, common subsumers need not be unique. Note that for target DLs that offer disjunction, the lcs is always trivial: $lcs(C_1, C_2) = C_1 \sqcup C_2$. Thus target DLs without disjunction may yield more informative lcs.

Similarly to the lcs, the msc does not need to exist if computed w.r.t. cyclic ABoxes. Again we compute here approximations of the msc by limiting the role-depth of the resulting concept as suggested in [13].

Definition 2. *Let $\mathcal{K} = (\mathcal{T}, \mathcal{A})$ be a KB written in $\mathcal{L}_s$ and a be an individual from $\mathcal{A}$. An $\mathcal{L}_t$-concept description C is the most specific concept of a w.r.t. $\mathcal{K}$ (written $msc_\mathcal{K}(a)$) if it satisfies:*

1. *$\mathcal{K} \models C(a)$, and*
2. *for all $\mathcal{L}_t$-concepts D, $\mathcal{K} \models D(a)$ implies $C \sqsubseteq_\mathcal{T} D$.*

If the concept C has a role-depth up to k and Condition 2 holds for all such D with role-depth up to k, then C is the role depth bounded msc of a w.r.t. $\mathcal{K}$ and k (k-$msc_\mathcal{K}(a)$).

The *msc* and the *k-msc* are unique up to equivalence in $\mathcal{EL}$ and $\mathcal{ELOR}$. In $\mathcal{ELOR}$ the *msc* is trivial, since $msc_\mathcal{K}(a) = \{a\}$. Thus we consider in this paper a more interesting case, where the target DL $\mathcal{L}_t$ for the resulting concept is a less expressive one without nominals, namely $\mathcal{EL}$ or $\mathcal{ELR}$.

3   Computing the *k*-lcs in $\mathcal{ELOR}$

The algorithms to compute the role-depth bounded lcs are based on completion-based classification algorithms for the corresponding DL. For the DL $\mathcal{ELOR}$, a consequence-based algorithm for classification of TBoxes was presented in [12], building upon the completion algorithm developed in [3]. The completion algorithm presented next adapts the ideas of the complete algorithm.

3.1   Completion Algorithm for $\mathcal{ELOR}$-TBoxes

The completion algorithms work on normalized TBoxes. We define for $\mathcal{ELOR}$ the set of *basic concepts* for a TBox $\mathcal{T}$:

$$\mathsf{BC}_\mathcal{T} = (\mathsf{Sig}(\mathcal{T}) \cap (N_C \cup N_I)) \cup \{\top\}.$$

Let $\mathcal{T}$ be an $\mathcal{ELOR}$-TBox and $A, A_1, A_2, B \in \mathsf{BC}_\mathcal{T}$; then $\mathcal{T}$ is in *normal form* if

- each GCI in $\mathcal{T}$ is of the form: $A \sqsubseteq B$, $A_1 \sqcap A_2 \sqsubseteq B$, $A \sqsubseteq \exists r.B$, or $\exists r.A \sqsubseteq B$.
- each RIA in $\mathcal{T}$ is of the form: $r \sqsubseteq s$ or $r_1 \circ r_2 \sqsubseteq s$.

Every $\mathcal{ELOR}$-TBox can be transformed into normal form in linear time by applying a set of normalization rules given in [3]. These normalization rules essentially introduce new named concepts for complex concepts used in GCIs or new roles used in complex RIAs.

Before describing the completion algorithm in detail, we introduce the reachability relation $\leadsto_R$, which plays a fundamental role in the correct treatment of nominals in TBox classification algorithms [3,12].

Definition 3 ($\leadsto_R$). *Let $\mathcal{T}$ be an $\mathcal{ELOR}$-TBox in normal form, $G \in N_C$ a concept name, and $D \in \mathsf{BC}_\mathcal{T}$. $G \leadsto_R D$ iff there exist roles $r_1, \ldots, r_n \in N_R$ and basic concepts $A_0, \ldots, A_n, B_0, \ldots, B_n \in \mathsf{BC}_\mathcal{T}$, $n \geq 0$ such that $A_i \sqsubseteq_\mathcal{T} B_i$ for all $0 \leq i \leq n$, $B_{i-1} \sqsubseteq \exists r_i.A_i \in \mathcal{T}$ for all $1 \leq i \leq n$, A_0 is either G or a nominal, and $B_n = D$.*

Informally, the concept name D is reachable from G if there is a chain of existential restrictions starting from G or a nominal and ending in D. This implies that, for $G \leadsto_R D$, if the interpretation of G is not empty, then the interpretation of D cannot be empty either. This in turn causes additional subsumption relationships to hold. Note that, if D is reachable from a nominal, then $G \leadsto_R D$ holds for all concept names G, since the interpretation of D can never be empty.

The basic idea of completion algorithms in general is to generate canonical models of the TBox. To this end, the elements of the interpretation domain are represented by named concepts or nominals from the normalized TBox. These elements are then related via roles according to the existential restrictions derived for the TBox. More precisely, let $\mathcal{T}$ be a normalized TBox, $G \in \mathsf{Sig}(\mathcal{T}) \cap N_C \cup \{\top\}$ and $A \in \mathsf{BC}_\mathcal{T}$, we introduce a *completion set* $S^G(A)$. We store all basic concepts that subsume a basic concept A in the completion set $S^A(A)$ and all basic concepts B for which $\exists r.B$ subsumes A in the completion set $S^A(A, r)$. These completion sets are then extended using a set of rules. However, the algorithm needs to keep track also of completion sets of the form $S^G(A)$ and $S^G(A, r)$ for every $G \in (\mathsf{Sig}(\mathcal{T}) \cap N_C) \cup \{\top\}$, since the non-emptiness of an interpretation of a concept G may imply additional subsumption relationships for A. The completion set $S^G(A)$ therefore stores all basic concepts that subsume A under the assumption that G is not empty. Similarly, $S^G(A, r)$ stores all concepts B for which $\exists r.B$ subsumes A under the same assumption.

For every $G \in (\mathsf{Sig}(\mathcal{T}) \cap N_C) \cup \{\top\}$, every basic concept A and every role name r, the completion sets are initialized as $S^G(A) = \{A, \top\}$ and $S^G(A, r) = \emptyset$. These sets are then extended by applying the completion rules shown in Figure 1 (adapted from [12]) exhaustively.

To compute the reachability relation $\leadsto_R$ used in rule **OR7**, the algorithm can use Definition 3 with all previously derived subsumption relationships; that is, $A_i \sqsubseteq B_i$ if it finds $B_i \in S^{A_i}(A_i)$. Thus the computation of $\leadsto_R$ and the application of the completion rules need to be carried out simultaneously.

It can be shown that the algorithm terminates in polynomial time, and is sound and complete for classifying the TBox $\mathcal{T}$. In particular, when no rules are applicable anymore the completion sets have the following properties.

Proposition 1. *Let $\mathcal{T}$ be an $\mathcal{ELOR}$-TBox in normal form, $C, D \in \mathsf{BC}_\mathcal{T}$, $r \in \mathsf{Sig}(\mathcal{T}) \cap N_R$, and $G = C$ if $C \in N_C$ and $G = \top$ otherwise. Then, the following properties hold:*

$C \sqsubseteq_\mathcal{T} D$ *iff* $D \in S^G(C)$*, and*
$C \sqsubseteq_\mathcal{T} \exists r.D$ *iff*   *there exists $E \in \mathsf{BC}_\mathcal{T}$ such that $E \in S^G(C, r)$ and $D \in S^G(E)$.*

We now show how to use these completion sets for computing the role-depth bounded lcs for $\mathcal{ELOR}$-concept w.r.t. a general $\mathcal{ELOR}$-TBox.

OR1 If $A_1 \in S^G(A)$, $A_1 \sqsubseteq B \in \mathcal{T}$ and $B \notin S^G(A)$,
then $S^G(A) := S^G(A) \cup \{B\}$

OR2 If $A_1, A_2 \in S^G(A)$, $A_1 \sqcap A_2 \sqsubseteq B \in \mathcal{T}$ and $B \notin S^G(A)$,
then $S^G(A) := S^G(A) \cup \{B\}$

OR3 If $A_1 \in S^G(A)$, $A_1 \sqsubseteq \exists r.B \in \mathcal{T}$ and $B \notin S^G(A, r)$,
then $S^G(A, r) := S^G(A, r) \cup \{B\}$

OR4 If $B \in S^G(A, r)$, $B_1 \in S^G(B)$, $\exists r.B_1 \sqsubseteq C \in \mathcal{T}$ and $C \notin S^G(A)$,
then $S^G(A) := S^G(A) \cup \{C\}$

OR5 If $B \in S^G(A, r)$, $r \sqsubseteq s \in \mathcal{T}$ and $B \notin S^G(A, s)$,
then $S^G(A, s) := S^G(A, s) \cup \{B\}$

OR6 If $B \in S^G(A, r_1)$, $C \in S^G(B, r_2)$, $r_1 \circ r_2 \sqsubseteq s \in \mathcal{T}$ and $C \notin S^G(A, s)$,
then $S^G(A, s) := S^G(A, s) \cup \{C\}$

OR7 If $\{a\} \in S^G(A_1) \cap S^G(A_2)$, $G \leadsto_R A_2$, and $A_2 \notin S^G(A_1)$,
then $S^G(A_1) := S^G(A_1) \cup \{A_2\}$

Fig. 1. Completion rules for $\mathcal{ELOR}$

3.2 Computing the Role-Depth Bounded $\mathcal{ELOR}$-lcs

In order to compute the role-depth bounded lcs of two $\mathcal{ELOR}$-concepts C and D, we extend the methods from [17] for $\mathcal{EL}$-concepts and from [10] for $\mathcal{ELR}$-concepts, where we compute the cross-product of the tree unravelings of the canonical model represented by the completion sets for C and D up to the role-depth k. Clearly, in the presence of nominals, the right completion sets need to be chosen that preserve the non-emptiness of the interpretation of concepts derived by the reachability relation $\leadsto_R$.

An algorithm that computes the role-depth bounded $\mathcal{ELOR}$-lcs using completion sets is shown in Figure 2. In the first step, the algorithm introduces two new concept names A and B as abbreviations for the (possibly complex) input concepts C and D, and the augmented TBox is normalized. The completion sets are then initialized and the completion rules from Figure 1 are applied exhaustively, yielding the saturated completion sets $S_{\mathcal{T}}$. In the recursive procedure k-lcs-r for concepts A and B, we first obtain all the basic concepts that subsume both A and B from the sets $S^A(A)$ and $S^B(B)$. For every role name r, the algorithm then recursively computes the $(k-1)$-lcs of the concepts A' and B' in the subsumer sets $S^A(A, r)$ and $S^B(B, r)$, i.e., for which $A \sqsubseteq_{\mathcal{T}} \exists r.A'$ and $B \sqsubseteq_{\mathcal{T}} \exists r.B'$. These concepts are conjoined as existential restrictions to the k-lcs concept.

The algorithm only introduces concept and role names that occur in the original TBox $\mathcal{T}$. Therefore those names introduced by the normalization are not used in the concept for the k-lcs and an extra denormalization step as in [17,10] is not necessary.

Notice that for every pair (A', B') of r-successors of A and B it holds that $A \leadsto_R A'$ and $B \leadsto_R B'$. Intuitively, we are assuming that the interpretation of both A and B is non-empty. This in turn causes the interpretation of $\exists r.A'$

Procedure k-lcs($C, D, \mathcal{T}, k$)
Input: C, D: $\mathcal{ELOR}$-concepts; $\mathcal{T}$: $\mathcal{ELOR}$-TBox; $k \in \mathbb{N}$
Output: role-depth bounded $\mathcal{ELOR}$-lcs of C, D w.r.t. $\mathcal{T}$ and k

1: $\mathcal{T}' := \mathsf{normalize}(\mathcal{T} \cup \{A \equiv C, B \equiv D\})$
2: $\mathsf{S}_{\mathcal{T}} := \mathsf{apply\text{-}completion\text{-}rules}(\mathcal{T}')$
3: **return** k-lcs-r($A, B, \mathsf{S}_{\mathcal{T}}, k, A, B, \mathsf{Sig}(\mathcal{T})$)

Procedure k-lcs-r($X, Y, \mathsf{S}_{\mathcal{T}}, k, A, B, \mathsf{Sig}(\mathcal{T})$)
Input: A, B: concept names, X, Y: basic concepts with $A \rightsquigarrow_R X, B \rightsquigarrow_R Y$; $k \in \mathbb{N}$;
          $\mathsf{S}_{\mathcal{T}}$: set of saturated completion sets; $\mathsf{Sig}(\mathcal{T})$: signature of $\mathcal{T}$
Output: role-depth bounded $\mathcal{ELOR}$-lcs of X, Y w.r.t. $\mathcal{T}$ and k

1: common-names := $S^A(X) \cap S^B(Y) \cap \mathsf{BC}_{\mathcal{T}}$
2: **if** $k = 0$ **then**
3:    **return** $\displaystyle\prod_{P \in \text{common-names}} P$
4: **else**
5:    **return** $\displaystyle\prod_{P \in \text{common-names}} P \sqcap$

$$\prod_{r \in \mathsf{Sig}(\mathcal{T}) \cap N_R} \left(\prod_{\substack{E \in S^A(X,r), \\ F \in S^B(Y,r)}} \exists r.\text{k-lcs-r}\big(E, F, \mathsf{S}_{\mathcal{T}}, k-1, A, B, \mathsf{Sig}(\mathcal{T})\big) \right)$$

Fig. 2. Computation algorithm for role-depth bounded $\mathcal{ELOR}$-lcs

and $\exists r.B'$ to be not empty, either. Thus, it suffices to consider the completion sets S^A and S^B, without the need to additionally compute $S^{A'}$ and $S^{B'}$, or the completion sets S^C for any other basic concept C encountered during the recursive computation of the k-lcs. This allows for a goal-oriented optimization in cases where there is no need to classify the full TBox.

3.3   Computing the Role-Depth Bounded msc w.r.t. $\mathcal{ELOR}$-KBs

We now turn our attention to the other generalization inference: the computation of the most specific concept representing a given individual. Recall that, since $\mathcal{ELOR}$ allows the use of nominals, computing the (exact) $\mathcal{ELOR}$-msc for a given individual is a trivial task: the most specific $\mathcal{ELOR}$-concept describing an individual $a \in N_I$ is simply the nominal $\{a\}$. However, it may be of interest to compute the msc w.r.t. a less expressive target DL. Next, we describe how to compute the depth-bounded $\mathcal{EL}$-msc of an individual w.r.t. an $\mathcal{ELOR}$-KB.

As we have defined them, KBs consist of two parts: the TBox, which represents the conceptual knowledge of the domain, and the ABox, which states information about individuals. In the presence of nominals, this division between concepts and individuals is blurred. In fact, it is easy to see that ABox assertions can be simulated using GCIs as described by the following proposition.

Procedure k-msc $(a, \mathcal{K}, k)$
Input: a: individual from $\mathcal{K}$; $\mathcal{K} = (\mathcal{T}, \mathcal{A})$ an $\mathcal{ELOR}$-KB; $k \in \mathbb{N}$
Output: role-depth bounded $\mathcal{EL}$-msc of a w.r.t. $\mathcal{K}$ and k.
1: $\mathcal{T}' := \mathcal{T} \cup$ absorb-ABox$(\mathcal{K})$
2: $\mathcal{T}'' :=$ normalize$(\mathcal{T}')$
3: $S_\mathcal{K} :=$ apply-completion-rules$(\mathcal{T}'')$
4: **return** traversal-concept $(\{a\}, S_\mathcal{K}, k, \mathsf{Sig}(\mathcal{K}))$

Procedure traversal-concept $(A, S_\mathcal{K}, k, \mathsf{Sig}(\mathcal{K}))$
Input: A: basic concept from $\mathcal{T}'$; $S_\mathcal{K}$: set of completion sets; $k \in \mathbb{N}$;
$\quad\quad$ $\mathsf{Sig}(\mathcal{K})$: signature of original KB $\mathcal{K}$
Output: role-depth bounded traversal concept w.r.t. $\mathcal{K}$ and k.

1: **if** $k = 0$ **then**
2: $\quad$ **return** $\bigsqcap_{B \in S^\top(A) \cap (\mathrm{BC}_\mathcal{T} \setminus N_I)} B$
3: **else**
4: $\quad$ **return** $\displaystyle\bigsqcap_{B \in S^\top(A) \cap (\mathrm{BC}_\mathcal{T} \setminus N_I)} B \sqcap$
$$\bigsqcap_{r \in \mathsf{Sig}(\mathcal{K}) \cap N_R} \bigsqcap_{B \in S^\top(A,r)} \exists r.\text{traversal-concept}\,(B, S_\mathcal{K}, k-1, \mathsf{Sig}(\mathcal{K}))$$

Fig. 3. Computation algorithm for the role-depth bounded $\mathcal{EL}$-msc w.r.t. $\mathcal{ELOR}$-KBs

Lemma 1. *An interpretation $\mathcal{I}$ satisfies the concept assertion $C(a)$ iff it satisfies the GCI $\{a\} \sqsubseteq C$. It satisfies the role assertion $r(a, b)$ iff it satisfies the GCI $\{a\} \sqsubseteq \exists r.\{b\}$.*

Using this result, we can 'absorb' the ABox into the TBox and restrict our attention to reasoning w.r.t. TBoxes only, without losing generality. Figure 3 describes the algorithm for computing the $\mathcal{EL}$-k-msc w.r.t. an $\mathcal{ELOR}$-KB.

As before, correctness of this algorithm is a consequence of the invariants described by Proposition 1. The set $S^\top(\{a\})$ contains all the basic concepts that subsume the nominal $\{a\}$; that is, all concepts whose interpretation must contain the individual $a^\mathcal{I}$. Likewise, $S^\top(\{a\}, r)$ contains all the existential restrictions subsuming $\{a\}$. Thus, a recursive conjunction of all these subsumers provides the most specific representation of the individual a.

Since the target language is $\mathcal{EL}$, no nominals may be included in the output. However, the recursion includes also the $\mathcal{EL}$-msc of the removed nominals, hence indeed providing the most specific $\mathcal{EL}$ representation of the input individual. As in the computation of the lcs presented above, the only completion sets relevant for computing the msc are those of the form $S^\top(A)$ and $S^\top(A, r)$. Once again, this means that it is possible to implement a goal-oriented approach that computes only these sets, as needed, when building the msc for a given individual.

In this section we have shown how to compute generalization inferences with a bounded role-depth w.r.t. KBs written in the DL $\mathcal{ELOR}$, which extends $\mathcal{EL}$ by allowing nominals and complex role inclusion axioms. With the exception of data-types and disjointness axioms, this covers the full expressivity of the OWL 2 EL profile of the standard ontology language OWL 2. Given its status as W3C standard, it is likely that more and bigger ontologies built using this profile, thus the generalization inferences investigated in this paper and their computation algorithms will become useful to more ontology engineers. In fact, there already exist ontologies that use nominals in their representation. For example, the FMA ontology [19] is written in $\mathcal{ELOR}$ and currently contains already 85 nominals.

4   Conclusions

We have studied reasoning services for computing generalizations in extensions of the light-weight description logic $\mathcal{EL}$ by nominals and role inclusions, which yields the DL $\mathcal{ELOR}$. One of the characterizing features of $\mathcal{EL}$ and its extension $\mathcal{ELOR}$ is that they allow for polynomial time standard reasoning reasoning— such as subsumption. Efficient reasoning becomes expedient when dealing with huge knowledge bases such as, for instance, the biomedical ontologies SNOMED and the Gene Ontology. Additionally, $\mathcal{ELOR}$ covers a large part of the OWL 2 EL profile. Given its status as a W3C recommendation, it is likely that the usage of the $\mathcal{EL}$-family of DLs becomes more widespread in the future.

Especially for the huge ontologies written in extensions of $\mathcal{EL}$, tools that aid the user with the construction and maintenance of the knowledge base become necessary. As previous work has shown, the generalization inferences lcs and msc can be effectively used for such tasks. Besides this application, the generalizations can be used as a basis for other inferences, like the construction of semantic similarity measures and information retrieval procedures. The algorithms presented in this paper are a basis for employing these services for $\mathcal{ELOR}$-knowledge bases.

The contributions of this paper are manyfold. First, we have given a completion algorithm for $\mathcal{ELOR}$-knowledge bases, inspired by a consequence-based classification algorithm for $\mathcal{EL}$ with nominals [12]. This completion algorithm is then employed to extend the algorithms for computing approximations of the lcs and of the msc for the DL $\mathcal{ELOR}$. In general, the lcs and msc do not need to exist, even for $\mathcal{EL}$, thus we approximate them by limiting the role-depth of the resulting concept description, up to a maximal bound to be specified by the user.

We extended here the computation algorithm of the k-lcs to the DL $\mathcal{ELOR}$, using the new completion algorithm, by allowing nominals as part of the resulting concept. Since the k-msc is trivial in $\mathcal{ELOR}$ due to nominals, we give a computation algorithm for the k-msc for the target language $\mathcal{EL}$, which works w.r.t. the axioms and assertions of $\mathcal{ELOR}$-KBs. Using these algorithms, the generalization inferences can be used for a set of ontologies built for the OWL 2 EL profile. Both algorithms have the property that, if the exact lcs or msc exist, then our algorithms compute the exact solution for a sufficiently large role-depth bound k. Such a k can be computed using the necessary and sufficient conditions for the existence of the lcs and msc given for for $\mathcal{EL}$ in [23] and for $\mathcal{ELR}$ in [21].

As future work we intend to study methods of finding these generalizations in further extensions of $\mathcal{EL}$. Initial steps in this direction have been made by considering $\mathcal{EL}$ with subjective probability constructors [18]. In a different direction, we also intend to implement a system that can compute the lcs and the msc, by modifying and improving existing completion-based reasoners.

References

1. Baader, F.: Least common subsumers and most specific concepts in a description logic with existential restrictions and terminological cycles. In: Gottlob, G., Walsh, T. (eds.) Proc. of the 18th Int. Joint Conf. on Artificial Intelligence (IJCAI 2003), pp. 325–330. Morgan Kaufmann (2003)
2. Baader, F.: Terminological cycles in a description logic with existential restrictions. In: Gottlob, G., Walsh, T. (eds.) Proc. of the 18th Int. Joint Conf. on Artificial Intelligence (IJCAI 2003), pp. 319–324. Morgan Kaufmann (2003)
3. Baader, F., Brandt, S., Lutz, C.: Pushing the $\mathcal{EL}$ envelope. In: Proc. of the 19th Int. Joint Conf. on Artificial Intelligence (IJCAI 2005), Edinburgh, UK. Morgan-Kaufmann Publishers (2005)
4. Baader, F., Calvanese, D., McGuinness, D., Nardi, D., Patel-Schneider, P. (eds.): The Description Logic Handbook: Theory, Implementation, and Applications. Cambridge University Press (2003)
5. Baader, F., Küsters, R., Molitor, R.: Computing least common subsumers in description logics with existential restrictions. In: Dean, T. (ed.) Proc. of the 16th Int. Joint Conf. on Artificial Intelligence (IJCAI 1999), Stockholm, Sweden, pp. 96–101. Morgan Kaufmann, Los Altos (1999)
6. Borgida, A., Walsh, T., Hirsh, H.: Towards measuring similarity in description logics. In: Proc. of the 2005 Description Logic Workshop (DL 2005). CEUR Workshop Proceedings, vol. 147 (2005)
7. Brandt, S., Turhan, A.-Y.: Using non-standard inferences in description logics — what does it buy me? In: Görz, G., Haarslev, V., Lutz, C., Möller, R. (eds.) Proc. of the 2001 Applications of Description Logic Workshop (ADL 2001), Vienna, Austria. CEUR Workshop, vol. (44). RWTH Aachen (September 2001), http://CEUR-WS.org/Vol-44/
8. d'Amato, C., Fanizzi, N., Esposito, F.: A semantic similarity measure for expressive description logics. In: Proc. of Convegno Italiano di Logica Computazionale (CILC 2005) (2005)
9. Ecke, A., Peñaloza, R., Turhan, A.-Y.: Towards instance query answering for concepts relaxed by similarity measures. In: Workshop on Weighted Logics for AI (in conjunction with IJCAI 2013), Beijing, China (to appear, 2013)
10. Ecke, A., Turhan, A.-Y.: Role-depth bounded least common subsumers for $\mathcal{EL}^+$ and $\mathcal{ELI}$. In: Kazakov, Y., Lembo, D., Wolter, F. (eds.) Proc. of the 2012 Description Logic Workshop (DL 2012). CEUR Workshop Proceedings, vol. 846. CEUR-WS.org (2012)
11. Kazakov, Y., Krötzsch, M., Simančík, F.: ELK reasoner: Architecture and evaluation. In: Horrocks, I., Yatskevich, M., Jimenez-Ruiz, E. (eds.) Proceedings of the OWL Reasoner Evaluation Workshop (ORE 2012). CEUR Workshop Proceedings, vol. 858. CEUR-WS.org (2012)

12. Kazakov, Y., Krötzsch, M., Simančík, F.: Practical reasoning with nominals in the $\mathcal{EL}$ family of description logics. In: Brewka, G., Eiter, T., McIlraith, S.A. (eds.) Proc. of the 12th Int. Conf. on the Principles of Knowledge Representation and Reasoning (KR 2012), pp. 264–274. AAAI Press (2012)

13. Küsters, R., Molitor, R.: Approximating most specifc concepts in description logics with existential restrictions. In: Baader, F., Brewka, G., Eiter, T. (eds.) KI 2001. LNCS (LNAI), vol. 2174, pp. 33–47. Springer, Heidelberg (2001)

14. Lehmann, K., Turhan, A.-Y.: A framework for semantic-based similarity measures for $\mathcal{ELH}$-concepts. In: del Cerro, L.F., Herzig, A., Mengin, J. (eds.) JELIA 2012. LNCS, vol. 7519, pp. 307–319. Springer, Heidelberg (2012)

15. Mendez, J.: jCel: A modular rule-based reasoner. In: Proc. of the 1st Int. Workshop on OWL Reasoner Evaluation (ORE 2012). CEUR, vol. 858 (2012)

16. Motik, B., Cuenca Grau, B., Horrocks, I., Wu, Z., Fokoue, A., Lutz, C.: OWL 2 web ontology language profiles. W3C Recommendation (October 27, 2009), http://www.w3.org/TR/2009/REC-owl2-profiles-20091027/

17. Peñaloza, R., Turhan, A.-Y.: A practical approach for computing generalization inferences in $\mathcal{EL}$. In: Antoniou, G., Grobelnik, M., Simperl, E., Parsia, B., Plexousakis, D., De Leenheer, P., Pan, J. (eds.) ESWC 2011, Part I. LNCS, vol. 6643, pp. 410–423. Springer, Heidelberg (2011)

18. Peñaloza, R., Turhan, A.-Y.: Instance-based non-standard inferences in $\mathcal{EL}$ with subjective probabilities. In: Bobillo, F., Costa, P.C.G., d'Amato, C., Fanizzi, N., Laskey, K.B., Laskey, K.J., Lukasiewicz, T., Nickles, M., Pool, M. (eds.) URSW 2008-2010/UniDL 2010. LNCS, vol. 7123, pp. 80–98. Springer, Heidelberg (2013)

19. Rosse, C., Mejino, J.L.V.: A reference ontology for biomedical informatics: the foundational model of anatomy. Journal of Biomedical Informatics 36, 478–500 (2003)

20. Spackman, K.: Managing clinical terminology hierarchies using algorithmic calculation of subsumption: Experience with SNOMED-RT. Journal of the American Medical Informatics Assoc. (2000) (Fall Symposium Special Issue)

21. Turhan, A.-Y., Zarrieß, B.: Computing the lcs w.r.t. general $\mathcal{EL}+$ TBoxes. In: Proceedings of the 26th International Workshop on Description Logics (DL 2013), Ulm, Germany, CEUR Workshop Proceedings. CEUR-WS.org. (to appear, July 2013)

22. W3C OWL Working Group. OWL 2 web ontology language document overview. W3C Recommendation (October 27, 2009), http://www.w3.org/TR/2009/REC-owl2-overview-20091027/.

23. Zarrieß, B., Turhan, A.-Y.: Most specific generalizations w.r.t. general $\mathcal{EL}$-TBoxes. In: Proceedings of the 23rd International Joint Conference on Artificial Intelligence (IJCAI 2013), Beijing, China. AAAI Press (to appear, 2013)

Parallel Variable Elimination on CNF Formulas

Kilian Gebhardt and Norbert Manthey

Knowledge Representation and Reasoning Group
Technische Universität Dresden

Abstract. Formula simplification is important for the performance of SAT solvers. However, when applied until completion, powerful preprocessing techniques like variable elimination can be very time consuming. Therefore, these techniques are usually used with a resource limit. Although there has been much research on parallel SAT solving, no attention has been given to parallel preprocessing. In this paper we show how the preprocessing techniques subsumption, clause strengthening and variable elimination can be parallelized. For this task either a high-level variable-graph formula partitioning or a fine-grained locking schema can be used. By choosing the latter and enforcing clauses to be ordered, we obtain powerful parallel simplification algorithms. Especially for long pre-processing times, parallelization is beneficial, and helps MINISAT to solve 11 % more instances of recent competition benchmarks.

1 Introduction

Since the development of the *Conflict Driven Clause Learning*(CDCL) algorithm [1], hard problems from applications like model checking, routing or scheduling can be solved [2,3,4]. Sequential SAT solvers have been equipped with efficient data structures resulting in a high efficiency [5,6,7], but more importantly have been extended with advanced heuristics that drive their search [5,8,9]. Furthermore, formula simplification has been added, which enables these tools to either solve previously unsolvable instances or to solve problems faster.

Recently, the extraction of *minimal unsatisfiable subformulas* has been enhanced with formula simplification, resulting in an improved performance [10]. Another demonstration of the utility of preprocessing is the application of preprocessing to incremental SAT solving, which is used for example for bounded model checking [11]. Already these examples show that SAT preprocessing is crucial for the overall solving tool chain. Preprocessing techniques are usually polynomially bounded. Still, their execution can be very resource consuming, and therefore these techniques usually ship with a cut off (e.g. [12]). In practice, SAT solvers use simplifications usually before search, and apply a cut off. The alternative is to use these techniques also during search – known as *inprocessing* – and to restrict their execution time even more. In contrast to limiting preprocessing, running simplifications until fix point might have positive effects on solving difficult problems. Since the run time of the overall tool chain should be optimal, cut offs seem to be a reasonable compromise. By exploiting the omnipresent multicore architecture, it should be possible to speed up CNF simplifications.

In this paper, we present a parallelization of the widely used techniques *variable elimination, (clause) strengthening* and *subsumption*. There are two important goals that we reach with this approach: the overall run time when running these techniques

I.J. Timm and M. Thimm (Eds.): KI 2013, LNAI 8077, pp. 61–73, 2013.
© Springer-Verlag Berlin Heidelberg 2013

until completion is reduced, and with parallel formula simplifications we enable parallel SAT solvers to become more scalable. The presented parallelization uses workers that execute a fine grained low-level parallelization based on *critical sections*. All clauses and variables that are necessary for the next step of the algorithm are reserved exclusively for the current worker. The approach scales with the size of the formula. This is an advantage compared to the alternative high-level parallelization approach: partitioning the formula and then process each partition without locking, because each worker has exclusive access to its partition. We implemented the modified algorithms into the preprocessor COPROCESSOR [13]. To reduce the overall overhead of the approach, we add the invariant that all variables in a clause of the formula have to be sorted. Based on this invariant, a deadlock-free implementation is guaranteed. Our experimental evaluation reveals that the run time of the parallel algorithm improves with the number of available resources for all the presented techniques. The overall performance of MINISAT 2.2 is improved with the parallel preprocessor: 11 % more instances of a benchmark combined from recent SAT competitions can be solved.

The paper is structured as follows: first, we briefly introduce the notions which we use throughout the paper in Section 2. Afterwards, we present the sequential algorithms of the chosen preprocessing techniques in Section 3. Then, we discuss in Section 4 how these techniques can be parallelized with locks, and provide an experimental evaluation in Section 5. Finally, we conclude and give an outlook on future work in Section 6.

2   Preliminaries

2.1   Notions and Basic Concepts

We assume a fixed set $\mathcal{V}$ of Boolean variables, or briefly just *variables* or *atoms*. A *literal* is a variable x (*positive literal*) or a negated variable $\overline{x}$ (*negative literal*). We overload the overbar notation: The *complement* $\overline{l}$ of a positive (negative, resp.) literal l is the negative (positive, resp.) literal with the same variable as l. A *clause* is a finite set of literals, a *formula* (short for *formula in conjunctive normal form*) is a finite set of clauses.

An *interpretation* is a mapping from the set $\mathcal{V}$ of all Boolean variables to the set $\{\top, \bot\}$ of truth values. In the following, we assume the reader to be familiar with propositional logic, and how propositional formulas are evaluated under interpretations. More details can be found in [14].

A clause that contains exactly one literal is called a *unit clause*. A clause that contains a literal and its complement is called a *tautology*. A clause C *subsumes* a clause D if and only if $C \subseteq D$. The set of all atoms occurring in a formula F (in positive or negative literals) is denoted by $\mathsf{atoms}(F)$. We define a total order $\leq$ on $\mathsf{atoms}(F)$. The function atom maps each literal to the corresponding variable. If F is a formula and l is a literal, then the formula consisting of all clauses in F that contain l is denoted by F_l. If x is a Boolean variable and $C = \{x\} \cup C'$ as well as $D = \{\overline{x}\} \vee D'$ are clauses, then the clause $C' \cup D'$ is called the *resolvent of C and D upon x*. For two formulas F, G and variable x, the set of all resolvents of a clause in F with a clause in G upon x is denoted by $F \otimes_x G$.

The SAT problem is to answer whether a given formula F is satisfiable. Since [15], SAT is known to be $\mathcal{NP}$-complete. There are two ways to solve SAT: using local search algorithms [16], or by using structured search [14].

2.2 Concepts of Parallel Algorithms

Let T_1 denote the run time needed by a sequential algorithm to solve a given problem, and T_n the run time a parallel algorithm with n computing resources needs. Then, we calculate the *speedup* $S = \frac{T_1}{T_n}$. A speedup is called *linear*, if $S = n$. If $T_1 < T_n$, we say the parallel algorithm *slows down*.

In the following we refer to *workers* to talk about parts of the algorithm being executed in parallel. When showing that the implementation of a parallel algorithm is deadlock free, the *Coffman Conditions* [17] can be used. They state that in a concurrent environment deadlocks arise only, if the following four conditions are met simultaneously: only a single worker can execute a part of the algorithm at a time (mutual exclusion condition), resources are not acquired *atomically* (lock a resource, wait for the next one), locks cannot be preempted (return lock, if overall locking procedure fails), and resources can be locked in a circular manner (circular wait condition). As long as it is ensured that at each step of the algorithm at least one of the above four conditions is violated, the algorithm cannot get stuck in a deadlock.

3 SAT Preprocessing

Simplifying the formula before giving it to the SAT solver is a crucial part of the solving chain. Several techniques, such as bounded variable elimination [18], blocked clause elimination [19], equivalent literal elimination [20], probing [21] or automated re-encoding by using extended resolution [12,22], have been proposed as formula simplifications.

Successful SAT solvers either use simplifications only before search in an incomplete way, or utilize these techniques also during search – known as *inprocessing* – and spend even less time per simplification. This treatment points exactly to the weakness of simplification techniques: applying them until completion can take more time then solving the initial formula. Therefore, inprocessing seems a appealing idea to follow. Here we do not want to discuss when preprocessing and inprocessing can be exchanged, but focus on another point in parallel SAT solving: powerful parallel SAT solvers as PENELOPE use the *sequential* preprocessor SATELITE [18], which has been developed in 2005. Although PENELOPE can utilize up to 32 computing units, during preprocessing only a single core is used. By parallelizing the preprocessor, the efficiency of any parallel SAT solver could be improved – however to the best of the authors' knowledge, there exists no publicly available work on parallel formula simplification. After introducing the most widely used simplification techniques, we address their parallelization in Section 4[1].

Unit Propagation (UP) applies a (partial) interpretation to the formula. The partial interpretation is represented as the set of all unit clauses in the formula. The pseudo code of the algorithm is presented in Fig. 1. The propagation queue Q is initialized with the set of literals of the unit clauses of the formula F (line 1). For each literal l in the propagation queue Q (line 2), all clauses containing l are removed, except the unit clause

---

[1] We do not discuss the effectiveness of the chosen techniques here. The effectiveness of simplification techniques has been compared in [23], showing that BVE is the most powerful technique.

UnitPropagation (CNF formula F)

1    $Q = \{l \mid C \in F, |C| = 1, l \in C\}$

2   **for** $l \in Q$ **do**

3        $Q := Q \setminus \{l\}$

4        $F := (F \setminus F_l) \cup \{l\}$

5   **for** $C \in F_{\bar{l}}$ **do**

6            $C := C \setminus \{\bar{l}\}$

7   **if** $|C| = 1$ **then** $Q = Q \cup C$

Subsumption (CNF formulas F,G)

1   **for** $C \in G$ **do**

2        $l = \text{argmin}_{l \in C} |F_l|$

3   **for** $D \in F_l$ **do**

4   **if** $C \subseteq D \wedge C \neq D$

5   **then** $F = F \setminus \{D\}$

Strengthening (CNF formulas F, G)

1    $Q = G$

2   **for** $C \in Q$ **do**

3        $Q := Q \setminus \{C\}$

4        $l = \text{argmin}_{l \in C} |F_l \cup F_{\bar{l}}|$

5   **for** $D \in F_l \cup F_{\bar{l}}$ **do**

6   **if** $(C \otimes D) \subseteq D$ **then**

7                $D := (C \otimes D)$

8                $Q := Q \cup \{D\}$

SubSimp (CNF formulas F,G)

1   Subsumption(F,G)

2   Strengthening(F,G)

3    $H := \{C \mid C \in F, \text{changed}\}$

4   Subsumption(F,H)

Fig. 1. Pseudo code the simplification algorithms Unit Propagation, Subsumption and Strengthening

itself (line 4), and all occurrences of $\bar{l}$ are removed (line 5–6). To compute the transitive closure, newly created clauses are added to the propagation queue again (line 7). The application of UP preserves equivalence of the formula F. Since new unit clauses can be derived, performing unit propagation might touch all clauses of the formula, independently of the initial Q.

Subsumption (SUB) removes redundant clauses from the formula. A clause $D \in F$ is subsumed, if it is a superset of another clause $C \in F$, because in this case any model of C is also a model of D. The implementation is also given in Fig. 1, and provides the formula F to be reduced and the set of candidates $G \subseteq F$, which are used for the check. To perform all checks, the method would be called with Subsumption(F,F). For each clause of the set of candidates G, the algorithm performs the redundancy check (line 1). Since the presented algorithm is confluent, its result is independent of the execution order. Therefore, the workload is minimized by choosing the minimally occurring literal l (line 2) to determine which clauses have to be removed. To subsume a clause, l has to be part of both C and D. If a clause D can be subsumed, it is removed (line 5), without deleting the clause itself(line 4).

(Clause) Strengthening (STR), also called *self-subsuming resolution*, removes a literal l from a clause $D \in F$, if there exists another clause $C \in F$, so that there exists a resolvent $C' = C \otimes D$, and C' subsumes the clause D. Instead of removing D and adding the resolvent $C \otimes D$, the implementation usually removes the literal l from D, which has been removed due to resolution. Strengthening is not confluent. The pseudo code of the algorithm is given in Fig. 1. Similar to subsumption, a candidate set of clauses G is given. Since a strengthened clause should be re-tested, a working clause set Q is introduced and initialized with all candidates (line 1). For each clause C it is checked, whether it can strengthen other clauses, again with the most cost efficient literal l (line 4). The clause C can strengthen only clauses D that either also contain l or that contain $\bar{l}$. In all cases, the following precondition has to be fulfilled: $\exists l' \in C$:

VariableElimination (CNF formula F)

```
1    Q = atoms(F)
2    do
3        SubSimp(F,F)                    // remove all redundant clauses
4        for v ∈ Q do                    // use heuristic for order
5            Q := Q \ {v}
6            S := F_v ⊗ F_v̄              // create all resolvents, could consider gates
7            if |S| ≤ |F_v| + |F_v̄| then   // check heuristic
8                F := F \ (F_v ∪ F_v̄)
9                F := F ∪ S
10               SubSimp(F,S)             // check redundancy based on new clauses
11           update(Q)                    // add variables of modified clauses
12   while changed                        // repeat, if changes have been performed
```

Fig. 2. Pseudo code of variable elimination

$(C \setminus \{l'\}) \subset D$. Thus all candidate clauses $D \in F_l \cup F_{\bar{l}}$ are checked (line 5). If a clause D can be reduced (lines 6–7), this clause is added to the working queue Q again (line 8). If G is a subset of F, the execution of the algorithm might still visit all clauses of F, because reduced clauses are revisited.

SubSimp is a combination of subsumption and strengthening. Instead of performing both subsumption and strengthening in one routine, we split the two into separate routines. The routine also supports working with candidates G. After calling strengthening, the reduced clauses are new candidates to subsume other clauses of the formula, and thus a new set H is generated (line 3), and subsumption is executed again (line 4). Note, it is not necessary to re-check the clauses in G.

(Bounded) Variable Elimination (BVE) [18] eliminates a variable v by pairwise resolving all clauses $C \in F_l$ and $D \in F_{\bar{l}}$. Then, the original clauses are replaced by the set of resolvents: $F := (F \cup (F_v \otimes_v F_{\bar{v}})) \setminus (F_v \cup F_{\bar{v}})$. The implementation of the algorithm (pseudo code presented in Fig. 2) is based on a variable queue Q, which is initialized with all atoms of the formula F (line 1). The whole algorithm is usually repeated until it reaches a fix point (lines 2, 12). After removing all redundant clauses (line 3), variable elimination is tested for each variable v of the queue Q, where the selection order depends on a heuristic (line 4). Here, we select a variable that occurs least frequent in the current formula. Next, the set of resolvents S is generated (line 6). This process can take into account that v is defined as output of a gate (see [18] for details). If the set of resolvents S is smaller than the set $F_v \cup F_{\bar{v}}$ (line 7), the substitution of these sets if performed (lines 8–9). Furthermore, it is checked whether the new clauses can be used to remove redundant clauses (line 10). After all variables of Q have been checked, all variables of the current formula that occur in any clause that has been changed or removed by the steps above becomes candidate for further eliminations. Therefore, these variables are reinserted into the queue Q (line 11), and the algorithm is repeated (line 12).

In preparation of the parallel execution, note that the outcome of two variable eliminations with different variable orderings (line 4) can be different. Since the new clauses are created by resolution, eliminating variable v_1 might change the formula, so that eliminating v_2 is not possible any more (due to the limiting heuristics), although the latter elimination would have been possible for the original formula. Furthermore, since strengthening is also called during the algorithm execution, this gives another diversification.

4   Parallel Preprocessing

A survey on parallel SAT solving can be found in [24,25]. Although there has been much research on parallel search, there is no work on parallel preprocessing publicly available. This comes as a surprise, because preprocessing techniques are much more likely to be apt for parallelization, since their complexity class usually is $\mathcal{P}$. We picked the most widely used preprocessing techniques, that are present in the modern prepro-cessors SATELITE [18] and COPROCESSOR [13], and present a way to parallelize them. After discussing the alternative approach based on formula partitioning, we present par-allel versions of the preprocessing algorithms presented above for current multi-core architectures. As an abstraction let $W = \{W_1, \ldots, W_n\}$ be a set of workers, that will execute specified algorithms with individual arguments, private and shared resources.

Variable Graph Partitioning can be used to divide the formula in pairwise disjoint sets on which the workers can perform simplifications without additional synchronization. It seems to be desirable to find the partition with the fewest connections between the subgraphs, because the border variables cannot be processed by any worker. On the other hand, BVE and strengthening are not confluent and a partition heavily effects which of the sequential simplification steps can actually be performed. This property makes it difficult to predict the utility of a partition in advance. Finally, as already the minimum graph bisection is $\mathcal{NP}$-hard [26], it is unexpected to obtain an efficient parallelization with graph partitioning, in which all parts of the algorithm are executed in parallel. Therefore, the authors preferred a locking-based parallelization approach.

Locking-Based Parallel Preprocessing tries to overcome the shortcomings of *Variable Graph Partitioning* by creating only temporary partitions. With regard to the simpli-fication technique, exclusive access rights to a subformula F_i are granted to a worker W_i. After a simplification step has been performed, W_i returns its privileges. Exclusive access rights are ensured with the help of locks.

Subsumption has no critical sections, since the only manipulation of F is the removal of clauses (line 5). If a worker W_i tests whether C subsumes other clauses, and C is removed by W_j, further subsumption checks with C will not lead to wrong results, due to transitivity of $\subseteq$. F_l is changed only, if another worker removed a clause containing l, which will even reduce the workload for W_i. Therefore, *Subsumption* can be paral-lelized by dividing F in subsets F_i, such that $F = \bigcup_{i=1}^{n} F_i$. Then each worker W_i executes $Subsumption(F, F_i)$.

Strengthening requires each worker W_i to have exclusive access rights to the clauses C and D while performing the strengthening test and overwriting D when indicated (Fig. 1, lines 6, 7). The authors favored a locking approach that introduces a lock for each $v \in \text{atoms}(F)$ which is shared among all workers. If W_i holds a lock on an atom v, it has exclusive access to all clauses whose smallest literal is v or $\overline{v}$. The total order $\leq$ on $\text{atoms}(F)$ is exploited to avoid deadlocks: After W_i locked v it may request locks

ParallelVariableElimination (CNF formula F, $Q \subseteq$ atoms(F))

1 **while** $Q \neq \emptyset$ **do**
2    $Q_S := \emptyset$ // reset SubSimp queue
3   **atomic** $v := v' \in Q$, $Q := Q \setminus \{v'\}$ // get variable from Q
4   lock v, readlock CDB   // freeze neighbors
5    $N = \emptyset$
6   **for** $C \in F_v \cup F_{\overline{v}}$ **do**   // calculate neighbors
7   lock C, $N := N \cup$ atoms($\{C\}$), unlock C
8    $ts := $ *current_time_stamp*   // time stamp for neighborhood
9   unlock CDB, unlock v

10   lock all $v' \in N$, readlock CDB
11   **if** *time_stamp*(v) $> ts$ **then**   // check correctness of neighbors
12   unlock all $v' \in N$, unlock CDB
13   **goto 4**
14   $c_{old} := |F_v| + |F_{\overline{v}}|$ // simulate elimination
15   $c_{new} := |F_v \otimes F_{\overline{v}}|$
16   $size := \sum_{C \in F_v \otimes F_{\overline{v}}} |C|$ // total size of resolvents
17   unlock CDB

18   **if** $c_{new} \leq c_{old}$ **then**
19   **atomic** reserveMemory($size$, c_{new}, CDB)   // reserve memory for resolvents
20   readlock CDB
21     $S := F_v \otimes F_{\overline{v}}$
22     $F := (F \cup S) \setminus (F_v \cup F_{\overline{v}})$
23     $Q_S := S$ // add resolvents to SubSimp queue
24   unlock CDB
25   **atomic inc** *current_time_stamp*   // increment time stamp
26   **for** $v' \in N$ **do**   // set time stamp to all neighbors
27   *time_stamp*(v') := *current_time_stamp*
28   unlock all $v' \in N$

29   **for** $C \in Q_S$ **do**   // SubSimp
30   lock $v = \min_{l \in C}$ atom(l), lock CDB, C
31   **if** $v \neq \min_{l \in C}$ atom(l) **then**   // if smallest atom of C changed
32   unlock C, CDB, v, **goto 30**   // renew locks
33     $l = \operatorname{argmin}_{l \in C} |F_l \cup F_{\overline{l}}|$
34   **for** $D \in (F_l \cup F_{\overline{l}}) \setminus \{C\}$ **do**
35   **if** preemptableLock $D = $ *success* **then**   // abort, if $\min_{l \in D}$ atom(l) $> v$
36   **if** $C \subseteq D$ **then** $F := F \setminus \{D\}$
37   **else if** $C \otimes D \subseteq D$ **then**
38           $D := C \otimes D$, $Q := Q \cup \{D\}$
39   unlock D
40   unlock C, unlock CDB, unlock v

Fig. 3. Pseudo code of parallel variable elimination, with phases neighbor calculation (l. 4–9), elimination simulation (l. 10–17), elimination (l. 18–28) , SubSimp (l. 29–40)

only on smaller atoms. Since $C \otimes D \subseteq D \implies \min_{l \in C}$ atom(l) $\geq \min_{l \in D}$ atom(l), the smallest atom v' of D needs to be locked only if it is smaller than v. We discuss a slightly modified parallel strengthening algorithm, that exploits the same idea, during the presentation of the parallel BVE.

Variable Elimination requires a more complex locking scheme: An elimination of v requires a worker to have exclusive access to the set of clauses $F_v \cup F_{\overline{v}}$ while the steps in lines 6–9 of the sequential algorithm are performed (Fig. 2). We will use the stronger condition of exclusive access to all clauses that consist of *neighbor-variables* (or *neighbors*) of v, i.e. atoms($F_v \cup F_{\overline{v}}$). A further difficulty is the creation of new clauses: In current SAT solvers a *multiple reader - single writer* synchronization to the clause database (CDB) is necessary. Finally, *SubSimp* shall be executed in parallel to BVE.

To meet all requirements three kinds of locks are used: variable locks, a RW-lock for the CDB and a lock per clause. A worker W_i may access clauses only, if the clause storage was readlocked, and writes clauses only in previously reserved memory. W_i has exclusive access to a clause C (with the semantics that consistent reading and writing is guaranteed), if W_i locked all atoms of C or if W_i locked at least one of the atoms of C and the clause lock corresponding to C. Obviously, if all modifications of the formula result from exclusive read and write operations, these conditions will lead to a correct concurrent algorithm.

To circumvent deadlocks, variables are always locked orderly, afterwards the clause storage is locked and finally at most two clause locks are acquired, where the second clause lock must be preemptable. Hence, the third (non-preemptable locks) or fourth (circular-wait) Coffman condition are violated respectively.

The pseudo code for the parallel BVE algorithm is given in Fig. 3 and it consists only of the inner for-loop of the sequential BVE algorithm, which is given in Fig. 1(lines 4–10). The call to a parallel SubSimp (Fig. 1 lines 3) is executed before the outlined algorithm. All workers share a variable queue Q and request atoms v to process (line 3). Afterwards v is locked, to prevent other workers to change v's neighborhood, and the CDB is readlocked (line 6) for clause access. All neighbors are determined (lines 6–7), which requires to lock each clause for consistent reading, and the current time stamp is requested successively (line 8), to cheaply check whether the neighborhood of some variable has been altered since previous locking. After unlocking v and the CDB (line 9), to keep the locking order, all $v' \in N$ are locked and the CDB is readlocked again (line 10). If another worker modified the formula in the meantime such that $F_v \cup F_{\overline{v}}$ changed (line 11), the variable locks have to be renewed (lines 12–13). Otherwise the underlying data for the utility of the elimination is computed as usual: number of clauses before resolution (line 14), number of clauses after after resolution (line 15) and additionally the total size of the resolvents (line 16). After the CDB lock was released (line 17), it is decided whether an elimination should be performed (line 18). If this is the case, a space reservation in CDB for the resolvents is created (line 19). In this period a memory relocation of the CDB is possible, which makes a CDB writelock necessary. While the CDB is readlocked (line 20–24) the usual clause elimination is performed and all resolvents are added to the SubSimp queue (lines 21–23). Afterwards the global time stamp is incremented (line 25) and assigned to all neighboring variables(lines 26–27), since their neighborhood could have been extended as a consequence of the elimination. Finally all variable locks are released (line 28) and the SubSimp phase begins: The smallest atom v of C is determined and locked (which indeed requires an enclosing CDB lock), followed by locking the CDB and C (line 30). If v is not the smallest atom of C any more (C was changed in the meantime), this step is repeated (lines 31–32). Then all candidate clauses are locked with preemptableLock (line 35), which verifies that the smallest atom of D is still less or equal to v while waiting for the lock. Then tests for subsumption (line 36) and strengthening (line 37) are performed and strengthened clauses are added to the SubSimp queue (line 38). Notice that a worker has exclusive access to D only, if D contains the atom v, but this is a necessary condition for $C \subseteq D$ or $C \otimes D \subseteq D$. In contrast to the sequential SubSimp, we joined the single loops for SUB and STR to reduce the locking overhead.

Implementation. The above algorithms are implemented as part of the COPROCESSOR project [13]. Clauses are represented as a vector of literals and a header, that, amongst others, contains the size information and a delete flag. The literals of a clause are always ordered, which makes the determination of the smallest atom of a clause efficient and is also profitable for subsumption and resolution computations. Variable and clause locks are implemented as spin locks based on an atomic *compare-and-exchange* operation. Hence, kernel level switches can be avoided and the required amount of locks can be supplied.

5 Evaluation

In this section we want to point out that exploiting parallel resources is beneficial for instances for which sequential preprocessing consumes a lot of time. Therefore, we created a benchmark of 880 instances, by merging the application benchmarks from the SAT competition 2009, the SAT Challenge 2012, and the instances which have not been selected for the SAT Challenge 2012, but which have not been selected due to being too hard. We implemented the parallel preprocessing methods into the preprocessor COPROCESSOR, which already provides the sequential routines [13] and uses step limits for each technique. To see these limits, we disabled the step limit, and ran each technique until completion[2]. The timeout for the preprocessor and the solver in

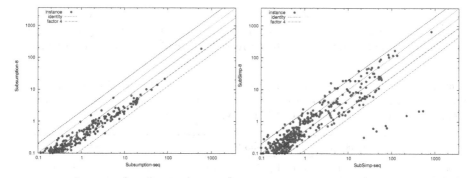

Fig. 4. Comparing the run time of sequential subsumption (left) and SubSimp (right) on the y-axis with their parallel version, which utilizes eight cores

---

[2] COPROCESSOR as well as the list of instances used during preprocessing are available at http://tools.computational-logic.org.

combination is set to 3600 seconds. After preprocessing, we run the sequential SAT solver MINISAT 2.2.

For the experiment we use a AMD Opteron 6274 with 2.2 GHz. This CPU provides 16 cores. Every two consecutive cores share a L2 cache of 2 MB , and the first and second 8 cores share a L3 cache of 16 MB. Before presenting the empirical evaluation, we point the reader to an artefact in the results, which seems to stem from the provided architecture: if up to eight cores are used, communication among the cores can be done via the shared L3 cache. However, note that once more cores are used, there is no L3 cache among all the cores. Therefore, the overall performance might drop due to communication overhead.

5.1 Analyzing the Simplification Time

First, we compare the more basic techniques subsumption and strengthening. Each parallel version pays a small overhead for initializing the work for all threads. Therefore, for very small execution times, the overhead of the parallel implementation is comparably high. The run times of the sequential algorithm (x-axis) and the parallel algorithm (y-axis) are compared in Fig. 4. For subsumption, a lock free implementation is used, so that there is almost no slowdown for the parallel algorithm. Note, that for large sequential run times the speedup of the parallel algorithm increases, and for large times a speedup of up to an order of magnitude has been measured. Note in addition, that the parallel algorithm is confluent, and thus the resulting CNF formula is equivalent to the input formula.

For SubSimp the picture is not that clear. Still, the speedup of the parallel algorithm increases with the runtime the sequential algorithm needs. For eight workers, there exists formulas with a superior speedup. However, there are also formulas that show a slowdown. This effect can be explained with properties of the algorithm: as discussed in section 3, strengthening is not confluent, and therefore the parallel as well as the sequential algorithm might be able to perform more reductions, depending on the execution order. This effect can result in an increased run time. All in all, the results still show that by parallelizing the algorithm, and improvement can be achieved.

Finally, we compare the effect on variable elimination: when using more cores, the average simplification time can be decreased. Especially for long runs of variable

Table 1. The table gives the average simplification time and the number of satisfiable and unsatisfiable solved instances per preprocessing technique. The average simplification time is calculated for all instances of the benchmark, including unsolved instances.

	Subsumption				SubSimp					BVE						
Cores	seq	1	8	16	seq	1	4	8	16	seq	R_{seq}	1	4	8	R_8	16
T_{Simp}	1.8	2.5	**0.5**	1.8	7.7	8.7	5.6	4.0	**3.7**	19.8	18.2	27.6	20.4	19.6	**16.8**	28.8
SAT	240	240	**268**	263	246	254	262	**264**	263	255	**270**	249	**270**	264	269	262
UNSAT	229	227	259	**261**	222	245	257	**259**	256	252	283	257	**295**	287	284	286
Total	469	467	**527**	524	468	499	519	**523**	519	507	553	506	**565**	551	553	548

elimination, we can see a clear improvement. The following numbers are calculated when using eight cores: For formulas where the sequential algorithm uses more than 10 seconds, the average speedup is 1.55. When moving this limit further and considering only instances that require at least 50 seconds for variable elimination, the speedup increases to 1.88, and when moving to 100 seconds, the speedup stays 1.88.

5.2 Analyzing the Simplification Quality

Next, we want to argue that the *quality* of the resulting formula does not decrease when a parallel algorithm (especially strengthening and BVE) is used. We measure the quality with the number of solved satisfiable and unsatisfiable instances, when using MINISAT 2.2 after running parallel preprocessing. Table 1 provides this data for all three preprocessing techniques. The sequential implementation is given in the columns *seq*. For subsumption, the number of solved instances increases with the number of cores, until 16 cores are used, where this number decreases again. Especially the average simplification time drops again, where small instances use more run time. However, the number of solved instances increases, underlining that especially long preprocessing runs benefit. When measuring the quality of parallel preprocessing with respect to the number of solved instances, using parallel procedures clearly results in a performance improvement – when using eight cores, 527 instead of 469 instances can be solved.

For SubSimp, the data is similar, but now the average simplification time decreases continuously. With respect to the number of solved instances, the algorithm also benefits from parallelization: 523 instead of 468 instances are solved, when eight cores are used.

Finally, we also performed experiments with parallel variable elimination. Note that due to locking neighboring variables, this method ships with more overhead than the previous algorithms. Still, by increasing the number of available resources, the run time of the simplification method can be decreased. Similarly to SubSimp, the result of BVE is non-deterministic for the parallel algorithm. Furthermore, for long running instances, improvement due to the parallelization increases. From this improvement on long running instances, also the number of solved instances increases. When following the usual heuristic to process variables within the algorithm, it can be seen that the parallel algorithm slows down, because it waits for locking neighboring variables. After changing the process order (in R configurations), the average simplification run time drops significantly, surprisingly also for the sequential algorithm. Again, this effect may be caused by the algorithms not being confluent.

Exact numbers are given in Table 1. The sequential algorithm can solve 507 instances from the benchmark, and requires 19.8 seconds in average to simplify an instance. When calculating the overhead of the parallelization by using one core with the parallel algorithm, the average simplification time increases by 8 seconds. Only when eight cores are used, the speedup of the parallel execution can cope with this overhead. However, the algorithm still waits for neighboring variables, because similar variables are scheduled after each other, thus blocking working threads. Therefore, a randomized variable order has been used in the R configurations. Since the parallel simplification improves long running instances most (see above), the number of solved instances within the timeout increases. When eight cores are used, 551 instances can be solved. When using the randomized order, another two instances are solved. Surprisingly, using four cores results in the even higher number of 565 solved instances. This effect can be due to less blocking and due to the indeterministic result of the parallel simplification algorithm.

All in all, the provided experimental evaluation shows that the parallel version improves the state of the art, not only by improving the run time that is required to simplify a formula, but also by improving the performance when being combined with a sequential solver. When using the simplifier in a real world scenario, a heuristic needs to be applied to determine when to use the sequential and when to use the parallel implementation, since for small run times the overhead of the parallel algorithm cannot be neglected.

6   Conclusion

In this paper we have shown how the widely used CNF simplification techniques subsumption, strengthening and variable elimination can be parallelized. We chose a fine grained lock based approach and introduced global locks, locks per variable and per clause, and forced clauses to be sorted. For this setup we can show that the parallelization is deadlock free by ensuring that at least one of the Coffman Conditions is violated. After implementing the parallel algorithms into the preprocessor COPROCESSOR, we evaluated the performance of the algorithms when being executed until completion. Especially on formulas where the sequential algorithm requires much run time, using the parallel algorithm results in a speedup of the simplification. For confluent subsumption, the execution time can be reduced by a factor up to 3.6, where the same resulting formula is obtained. Parallelizing strengthening and variable elimination usually results in a different formula, since these algorithms are not confluent. Still, for large sequential run times (more than 100 seconds), an average speedup of 2.3 for combining strengthening with subsumption, and a speedup of 1.88 for variable elimination can be obtained.

Acknowledgements. The authors would like to thank Mate Soos for fruitful discussions on the efficient implementation of subsumption and self-subsuming resolution.

References

1. Marques-Silva, J.P., Sakallah, K.A.: Grasp – a new search algorithm for satisfiability. In: Proc. 1996 IEEE/ACM International Conference on Computer-Aided Design, ICCAD 1996, pp. 220–227 (1996)
2. Biere, A., Cimatti, A., Clarke, E.M., Fujita, M., Zhu, Y.: Symbolic model checking using SAT procedures instead of BDDs. In: Proc. 36th Annual ACM/IEEE Design Automation Conference, DAC 1999, pp. 317–320. ACM, New York (1999)
3. Aloul, F.A., Ramani, A., Markov, I.L., Sakallah, K.A.: Solving difficult SAT instances in the presence of symmetry. In: DAC 2002, pp. 731–736 (2002)
4. Großmann, P., Hölldobler, S., Manthey, N., Nachtigall, K., Opitz, J., Steinke, P.: Solving periodic event scheduling problems with SAT. In: Jiang, H., Ding, W., Ali, M., Wu, X. (eds.) IEA/AIE 2012. LNCS, vol. 7345, pp. 166–175. Springer, Heidelberg (2012)
5. Moskewicz, M.W., Madigan, C.F., Zhao, Y., Zhang, L., Malik, S.: Chaff: engineering an efficient SAT solver. In: Proc. 38th Annual Design Automation Conference, DAC 2001, pp. 530–535 (2001)

6. Ryan, L.O.: Efficient algorithms for clause learning SAT solvers. Master's thesis, Simon Fraser University, Canada (2004)
7. Hölldobler, S., Manthey, N., Saptawijaya, A.: Improving resource-unaware SAT solvers. In: Fermüller, C.G., Voronkov, A. (eds.) LPAR-17. LNCS, vol. 6397, pp. 519–534. Springer, Heidelberg (2010)
8. Audemard, G., Simon, L.: Predicting learnt clauses quality in modern SAT solvers. In: Proc. 21st Int. Joint Conf. on Artifical Intelligence, IJCAI 2009, pp. 399–404 (2009)
9. Huang, J.: The effect of restarts on the efficiency of clause learning. In: Proc. 20th International Joint Conference on Artifical Intelligence, IJCAI 2007, pp. 2318–2323 (2007)
10. Belov, A., Järvisalo, M., Marques-Silva, J.: Formula preprocessing in mus extraction. In: Piterman, N., Smolka, S.A. (eds.) TACAS 2013 (ETAPS 2013). LNCS, vol. 7795, pp. 108–123. Springer, Heidelberg (2013)
11. Nadel, A., Ryvchin, V., Strichman, O.: Preprocessing in incremental sat. In: Cimatti, A., Sebastiani, R. (eds.) SAT 2012. LNCS, vol. 7317, pp. 256–269. Springer, Heidelberg (2012)
12. Manthey, N., Heule, M.J.H., Biere, A.: Automated reencoding of boolean formulas. In: Biere, A., Nahir, A., Vos, T. (eds.) HVC 2012. LNCS, vol. 7857, pp. 102–117. Springer, Heidelberg (2013)
13. Manthey, N.: Coprocessor 2.0: a flexible CNF simplifier. In: Cimatti, A., Sebastiani, R. (eds.) SAT 2012. LNCS, vol. 7317, pp. 436–441. Springer, Heidelberg (2012)
14. Biere, A., Heule, M., van Maaren, H., Walsh, T. (eds.): Handbook of Satisfiability. Frontiers in Artificial Intelligence and Applications, vol. 185. IOS Press (2009)
15. Cook, S.A.: The complexity of theorem-proving procedures. In: Proc. 3rd Annual ACM Symposium on Theory of Computing, pp. 151–158 (1971)
16. Hoos, H., Stützle, T.: Stochastic Local Search. Morgan Kaufmann / Elsevier, San Francisco (2005)
17. Coffman, E.G., Elphick, M., Shoshani, A.: System deadlocks. ACM Comput. Surv. 3(2), 67–78 (1971)
18. Eén, N., Biere, A.: Effective preprocessing in SAT through variable and clause elimination. In: Bacchus, F., Walsh, T. (eds.) SAT 2005. LNCS, vol. 3569, pp. 61–75. Springer, Heidelberg (2005)
19. Järvisalo, M., Biere, A., Heule, M.: Blocked clause elimination. In: Esparza, J., Majumdar, R. (eds.) TACAS 2010. LNCS, vol. 6015, pp. 129–144. Springer, Heidelberg (2010)
20. Van Gelder, A.: Toward leaner binary-clause reasoning in a satisfiability solver. Annals of Mathematics and Artificial Intelligence 43(1-4), 239–253 (2005)
21. Lynce, I., Marques-Silva, J.: Probing-Based Preprocessing Techniques for Propositional Satisfiability. In: Proc. 15th IEEE International Conference on Tools with Artificial Intelligence, ICTAI 2003, pp. 105–110 (2003)
22. Tseitin, G.S.: On the complexity of derivations in propositional calculus. In: Slisenko, A.O. (ed.) Studies in Constructive Mathematics and Mathematical Logic, pp. 115–125. Consultants Bureau, New York (1970)
23. Balint, A., Manthey, N.: Boosting the Performance of SLS and CDCL Solvers by Preprocessor Tuning. In: Pragmatics of SAT (POS 2013) (2013)
24. Hölldobler, S., Manthey, N., Nguyen, V., Stecklina, J., Steinke, P.: A short overview on modern parallel SAT-solvers. In: Wasito, I., Hasibuan, Z., Suhartanto, H. (eds.) Proc. of the International Conference on Advanced Computer Science and Information Systems, pp. 201–206 (2001) ISBN 978-979-1421-11-9
25. Martins, R., Manquinho, V., Lynce, I.: An overview of parallel SAT solving. Constraints 17(3), 304–347 (2012)
26. Garey, M.R., Johnson, D.S., Stockmeyer, L.: Some simplified NP-complete problems. In: Proc. Sixth Annual ACM Symposium on Theory of Computing, STOC 1974, pp. 47–63 (1974)

Agent-Based Multimodal Transport Planning in Dynamic Environments

Christoph Greulich[1], Stefan Edelkamp[2], and Max Gath[2]

[1] International Graduate School for Dynamics in Logistics
[2] Institute for Artificial Intelligence
University of Bremen, Germany
{greulich,edelkamp,mgath}@tzi.de

Abstract. The development and maintenance of traffic concepts in urban districts is expensive and leads to high investments for altering transport infrastructures or for the acquisition of new resources. We present an agent-based approach for modeling, simulation, evaluation, and optimization of public transport systems by introducing a dynamic microscopic model. Actors of varying stakeholders are represented by intelligent agents. While describing the inter-agent communication and their individual behaviors, the focus is on the implementation of information systems for traveler agents as well as on the matching between open source geographic information systems, and standardized transport schedules provided by the Association of German Transport Companies. The performance, efficiency, and limitations of the system are evaluated within the public transport infrastructure of Bremen. We discuss the effects of passengers' behaviors to the entire transport network and investigate the system's flexibility as well as consequences of incidents in travel plans.

1 Introduction

Public transport networks (PTN) were introduced to urban regions in the 19th century [6] and underwent radical changes throughout history. The development of combustion engines and the discovery of electricity had huge influence on the means of public transport. Optimization of such PTNs grew into a diversified research area which ranges from developing optimization processes [14] to analysis of passenger behavior [2,4,7].

Applying new traffic concepts or changes to a given PTN or the infrastructure of an urban region can be very expensive. Several authors approach the evaluation of those changes by agent-based simulation of PTNs [8,10,11]. A crucial part of the simulation-based approach is multimodal route planning which considers various means of public and individual transportation. Unfortunately, multimodal route planning using public transportation (e.g., buses, trams, metros) and individual transportation (e.g., cars, bikes, or foot) requires an accurate linkage of the street map to the one for public transportation. Therefore, previous approaches have been limited to a specific area, such as Belfort [11] or Bangalore [8].

I.J. Timm and M. Thimm (Eds.): KI 2013, LNAI 8077, pp. 74–85, 2013.

Even though publicly available and community-edited maps often contain information on stops and travel routes for public transportation, in multimodal route planning most frequently the resources of the two are diverse, especially if exact time scheduling constraints are involved. Timetables for public transportation units are, e.g., extracted from public transport company (PTC) databases and geo-located to the maps.

While this problem is conceptually easy, real-word challenges for the mapping include varying wordings of stops, and missing or reduced line information, where an line is a sequence of stops. Moreover, given geo-coordinates may not distinguish between multiple locations of stops for diverse travel directions at crossings. To resolve various namings for the geo-location and matching problem, we applied a generalization of the Needleman-Wunsch [13] algorithm for computing the alignment of genome strings. The layered algorithm is implemented in a database query language. Similarity matrices are extracted from a low-level approximate string matching, while the top-level alignment compares every two different lines passing a certain stop.

Inferred timetables are additionally fed into a public transport information system providing route information for individual passenger agents. They take the information as a guideline to plan their travel. The information system supports several implementations for shortest route queries.

The bijection between public transport and street map data combined with time-tabling information on travel and waiting times of mobile vehicles enables realistic travel simulation. Since the considered scenario provides a natural mapping of traffic stakeholder to software agents, we apply our multiagent-based simulation framework PlaSMA for evaluation. This enables fine-grained modeling of individual traffic participants on real-world transport infrastructures.

2 Simulation Model

To reach their individual goals, the agent-based simulation model contains three types of agents that interact with each other as well as with the environment. The transport infrastructure of the simulation environment is modeled as a directed graph. Nodes represent traffic junctions, dead ends, or stops of the PTN, while edges represent different types of ways, e.g., roads, motorways, and trails.

The *PublicTransportCompany-Agent* (*PTC-Agent*) receives a timetable upon creation. This timetable contains all departures and arrivals of every line of its fleet. According to the given timetable, the *PTC-Agent* creates *Vehicle-Agents* having a specific timetable for the journey from the first to the last stop of the line. In addition, the *PTC-Agent* provides a public transport information system for answering transport requests of potential passengers. To reduce communication, transportation contracts will be concluded between *Traveler-Agents* and *PTC-Agents* directly. Upon creation, the *Vehicle-Agent* drives its tour according to the timetable. *Traveler-Agents* are loaded or unloaded at stops, depending on their destination and their contract status. Finally, the *Traveler-Agent* tries to determine the most satisfying traveling option between its current position and its destination. The goal of the *Traveler-Agent* is to find the route with the earliest arrival time. If the distance between the origin and destination is above a predefined threshold, the *Traveler-Agent* avoids walking and acquires alternatives from the *PTC-Agent*. It reacts to problems (e.g., missed connections or inadmissible delays) by replanning which implies acquiring new alternative routes to reach the destination. The simulation model has already been introduced in [8].

3 Matching Data Sets

Since the simulation model is independent from the environment, the infrastructure and the simulated PTN can be exchanged easily. The underlying PlaSMA simulation platform[1] supports the import of OpenStreetMap[2] (OSM) datasets. These datasets contain PTN-related information, such as the public transport lines as well as the positions and names of their stops. Due to the fact that data is added to OSM manually, it is not guaranteed that the geographic information system is complete and accurate. Therefore, recent changes to the infrastructure or the PTN may not been transfered and stops or lines may be missing or tagged with wrong coordinates. Unfortunately, OSM does not provide information about the timetable of each line.

On the other hand, data sets of PTCs essentially consist of timetables. The Association of German Transport Companies (VDV) introduced standardized data models for the storage of PTN-related information [16]. The standard allows but not necessarily requires the storage of geographical information for each stop. Therefore, the operating data of a PTC does not provide enough information to map the stops' IDs to their geographical position which is necessary for an accurate simulation model.

Consequently, the mapping of street map data and the PTCs own timetable data is an essential problem as illustrated in Fig. 1. Names and identifiers of various stops and lines in each data set may vary significantly. Even if stops have the same names stops may form a stop area and, therefore, share the same name, e.g., two stops on opposite sides of the street. As a result, a name-to-name matching approach is not applicable. A solution is to distinguish the stops of a stop area by identifying their associated lines.

The similarity of two lines is given by the similarity of their stops and their respective indices alike. Finding pairs of two lines (one from each data set) allows to determine pairs of stops. Thus, each stop position in the street map can be mapped to the stop identifier in the PTC's data set.

3.1   The Needleman-Wunsch Algorithm

The Needleman-Wunsch algorithm [13] has originally been designed to align two nucleotide or peptide sequences but is commonly used to solve string alignment

---

[1] http://plasma.informatik.uni-bremen.de
[2] http://www.openstreetmap.org

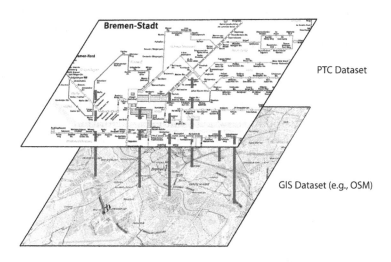

Fig. 1. Linkage of PTN information from two different data sets

problems. A similarity value $S(x, y)$ specificies the similarity score of x and y, where $x, y \in \Sigma$ and Σ is the given alphabet.

The Needleman-Wunsch-algorithm computes a matrix M with a size of $(|A| + 1) \times (|B| + 1)$ where A and B are two strings over Σ. The matrix contains a column for each element of a string $A = a_1 \ldots a_n$ and a row j for each element of a string $B = b_1 \ldots b_n$. Additionally, the first row and column is reserved for multiples of the gap penalty p. Although the algorithm relies on matrix recurrences it can be solved in time $O(nm)$ by dynamic programming [9]. For $M_{i,0} = p \cdot i, i \in \{1, \ldots, n\}$ and $M_{0,j} = p \cdot j, j \in \{1, \ldots, m\}$ we have

$$M_{i,j} = max \begin{pmatrix} M_{i-1,j-1} + S(a_i, b_j), \\ M_{i,j-1} + p, \\ M_{i+1,j} + p \end{pmatrix}, i, j \in \{1, \ldots, n\} \times \{1, \ldots, m\}$$

3.2 Stop and Line Matching

We apply the above algorithm to the given matching problem. Let $\mathbb{I}$ be a set of lines and $\mathcal{E}, \mathcal{F} \subset \mathbb{I}$. In order to align two lines $E \in \mathcal{E}$ and $F \in \mathcal{F}$ of two different data sets $\mathcal{E}$ and $\mathcal{F}$, the similarity matrix S is substituted by the function $s(e, f)$, which determines the similarity between two stops $e \in E$ and $f \in F$ by the comparison of their names. For solving the corresponding alignment problem to compute $s(e, f)$, we apply the trigram matching algorithm which counts the number of trigrams (sequences of 3 consecutive characters) that are included in both stop names to determine similarity [15].

Additionally, geographical information is taken into account, e.g., the distance between e and f. The value of the gap penalty p a threshold and depends on the implementation of the similarity function. The penalty score for creating a gap must be greater than the similarity score of two stops with an unlikely match.

For each line of the PTC data set, we determine the most similar line from the OSM data set. The resulting Needleman-Wunsch matrix of the best matching pair is saved. After the investigation of all line pairs, pairs of stops are computed by applying a backtracking algorithm to the Needleman-Wunsch-matrices of the line pairs. As a result, the node IDs of stops from the OSM data set are linked to the equivalent stop in the PTC's data set. Algorithms 1.1 to 1.3 show implementations of the necessary functions in pseudo code.

function FINDMATCHINGLINES($\mathcal{E},\mathcal{F}$)
    $R \leftarrow \emptyset$
    for each $E \in \mathcal{E}$ **do**
        $P.Line \leftarrow E$
        $Similarity \leftarrow 0$
        for each $F \in \mathcal{F}$ **do**
            $M \leftarrow$ CREATENEEDLEMANWUNSCHMATRIX(E, F)
            if $M_{|E|,|F|} > Similarity$ **then**
                $P.BestMatch \leftarrow F$
                $P.BestMatrix \leftarrow M$
                $Similarity \leftarrow M_{|E|,|F|}$
        $R \leftarrow R \cup \{P\}$
    return R

Algorithm 1.1. Determining best matching lines of two data sets $\mathcal{E}$ and $\mathcal{F}$

function CREATENEEDLEMANWUNSCHMATRIX(E, F)
    M is a matrix with the size of $(|E| + 1) \times (|F| + 1)$
    p is the penalty for skipping an element
    for $i = 0$ to $|E|$ **do**
        $M_{i,0} = i \cdot p$
    for $j = 0$ to $|F|$ **do**
        $M_{0,j} = j \cdot p$
    for $i = 1$ to $|E|$ **do**
        for $j = 1$ to $|F|$ **do**

$$M_{i,j} \leftarrow max \begin{pmatrix} M_{i-1,j-1} + s(e_i, f_j)\ , \\ M_{i-1,j} + p, \\ M_{i,j-1} + p \end{pmatrix}$$

    return M

Algorithm 1.2. The Needleman-Wunsch Algorithm

function CREATESTOPPAIRS(E, F, M)
    p is the penalty for skipping an element
    $i \leftarrow |E|$
    $j \leftarrow |F|$
    while $i > 0$ **or** $j > 0$ **do**
        if $M_{i,j} = M_{i-1,j-1} + s(e_i, f_j)$ **then**
            MEMORIZEPAIR(e_i, f_j)
            $i \leftarrow i - 1$
            $j \leftarrow j - 1$
        else if $M_{i,j} = M_{i-1,j} + p$ **then**
            $i \leftarrow i - 1$
        else if $M_{i,j} = M_{i,j-1} + p$ **then**
            $j \leftarrow j - 1$

Algorithm 1.3. Backtracking for the Needleman-Wunsch Algorithm

4 Public Transport Information Systems

In order to satisfy transport requests of customers and to determine the route with the earliest arrival time, we implemented a public transport information system solving the *Earliest-Arrival-Problem* (EAP) [12] with stop-specific transfer times. In addition, the route which minimizes the number of transfers should be preferred if several routes arrive at the same time. Moreover, undesired lines have to be excluded. Next, we present three different approaches for solving the EAP. The search algorithms extend the well-known Dijkstra algorithm [5].

4.1 Time-Expanded Graph

We extend the *time-expanded graph* (TEG) approach [12]. Let S denote the set of stop areas and L denote the set of lines. A time-expanded graph includes a set of nodes N and a set of edges E. Each node $(l, s) \in (L \times S)$ represents the arrival or departure of an line $l \in L$ at a stop area $s \in S$. Edges connecting nodes represent transport routes of vehicles between stops as well as transfers of passengers at a certain stop area. The weights of edges determine the travel time. As a result, a shortest-path search is applied to satisfy a certain transport request from a start node to a goal node. To fulfill the requirements for passenger transport, the search is altered: edges which are served by undesired lines are excluded and edges that require passenger transfers are only considered if the current line does not reach the stop area within the same time. Consequently, these conditions ensure that routes with more transfers are avoided if the arriving time is equal to a route with less transfers.

4.2 Time-Dependent Graph

Within a *time-dependent graph* (TDG) [12] each stop area is represented by only one node. Two nodes are linked by exactly one edge if there is at least one

function FINDSHORTESTPATH(n_{source}, n_{sink}, t_0, I, X)
   $M \leftarrow \{n_{source}\}$
   SETTIMEDISTANCE(n_{source}, t_0)
   SETSUBEDGE(n_{source}, **null**)
   while $M \neq \emptyset$ **do**
      $u \leftarrow$ GETNODEWITHMINDISTANCE(M)
      $M \leftarrow M \backslash \{u\}$
      if $u = n_{sink}$ **then**
         return CREATEPATH(u)
      $e_u \leftarrow$ GETSUBEDGE(u)
      for all $E \in$ GETEDGES(u) **do**
         $v \leftarrow$ SINK(E)
         for all $e \in E$ **do**
            $d_{departure} \leftarrow$ DEPARTURE(e) - GETTIMEDISTANCE(u)
            if $((I = \emptyset \vee$ LINE(e) $\in I) \wedge$ LINE(e) $\notin X) \wedge$
                  $((e_u =$ **null** $\wedge$ARRIVAL(e)$<$ GETTIMEDISTANCE(v)) $\vee$
                  $(e_u \neq$ **null** $\wedge$ARRIVAL(e)$<$ GETTIMEDISTANCE(v) $\wedge$
                    LINE(e_u) $\neq$ LINE(e) $\wedge$
                    $d_{departure} \geq$ GETTRANSFERTIME(u)) $\vee$
                  $(e_u \neq$ **null** $\wedge$ARRIVAL(e)$\leq$ GETTIMEDISTANCE(v) $\wedge$
                  LINE(e_u) $=$ LINE(e))) **then**
               if $v = n_{source}$ **then**
                  SETSUBEDGE(SINK(E), **null**)
               else
                  SETSUBEDGE(SINK(E), e)
               SETTIMEDISTANCE(SINK(E), d)
               $M \leftarrow M \cup \{$SINK(E)$\}$
   return new empty path

Algorithm 1.4. Implementation of the Shortest-Path Algorithm on a TDG

direct connection between each other. As a result, the search space is decreased significantly in contrast to a TEG. However, each edge contains several subedges with specific arrival and departure times as well as a dedicated line. The shortest-path search has to be adapted to the sub-edge graph structure. The pseudo code is shown in Algorithm 1.4.

Input parameters next to the start and goal node include the start time t_0, a set of allowed lines I, and a set of lines X which should be avoided. If I is an empty set, all lines which are not in X are considered. The shortest path search for a TDG considers only predecessor edges instead of predecessor nodes. The functions SETSUBEDGE(A, e) and GETSUBEDGE(A) save and return the best sub-edge e to the node A. The algorithm chooses the node with the shortest distance and iterates over all outgoing edges including their sub-edges. The procedure ARRIVAL(e) determines the estimated arrival time at the node that is reachable by e. In addition, the distance between nodes is computed by the travel time from node A to node B. In order to prefer routes with the earliest time of arrival, conditions for choosing the best edge are imposed.

4.3   Reduced Time-Expanded Graph

In a time-dependent graph (TDG), the graph is reduced and only the shortest-route with the earliest departure time from one node to another is considered. However, this may result in undesirable transfers between lines. Thus, we reduce the number of edges of the TEG without cutting relevant solutions. Let (v, u) denote an edge from node $v \in N$ to node $u \in N$, $s_i \in S$ the stop at node $i \in N$, and t_i the time of arrival or departure. While the classic TEG contains all edges (v, u) with $s_v = s_u \land t_v \leq t_u$, the reduced TEG includes only the edge (v, u) representing the next departure per line $l_u \in L$ at stop u:

$$s_v = s_u \land t_v = t_u \land (\neg \exists u' : u' \neq u \land s_v = s_{u'} \land t_v \leq t_{u'} \land t_{u'} < t_u \land l_{u'} = l_u).$$

5   Evaluation

The BSAG[3], the local PTC of Bremen (Germany), provided a set of operating data which meets the VDV-standard. The monday schedule of the PTC data set contains 116 lines. Lines may have a set of variants, e.g., for the opposite direction or for shorter/alternative routes. A lot of these variants are not accessible for passengers but merely for service maintenance and can be ignored for the purpose of simulation. Additionally, each line variation may have not one but several timetables depending on the current time of day. This results in 560 line timetables. More than 1,990 stops are served by these lines.

The PTC data set is matched against an OSM data set which contains 76 line variants and a variety of 768 stops. The OSM data set does not usually contain more than two variants of the same line (one for each direction). Unfortunately, several information in the OSM is outdated due to recent changes to infrastructure and PTN. Hence, the OSM data set contains stops that are not served anymore by any line in the PTC data set. Additionally, not all PTN information could be exported from the OSM data set. Several lines and stops are not tagged correctly or by an outdated tagging standard that is neither compatible with the new one, nor with the applied importer software.

However, 65 line variations from OSM could be successfully linked to lines from the PTC data set and 549 stops could be linked to their respective node ID. Hence, 314 of 560 line timetables can be simulated without any manual modeling. The compressed infrastructure itself is represented by a graph with 26,121 nodes and 59,950 edges.

Based on this data, a series of experiments was run to determine the capability and limitations of the simulation model and its implementation. In each experiment, we simulated a PTN with a 24 hours monday schedule. The start and destination locations of each traveler are chosen randomly. Therefore, the simulation results do not reflect real world utilization yet. In future work, varying population density and areas which are frequently visited have to be taken into account. All experiments are computed on a dedicated machine with 8 dual-core AMD processors and 64 GB of RAM.

---

[3] http://www.bsag.de

5.1   Ressource Limitations and Scalability

According to real world data, about 281,000 passengers are transported per day by the BSAG [1]. Therefore, nearly 2,000 passengers have to be created every ten minutes in order to approximate real world statistics. However, no more than about 7,000 active agents can be handled by the given machine due to a lack of memory. Another experiment with 200 passengers every ten minutes was aborted due to the same memory issues after about 90% of the simulation was already completed. Hence, a simulation of 100 passengers every ten minutes is manageable which corresponds to a scale of 1:20.

In the experiments, varying distributions (e.g. due to rush hours) have not been taken into account. It has to be considered that peak values may be much greater if a more accurate distribution is applied. Therefore, memory usage has to be reduced significantly. This may be achieved by reducing the number of agents without reducing the number of passengers.

5.2   Comparison of Information Systems

Both computing time and quality of results vary between the three different graph types due to the diverse size and complexity. Creating a complete TEG for the PTN timetable took 106.5 seconds. Furthermore, a reduced TEG was created within 10.8 seconds. The creation of a TDG took about 0.1 seconds.

The TDG always proved itself to be the fastest variant. The results of five randomly chosen transport requests are shown in Table 1. To generate more representative numbers, experiments on a scale of 1:100 have been run with each graph type. However, the TEG-experiment was aborted manually after about 36 hours and a simulation progress of less than 40%. In comparison, finishing the experiment took 14.3 hours with the reduced TEG and only 0.5 hours with the TDG. Each one of the 2,863 transport requests has been solved in 17.2 seconds with the reduced TEG and in 0.006 seconds with the TDG on average.

Table 1. Computing time of randomly chosen transport requests

Request (time 08:00)	TEG	red. TEG	TDG
Kriegerdenkmal → Hasenb. Jachthafen	146.184s	2.995s	0.076s
Hasenb. Jachthafen → Sebaldsbrück	243.908s	6.553s	0.105s
Groepelingen → Polizeipraesidium	182.154s	4.126s	0.088s
Waller Friedhof → Ricarda-Huch-Strasse	124.414s	2.307s	0.079s
Roland-Center → Julius-Brecht-Allee	62.868s	0.641s	0.064s
Average	151.905s	3.324s	0.082s

Even though the recuded TEG variant is significantly faster than the complete TEG, both variants produce identical results. Unfortunately, the solution quality varies between the TEG variants and the TDG. All variants solve the EAP correctly by computing a shortest path with the ideal arrival time. However, the

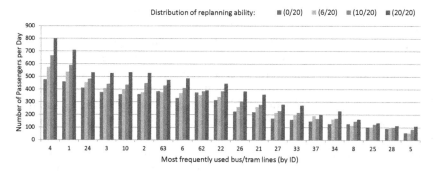

Fig. 2. Line utilization with diverse distribution of replanning ability

TDG is not capable of minimizing the number of transfers while searching for a shortest path. Consequently, passengers would not choose all of the computed routes based on a TDG because they contain unnecessary transfers a real passenger would try to avoid. From this point of view, the reduced TEG variant is the best choice for a simulation of passenger behavior, even though it is not the fastest variant.

5.3 Application: Effects of Passengers' Behaviors to the PTN

In 2013, 40% of Germans already own a smartphone [3]. Hence, two out of five Germans are able to revise their current traveling plans in case of unexpected disruptions by looking up alternative options. As a result, passengers can switch lines more often in case of delays and disruptions. This affects the utilization of the failed line and other lines alike. The goal of public transport providers

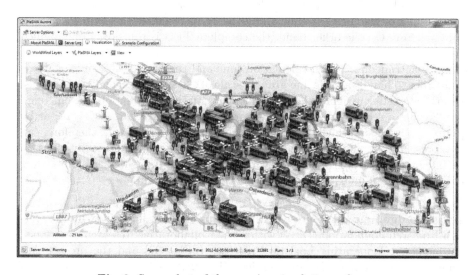

Fig. 3. Screenshot of the running simulation software

is to anticipate the passengers' behaviors in predictable situations (e.g., road construction or public demonstrations) as well as in unexpected situations (e.g., in case of a fire or in natural disasters) to adapt timetables and schedules appropriately. The model enables strategy and scenario analysis.

Several performance indicators, such as the utilization of each line or departures and arrivals at each stop are measured by the simulation system. The share of replanning agents and the probability of line failure are given by simulation parameters. As an example, we set up a series of experiments with a high failure possibility of 33% for every vehicle and a diverse distribution of replanning ability (0%, 30%, 50%, 100%). Fig. 2 shows the utilization of the BSAG's frequently used lines according to that experiment. Though the chosen scenario setup is rather generic, it is also possible to simulate specific situations where a only certain lines fail. Therefore, the PTC can predict passenger behavior by applying the simulation model to a specific problem. Fig. 3 shows the running simulation software.

6   Conclusion and Outlook

In this paper we presented an adaptation of the Needleman-Wunsch Algorithm in order to match line information from VDV-compliant data sets to excerpts from the OSM. The approach allows the simulation model to be applied to any compatible combination of PTN and infrastructure. Furthermore, real world data sets of the PTN of Bremen (Germany) were used as an example to determine bottlenecks of a microscopic simulation of PTNs. One bottleneck is the available RAM due to the large number of more than 6,000 concurrently active agents. Another bottleneck is the graph-based approach to intermodal routing. We pinpointed by comparison that EAPs could be solved by complete TEG, reduced TEG, and TDG alike. However, while TDG is a lot faster than both TEG variants, results of the TDG are not always likely to resemble the routes a human would choose. On the other hand, the complete TEG is too slow to be applied to a simulation on larger PTN. The reduced variant of the TEG provides an acceptable tradeoff between calculation time and the quality of results.

In order to handle a more fine-grained scale of the simulation and larger PTNs, we are interested in increasing the efficiency of the information system (e.g., by adapting a recently developed K-shortest-paths search for TDGs [17] or by grouping passengers which have similar or identical interests and, therefore, can be represented by one single agent). Further research will additionally focus on the integration of traffic simulation within our framework as well as on modeling and simulation of unexpected changes to the infrastructure.

Acknowledgement. The presented research was partially funded by the German Research Foundation (DFG) within the Collaborative Research Centre 637 Autonomous Cooperating Logistic Processes (SFB 637) and the project Autonomous Courier and Express Services (HE 989/14-1) at the University of Bremen, Germany. We thank the BSAG for providing real-world timetable data.

References

1. Bremer Straßenbahn AG: Blickpunkte. Geschäftsbericht 2011 (2012)
2. Buehler, R.: Determinants of transport mode choice: a comparison of Germany and the USA. Journal of Transport Geography 19(4), 644–657 (2011)
3. Bundesverband Informationswirtschaft, Telekommunikation und neue Medien e.V. (BITKOM): Auch Ältere steigen auf Smartphones um. 40 Prozent aller Deutschen haben ein Smartphone (2013)
4. Collins, C.M., Chambers, S.M.: Psychological and situational influences on commuter-transport-mode choice. Env. and Beh. 37(5), 640–661 (2005)
5. Dijkstra, E.W.: A note on two problems in connexion with graphs. Numerische Mathematik 1, 269–271 (1959)
6. Divall, C., Schmucki, B.: Introduction: Technology (sub)urban development and the social construction of urban transport. In: Suburbanizing The Masses. Public Transport and Urban Development in Historical Perspective. Ashgate (2003)
7. de Donnea, F.: Consumer behaviour, transport mode choice and value of time: Some micro-economic models. Regional and Urban Economics 1(4), 55–382 (1972)
8. Greulich, C., Edelkamp, S., Gath, M., Warden, T., Humann, M., Herzog, O., Sitharam, T.: Enhanced shortest path computation for multiagent-based intermodal transport planning in dynamic environments. In: ICAART (2), pp. 324–329 (2013)
9. Gusfield, D.: Algorithms on Strings, Trees and Sequences. Cambridge University Press (1997)
10. Klügl, F., Rindsfüser, G.: Agent-based route (and mode) choice simulation in real-world networks. In: WI-IAT, vol. 2, pp. 22–29 (2011)
11. Meignan, D., Simonin, O., Koukam, A.: Multiagent approach for simulation and evaluation of urban bus networks. In: AAMAS, pp. 50–56 (2006)
12. Müller-Hannemann, M., Schulz, F., Wagner, D., Zaroliagis, C.: Timetable information: Models and algorithms. In: Geraets, F., Kroon, L.G., Schoebel, A., Wagner, D., Zaroliagis, C.D. (eds.) Railway Optimization 2004. LNCS, vol. 4359, pp. 67–90. Springer, Heidelberg (2007)
13. Needleman, S.B., Wunsch, C.D.: A general method applicable to the search for similarities in the amino acid sequence of two proteins. Journal of Molecular Biology 48(3), 443–453 (1970)
14. van Nes, R., Hamerslag, R., Immers, B.H.: Design of public transport networks. Transportation Research Record 1202, 74–83 (1988)
15. Tardelli, A.O., Anção, M.S., Packer, A.L., Sigulem, D.: An implementation of the trigram phrase matching method for text similarity problems. In: Bos, L., Laxminarayan, S., Marsh, A. (eds.) Medical and Care Compunetics 1, 1st edn., vol. 103. IOS Press (2004)
16. Verband Deutscher Verkehrsunternehmen: ÖPNV-Datenmodell 5.0. "Schnittstellen-Initiative". VDV Standardschnittstelle. Liniennetz/Fahrplan. Version: 1.4 (2008)
17. Yang, Y., Wang, S., Hu, X., Li, J., Xu, B.: A modified k-shortest paths algorithm for solving the earliest arrival problem on the time-dependent model of transportation systems. In: International MultiConference of Engineers and Computer Scientists, pp. 1562–1567 (2012)

On GPU-Based Nearest Neighbor Queries for Large-Scale Photometric Catalogs in Astronomy

Justin Heinermann[1], Oliver Kramer[1], Kai Lars Polsterer[2], and Fabian Gieseke[3]

[1] Department of Computing Science
University of Oldenburg, 26111 Oldenburg, Germany
{justin.philipp.heinermann,oliver.kramer}@uni-oldenburg.de
[2] Faculty of Physics and Astronomy
Ruhr-University Bochum, 44801 Bochum, Germany
polsterer@astro.rub.de
[3] Department of Computer Science
University of Copenhagen, 2100 Copenhagen, Denmark
fabian.gieseke@diku.dk

Abstract. Nowadays astronomical catalogs contain patterns of hundreds of millions of objects with data volumes in the terabyte range. Upcoming projects will gather such patterns for several billions of objects with peta- and exabytes of data. From a machine learning point of view, these settings often yield unsupervised, semi-supervised, or fully supervised tasks, with large training and huge test sets. Recent studies have demonstrated the effectiveness of prototype-based learning schemes such as simple nearest neighbor models. However, although being among the most computationally efficient methods for such settings (if implemented via spatial data structures), applying these models on all remaining patterns in a given catalog can easily take hours or even days. In this work, we investigate the practical effectiveness of GPU-based approaches to accelerate such nearest neighbor queries in this context. Our experiments indicate that carefully tuned implementations of spatial search structures for such multi-core devices can significantly reduce the practical runtime. This renders the resulting frameworks an important algorithmic tool for current and upcoming data analyses in astronomy.

1 Motivation

Modern astronomical surveys such as the *Sloan Digital Sky Survey* (SDSS) [16] gather terabytes of data. Upcoming projects like the *Large Synoptic Sky Telescope* (LSST) [8] will produce such data volumes *per night* and the anticipated overall catalogs will encompass data in the peta- and exabyte range. Naturally, such big data scenarios render a manual data analysis impossible and machine learning techniques have already been identified as "increasingly essential in the era of data-intensive astronomy" [4]. Among the most popular types of data are *photometric patterns* [16], which stem from grayscale images taken at different

I.J. Timm and M. Thimm (Eds.): KI 2013, LNAI 8077, pp. 86–97, 2013.

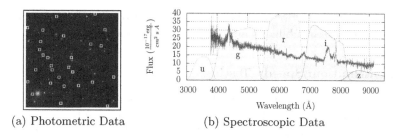

(a) Photometric Data   (b) Spectroscopic Data

Fig. 1. The telescope of the SDSS [16] gathers both photometric and spectroscopic data. Photometric data are given in terms of grayscale images, which are extracted via five filters covering different wavelength ranges (called the **u**, **g**, **r**, **i**, and **z** bands). Such data can be composed to (single) RGB images, see Figure (a). For a small subset of the detected objects (white squares), detailed follow-up observations are made in terms of spectra, see Figure (b).

wavelength ranges. One group of these photometric features are the so-called *magnitudes*, which depict logarithmic measures of the brightness. From a machine learning point of view, these features usually lead to low-dimensional feature spaces (e.g., $\mathbb{R}^4$ or $\mathbb{R}^5$). For a small subset of objects, detailed information in terms of spectra is given, see Figure 1. One of the main challenges in astronomy is to detect new and rare objects in the set of photometric objects that to do not yet have an associated spectrum. Hence, one aims at selecting valuable, yet unlabeled objects for spectroscopic follow-up observations, based on training sets that consist of photometric patterns *with* associated spectra.

1.1 Big Training and Huge Test Data

Given the data in the current data release of the SDSS (DR9) [16], for instance, requires building the corresponding models on training sets containing up to 2.3 million objects. Further, the resulting models have to be (recurrently) applied on the massive amount of remaining photometric objects in the catalog (about one billion astronomical objects). Recent studies [14] have shown that prototype-based learning frameworks like *nearest neighbor regression* models depict excellent learning frameworks, often out-competing other sophisticated schemes like *support vector machines* or *neural networks* [7].

A crucial ingredient of such nearest neighbor models is to take *as many as possible* of the available training patterns into account to obtain accurate local estimates of the conditional probabilities. While well-known spatial data structures such as k-d trees [2] can be used to reduce the runtime needed per pattern to $\mathcal{O}(\log n)$ in practice, the implicit constants hidden in the big-$\mathcal{O}$-notation can still render the processing of large test sets very time-consuming. For instance, applying a nearest neighbor model that is based on two million training patterns on a test set of size one billion can take days on a standard desktop machine.[1]

1.2   Contribution: Speedy Testing

In contrast to the particular application of such models, a simple *scan* over the test data can usually be performed in minutes only (due to the data being stored consecutively on disk). In this work, we aim at investigating the potential of *graphics processing units* (GPUs) to accelerate the testing phase of nearest neighbor models in this context. For this sake, we consider several implementations of the classical k-d tree data structure [2] on GPUs and show how to shorten the influence of undesired side-effects that can occur when making use of such multi-core devices. The final nearest neighbor implementation reduces the runtime needed per test instance by an order of magnitude and, thus, demonstrates the potential of GPUs for the data analysis of large-scale photometric catalogs in astronomy.

2   Background

We start by providing the background related to GPUs and nearest neighbor queries that will be of relevance for the remainder of this work.

2.1   Graphics Processing Units

GPUs have become powerful parallel processing devices that can also be used for general purpose computations. Typical examples, in which GPUs usually outperform CPUs, are image processing tasks or numerical computations like matrix multiplication. In addition, developing code for GPUs has become much easier since the hardware manufacturers offer toolkits such as *nVidia CUDA* and *AMD Stream*, which provide high-level programming interfaces. Furthermore, with programming languages like *OpenCL*, there exists hardware- and platform-independent interfaces that are available for parallel computations using many- and multi-core processors [10].

To develop efficient code for GPUs, one needs profound knowledge about the architecture of the computing device at hand. Due to a lack of space, we only introduce the basic principles that are needed for the remainder of this work: GPUs, designed as highly parallel processors, consist of a large number of cores (e.g., 384 cores on the nVidia Geforce GTX 650). Whereas CPUs exhibit

---

[1] In the worst case, all leaves of a k-d tree need to be visited for a given query. However, for low-dimensional feature spaces, a small number of leaves need to be checked in practice, and this leads to the desired logarithmic runtime behavior. It is worth pointing out, however, that the logarithmic runtime of such nearest neighbor models needed per test query already depicts a very efficient way to process large test sets. Other schemes like support vector models or neural networks (with a reasonable amount of neurons) do not exhibit a better runtime behavior in practice.

complex control logic functions and large caches and are optimized with respect to the efficiency of sequential programs, the GPU cores are designed for "simple" tasks. The differences to CPUs include, for instance, the chip-design (of ALUs) and a higher memory-bandwidth [9]. A GPU-based program consists of a *host program* that runs on the CPU and a *kernel program* (or *kernel* for short). The latter one is *distributed* to the cores of the GPU and run as *threads*, also called *kernel instances*. The kernel programs are mostly based on the *single instruction multiple data*-paradigm (SIMD), which means that all threads are executing exactly the same instruction in one clock cycle, but are allowed to access and process different pieces of data that are available in the memory of the GPU.[2] In addition, several restrictions are given when developing code for GPUs (e.g., recursion is prohibited). Similar to standard memory hierarchies of the host systems, a GPU exhibits a hierarchical memory layout with different access times per memory type [10,12].

2.2 Nearest Neighbor Queries Revisited

A popular data mining technique are *nearest neighbor models* [7], which can be used for various supervised learning tasks like *classification* or *regression*.[3] For supervised learning problems, one is usually given a labeled training set of the form $T = \{(\mathbf{x}_1, y_1), \ldots, (\mathbf{x}_n, y_n)\} \subset \mathbb{R}^d \times \mathbb{R}$, and predictions for a query object $\mathbf{x}$ are made by averaging the label information of the k nearest neighbors (kNN), i.e., via

$$f(\mathbf{x}) = \sum_{\mathbf{x}_i \in N_k(\mathbf{x})} y_i, \qquad (1)$$

where N_k denotes the set of indices for the k nearest neighbors in T. Thus, a direct implementation of such a model given a test set S takes $\mathcal{O}(|S||T|d)$ time, which can very time-consuming even given moderate-sized sets of patterns.

Due to its importance, the problem of finding nearest neighbors has gained a lot of attention over the last decades: One of the most prominent ways to accelerate such computations are spatial search structures like k-d trees [2] or *cover trees* [3]. Another acceleration strategy is *locality-sensitive hashing* [1,15], which aims at computing $(1 + \varepsilon)$-approximations (with high probability). The latter type of schemes mostly address learning tasks in high-dimensional feature spaces (for which the former spatial search structures usually do not yield any speed-up anymore). Due to a lack of space, we refer to the literature for an overview [1,15].

Several GPU-based schemes have been proposed for accelerating nearest neighbor queries. In most cases, such approaches aim at providing a decent speed-up for medium-sized data sets, but fail for large data sets. As an example, consider the implementation proposed by Bustos *et al.* [5], which resorts to sophisticated texture-image-techniques. An approach related to what is proposed in this work

---

[2] More precisely, all threads of a *work-group*, which contains, e.g., 16 or 32 threads.

[3] As pointed out by Hastie *et al.* [7], such a model "is often successful where each class has many possible prototypes, and the decision boundary is very irregular".

Table 1. Runtime comparison of a brute-force approach for nearest neighbor queries on a GPU (`bfgpu`) and on a CPU (`bfcpu`) as well as a k-d tree-enhanced version (`kdcpu`) on a CPU using $k = 10$. The patterns for both the training and the test set of size $|T|$ and $|S|$, respectively, stem from a four-dimensional feature space, see Section 4.

$|T|$	$|S|$	`bfgpu`	`bfcpu`	`kdcpu`
50,000	50,000	**0.751**	347.625	0.882
500,000	500,000	68.864	-	**13.586**

is the k-d tree-traversal framework given by Nakasato [11], which is used to compute the forces between particles. An interesting approach is proposed by Garcia *et al.* [6]: Since matrix multiplications can be performed efficiently on GPUs, they resort to corresponding (adapted) implementations to perform the nearest neighbor search. The disadvantage of these schemes is that they cannot be applied in the context of very large data sets as well due to their general quadratic running time behavior and memory usage.

3   Accelerating the Testing Phase via GPUs

In the following, we will show how to accelerate nearest neighbor queries by means of GPUs and k-d trees for the case of massive photometric catalogs. As mentioned above, programming such parallel devices in an efficient way can be very challenging. For the sake of demonstration, we provide details related to a simple brute-force approach, followed by an efficient implementation of a corresponding k-d tree approach. While the latter one already yields significant speed-ups for the task at hand, we additionally demonstrate how to improve its performance by a carefully selected layout of the underlying tree structure.

3.1   Brute-Force: Fast for Small Reference Sets

A direct implementation that makes use of GPUs is based on either distributing the test queries to the different compute units or on distributing the computation of the nearest neighbors in the training set for a single query. Thus, every test instance is assigned to a thread that searches for the k nearest neighbors in the given training set. Due to its simple conceptual layout, this approach can be implemented extremely efficient on GPUs, as described by several authors (see Section 2.1). As an example, consider the runtime results in Table 1: For a medium-sized data set (top row), the brute-force scheme executed on a GPU (`bfgpu`) outperforms its counterpart on the CPU (`bfcpu`) by far, and is even faster than a well-tuned implementation that resorts to k-d trees (`kdcpu`) on CPUs. However, this approach is not suited for the task at hand due to its quadratic running time behavior (bottom row) and becomes inferior to spatial loop-up strategies on CPUs. Thus, a desirable goal is the implementation of such spatial search structures on GPUs, and that is addressed in the next sections.

3.2 Spatial Lookup on GPUs: Parallel Processing of k-d trees

A k-d tree is a well-known data structure to accelerate geometric problems including nearest neighbor computations. In the following, we will describe both the construction and layout of such a tree as well as the traversal on a GPU for obtaining the nearest neighbors in parallel.

Construction Phase. A standard k-d tree is a balanced binary tree defined as follows: The root of the tree $\mathcal{T}$ corresponds to all points and its two children correspond to (almost) equal-sized subsets. Splitting the points into such subsets is performed in a level-wise manner, starting from the root (level $i = 0$). For each node v at level i, one resorts to the median in dimension $i \bmod d$ to partition the points of v into two subsets. The recursion stops as soon as a node v corresponds to a singleton or as soon as a user-defined recursion level is reached. Since it takes linear time to find a median, the construction of such a tree can be performed in $\mathcal{O}(n \log n)$ time for n patterns in $\mathbb{R}^d$ [2].

Memory Layout. In literature, several ways of representing such a data structure can be found [2]. One way, which will be considered in the following, is to store the median in each node v (thus consuming $\mathcal{O}(n)$ additional space in total). Further, such a tree can be represented in a pointerless manner (necessary for a GPU-based implementation): Here, the root is stored at index 0 and the children of a node v with index i are stored at $2i+1$ (left child) and at $2i+2$ (right child). Since the median is used to split points into subsets, the tree has a maximum height of $h = \lceil \log n \rceil$. Note that one can stop the recursion phase as soon as a certain depth is reached (e.g. $i = 10$). In this case, a leaf corresponds to a d-dimensional box and all points that are contained in this box.

For the nearest neighbor queries described below, we additionally sort the points *in-place* per dimension $i \bmod d$ while building the tree. This permits an efficient access to the points that are stored consecutively in memory for each leaf. Both, the array containing the median values as well as the reordered (training) points, can be transferred from host system to the memory of the GPU prior to the parallel nearest neighbor search, which is described next.

Parallel Nearest Neighbor Queries. Given an appropriately built k-d tree, one can find the nearest neighbor for a given test query $\mathbf{q} \in \mathbb{R}^d$ as follows: In the first phase, the tree is traversed from top to bottom. For each level i and internal node v with median m, one uses the distance $d = \mathbf{q}_i - m_i$ between $\mathbf{q}$ and the corresponding splitting hyperplane to navigate to one of the children of v. If $d \leq 0$, the left child is processed in the next step, otherwise the right one. As soon as a leaf is reached, one computes the distances between $\mathbf{q}$ and all points that are stored in the leaf. In the second phase, one traverses the tree from bottom to top. For each internal node v, one checks if the distance to the splitting hyperplane is less than the distance to the best nearest neighbor candidate found so far. If this is the case, then one recurses to the child that has not yet been visited. Otherwise, one goes up to the parent of the current node. As soon as the root has been reached (and both children have been processed), the recursive calls stop. The generalization to finding the k nearest neighbors is straightforward.

Instead of using the nearest point as intermediate candidate solution, one resorts to the current k-th neighbor of $\mathbf{q}$, see Bentley [2] for further details.

To efficiently process a large number of test queries in parallel, one can simply assign a thread to each query instance. Further, for computing the nearest neighbors in a leaf of the tree, one can resort to a simple GPU-based brute-force approach, see above.

3.3 Faster Processing of Parallel Queries

Compared to the effect of using k-d trees in a program on the CPU, the performance gain reached by the approach presented in the previous section is not as high as expected when considering $\mathcal{O}(\log n)$ time complexity per query (i.e., a direct parallel execution of such nearest neighbor queries does yield an optimal performance gain). Possible reasons are (a) *flow divergence* and (b) *non-optimal memory access*. The former issue is due to the SIMD architecture of a GPU, which enforces all kernel instances of a workgroup to perform the same instructions simultaneously.[4] The latter one describes various side-effects that can occur when the kernel instances access shared memory resources such as local or global memory (e.g., *bank conflicts*). Accessing the global memory can take many more block cycles compared to size-limited on-chip registers. We address these difficulties by proposing the following modifications to optimize the parallel processing of k-d trees on GPUs:

1. *Using private memory for test patterns:* The standard way to transfer input parameters to the kernel instances is to make use of the global memory (which depicts the largest part of the overall memory, but is also the slowest one). We analyzed the impact of using registers for the test instances. Each entry is unique to one kernel instance, because one thread processes the k-d tree for one test instance. Thus, every time the distance between the test instance and some training instance is computed, only the private array is accessed.
2. *Using private memory for the nearest neighbors:* During the execution of each kernel instance, a list of the k nearest neighbors found so far has to be updated. In case a training pattern in a leaf is closer to the corresponding test instance than one of the points stored in this list, it has to be inserted, which can result in up to k read- and write-operations. Further, the current k-th nearest neighbor candidate is accessed multiple times during the traversal of the top of the k-d tree (for finding the next leaf that needs to be checked). Hence, to optimize the recurrent access to this list, we store the best k nearest neighbor candidates in private memory as well.
3. *Utilizing vector data types and operations:* GPUs provide optimized operations for vector data types. As described below, we focus on a particular four-dimensional feature space that is often used in astronomy. Thus, to store both the training T and test set S, we make use of `float4`-arrays. This

---

[4] For instance, the processing of an *if*- and the corresponding *else*-branch can take as long as the sequential processing of both branches.

renders the application of the built-in function distance possible to compute the Euclidean distances.[5]

As we will demonstrate in the next section, the above modifications can yield a significant speed-up compared to a direct (parallel) implementation on GPUs.

4   Experimental Evaluation

In this section, we describe the experimental setup and provide practical runtime evaluations for the different implementations.

4.1   Experimental Setup

We will first analyze the performance gain achieved by the particular optimizations described in Section 3. Afterwards, we will give an overall comparison of the practical performances of the different nearest neighbor implementations. For all performance measurements, a desktop machine with specifications given below was used (using only one of the cores of the host system). For the CPU-based implementation, we resort to the k-d tree-kNN-implementation of the *sklearn*-package (which is based on Fortran) [13].

Implementation. The overall framework is implemented in *OpenCL*. This ensures a broad applicability on a variety of systems (even not restricted to GPUs only). Further, we make use of *PyOpenCL* to provide a simple yet effective access to the implementation. The experiments are conducted on a standard PC running *Ubuntu 12.10* with an *Intel Quad Core CPU 3.10 GHz*, 8GB RAM, and a *Nvidia GeForce GTX 650* with 2GB RAM.

Astronomical Data. We resort to the data provided by the SDSS, see Section 1. In particular, we consider a special type of features that are extracted from the image data, the so-called *PSF magnitudes*, which are used for various tasks in the field of astronomy including the one of detecting distant *quasars* [14].[6] A well-known set of induced features in astronomy is based on using the so-called *colors* $u - g, g - r, r - i, i - z$ that stem from the (PSF) magnitudes given for each of the five bands. This feature space can be used, for instance, for the task of estimating the redshift of quasars, see Polsterer *et al.* [14] for details. For the experimental evaluation conducted in this work, we will therefore explicitly focus on such patterns in $\mathbb{R}^4$. In all scenarios considered, the test sets are restricted to less than two million objects. The more general case (with hundreds of millions of objects) can be simply considering chunks of test patterns.[7]

---

[5] Note that there exists an even faster function (*fast_distance*) which returns an approximation; however, we used the standard function (*distance*) to keep the needed numerical precision.

[6] A quasar is the core of a distant galaxy with an active nucleus. Quasars, especially those with a high redshift, can help understanding the evolution of the universe.

[7] Since these patterns are stored consecutively on hard disk, one can efficiently transfer the data from disk to main memory (reading two million test patterns into main memory took less than half a second on our test system, and is thus negligible compared to the application of the overall model).

Table 2. Performance comparison for k-d tree kNN search on the GPU using global vs. private memory for the test instances ($|S|$) given four-dimensional patterns and $k = 10$ neighbors. The number of training patterns is $200,000$.

$|S|$	10,000	20,000	50,000	100,000	200,000	500,000	1,000,000
global	0.063	0.130	0.306	0.605	1.170	2.951	5.743
private	**0.052**	**0.107**	**0.253**	**0.499**	**0.974**	**2.438**	**4.709**

Performance Measures. We will only report the time needed for the testing phase, i.e., the runtimes needed for the construction of the appropriate k-d trees will not be reported. Note that, for the application at hand, one only needs to build the tree once at during the training phase, and it can be re-used for the nearest neighbor queries of millions or billions of test queries. In addition, the runtime is very small also (less than a second for all the experiments considered).

4.2   Fine-Tuning

As pointed out in Section 3, a k-d tree-based implementation of the nearest neighbor search on GPUs can be tuned with different optimization approaches in order to obtain a better practical performance. In the following, we compare the runtime improvements achieve via the different modifications proposed.

Using Private Memory for Test Patterns. The first optimization we analyze is the usage of private memory for the test instance processed by a particular thread. The influence of this rather simple modification indicates that it pays off to use registers instead of the given global memory structures, see Table 2. For $1,000,000$ test instances, a speed-up of 18% was achieved.

Using Private Memory for the Nearest Neighbors. In Section 3, we proposed to use registers instead of global memory for the list of neighbors. This modification gives a large speed-up, especially if the number k of nearest neighbors is large. The performance results are shown in Figure 2 (a): For the case of $k = 50$ nearest neighbors, $|S| = 1,000,000$ test instances, and a training set size of $|T| = 200,000$, only half of the time is needed given the optimized version.

Utilizing Vector Data Types and Operations. A large amount of work in astronomy is conducted in the four-dimensional feature space described above. We can make use of the high-performance operations available for vector data types in *OpenCL*. The performance comparison given in Figure 2 (b) shows that one can achieve a significant speed-up of more than 30% by simply resorting to these vector data types and operations.

4.3   Runtime Performances

In the remainder of this section, we compare four different nearest neighbor approaches:

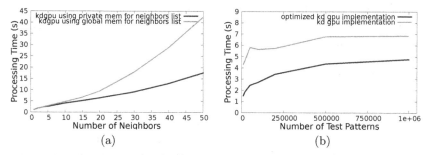

Fig. 2. Experimental results for (a) the usage of private memory for test instances with $200,000$ training and $1,000,000$ test patterns. The plot shows the processing time for varying numbers of k. In Figure (b), the usage of vector data types and operations is depicted with $200,000$ training patterns, $k = 10$, and 4-dimensional patterns. The plot shows the processing time for varying test set sizes.

- *knn-brute-gpu*: brute-force approach on the GPU
- *knn-kd-cpu*: k-d tree-based search on the CPU
- *knn-kd-gpu*: standard k-d tree approach on the GPU
- *knn-kd-fast-gpu*: k-d tree approach on the GPU with additional modifications

As shown in Figure 3, the runtime of the brute-force version is only good for relatively small training data sets. In case the size of both the training and test set is increased, such a brute-force implementation (naturally) gets too slow. For larger data sets, the CPU version based on k-d tree yields better results: Given $1,000,000$ patterns in both the training and test set, the brute-force implementation takes about 274 seconds, whereas the k-d tree-based CPU implementation only takes about 33 seconds. That said, the fulfillment of our main motivation has to be analyzed: Can we map this performance improvement to GPUs? Figure 3 (a) shows that the direct k-d tree implementation already provides a large performance gain. For $1,000,000$ patterns used as training and test data, it takes only less than 7 seconds. However, the additional modifications proposed

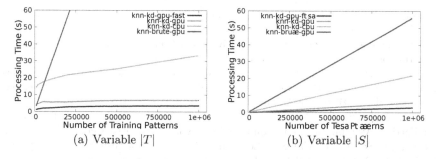

Fig. 3. Runtime comparison for $k = 10$ and four-dimensional patterns: (a) Processing time for variable training set size $|T|$ and test set size $|S| = 1,000,000$. (b) Processing time for variable test set size and training set size of $|T| = 200,000$.

in Section 3 can even reduce the needed runtime to about 3.6 seconds (thus, a speed-up of about ten is achieved compared to the corresponding CPU version). Figure 3 (b) also shows that the amount of test data has a much lower impact on our k-d tree implementation, which is especially useful for the mentioned application in astronomy with petabytes of upcoming data.

5   Conclusions

In this work, we derived an effective implementation for nearest neighbor queries given huge test and large training sets. Such settings are often given in the field of astronomy, where one is nowadays faced with the semi-automated analysis of billions of objects. We employ data structures on GPUs and take advantage of the vast of amount of computational power provided by such devices. The result is a well-tuned framework for nearest neighbor queries. The applicability is demonstrated on current large-scale learning tasks in the field of astronomy.

The proposed framework makes use of standard devices given in current machines, but can naturally also be applied in the context of large-scale GPU systems. In the future, the amount of astronomical data will increase dramatically, and the corresponding systems will have to resort to cluster systems to store and process the data. However, a significant amount of research will always be conducted using single workstation machines, which means there is a need for efficient implementations of such specific tasks.

Acknowledgements. This work was partly supported by grants of the German Academic Exchange Service (DAAD). The data used for the experimental evaluation are based the Sloan Digital Sky Survey (SDSS).[8]

---

[8] Funding for the SDSS and SDSS-II has been provided by the Alfred P. Sloan Foundation, the Participating Institutions, the National Science Foundation, the U.S. Department of Energy, the National Aeronautics and Space Administration, the Japanese Monbukagakusho, the Max Planck Society, and the Higher Education Funding Council for England. The SDSS Web Site is http://www.sdss.org/. The SDSS is managed by the Astrophysical Research Consortium for the Participating Institutions. The Participating Institutions are the American Museum of Natural History, Astrophysical Institute Potsdam, University of Basel, University of Cambridge, Case Western Reserve University, University of Chicago, Drexel University, Fermilab, the Institute for Advanced Study, the Japan Participation Group, Johns Hopkins University, the Joint Institute for Nuclear Astrophysics, the Kavli Institute for Particle Astrophysics and Cosmology, the Korean Scientist Group, the Chinese Academy of Sciences (LAMOST), Los Alamos National Laboratory, the Max-Planck-Institute for Astronomy (MPIA), the Max-Planck-Institute for Astrophysics (MPA), New Mexico State University, Ohio State University, University of Pittsburgh, University of Portsmouth, Princeton University, the United States Naval Observatory, and the University of Washington.

References

1. Andoni, A., Indyk, P.: Near-optimal hashing algorithms for approximate nearest neighbor in high dimensions. Communications of the ACM 51(1), 117–122 (2008)
2. Bentley, J.L.: Multidimensional binary search trees used for associative searching. Communications of the ACM 18(9), 509–517 (1975)
3. Beygelzimer, A., Kakade, S., Langford, J.: Cover trees for nearest neighbor. In: Proceedings of the 23 International Conference on Machine Learning, pp. 97–104. ACM (2006)
4. Borne, K.: Scientific data mining in astronomy, arXiv:0911.0505v1 (2009)
5. Bustos, B., Deussen, O., Hiller, S., Keim, D.: A graphics hardware accelerated algorithm for nearest neighbor search. In: Alexandrov, V.N., van Albada, G.D., Sloot, P.M.A., Dongarra, J. (eds.) ICCS 2006, Part IV. LNCS, vol. 3994, pp. 196–199. Springer, Heidelberg (2006)
6. Garcia, V., Debreuve, E., Barlaud, M.: Fast k nearest neighbor search using GPU. In: CVPR Workshop on Computer Vision on GPU, Anchorage, Alaska, USA (June 2008)
7. Hastie, T., Tibshirani, R., Friedman, J.: The Elements of Statistical Learning, 2nd edn. Springer (2009)
8. Ivezic, Z., Tyson, J.A., Acosta, E., Allsman, R., andere: Lsst: from science drivers to reference design and anticipated data products (2011)
9. Kirk, D.B., Wen-mei, H.: Programming Massively Parallel Processors: A Hands-on Approach, 1st edn. Morgan Kaufmann Publishers Inc., San Francisco (2010)
10. Munshi, A., Gaster, B., Mattson, T.: OpenCL Programming Guide. OpenGL Series. Addison-Wesley (2011)
11. Nakasato, N.: Implementation of a parallel tree method on a gpu. CoRR, abs/1112.4539 (2011)
12. nVidia Corporation. Opencl ^{TM} best practices guide (2009), http://www.nvidia.com/content/cudazone/CUDABrowser/downloads/papers/NVIDIA_OpenCL_BestPracticesGuide.pdf
13. Pedregosa, F., Varoquaux, G., Gramfort, A., Michel, V., Thirion, B., Grisel, O., Blondel, M., Prettenhofer, P., Weiss, R., Dubourg, V., Vanderplas, J., Passos, A., Cournapeau, D., Brucher, M., Perrot, M., Duchesnay, E.: Scikit-learn: Machine Learning in Python. Journal of Machine Learning Research 12, 2825–2830 (2011)
14. Polsterer, K.L., Zinn, P., Gieseke, F.: Finding new high-redshift quasars by asking the neighbours. Monthly Notices of the Royal Astronomical Society (MNRAS) 428(1), 226–235 (2013)
15. Shakhnarovich, G., Darrell, T., Indyk, P.: Nearest-Neighbor Methods in Learning and Vision: Theory and Practice (Neural Information Processing). MIT Press (2006)
16. York, D.G., et al.: The sloan digital sky survey: Technical summary. The Astronomical Journal 120(3), 1579–1587

On Mutation Rate Tuning and Control for the (1+1)-EA

Oliver Kramer

Computational Intelligence Group
Department of Computing Science
University of Oldenburg

Abstract. The significant effect of parameter settings on the success of the evolutionary optimization has led to a long history of research on parameter control, e.g., on mutation rates. However, few studies compare different tuning and control strategies under the same experimental condition. Objective of this paper is to give a comprehensive and fundamental comparison of tuning and control techniques of mutation rates employing the same algorithmic setting on a simple unimodal problem. After an analysis of various mutation rates for a (1+1)-EA on OneMax, we compare meta-evolution to Rechenberg's 1/5th rule and self-adaptation.

1 Introduction

Parameter control is an essential aspect of successful evolutionary search. Various parameter control and tuning methods have been proposed in the history of evolutionary computation, cf. Figure 1 for a short taxonomy. The importance of parameter control has become famous for mutation rates. Mutation is a main source of evolutionary changes. According to Beyer and Schwefel [1], a mutation operator is supposed to fulfill three conditions. First, from each point in the solution space each other point must be reachable. Second, in unconstrained solution spaces a bias is disadvantageous, because the direction to the optimum is unknown, and third, the mutation strength should be adjustable, in order to adapt exploration and exploitation to local solution space conditions. Mutation rates control the magnitude of random changes of solutions. At the beginning of the history of evolutionary computation, researchers argued about proper settings. De Jong's [6] recommendation was the mutation strength $\sigma = 0.001$, Schaffer *et al.* [9] recommended the setting $0.005 \leq \sigma \leq 0.01$, and Grefenstette [5] $\sigma = 0.01$. Mühlenbein [8] suggested to set the mutation probability to $\sigma = 1/N$ depending on the length N of the representation. But early, the idea appeared to control the mutation rate during the optimization run, as the optimal rate might change during the optimization process, and different rates are reasonable for different problems. Objective of this paper is to compare the parameter tuning and control techniques of a simple evolutionary algorithm (EA) on a simple function, i.e. *OneMax*, to allow insights into the interplay of mutation rates and parameter

I.J. Timm and M. Thimm (Eds.): KI 2013, LNAI 8077, pp. 98–105, 2013.

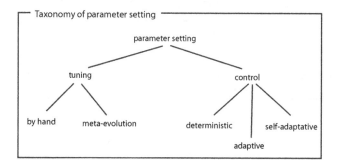

Fig. 1. Taxonomy of parameter setting of this work oriented to Eiben *et al.* [3] and complemented on the parameter tuning branch (cf. Kramer [7])

control mechanisms. *OneMax* is a maximization problem defined on $\{0,1\}^N \to \mathbb{N}$ that counts the number of ones in bit string $\mathbf{x}$

$$OneMax(\mathbf{x}) = \sum_{i=1}^{N} x_i. \tag{1}$$

The optimal solution is $\mathbf{x}^* = (1,\dots,1)^T$ with fitness $f(\mathbf{x}) = N$.

This paper is structured as follows. Section 2 repeats the (1+1)-EA and a known runtime result on *OneMax*. In Section 3, we study mutation rates of the (1+1)-EA on *OneMax*. In Section 4, we tune the mutation rate of the (1+1)-EA with a $(\mu + \lambda)$-ES, an approach known as meta-evolution. In Section 5, we employ Rechenberg's 1/5th rule to control the mutation rates, while we analyze self-adaptive mutation rates in Section 6. Conclusions are drawn in Section 7.

2   The (1+1)-EA

Evolutionary optimization is a class of black box optimization algorithms that mimics the biological process of optimization known as evolution. Evolutionary algorithms are based on evolutionary operators that model problem-specific processes in natural evolution, of which the most important are (1) crossover, (2) mutation, and (3) selection. Basis of most evolutionary methods is a set of candidate solutions. Crossover combines the most promising characteristics of two or more solutions. Mutation adds random changes, while carefully balancing exploration and exploitation. Selection chooses the most promising candidate solutions in an iterative kind of way, alternately with recombination and mutation. Evolutionary algorithms have developed to strong optimization algorithms for difficult continuous optimization problems. The long line of research on evolutionary computation was motivated by the goal of applying evolutionary algorithms to a wide range of problems. Applying evolutionary algorithms

---

Algorithm 1.1. Standard $(1 + 1)$-EA

1: choose $\mathbf{x} \in \{0, 1\}^N$ uniform at random
2: **repeat**
3:     produce $\mathbf{x}'$ by flipping each bit of $\mathbf{x}$ with probability $1/N$
4:     replace $\mathbf{x}$ with $\mathbf{x}'$ if $f(\mathbf{x}') \leq f(\mathbf{x})$
5: **until** termination condition

---

is comparatively easy, if the modeling of the problem is conducted carefully and appropriate representations and parameters are chosen.

The $(1 + 1)$-EA works on bit string representations $\mathbf{x} = (x_1, \ldots, x_N)^T \in \{0, 1\}^N$ with only one individual, which is changed with bit-flip mutation. Bit-flip mutation means that each bit x_i of bit-string $\mathbf{x}$ is flipped with probability $\sigma = 1/N$. No recombination is employed, as no population is used. Furthermore, the selection operator can be reduced to a simple selection of the better one of two solutions. The pseudocode can be found in Algorithm 1.1. The number of fitness function calls of a $(1+1)$-EA complies with the number of generations.

For the $(1+1)$-EA, a runtime analysis on the simple *OneMax* problem demonstrates its properties. The runtime analysis is based on the method of fitness-based partitions, and shows that the $(1 + 1)$-EA's runtime is upper bounded by $O(N \log N)$ on *OneMax* [2]. In the remainder of this work, we will experimentally analyze and compare a selection of important parameter control and tuning techniques.

3   A Study on Mutation Rates

The question comes up, if our experiments can confirm the theoretical result, i.e., if the mutation rate $1/N$ leads to $N \log N$ generations in average. For this sake, we test the $(1+1)$-EA with various mutation rates on *OneMax* with various problem sizes. This extensive analysis is similar to tuning by hand, which is probably the most frequent parameter tuning method. Figure 2 shows the analysis with problem sizes $N = 10, 20$ and 30. The results show that the optimal

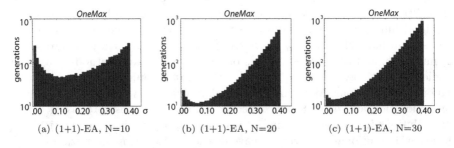

(a) $(1+1)$-EA, N=10   (b) $(1+1)$-EA, N=20   (c) $(1+1)$-EA, N=30

Fig. 2. Analysis of mutation strength σ for $(1 + 1)$-EA on *OneMax* for three problem sizes

mutation rate is close to $1/N$, which leads to the runtime of $O(N \log N)$. Our experiments confirm this result with the exception of a multiplicative constant, i.e., the runtime is about two times higher than $N \log N$. In the the following section, we employ evolutionary computation to search for optimal mutation rates, an approach called meta-evolution.

4   Meta-evolution

Meta-evolution is a parameter tuning method that employs evolutionary computation to tune evolutionary parameters. The search for optimal parameters is treated as optimization problem. We employ a $(\mu + \lambda)$-ES, i.e., an evolution strategy (ES) for continuous optimization [1], to tune the mutation rate of an inner (1+1)-EA. The $(\mu+\lambda)$-ES employs arithmetic recombination and isotropic Gaussian mutation $\mathbf{x}' = \mathbf{x} + \mathcal{N}(0, \sigma)$ with a decreasing σ depending on generation t. Algorithm 1.2 shows the pseudocode of the meta-evolutionary approach.

Algorithm 1.2. Meta-$(1 + 1)$-EA

```
 1: initialize mutation rates σ₁,...,σμ ∈ P, τ
 2: repeat
 3:    for i = 1 to λ do
 4:       select ρ parents from P
 5:       create σᵢ by recombination
 6:       decrease τ
 7:       mutate σᵢ = σᵢ + τ · N(0,1)
 8:       run (1+1)-EA with σᵢ
 9:       add σᵢ to P'
10:    end for
11:    select μ parents from P' → P
12: until termination condition
```

In our experimental analysis, we employ a $(10 + 100)$-ES optimizing the mutation rate of the underlying (1+1)-EA that solves problem *OneMax* for various problem sizes N. The ES starts with an initial mutation rate of $\tau = 0.2$. In each generation, τ is decreased deterministically by multiplication, i.e., $\tau = \tau \cdot 0.95$. The inner (1+1)-EA employs the evolved mutation rate σ of the upper ES and is run 25 times with this setting. The average number of generations until the optimum of *OneMax* is found employing the corresponding σ is the fitness $f(\sigma)$. The ES terminates after 50 generations, i.e., $50 \cdot 100 = 5000$ runs of the (1+1)-EA are conducted. Table 1 shows the experimental results of the meta-evolutionary approach. The table shows the average number t of generations until the optimum has been found by the (1+1)-EA in the last generation of the ES, the evolved mutation rate σ^* and the number of generations, the ES needed to find σ^*. The achieved speed of convergence by the inner (1+1)-EA, e.g., 170.6 generations for $N = 30$ is a fast result.

Table 1. Experimental results of meta-evolutionary approach of a (10+100)-EA tuning the mutation rates of a (1+1)-EA on *OneMax*

N	t	σ^*	gen.
5	8.80	0.252987	37
10	31.84	0.134133	14
20	90.92	0.071522	42
30	170.60	0.055581	41

5   Rechenberg's 1/5th Rule

The idea of Rechenberg's 1/5th rule is to increase the mutation rate, if the success probability is larger than 1/5th, and to decrease it, if the success probability is smaller. The success probability can be measured w.r.t. a fix number G of generations. If the number of successful generations of a (1+1)-EA, i.e., the offspring employs a better fitness than the parent, is g, then g/G is the success rate. If $g/G > 1/5$, σ is increased by $\sigma = \sigma \cdot \tau$ with $\tau > 1$, otherwise, it is decreased by $\sigma = \sigma/\tau$. Algorithm 1.3 shows the pseudocode of the (1+1)-EA with Rechenberg's 1/5th rule.

Algorithm 1.3. $(1 + 1)$-EA with Rechenberg's 1/5th rule

 1: choose $\mathbf{x} \in \{0,1\}^N$ uniform at random
 2: **repeat**
 3:     **for** $i = 1$ **to** G **do**
 4:         produce $\mathbf{x}'$ by flipping each bit of $\mathbf{x}$ with probability σ
 5:         replace $\mathbf{x}$ with $\mathbf{x}'$ if $f(\mathbf{x}') \le f(\mathbf{x})$ and set $g+ = 1$
 6:     **end for**
 7:     **if** $g/G > 1/5$ **then**
 8:         $\sigma = \sigma \cdot \tau$
 9:     **else**
10:         $\sigma = \sigma/\tau$
11:     **end if**
12: **until** termination condition

Figure 3 shows the corresponding experimental results for various values for τ and $N = 10, 20$ and 30. The results show that Rechenberg's rule is able to automatically tune the mutation rate and reach almost as good results as the runs with tuned settings. We can observe that smaller settings for τ, i.e., settings close to 1.0 achieve better results than larger settings in all cases. Further experiments have shown that settings over $\tau > 10.0$ lead to very long runtimes (larger than 10^5 generations). In such cases, σ cannot be fine-tuned to allow a fast approximation to the optimum.

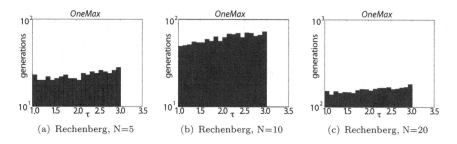

| (a) Rechenberg, N=5 | (b) Rechenberg, N=10 | (c) Rechenberg, N=20 |

Fig. 3. Experimental results of parameter control with Rechenberg's 1/5th rule

6   Self-adaptation

Self-adaptation is an automatic evolutionary mutation rate control. It was originally introduced by Rechenberg and Schwefel [10] for ES, later independently in the United States by Fogel [4] for evolutionary programming. The most successful self-adaptively controlled parameters are mutation parameters. This is a consequence of the direct influence of the mutation operator on the exploration behavior of the optimization algorithm: Large mutation strengths cause large changes of solutions, decreasing mutation strengths allow an approximation of the optimum, in particular in continuous solution spaces.

The mutation rate σ is added to each individual $\mathbf{x}$ and is at the same time subject to recombination, mutation and selection. For a (1+1)-EA, self-adaptation means that the mutation rate σ is mutated with log-normal mutation

$$\sigma' = \sigma \cdot e^{\tau \mathcal{N}(0,1)} \tag{2}$$

with a control parameter τ. Afterwards, the mutation operator is applied. Appropriate mutation rates are inherited and employed in the following generation. The log-normal mutation allows an evolutionary search in the space of strategy parameters. It allows the mutation rates to scale in a logarithmic kind of way from values close to zero to infinity. Algorithm 1.4 shows the pseudocode of the SA-(1+1)-EA with σ-self-adaptation.

Algorithm 1.4. SA-$(1+1)$-EA

  1: choose $\mathbf{x} \in \{0,1\}^N$ uniform at random
  2: choose $\sigma \in \{0,1\}$ at random
  3: **repeat**
  4:    produce $\sigma' = \sigma \cdot e^{\tau \mathcal{N}(0,1)}$
  5:    produce $\mathbf{x}'$ by flipping each bit of $\mathbf{x}$ with probability σ'
  6:    replace $\mathbf{x}$ with $\mathbf{x}'$ and σ with σ', if $f(\mathbf{x}') \leq f(\mathbf{x})$
  7: **until** termination condition

Figure 4 shows typical developments[1] of fitness $f(\mathbf{x})$ and mutation rate σ of the SA-(1+1)-EA on $N = 10, 50$ and 100 for $\tau = 0.1$. Due to the plus selection scheme, the fitness is decreasing step by step. The results show that the mutation rate σ is adapting during the search. In particular, in the last phase of the search for $N = 100$, σ is fast adapting to the search conditions and accelerates the search significantly.

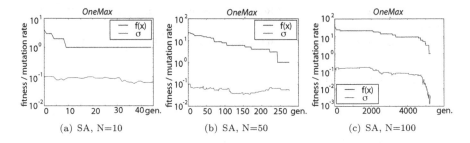

(a) SA, N=10   (b) SA, N=50   (c) SA, N=100

Fig. 4. SA-(1+1)-EA on *OneMax* with $N = 10, 50$ and 100

Table 2 shows the experimental results of the SA-(1+1)-EA with various settings for τ on *OneMax* with problem sizes $N = 10, 20, 30, 50$, and 100. The results show that the control parameter, i.e., the mutation rate τ of the mutation rate σ, has a significant impact on the success of the SA-(1+1)-EA. Both other setting, i.e., $\tau = 0.01$ and $\tau = 1.0$ lead to worse results. In particular on the large problem instance with $N = 100$, both settings fail and lead to long optimization runs.

Table 2. Number of generations the SA-(1+1)-EA needs to reach the optimum

N	10	20	30	50	100
$\tau = 0.01$	48.3 ± 29.03	162.0 ± 83.1	359.0 ± 175.0	$2.4e3 \pm 552.8$	$> 10^5$
$\tau = 0.1$	46.1 ± 36.3	142.9 ± 47.1	274.0 ± 97.4	$1.0e3 \pm 770.7$	$3.6e3 \pm 3.3e3$
$\tau = 1.0$	$2.7e3 \pm 4.9e3$	$5.0e3 \pm 1.2e4$	$8.9e3 \pm 9.5e3$	$1.9e4 \pm 1.4e4$	$> 10^5$

7   Conclusions

The success of evolutionary algorithms depends on the choice of appropriate parameter settings, in particular mutation rates. Although a lot of studies are known in literature, only few compare different parameter control techniques employing the same algorithmic settings on the same problems. But only such a comparison allows insights into the underlying mechanisms and common principles. The analysis has shown that optimally tuned mutation rates can automatically been found with meta-evolution. The effort spent into the search is

---

[1] Employing a logarithmic scale.

comparatively high, but the final result is competitive or better than the control techniques. But more flexible and still powerful is the adaptive mutation rate control with Rechenberg's rule. Self-adaptation turns out to be the most flexible control technique with its automatic mutation rate control. Although self-adaptation depends on the control parameter τ, it is quite robust w.r.t. the problem size. It became famous in ES for continuous optimization and also has shown the best results in our parameter control study. As future work, we plan to extend our analysis to further EA variants, parameter control techniques, and problem types.

References

1. Beyer, H.-G., Schwefel, H.-P.: Evolution strategies - A comprehensive introduction. Natural Computing 1, 3–52 (2002)
2. Droste, S., Jansen, T., Wegener, I.: On the analysis of the (1+1) evolutionary algorithm. Theoretical Computer Science 276(1-2), 51–81 (2002)
3. Eiben, A.E., Hinterding, R., Michalewicz, Z.: Parameter control in evolutionary algorithms. IEEE Transactions on Evolutionary Computation 3(2), 124–141 (1999)
4. Fogel, D.B., Fogel, L.J., Atma, J.W.: Meta-evolutionary programming. In: Proceedings of 25th Asilomar Conference on Signals, Systems & Computers, pp. 540–545 (1991)
5. Grefenstette, J.: Optimization of control parameters for genetic algorithms. IEEE Trans. Syst. Man Cybern. 16(1), 122–128 (1986)
6. Jong, K.A.D.: An analysis of the behavior of a class of genetic adaptive systems. PhD thesis, University of Michigan (1975)
7. Kramer, O.: Self-Adaptive Heuristics for Evolutionary Computation. Springer, Berlin (2008)
8. Mhlenbein, H.: How genetic algorithms really work: Mutation and hill-climbing. In: Proceedings of the 2nd Conference on Parallel Problem Solving from Nature (PPSN), pp. 15–26 (1992)
9. Schaffer, J.D., Caruana, R., Eshelman, L.J., Das, R.: A study of control parameters affecting online performance of genetic algorithms for function optimization. In: Proceedings of the 3rd International Conference on Genetic Algorithms (ICGA), pp. 51–60 (1989)
10. Schwefel, H.-P.: Adaptive Mechanismen in der biologischen Evolution und ihr Einfluss auf die Evolutionsgeschwindigkeit. Interner Bericht Bionik, TU Berlin (1974)

Variable Neighborhood Search for Continuous Monitoring Problem with Inter-Depot Routes

Vera Mersheeva and Gerhard Friedrich

Alpen-Adria Universität,
Universitätsstraße 65–67, 9020 Klagenfurt, Austria
{vera.mersheeva,gerhard.friedrich}@uni-klu.ac.at

Abstract. In this paper we provide methods for the Continuous Monitoring Problem with Inter-Depot routes (CMPID). It arises when a number of agents or vehicles have to persistently survey a set of locations. Each agent has limited energy storage (e.g., fuel tank or battery capacity) and can renew this resource at any available base station. Various real-world scenarios could be modeled with this formulation. In this paper we consider the application of this problem to disaster response management, where wide area surveillance is performed by unmanned aerial vehicles. We propose a new method based on the Insertion Heuristic and the metaheuristic Variable Neighborhood Search. The proposed algorithm computes solutions for large real-life scenarios in a few seconds and iteratively improves them. Solutions obtained on small instances (where the optimum could be computed) are on average 2.6% far from optimum. Furthermore, the proposed algorithm outperforms existing methods for the Continuous Monitoring Problem (CMP) in both solution quality (in 3 times) and computational time (more than 400 times faster).

Keywords: Continuous Monitoring Problem, UAV route planning, Inter-depot routes, Variable Neighborhood Search, Heuristics.

1 Introduction

In this paper we consider a variant of the Continuous Monitoring Problem (CMP) [1] with Inter-Depot routes (CMPID). A set of vehicles has to periodically visit a set of locations. The major goal is to find a plan where a fleet visits locations uniformly and as often as possible. This means that the number of revisits should be maximized and the time between revisits should be equally distributed, i.e., long time intervals between revisits should be avoided. Vehicles are constrained by their energy storage (later referred to as capacity). In CMP each vehicle can renew its capacity at a predefined base station, whereas CMPID allows vehicles to refuel at any station.

In this paper we consider the exploration of a disaster scene (e.g., earthquake or train accident) using a fleet of unmanned aerial vehicles (UAVs) equipped with cameras. Micro-UAVs have limited flight height and they cannot carry

I.J. Timm and M. Thimm (Eds.): KI 2013, LNAI 8077, pp. 106–117, 2013.
© Springer-Verlag Berlin Heidelberg 2013

wide-angle lens cameras due to their weight. As a result, a single picture of the whole area cannot be taken in one shot. The way to resolve this problem is to split the overall area into rectangles. UAVs take a picture of each rectangle[1] and transmit this data to the ground station, where received pictures are stitched together into an overview image of high resolution. Obviously, the main intention of the aerial exploration is to always have the most up-to-date information for every rectangle. Therefore, the UAVs have to visit picture points as often as possible but avoiding long time spans between revisits.

Due to the additional constraints of the CMPID (e.g., capacity limitation, inter-depot routes), existing methods cannot be directly applied to it. We developed a metaheuristic based on the Variable Neighborhood Search algorithm (VNS) [2] that has proven its efficiency for the Vehicle Routing Problem. It iteratively improves the initial solution constructed by a modification of the Insertion Heuristic (IH) [3]. Later we will refer to our modification of IH as IDIH (Inter-Depot Insertion Heuristic). The proposed method returns near-optimal solutions (at most 8.5% far from optimum for cases where an optimum is computable). It also outperforms existing CMP methods [1] both in computational time (on average 481 times faster) and solution quality (on average in 3 times better). The method provides a feasible solution within seconds (e.g., in 10 seconds for a scenario with 800 points). Furthermore, in 10 minutes the method improves initial solution on 3–30% even for the large real-life scenarios.

The remainder of the paper is organized as follows. Section 2 gives a formal definition of the CMPID. In Section 3 we discuss the related problems and existing methods. Section 4 describes the proposed method in detail. An evaluation of the algorithm parameters as well as its performance is reported in Section 5. Finally, in Section 6 conclusions and directions for future work are discussed.

2 Problem Description

The base stations and target points[2] are given as a complete, undirected graph $G = \{W_b \cup W_p, E\}$, where E is a set of edges, $W_b = \{1, ..., n\}$ is a set of stations and $W_p = \{(n + 1), ..., (n + m)\}$ is a set of target points. The number of points and a number of stations are equal to n and m, respectively. The distance between way points i, j is depicted as a non-negative cost $d_{i,j}$. Every vehicle $v \in V$ is of a certain type, which is characterized by its speed and energy storage capacity. Each station $i \in W_b$ has a limited amount of energy sources of each type for renewal (e.g., number of batteries or amount of fuel).

Each vehicle $v \in V$ starts its route from the given initial position l_v. This initial position is either a base station or a target point. For instance, in our application the UAVs provide the first overview image of an area (with any existing method), so that the rescue team can start their mission. The last point visited by a drone is its initial position for the monitoring task that starts afterwards. This monitoring task is modeled as CMPID.

---

[1] We refer to locations where pictures are taken as picture points or target points.

[2] Later base stations and target points are referred to as way points.

The mission starts at time zero and ends at time mt. A mission is a set of routes for the whole fleet (one route for each vehicle), where a route is a sequence of way points. Every target has a time point when it was last visited before monitoring starts. This time point is measured from the beginning of the mission and is equal to zero if the target was not visited yet.

A set of routes is a feasible solution of the CMPID if it does not violate the following constraints:

1. The last target visit has to be before the end of the mission.
2. A vehicle can renew its capacity only at a base station with the available resources of a corresponding type.
3. At every base station a fleet cannot use more energy sources than available.
4. The fuel tank cannot be empty at any point of the route except the stations.

The goal function is expressed as a penalty function that has to be minimized [1]. Assume, each target point $i \in W_p$ has a certain number of visits $nvis(i)$ at the time points $T_i = \{t_{i,1}, t_{i,2}, ..., t_{i,nvis(i)}\}$. Then the goal function for the solution x is as follows:

$$f(x) = \sum_{i \in W_p} \left[\sum_{y=1}^{nvis(i)-1} (t_{i,y+1} - t_{i,y})^2 + (mT - t_{i,nvis(i)})^2 \right]. \qquad (1)$$

The growth of this function is polynomial if any point stays unvisited. The first summand leads to more equal visit frequencies. The second summand distributes visits equally over the total mission time.

3 Related Work

In this section we describe related problems, point out their differences from CMPID and state existing approaches.

CMP [1] is a generalization of the CMPID where each drone has to renew its capacity only in a particular station. Mersheeva and Friedrich [1] proposed two algorithms to compute initial routes, a modified Clarke and Wright algorithm (CW) and a Queue-based IH (QIH), and a VNS-based metaheuristic to improve them. Later we will refer to these methods as "CW+VNS" and "QIH+VNS". The main differences between our approach and QIH+VNS are explained in Section 4. Our algorithm is compared with these approaches in Section 5.3.

The problem considered in this paper is also similar to the Periodic Vehicle Routing Problem with Intermediate Facilities (PVRP-IF) [4]. The planning is done for a set of time units (e.g., days) where each customer has a predefined list of possible schedules of visits (e.g., either on Tuesday and Wednesday or on Monday and Friday). Vehicles can renew their capacity at intermediate facilities. In contrast to CMPID, those intermediate facilities have no energy source limit, and vehicles return to the base station at the end of each day. The goal of PVRP-IF is to minimize the total travel time. Angelelli and Speranza [4] solved this problem by a combination of IH and Tabu Search algorithm (TS).

Crevier et al. [5] introduced a multi-depot VRP with Inter-Depot Routes (VRPID). It can be seen as a VRP-IF where depots play the role of intermediate facilities. Crevier et al. applied the TS heuristic to solve the problem.

A waste collection problem is a special case of PVRP-IF. The objective is to collect the waste from the customers and deliver it to intermediate facilities. Before arriving at the base station each vehicle has to visit an intermediate facility and empty its storage. Nuortio et al. [6] propose a Guided Variable Neighborhood Thresholding algorithm for a real-life scenario. Kim et al. [7] solves a general case with an enhanced IH and Simulated Annealing (SA). Later this algorithm was outperformed by the methods proposed by Benjamin and Beasley [8]. They construct the routes with an IH and then improve them by either TS or VNS, or their combination. Hemmelmayr et al. [9] proposes a hybrid method based on a combination of VNS and an exact method. It performs well on scenarios for both PVRP-IF and VRPID.

Persistent visitation is a variation of the PVRP-IF where vehicles refill their fuel tanks at intermediate facilities and every customer visit has a predefined deadline. The goal is to minimize the amount of purchased fuel. Las Fargeas et al. [10] report results using only a single vehicle. They propose a three-step approach: first they compute every solution that satisfies all of the constraints; then they calculate the minimum possible amount of fuel for each solution. Finally, considering the results of the first two steps, they choose the best solution.

In the Patrolling Task [11] ground robots continuously follow routes where every target is visited exactly once. The goal is to minimize the time lag between two target visits. The main difference from the CMPID is the lack of capacity constraint. There are two main strategies for this problem. The first approach is to construct a circular path which robots will follow [12,13]. The second strategy is to split the area into subareas and assign a robot to each of them [14,15]. In the case of a static environment the first strategy is more efficient.

Oberlin et al. [16] deal with Heterogeneous, Multiple Depot, Multiple UAV Routing Problem where a fleet of drones visits every target exactly once. The algorithm proposed by Oberlin et al. transforms this problem into the Asymmetric TSP. Later this problem is solved with the Lin-Kernighan-Helsgaun heuristic. The obtained solution is transformed into a solution for the original problem.

There are two critical differences between CMPID and all of the previously stated problems except CMP. They have different goal functions and each one has a fixed number of visits. The goal of the CMPID is to maximize a number of visits while keeping visit frequency as even as possible. The related problems, on the other hand, minimize either total traveling time or exploitation cost. In these problems the number of visits at every customer is known beforehand.

4   Solution Method

Variable Neighborhood Search [2] is a framework for improvement heuristics. A general structure of VNS is presented in Algorithm 1. This method starts from the initial solution. At every iteration it applies one of the chosen neighborhood operators $N_k = \{n_1, n_2, ..., n_{k_{max}}\}$ to an incumbent solution (*shaking step*, line 4) and performs a *local search*, line 5. At the end of the iteration a decision is made to either accept the obtained solution or not (*acceptance phase*, line 6). This procedure repeats until a stopping condition is met. Stopping conditions can be a predetermined number of iterations or computational time.

Algorithm 1. Variable Neighborhood Search

> **input** : initial solution x, a set of neighborhood operators N_k
> **output**: improved solution x
>
> 1 **repeat**
> 2 $k \leftarrow 1$
> 3   **repeat**
> 4 $x' \leftarrow Shake(x, k)$;
> 5 $x'' \leftarrow LocalSearch(x')$;
> 6   **if** $f(x'') < f(x)$ **then**
> 7 $x \leftarrow x''$; $k \leftarrow 1$;
> 8   **else**
> 9 $k \leftarrow k + 1$;
> 10   **until** $k = k_{max}$;
> 11 **until** *stopping condition is met*;

Initial Solution. In order to provide an initial solution for the CMPID, a new algorithm, IDIH, was developed. As the work of Mersheeva and Friedrich [1], our insertion heuristic is based on the standard IH [3] for the TSP. In each step, the IH chooses a point and a position along the salesman's route with the lowest value of *evaluation function* and inserts this point at the selected position.

Mersheeva and Friedrich propose to use a queue $Q = \{q_1, q_2, ..., q_m\}$ of points. It is constructed by ordering the target points by their last visit time in increasing order. At every iteration the QIH selects a vehicle v with the minimum value of the following evaluation function:

$$g_1(v) = \alpha_1 \cdot d(v, q_1) \cdot scale + \alpha_2 \cdot t(v, q_1),$$

where $d(v, q_1)$ is a distance between the first queue point q_1 and the last point in the route of vehicle v. Time when vehicle v can arrive at the point q_1 is denoted as $t(v, q_1)$. Coefficients α_1 and $\alpha_2 = 1 - \alpha_1$ indicate how each of the correspondent parameters influences the final choice. Coefficient *scale* assures that mentioned distance and arrival time have the same order of magnitude.

Point q_1 is added to the end of the route of the selected vehicle v. In CMP a vehicle can renew its capacity only in a particular station assigned to it. Thus, if refueling is required, such station, assigned to the vehicle v, is inserted first. Finally point q_1 is moved to the end of the queue. If a point q_1 cannot be added to any of the routes, it is removed from the queue. The insertion process stops when the queue is empty, i.e., there is no point that can be inserted.

In order to increase efficiency, the method proposed in this paper selects both a point p and a vehicle v with the minimum value of the following formula:

$$g_2(p, v) = \alpha_1 * d(v, p) + \alpha_2 * \tau_p + \alpha_3 * t(v, p) \,. \tag{2}$$

In Equation (2), variable τ_p is the time of the last visit of point p. It leads to a more equal distribution of the visits over all points. Coefficients α_1, α_2 and $\alpha_3 = 1-(\alpha_1+\alpha_2)$ have the same function as in the method above. The *scale* coefficient did not improve solution quality and, therefore, it was eliminated. Choosing both a point and a vehicle allows exploring a wider solution neighborhood.

Algorithm 2 summarizes the whole work flow of IDIH. First of all, for every vehicle v a route is created by adding the given initial location l_v as the first element (line 2). Then the main loop in lines 3–19 inserts new points to the solution one at a time. It terminates when no point/vehicle is selected (line 15).

Algorithm 2. Inter-Depot Insertion Heuristic

    input : a scenario for CMPID
    output: a set of routes $R = \{r_v : v \in V\}$

1 **for** $v \in V$ **do**
2   add l_v to r_v;
3 **repeat**
4      $p_{best} \leftarrow null$; $v_{best} \leftarrow null$; $g_{min} \leftarrow \infty$; $b_{inter} \leftarrow null$;
5   **for** $p \in W_p$ **do**
6   **for** $v \in V$ **do**
7   **if** *NeedBatteryChange(v,p)* **then**
8               $b \leftarrow$ ChooseStation(v,p);
9   **if** $b \neq null$ *AND* $g_2(p, v) < g_{min}$ **then**
10                  $p_{best} \leftarrow p$; $v_{best} \leftarrow v$; $g_{min} \leftarrow g_2(p, v)$; $b_{inter} \leftarrow b$;
11   **else**
12   **if** $g_2(p, v) < g_{min}$ **then**
13                  $p_{best} \leftarrow p$; $v_{best} \leftarrow v$; $g_{min} \leftarrow g_2(p, v)$; $b_{inter} \leftarrow null$;
14   **if** $p_{best} = null$ **then**
15   **return** R;
16   **if** $b_{inter} \neq null$ **then**
17   add b_{inter} to route $r_{v_{best}}$;
18   add p_{best} to route $r_{v_{best}}$;
19 **until** *true*;

The main loop starts by setting initial values to the variables (line 4): a point p_{best} and a vehicle v_{best} (that will be inserted), their value g_{min} of the evaluation function (2) and intermediate base station b_{inter} where vehicle v_{best} will renew its capacity if it is required (otherwise, b_{inter} is equal to *null*).

A point-vehicle pair is selected if there is enough energy and their value of function (2) is lower than g_{min}. Function *NeedBatteryChange(v,p)* checks if vehicle v should change its battery in order to reach point p. This is necessary if v cannot reach p with the current battery or v can reach p but capacity is not sufficient to return to a base station. If the battery has to be changed then the most suitable station is chosen by the function *ChooseStation(v,p)* (Algorithm 3). In this way algorithm ensures that each drone has enough capacity to reach a station for refueling during the mission. If no base station was selected, i.e., *ChooseStation(v,p)* returns *null*, then this point-vehicle pair is not considered as a candidate for insertion.

Algorithm 3. ChooseStation(v,p)

---

1   $b_{best} \leftarrow null$; $d_{min} \leftarrow \infty$;
2   **for** $b \in W_b$ **do**
3   **if** $d_{v,b} + d_{b,p} < d_{min}$ *AND b has battery for v AND v can reach b* **then**
4         $d_{min} \leftarrow d_{v,b} + d_{b,p}$; $b_{best} \leftarrow b$;
5   return b_{best};

Shaking Step. In this step a solution is modified by an operator in order to choose another solution in the neighborhood. We introduce a new operator (*replace*) and we deploy three previously used operators: the *insert* operator [1] and the *move* and *cross-exchange* operators [17]. The *move(x, η)* operator relocates a sequence of η points from one route to another. The *cross-exchange(x,η)* operator exchanges two sequences of η points between two different routes. The *insert(x,η)* operator adds η new points, each at some position in a chosen route. Finally, the *replace(x,η)* operator substitutes η routed points with new points. All sequences, points and routes are selected randomly. These operators are applied in the following order: *insert(x,η)*, *replace(x,η)*, *move(x,η)*, *exchange(x,η)* with $\eta = 1$. The selection of both order and value of η is discussed in Section 5.1.

Local Search. Reduced Variable Neighborhood Search (RVNS) is a variation of VNS without local search [18]. Our approach is based on RVNS, as for the CMPID the local search requires large computational effort, especially in real-life instances.

Acceptance Phase. Lines 6–9 of Algorithm 1 show an example of the acceptance check as well as the resultant change of the neighborhood operator. It is called the first-accept strategy, as it allows only those solutions that improve a value of the goal function (1).

5 Computational Results

This section reports results of both tuning and evaluation of the proposed method. For one, we conduct a test to select coefficients α_1, α_2 and α_3 for IDIH, the order of the neighborhood operators and their parameter η. Afterwards, the algorithm is compared with the optimum on small scenarios and with the state-of-the-art methods on large instances. Finally, we check the scalability of the proposed algorithm, i.e., how its performance changes with increasing scenario size. All tests were performed on Intel Core i7 2.67 GHz system with 4GB RAM.

We have used two sets of benchmarks: large (48 real-life and 60 random) scenarios and 10 small scenarios where optimum can be obtained [19].

Picture points of *large scenarios* were generated in the following way. For *real-life* scenarios we calculate a rectangular terrain which will be covered in one shot. This is derived from the required image resolution and flight altitude. The area of this terrain and the minimum image overlap needed for stitching allow us to place the picture points. They are allocated evenly over the target area except no-fly zones – obstacles (e.g., high buildings or trees). In *random* scenarios (x, y) coordinates are chosen randomly within one of the following intervals: $[-300, 300]$ for 200–300 points, $[-400, 400]$ for 301–600 points and $[-500, 500]$ for 601–800 points. Real-life scenarios contain 46–441 picture points. In random instances number of points ranges from 200 to 800.

For every large scenario three or six base stations are placed randomly within intervals given for coordinates. Every benchmark has a set of four, seven or eight drones and a number of batteries sufficient to provide three or six overview images. Vehicles and their batteries are assigned to stations either *randomly* or as *equally* as possible. To provide the first overview image to the rescuers, we construct routes that cover the whole area once. The last point in a drone's route is its initial location for the monitoring task, i.e., input for the proposed algorithm. Finally, the speed of vehicles and their maximum travel time are set to 2.5 m/s and 1200 s, respectively, based on the specification of the micro-UAVs.

The "life_441p_3st_4dr_6ov_R" test case is a real-life benchmark that contains 441 target points, three base stations, four randomly assigned drones, and its area of interest can be covered six times.

Currently the optimum cannot be computed for our real-life scenarios due to their size and problem complexity. Hence, we have generated ten *smaller benchmarks* with six picture points, two base stations and two drones. In total there are five batteries which are sufficient to visit each point at least 2–3 times. Coordinates of the points and the base stations were chosen randomly in the domain [0,12]. Vehicles and batteries are located at the randomly chosen base stations. Optimal solutions for these scenarios were computed by a Gecode solver, where MiniZinc was used as a constraint programming language.

5.1 Tuning the Method

First of all, we have chosen the best combination of IDIH coefficients, α_1, α_2 and $\alpha_3 = 1 - \alpha_1 - \alpha_2$. All possible combinations of this coefficients within interval [0,1] with the step 0.25 were evaluated on large scenarios. Table 1 shows the best performing coefficients for the corresponding benchmark type. The best values of the coefficients showed dependency on both resource allocation (random or equal) and target points allocation (random or equal). However, they do not dependent on a number of targets, i.e., scenario size.

A good order of neighborhood operators increases efficiency of a metaheuristic [18]. To choose the best neighborhood structure, we evaluated all possible

Table 1. Best performing values of IDIH coefficients

Resource allocation	random		equal	
Points allocation	equal	rand	equal	rand
α_1	0.25	0.5	0.25	0
α_2	0.5	0.25	0.25	0.75

sequences with $\eta \in \{1, 2, 3\}$ on large scenarios with a random resource allocation. To evaluate the average performance of the metaheuristic, we run the VNS
10 times with 10^5 iterations for every scenario and operator sequence. Moreover,
results are not biased by a construction heuristic, as IDIH is deterministic.

Different orders of operators do not affect performance of the metaheuristic.
Hence, we ordered operators by the number of times they have been used. Thus,
the order *insert-replace-move-exchange* was selected. On the contrary, parameter
η had effect on the performance. *Move* or *exchange* of more than one point
leads to an unfeasible solution which violates the constraint of limited capacity.
Therefore, $\eta = 1$ obtained the best results and outperformed $\eta = 2$ on 8.59%
on average. We do not report the full numeric results in this paper, due to the
space limitations. All obtained computational results are available online [19].

5.2   Comparison with Optimum

For this evaluation we have used a set of 10 small instances. Results of this evaluation are presented in Table 2. The quality of the achieved solutions was measured
according to the following formula: $deviation = (f(x') - f(x)) * 100/f(x)$, where
x' is a solution obtained by the heuristic, x is an optimal solution, function f
represents the goal function (1).

Table 2. Comparison of the proposed method with optimum

Instance	1	2	3	4	5	6	7	8	9	10	Average
Optimal cost	69867	75250	5706	7826	6238	7044	7342	75317	75539	73351	
Deviation IDIH	7.08	2.64	12.48	5.75	2.85	4.86	8.50	5.65	3.39	2.72	5.59
from the IDIH	2.87	0.73	0.91	4.60	2.85	1.79	8.50	0.39	2.06	1.06	2.58
optimum +VNS											

5.3   Comparison with State of the Art

We compare our approach with the methods of Mersheeva and Friedrich [1]
using the large scenarios. Each metaheuristic was running for 10^4 iterations 10
times for each scenario. Performance of the heuristics are compared by both
solution quality and computational time (Fig. 1). Instances 1–54 have random
resource allocation. Instances 1–24, 55–78 are real-life scenarios. Due to the
new neighborhood structure, the proposed method outperformed CW+VNS and
QIH+VNS on average in 4.2 and 3.04 times, respectively. The absence of local

search results in a better computational time, i.e., on average in 245.41 times and 481.28 times better than time of CW+VNS and QIH+VNS, respectively. If the metaheuristic of [1] is applied without local search, it requires the same running time as the proposed method. However, its results are not reported here, since the solution quality is lower than the one of the original method.

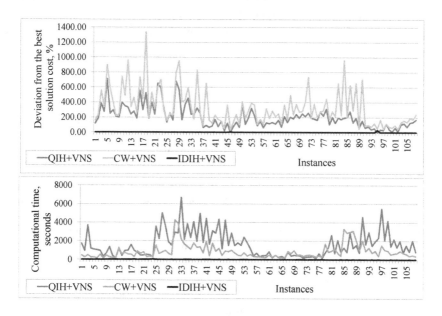

Fig. 1. Comparison of the proposed method "IDIH+VNS" with the CMP approaches

5.4 Scalability Evaluation

The final evaluation was conducted to check the scalability of the proposed improvement step, i.e., how well it performs on different scenario sizes. For this

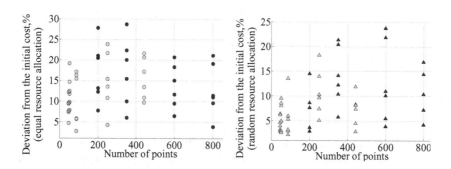

Fig. 2. Improvements of the solution quality after 10 minutes. Gray markers: real-world scenarios; black markers: scenarios with randomly placed picture points

the large scenarios were used. Firstly, IDIH computes an initial solution and its value of the goal function for a scenario. Then we ran the improvement algorithm 10 times, for 10 minutes each. The obtained improvement, i.e., deviation of the cost from the initial value, is averaged over these 10 runs. The left and the right charts of Fig. 2 report results for the scenarios with equal and random resource allocation respectively. Our metaheuristic provides improvements to the initial solution regardless of scenario size. Hence, the method obtains a good solution for the scenario of common size in a short time. Thus, it is useful for the team of first responders.

6   Conclusion

This paper focuses on a new extension of the Continuous Monitoring Problem – CMP with inter-depot routes. A real-world application to aerial surveillance of disaster sites shows the importance of this problem.

We proposed an algorithm based on the Insertion Heuristic and Variable Neighborhood Search. Our approach provides near-optimal results for the instances with known optimum (at most 8.5% and on average 2.58% far from optimum). Feasible solutions for the large real-world scenarios are found within seconds that allows quick plan adaptation to some scenario changes. However, the method is not designed for a highly dynamic or unknown environment, and online algorithm should be used instead. Initial solutions for tested scenarios were improved on 3–30% in only 10 minutes. The presented methods outperform existing approaches for the CMP in 3 times in solution quality and in 481 times in computational time. The evaluation shows that introducing inter-depot routes increases efficiency, i.e., vehicles visit more target points at a more uniform frequency. In our application this leads to more recent information updates which are important for situations where a small missed change can be critical.

Future work will focus on improving the heuristics, estimating the methodology performance for the environmental changes and introducing priorities for the picture points, i.e., points with higher priority are visited more often.

Acknowledgments. This work has been supported by the ERDF, KWF, and BABEG under grant KWF-20214/24272/36084 (SINUS). It has been performed in the research cluster Lakeside Labs. We would like to thank Sergey Alatartsev and John NA Brown for their valuable contribution.

References

1. Mersheeva, V., Friedrich, G.: Routing for continuous monitoring by multiple micro UAVs in disaster scenarios. In: European Conference on AI, pp. 588–593 (2012)
2. Mladenovic, N., Hansen, P.: Variable neighborhood search. Computers & Operations Research 24(11), 1097–1100 (1997)
3. Solomon, M.M.: Algorithms for the vehicle routing and scheduling problems with time window constraints. Operations Research 35(2), 254–265 (1987)

4. Angelelli, E., Speranza, M.G.: The periodic vehicle routing problem with intermediate facilities. European Journal of OR 137(2), 233–247 (2002)
5. Crevier, B., Cordeau, J.F., Laporte, G.: The multi-depot vehicle routing problem with inter-depot routes. European Journal of OR 176(2), 756–773 (2007)
6. Nuortio, T., Kytöjoki, J., Niska, H., Bräysy, O.: Improved route planning and scheduling of waste collection and transport. Expert Systems with Applications 30(2), 223–232 (2006)
7. Kim, B., Kim, S., Sahoo, S.: Waste collection vehicle routing problem with time windows. Computers & Operations Research 33(12), 3624–3642 (2006)
8. Benjamin, A., Beasley, J.: Metaheuristics for the waste collection vehicle routing problem with time windows, driver rest period and multiple disposal facilities. Computers & Operations Research 37(12), 2270–2280 (2010)
9. Hemmelmayr, V., Doerner, K.F., Hartl, R.F., Rath, S.: A heuristic solution method for node routing based solid waste collection problems. Journal of Heuristics 19(2), 129–156 (2013)
10. Las Fargeas, J., Hyun, B., Kabamba, P., Girard, A.: Persistent visitation with fuel constraints. In: Meeting of the EURO Working Group on Transportation, vol. 54, pp. 1037–1046 (2012)
11. Machado, A., Ramalho, G., Zucker, J.-D., Drogoul, A.: Multi-agent patrolling: an empirical analysis of alternative architectures. In: Sichman, J.S., Bousquet, F., Davidsson, P. (eds.) MABS 2002. LNCS (LNAI), vol. 2581, pp. 155–170. Springer, Heidelberg (2003)
12. Elmaliach, Y., Agmon, N., Kaminka, G.: Multi-robot area patrol under frequency constraints. Annals of Mathematics and AI 57(3), 293–320 (2009)
13. Elor, Y., Bruckstein, A.: Autonomous multi-agent cycle based patrolling. In: Dorigo, M., Birattari, M., Di Caro, G.A., Doursat, R., Engelbrecht, A.P., Floreano, D., Gambardella, L.M., Groß, R., Şahin, E., Sayama, H., Stützle, T. (eds.) ANTS 2010. LNCS, vol. 6234, pp. 119–130. Springer, Heidelberg (2010)
14. Smith, S.L., Rus, D.: Multi-robot monitoring in dynamic environments with guaranteed currency of observations. In: IEEE Conference on Decision and Control, pp. 514–521 (2010)
15. Portugal, D., Rocha, R.: MSP algorithm: multi-robot patrolling based on territory allocation using balanced graph partitioning. In: Proceedings of the 2010 ACM Symposium on Applied Computing, pp. 1271–1276. ACM (2010)
16. Oberlin, P., Rathinam, S., Darbha, S.: Today's travelling salesman problem. IEEE Robotics & Automation Magazine 17(4), 70–77 (2010)
17. Paraskevopoulos, D., Repoussis, P., Tarantilis, C., Ioannou, G., Prastacos, G.: A reactive variable neighborhood tabu search for the heterogeneous fleet vehicle routing problem with time windows. Journal of Heuristics 14, 425–455 (2008)
18. Hansen, P., Mladenović, N., Moreno Pérez, J.: Variable neighbourhood search: methods and applications. Annals of Operations Research 175(1), 367–407 (2010)
19. Mersheeva, V., Friedrich, G.: Benchmarks for the CMPID and the test results (2013), http://uav.lakeside-labs.com/test-data/

Advances in Accessing Big Data
with Expressive Ontologies

Ralf Möller[1], Christian Neuenstadt[1],
Özgür L. Özçep[1], and Sebastian Wandelt[2]

[1] Hamburg University of Technology, 21073 Hamburg, Germany
[2] Humboldt-Universität zu Berlin, 10099 Berlin, Germany

Abstract. Ontology-based query answering has to be supported w.r.t. secondary memory and very expressive ontologies to meet practical requirements in some applications. Recently, advances for the expressive DL $\mathcal{SHI}$ have been made in the dissertation of S. Wandelt for concept-based instance retrieval on Big Data descriptions stored in secondary memory. In this paper we extend this approach by investigating optimization algorithms for answering grounded conjunctive queries.[1]

1 Introduction

Triplestores, originally designed to store Big Data in RDF format on secondary memory with SPARQL as a query language, are currently more and more used in settings where query answering (QA) w.r.t. ontologies is beneficial. However, reasoning w.r.t. ontologies in secondary memory is provided for weakly expressive languages only (e.g., RDFS), if at all, and in some cases, query answering algorithms are known to be incomplete. For weakly expressive DL languages, such as DL-Lite, good results for sound and complete query answering w.r.t. large (virtual) Aboxes have already been achieved with OBDA based query rewriting techniques and schema specific mapping rules [1]. However, for expressive, more powerful DLs such as $\mathcal{ALC}$ and beyond only first steps have been made. Solving the problem of Accessing Big Data with Expressive Ontologies (ABDEO) is an important research goal.

A strategy to solve the ABDEO problem is to "summarize" Big Aboxes by melting individuals such that Aboxes fit into main memory [2]. In some situations inconsistencies occur, and summarization individuals must be "refined" (or unfolded) at query answering time in order to guarantee soundness and completeness, a rather expensive operation [3]. Other approaches make use of Abox modularization techniques and try to extract independent modules such that query answering is sound and complete. A first investigation of Abox modularization for answering instance queries w.r.t. the DL $\mathcal{SHIF}$ is presented in [5].

---

[1] This work has been partially supported by the European Commission as part of the FP7 project Optique (http://www.optique-project.eu/).

I.J. Timm and M. Thimm (Eds.): KI 2013, LNAI 8077, pp. 118–129, 2013.
© Springer-Verlag Berlin Heidelberg 2013

However, modularization with iterative instance checks over all individuals and modules of an Abox is not sufficient to ensure fast performance [5].[2]

The ABDEO approach presented here is based on a modularization approach developed by Wandelt [15,12,14] for really large Aboxes containing data descriptions for > 1000 universities in terms of LUBM scale measures [6], i.e., datasets in the range of billions of triples. Modules (islands) derived by Wandelt's techniques are usually small in practical applications and can be loaded into main memory such that a standard tableau prover can be used for instance checks. Iteration over all individuals gives sound and complete answers, in principle. Compared to [5], Wandelt (i) proposed extended modularization rules, (ii) implemented incremental ways of computing Abox modularizations, and (iii) investigated new ways to optimize sound and complete concept-based query answering (*instance queries*) with tableau-based reasoning systems for the logic $\mathcal{SHI}$. In particular, "similarities" between modules are detected such that a single instance query on a representative data structure (a so-called one-step node) yields multiple results at a time, and thus, instance checks are saved (the approach is reminiscent of but different from [3], see below or cf. [12] for details). Due to modularization rules, one-step node query answering is sound [12] and in many (well-defined) cases complete for eliminating candidates for a successive iterative instance checking process. In addition, to eliminate candidates, Wandelt and colleagues also investigate complete approximation techniques (see [15] for details).

In this paper we extend Wandelt's modularization based approach for query answering by investigating optimization techniques for answering *grounded conjunctive queries* w.r.t. $\mathcal{SHI}$ ontologies. Grounded conjunctive queries are more expressive from a user's point of view than instance queries. We argue that grounded conjunctive queries substantially narrow down the set of instance checking candidates if selective role atoms mentioned in queries are exploited for generating candidates for concept atoms, such that approximation techniques (to, e.g., DL-Lite) are not required in many cases. We demonstrate our findings using the LUBM benchmark as done, e.g., in [9] and [6]. As an additional extension to Wandelt's work, which uses specific storage layouts for storing Abox data descriptions and internal information in SQL databases, we investigate ontology-based access to existing data stores, namely triplestores, while providing query answering w.r.t. expressive ontologies.

2   Preliminaries

We assume the reader is familiar with description logic languages, ontologies (knowledge bases), inference problems, and optimized tableau-based reasoning algorithms (see, e.g., [11,7]). For the reader's convenience we define conjunctive queries in general, and grounded conjunctive queries in particular (adapted from [10]). In the following we use **AtCon**, **Con**, and **Rol** for the sets of atomic

---

[2] Note that Abox modularization is different from Tbox modularization, as for instance investigated in [4].

concept descriptions, concept descriptions, and role descriptions, respectively, in the ontology.

A *conjunctive query* (CQ) is a first-order query q of the form $\exists \boldsymbol{u}.\psi(\boldsymbol{u}, \boldsymbol{v})$ where ψ is a conjunction of concept atoms $A(t)$ and role atoms $R(t, t')$, with A and R being concept and role names, respectively. The parameters t, t' are variables from $\boldsymbol{u}$ or $\boldsymbol{v}$ or constants (individual names). The variables in $\boldsymbol{u}$ are the existentially quantified variables of q and $\boldsymbol{v}$ are the free variables, also called distinguished variables or answer variables of q. The query q is called a k-ary query iff $|\boldsymbol{v}| = k$. In a *grounded conjunctive query* (GCQ), $\boldsymbol{u}$ is empty. We only consider grounded conjunctive queries in this paper. We define an operator *skel* that can be applied to a CQ to compute a new CQ in which all concept atoms are dropped.

The query answering problem is defined w.r.t. an ontology $\mathcal{O} = (\mathcal{T}, \mathcal{R}, \mathcal{A})$. Let $Inds(\mathcal{A})$ denote the individuals in A. For $\mathcal{I}$ an interpretation, $q = \psi(\boldsymbol{v})$ a k-ary grounded conjunctive query, and $a_1, \dots, a_k \in Inds(\mathcal{A})$, we write $\mathcal{I} \models q[a_1, \dots, a_k]$ if $\mathcal{I}$ satisfies q (i.e., all atoms of q) with variables v_i replaced by $a_i, 1 \leq i \leq k$. A *certain answer* for a k-ary conjunctive query q and a ontology $\mathcal{O}$ is a tuple $(a_1, \dots, a_k)$ such that $\mathcal{I} \models q[a_1, \dots, a_k]$ for each model $\mathcal{I}$ of $\mathcal{O}$. We use $cert(q, \mathcal{O})$ to denote the set of all certain answers for q and $\mathcal{O}$. This defines the query answering problem. Given a $\mathcal{SHI}$ ontology $\mathcal{O}$ and a GCQ q, compute $cert(q, \mathcal{O})$. It should be noted that "tree-shaped" conjunctive queries can be transformed into grounded conjunctive queries, possibly with additional axioms in the Tbox [8]. The restriction to grounded conjunctive queries is not too severe in many practical applications.

Grounded conjunctive query answering can be implemented in a naive way by computing the certain answers for each atom and doing a join afterwards. Certain answers for concept atoms can be computed by iterating over $Inds(\mathcal{A})$ with separate instance checks for each individual. Rather than performing an instance check on the whole Abox, which is too large to fit in main memory in many application scenarios, the goal is to do an instance check on a module such that results are sound and complete. More formally, given an input individual a, the proposal is to compute a set of Abox assertions $\mathcal{A}_{isl}$ (a subset of the source Abox $\mathcal{A}$), such that for all atomic (!) concept descriptions A, we have $\langle \mathcal{T}, \mathcal{R}, \mathcal{A} \rangle \models A(a)$ iff $\langle \mathcal{T}, \mathcal{R}, \mathcal{A}_{isl} \rangle \models A(a)$.

3   Speeding Up Instance Retrieval

In order to define subsets of an Abox relevant for reasoning over an individual a, we define an operation which splits up role assertions in such a way that we can apply graph component-based modularization techniques over the outcome of the split.

Definition 1 (Abox Split). *Given*

- *a role description R,*
- *two distinct named individuals a and b,*

- *two distinct fresh individuals c and d, and,*
- *an Abox $\mathcal{A}$,*

an Abox split is a function $\downarrow_{c,d}^{R(a,b)}$: $\mathbf{SA} \rightarrow \mathbf{SA}$, defined as follows ($\mathbf{SA}$ is the set of Aboxes and $\mathcal{A} \in \mathbf{SA}$):

- *If $R(a,b) \in \mathcal{A}$ and $\{c,d\} \not\subseteq Ind(\mathcal{A})$, then*

$$\downarrow_{c,d}^{R(a,b)} (\mathcal{A}) = \mathcal{A} \setminus \{R(a,b)\} \cup \{R(a,d), R(c,b)\} \cup$$
$$\{C(c) \mid C(a) \in \mathcal{A}\} \cup$$
$$\{C(d) \mid C(b) \in \mathcal{A}\}$$

- *Else*

$$\downarrow_{c,d}^{R(a,b)} (\mathcal{A}) = \mathcal{A}.$$

In the following we assume that the Tbox is transformed into a normal form such that all axioms are "internalized" (i.e., on the lefthand side of a GCI there is only $\top$ mentioned. For a formal definition of the normal form of a Tbox, see [12]. Here we use an example to illustrate the idea.

Example 1 (Example for an Extended $\forall$-info Structure). Let

$$\mathcal{T}_{Ex1} = \{Chair \sqsubseteq \forall headOf.Department,$$
$$\exists memberOf.\top \sqsubseteq Person,$$
$$GraduateStudent \sqsubseteq Student\},$$
$$\mathcal{R}_{Ex1} = \{headOf \sqsubseteq memberOf\},$$

then the TBox in normal form is

$$\mathcal{T}_{Ex1norm} = \{\top \sqsubseteq \neg Chair \sqcup \forall headOf.Department,$$
$$\top \sqsubseteq \forall memberOf.\bot \sqcup Person,$$
$$\top \sqsubseteq \neg GraduateStudent \sqcup Student\}$$

and the extended $\forall$-info structure for $\mathcal{T}_{Ex1norm}$ and $\mathcal{R}_{Ex1}$ is:

$$extinfo_{\mathcal{T},\mathcal{R}}^{\forall}(R) = \begin{cases} \{Department, \bot\} & \text{if } R = headOf, \\ \{\bot\} & \text{if } R = memberOf, \\ \emptyset & \text{otherwise.} \end{cases}$$

Definition 2 (Extended $\forall$-info Structure). *Given a TBox $\mathcal{T}$ in normal form and an Rbox $\mathcal{R}$, an extended $\forall$-info structure for $\mathcal{T}$ and $\mathcal{R}$ is a function $extinfo_{\mathcal{T},\mathcal{R}}^{\forall} : \mathbf{Rol} \rightarrow \wp(\mathbf{Con})$, such that we have $C \in extinfo_{\mathcal{T},\mathcal{R}}^{\forall}(R)$ if and only if there exists a role $R_2 \in \mathbf{Rol}$, such that $\mathcal{R} \models R \sqsubseteq R_2$ and $\forall R_2.C \in clos(\mathcal{T})$, where $clos(\mathcal{T})$ denotes the set of all concept descriptions mentioned in $\mathcal{T}$.*

Now we are ready to define a data structure that allows us to check which concept descriptions are (worst-case) "propagated" over role assertions in $\mathcal{SHI}$-ontologies. If nothing is "propagated" that is not already stated in corresponding Abox assertions, a role assertion is called splittable. This is formalized in the following definition.

Definition 3 ($\mathcal{SHI}$-splittability of Role Assertions). *Given a $\mathcal{SHI}$-ontology $\mathcal{O} = \langle \mathcal{T}, \mathcal{R}, \mathcal{A} \rangle$ and a role assertion $R(a, b)$, we say that $R(a, b)$ is $\mathcal{SHI}$-splittable with respect to $\mathcal{O}$ iff*

1. *there exists no transitive role R_2 with respect to $\mathcal{R}$, such that $\mathcal{R} \models R \sqsubseteq R_2$,*
2. *for each $C \in extinfo_{\mathcal{T},\mathcal{R}}^{\forall}(R)$*
   - $C = \bot$ *or*
   - *there is a $C_2(b) \in \mathcal{A}$ and $\mathcal{T} \models C_2 \sqsubseteq C$ or*
   - *there is a $C_2(b) \in \mathcal{A}$ and $\mathcal{T} \models C \sqcap C_2 \sqsubseteq \bot$*

   and
3. *for each $C \in extinfo_{\mathcal{T},\mathcal{R}}^{\forall}(R^-)$*
   - $C = \bot$ *or*
   - *there is a $C_2(a) \in \mathcal{A}$ and $\mathcal{T} \models C_2 \sqsubseteq C$ or*
   - *there is a $C_2(a) \in \mathcal{A}$ and $\mathcal{T} \models C \sqcap C_2 \sqsubseteq \bot$.*

So far, we have introduced approaches to modularization of the assertional part of an ontology. In the following, we use these modularization techniques to define structures for efficient reasoning over ontologies.

We formally define a subset of assertions, called an *individual island*, which is worst-case necessary, i.e. possibly contains more assertions than really necessary for sound and complete instance checking. Informally speaking, we take the graph view of an Abox and, starting from a given individual, follow all role assertions in the graph until we reach a $\mathcal{SHI}$-splittable role assertion. We show that this strategy is sufficient for entailment of atomic concepts. The formal foundations for these subsets of assertions have been set up before, where we show that, under some conditions, role assertions can be broken up while preserving soundness and completeness of instance checking algorithms. First, in Definition 4, we formally define an individual island candidate with an arbitrary subset of the original Abox. The concrete computation of the subset is then further defined below.

Definition 4 (Individual Island Candidate).
Given an ontology $\mathcal{O} = \langle \mathcal{T}, \mathcal{R}, \mathcal{A} \rangle$ and a named individual $a \in Ind(\mathcal{A})$, an individual island candidate, is a tuple $ISL_a = \langle \mathcal{T}, \mathcal{R}, \mathcal{A}^{isl}, a \rangle$, such that $\mathcal{A}^{isl} \subseteq \mathcal{A}$. Given an individual island candidate $ISL_a = \langle \mathcal{T}, \mathcal{R}, \mathcal{A}^{isl}, a \rangle$ and an interpretation $\mathcal{I}$, we say that $\mathcal{I}$ is a model of ISL_a, denoted $\mathcal{I} \models ISL_a$, if $\mathcal{I} \models \langle \mathcal{T}, \mathcal{R}, \mathcal{A}^{isl} \rangle$. Given an individual island candidate $ISL_a = \langle \mathcal{T}, \mathcal{R}, \mathcal{A}^{isl}, a \rangle$, we say that ISL_a entails a concept assertion $C(a)$, denoted $\langle \mathcal{T}, \mathcal{R}, \mathcal{A}^{isl}, a \rangle \models C(a)$, if for all interpretations $\mathcal{I}$, we have $\mathcal{I} \models ISL_a \implies \mathcal{I} \models C(a)$. We say that ISL_a entails a role assertion $R(a_1, a_2)$, denoted $\langle \mathcal{T}, \mathcal{R}, \mathcal{A}^{isl}, a \rangle \models R(a_1, a_2)$, if for all interpretations $\mathcal{I}$, we have $\mathcal{I} \models ISL_a \implies \mathcal{I} \models R(a_1, a_2)$.

Please note that entailment of concept and role assertions can be directly reformulated as a decision problem over ontologies, i.e., we have $\langle \mathcal{T}, \mathcal{R}, \mathcal{A}^{isl}, a \rangle \models C(a) \iff \langle \mathcal{T}, \mathcal{R}, \mathcal{A}^{isl} \rangle \models C(a)$. In order to evaluate the quality of an individual island candidate, we define soundness and completeness criteria for individual island candidates.

Definition 5 (Soundness and Completeness for Island Candidates).
Given an ontology $\mathcal{O} = \langle \mathcal{T}, \mathcal{R}, \mathcal{A} \rangle$ and an individual island candidate $ISL_a = \langle \mathcal{T}, \mathcal{R}, \mathcal{A}^{isl}, a \rangle$, we say that ISL_a is sound *for instance checking in ontology $\mathcal{O}$ if for all atomic concept descriptions $C \in \mathbf{AtCon}$, $ISL_a \models C(a) \implies \langle \mathcal{T}, \mathcal{R}, \mathcal{A} \rangle \models C(a)$. ISL_a is* complete *for instance checking in ontology $\mathcal{O}$ if for all atomic concept descriptions $C \in \mathbf{AtCon}$, $\langle \mathcal{T}, \mathcal{R}, \mathcal{A} \rangle \models C(a) \implies ISL_a \models C(a)$.*

We say that ISL_a is sound *for relation checking in ontology $\mathcal{O}$ if for all role descriptions $R \in \mathbf{Rol}$ and all individuals $a_2 \in Inds(\mathcal{A})$*

- $ISL_a \models R(a, a_2) \implies \langle \mathcal{T}, \mathcal{R}, \mathcal{A} \rangle \models R(a, a_2)$ *and*
- $ISL_a \models R(a_2, a) \implies \langle \mathcal{T}, \mathcal{R}, \mathcal{A} \rangle \models R(a_2, a)$.

ISL_a *is* complete *for relation checking in ontology $\mathcal{O}$ if for all role descriptions $R \in \mathbf{Rol}$ and all individuals $a_2 \in Inds(\mathcal{A})$*

- $\langle \mathcal{T}, \mathcal{R}, \mathcal{A} \rangle \models R(a, a_2) \implies ISL_a \models R(a, a_2)$ *and*
- $\langle \mathcal{T}, \mathcal{R}, \mathcal{A} \rangle \models R(a_2, a) \implies ISL_a \models R(a_2, a)$.

We say that ISL_a is sound *for reasoning in ontology $\mathcal{O}$ if ISL_a is sound for instance and relation checking in $\mathcal{O}$. We say that ISL_a is* complete *for reasoning in $\mathcal{O}$ if ISL_a is complete for instance and relation checking in $\mathcal{O}$.*

Definition 6 (Individual Island).
Given an individual island candidate $ISL_a = \langle \mathcal{T}, \mathcal{R}, \mathcal{A}^{isl}, a \rangle$ for an ontology $\mathcal{O} = \langle \mathcal{T}, \mathcal{R}, \mathcal{A} \rangle$, ISL_a is called individual island *for $\mathcal{O}$ if ISL_a is sound and complete for reasoning in $\mathcal{O}$.*

An individual island candidate becomes an individual island if it can be used for sound and complete reasoning. It is easy to see that each individual island candidate is sound for reasoning since it contains a subset of the original Abox assertions.

In Fig. 1, we define an algorithm which computes an individual island starting from a given named individual a. The set **agenda** manages the individuals which have to be visited. The set **seen** collects already visited individuals. Individuals are visited if they are connected by a chain of $\mathcal{SHI}$-unsplittable role assertions to a. We add the role assertions of all visited individuals and all concept assertions for visited individuals and their direct neighbors.

Theorem 1 shows that the computed set of assertions is indeed sufficient for complete reasoning.

Theorem 1 (Island Computation yields Individual Islands for Ontologies). *Given an ontology $\mathcal{O} = \langle \mathcal{T}, \mathcal{R}, \mathcal{A} \rangle$ and an individual $a \in Inds(\mathcal{A})$, the algorithm in Fig. 1 computes an individual island $ISL_a = \langle \mathcal{T}, \mathcal{R}, \mathcal{A}^{isl}, a \rangle$ for a.*

Input: Ontology $\mathcal{O} = \langle \mathcal{T}, \mathcal{R}, \mathcal{A} \rangle$, individual $a \in Inds(\mathcal{A})$
Output: Individual island $ISL_a = \langle \mathcal{T}, \mathcal{R}, \mathcal{A}^{isl}, a \rangle$
Algorithm:
    Let agenda $= \{a\}$
    Let seen $= \emptyset$
    Let $\mathcal{A}^{isl} = \emptyset$
    While agenda $\neq \emptyset$ **do**
        Remove a_1 from **agenda**
        Add a_1 to **seen**
        Let $\mathcal{A}^{isl} = \mathcal{A}^{isl} \cup \{C(a_1) \mid C(a_1) \in \mathcal{A}\}$
        For each $R(a_1, a_2) \in \mathcal{A}$
            $\mathcal{A}^{isl} = \mathcal{A}^{isl} \cup \{R(a_1, a_2) \in \mathcal{A}\}$
            If $R(a_1, a_2) \in \mathcal{A}$ is $\mathcal{SHI}$-splittable with respect to $\mathcal{O}$ **then**
                $\mathcal{A}^{isl} = \mathcal{A}^{isl} \cup \{C(a_2) \mid C(a_2) \in \mathcal{A}\}$
            else agenda = **agenda** $\cup (\{a_2\} \setminus$ **seen**$)$
        For each $R(a_2, a_1) \in \mathcal{A}$
            $\mathcal{A}^{isl} = \mathcal{A}^{isl} \cup \{R(a_2, a_1) \in \mathcal{A}\}$
            If $R(a_2, a_1) \in \mathcal{A}$ is $\mathcal{SHI}$-splittable with respect to $\mathcal{O}$ **then**
                $\mathcal{A}^{isl} = \mathcal{A}^{isl} \cup \{C(a_2) \mid C(a_2) \in \mathcal{A}\}$
            else agenda = **agenda** $\cup (\{a_2\} \setminus$ **seen**$)$

Fig. 1. Schematic algorithm for computing an individual island

The proof is given in [12].

For each individual there is an associated individual island, and Abox consistency can be checked by considering each island in turn (islands can be loaded into main memory on the fly). Individual islands can be used for sound and complete instance checks, and iterating over all individuals gives a sound and complete (albeit still inefficient) instance retrieval procedure for very large Aboxes.

Definition 7 (Pseudo Node Successor). *Given an Abox* $\mathcal{A}$, *a pseudo node successor of an individual* $a \in Inds(\mathcal{A})$ *is a pair* $pns^{a,\mathcal{A}} = \langle \mathbf{rs}, \mathbf{cs} \rangle$, *such that there is an* $a_2 \in Ind(\mathcal{A})$ *with*

1. $\forall R \in \mathbf{rs}.(R(a, a_2) \in \mathcal{A} \vee R^-(a_2, a) \in \mathcal{A})$,
2. $\forall C \in \mathbf{cs}.C(a_2) \in \mathcal{A}$, *and*
3. $\mathbf{rs}$ *and* $\mathbf{cs}$ *are maximal.*

Definition 8 (One-Step Node).
Given $\mathcal{O} = \langle \mathcal{T}, \mathcal{R}, \mathcal{A} \rangle$ *and an individual* $a \in Inds(\mathcal{A})$, *the one-step node of* a *for* $\mathcal{A}$, *denoted* $osn^{a,\mathcal{A}}$, *is a tuple* $osn^{a,\mathcal{A}} = \langle \mathbf{rootconset}, \mathbf{reflset}, \mathbf{pnsset} \rangle$, *such that* $\mathbf{rootconset} = \{C|C(a) \in \mathcal{A}\}$, $\mathbf{reflset} = \{R|R(a, a) \in \mathcal{A} \vee R^-(a, a) \in \mathcal{A}\}$, *and* $\mathbf{pnsset}$ *is the set of all pseudo node successors of individual* a.

It should be obvious that for realistic datasets, multiple individuals in an Abox will be mapped to a single one-step node data structure. We associate the corresponding individuals with their one-step node. In addition, it is clear that one-step nodes can be mapped back to Aboxes. The obvious mapping function is called *Abox*. If $Abox(osn^{a,\mathcal{A}}) \models C(a)$ for a query concept C (a named concept), all associated individuals of $osn^{a,\mathcal{A}}$ are instances of C. It is also clear that not every *one-step node* is complete for determining whether a is not an instance of C. This is the case only if one-step nodes "coincide" with the islands derived for the associated individuals (splittable one-step nodes). Wandelt found that for LUBM in many cases islands are very small, and one-step nodes are indeed complete in the sense that if $Abox(osn^{a,\mathcal{A}}) \not\models C(a)$ then $\mathcal{A} \not\models C(a)$ (for details see [12]). In the following we assume that for instance retrieval, it is possible to specify a subset of Abox individuals as a set of possible candidates. If the set of candidates is small, with some candidates possibly eliminated by one-step nodes, then iterative instance checks give us a feasible instance retrieval algorithm in practice.

4   Answering Grounded Conjunctive Queries

In this section we will shortly describe an implementation of the introduced techniques with a triplestore database. As other groups we use the *Lehigh University Benchmark* or LUBM [6] for evaluating algorithms and data structures. This benchmark is an ontology system designed to test large ontologies with respect to OWL applications. With the LUBM generator, the user can generate n universities each consisting of a random number of departments and individuals. As the number of individuals and the number of assertions increases nearly linear with the number of universities, LUBM is an instrument to test the performance for query answering machines, especially for grounded conjunctive queries in a scalable Abox environment. If a system cannot handle LUBM with, say, a billion triples, it cannot deal with more complex scenarios occurring in future applications, either. The code we used in this paper for evaluating the optimization techiques is written in Java and can be downloaded at http://www.sts.tu-harburg.de/people/c.neuenstadt/. We store data in the triplestore AllegroGraph, which provides access to role instances (triples) w.r.t. RDFS plus transitive roles, i.e., role hierarchies and transitive roles are handled by AllegroGraph. Alternatively one could use materialization or query expansion in the OBDA style for role hierarchies. SPARQL is used as a query language for specifying queries to be executed on a particular triplestore database.

4.1   Setting Up an AllegroGraph Triplestore

AllegroGraph is run as a server program. In our setting, data is loaded directly into the server, whereas islands as well as one-step nodes are computed by a remote program run on a client computer (we cannot extend the server program easily). In a first step the whole data system has to be set up before we can start query answering. During the setup process, the communication between client and server system consists basically of sending SPARQL queries for data access required in the algorithm shown in Fig. 1 as well as sending AllegroGraph statements for adding additional triples (or changing existing ones) for storing islands and one-step nodes. Islands are indicated using the subgraph components of AllegroGraph triples (actually, quintuples).

The "similarity" of one-step nodes is deifned using hashvalues with a sufficient bitlength. We first compute a set from each island, compute a hashvalue for it, and store it together with the specific island in the triplestore. Identical hash values allow one to refer to "similar" one-step nodes (with additional checks applied to the collision list as usual for hashing).

Given the concept description C from the query and the named individual a from the tuple, we load the specific one-step node for a from the database and determine whether osn_a entails $C(a)$. Depending on the outcome, three states are possible:

- Osn_a entails $C(a)$, then a is actually an instance of C.
- Osn_a entails $\neg C(a)$ or does not entail $C(a)$ and is splittable, then a is actually not an instance of C.
- Osn_a is not splittable, then the client has to load and check the entire island associated with a to find out whether a actually is an instance of C.

Candidates for concept atoms are determined in our experiments by first doing a retrieval for a query q by executing $skel(q)$ (see above for a definition). Bindings for variables in $skel(q)$ define the candidates for retrieval with concept atoms. By eliminating all skeleton query result tuples that include individuals which do not belong to corresponding concept assertions used in the query, finally all remaining tuples are correct answers to the original conjunctive query.

Wandelt has already investigated the efficiency of Abox modularization techniques for an SQL database server. Here, instead, we work directly on an existing AllegroGraph triplesotore, convert the large ontology step by step into small chunks and compare the generated modules with the local modularization of Sebastian Wandelt on the SQL server [12]. The processing time for one university is about 5000 seconds on AllegroGraph server, where it is like one minute for Wandelt's approach. The modularization of one university takes nearly 200,000 queries. The decrease in performance is based on the huge number of SPARQL mini queries between server and the remote modularization client in the prototype implementation. Thus, only 5 universities are investigated for query answering experiments.

4.2 Evaluating Conjunctive Queries

For evaluating grounded conjunctive queries, LUBM provides 14 predefined test queries, which check several database criteria. We run the tests with an ontology, which uses the description logic language $\mathcal{SHI}$. LUBM queries differ in the amount of input, selectivity and reasoning behaviour for example by relying

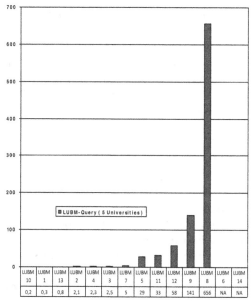

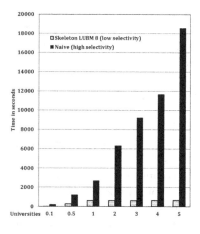

Fig. 2. Runtimes for all queries (in seconds)

Fig. 3. Comparison between skeleton query and naive approach (numbers for runtimes in seconds)

on inverse roles, role hierarchy, or transitivity inferences.[3] Selectivity basically means that the grounded conjunctive queries being considered have role atoms with large result sets to be reduced by atom queries, which we call less selective (proportion of the instances involved in the skeleton are high compared to those that actually satisfy the query criteria), or automatically excludes a lot of individuals, what we call a highly selective query. Rather than doing a join on the result sets of all atoms in a grounded conjunctive query, role atoms define candidates for concept atoms. Thus for selective queries, candidate sets for concept atoms are smaller. This reduces the number of instance checks that remain if, e.g., one-step node optimizations are not applicable (see above).

The result indicates that the less selective a query is w.r.t. role atoms, the more instance checks we need afterwards, and the more time consuming retrieval is (see Figure 2). Nevertheless, most of the LUBM queries are handled fast, even with the simple implementation for concept atoms with repetitive instance checks. Performance for Query 8 will be increased with an implementation of

---

[3] In the LUBM dataset, explict assertions about subrelations of degreeFrom are made (e.g., doctoralDegreeFrom). The relation degreeFrom is declared as an inverse to hasAlumnus. Thus, although, e.g., Query 13 contains a reference to University0 (asking for fillers of hasAlumnus), adding new universities with degreeFrom tuples with University0 on the righthand side causes the cardinality of the set of fillers for hasAlumnus w.r.t. University0 to increase, i.e., having a constant in the query does not mean the result set to be independent of the number of universities.

full one-step node retrieval (with multiple individuals returned at a time, see above). Queries 6 and 14 contain only concept atoms and are not tested here.

To demonstrate that our skeleton query candidate generator is able to significantly improve the results for queries with even low selectivity, we compare the approach of skeleton queries with the naive approach without skeleton queries in Figure 3. One can directly see the huge performance gain of the skeleton query even for less selective queries. We avoid lots of instance checks and can therefore decrease the answering time by orders of magnitude in many cases.

5   Conclusion

In this work we extended the Abox modularization strategies of Wandelt and colleagues to the efficient use of grounded conjunctive queries on triplestore servers. Results obtained with the techniques discussed in this paper are sound and complete. Note that query engines investigated in [6] are incomplete.

Our prototype needs linear time to add information to the triplestore in a setup phase. Therefore we were not able to run queries on billions of triples. We conclude that island computation needs to be built into the triplestore software iteself and cannot be done from a remote client.

In the average case, the size of the individual island (with respect to the number of assertion in its Abox) is considerably smaller than the original Abox. In our experiments the size is usually orders of magnitudes smaller. Please note that these modularization techniques allow traditional description logic reasoning systems to deal with ontologies which they cannot handle without modularizations (because the data or the computed model abstraction does not fit into main memory).

In addition, the evaluation of the prototype showed how grounded conjuctive queries on triplestore servers w.r.t. expressive ontologies ($\mathcal{SHI}$) can be implemented using only a small size of main memory. The main strategy is to use a skeleton query and try to keep the necessary amount of instance checks in the second step as small as possible. If the number of results for less selective skeleton queries gets larger, the number of instance checks increases rapidly. In some cases it would obviously have been better to reduce the set of possible tuples by considering concept atoms first. This observation has also been made in [9] and, much earlier, in [16] where more elaborate query plan generation techniques are investigated, albeit for main memory systems.

We would like to emphasize that the proposed optimizations can be used for parallel reasoning over ontologies [13]. This will be further investigated in future work such that ABDEO will become possible for practically relevant datasets and ontologies that are more demanding than LUBM.

References

1. Calvanese, D., De Giacomo, G., Lembo, D., Lenzerini, M., Poggi, A., Rodriguez-Muro, M., Rosati, R.: Ontologies and databases: The DL-Lite approach. In: Reasoning Web. Semantic Technologies for Information Systems, pp. 255–356 (2009)

2. Dolby, J., Fokoue, A., Kalyanpur, A., Kershenbaum, A., Schonberg, E., Srinivas, K., Ma, L.: Scalable semantic retrieval through summarization and refinement. In: Proceedings of the National Conference on Artificial Intelligence, p. 299. AAAI Press, MIT Press, Cambridge, Menlo Park (1999, 2007)
3. Dolby, J., Fokoue, A., Kalyanpur, A., Schonberg, E., Srinivas, K.: Scalable highly expressive reasoner (SHER). J. Web Sem. 7(4), 357–361 (2009)
4. Grau, B.C., Parsia, B., Sirin, E., Kalyanpur, A.: Modularity and web ontologies. In: Proc. KR 2006 (2006)
5. Guo, Y., Heflin, J.: A scalable approach for partitioning owl knowledge bases. In: Proc. of the 2nd International Workshop on Scalable Semantic Web Knowledge Base Systems, SSWS 2006 (2006)
6. Guo, Y., Pan, Z., Heflin, J.: LUBM: A benchmark for OWL knowledge base systems. Web Semantics: Science, Services and Agents on the World Wide Web 3(2), 158–182 (2005)
7. Haarslev, V., Möller, R.: On the scalability of description logic instance retrieval. Journal of Automated Reasoning 41(2), 99–142 (2008)
8. Horrocks, I., Tessaris, S.: A conjunctive query language for description logic ABoxes. In: Proc. of the 17th Nat. Conf. on Artificial Intelligence (AAAI 2000), pp. 399–404 (2000)
9. Kollia, I., Glimm, B., Horrocks, I.: SPARQL query answering over OWL ontologies. In: Antoniou, G., Grobelnik, M., Simperl, E., Parsia, B., Plexousakis, D., De Leenheer, P., Pan, J. (eds.) ESWC 2011, Part I. LNCS, vol. 6643, pp. 382–396. Springer, Heidelberg (2011)
10. Lutz, C., Toman, D., Wolter, F.: Conjunctive query answering in the description logic EL using a relational database system. In: Boutilier, C. (ed.) IJCAI, pp. 2070–2075 (2009)
11. Möller, R., Haarslev, V.: Tableaux-based reasoning. In: Staab, S., Studer, R. (eds.) Handbook of Ontologies, pp. 509–528. Springer (2009)
12. Wandelt, S.: Efficient instance retrieval over semi-expressive ontologies. PhD thesis, Hamburg University of Technology (2011)
13. Wandelt, S., Moeller, R.: Distributed island-based query answering for expressive ontologies. In: Bellavista, P., Chang, R.-S., Chao, H.-C., Lin, S.-F., Sloot, P.M.A. (eds.) GPC 2010. LNCS, vol. 6104, pp. 461–470. Springer, Heidelberg (2010)
14. Wandelt, S., Möller, R.: Towards Abox modularization of semi-expressive description logics. Journal of Applied Ontology 7(2), 133–167 (2012)
15. Wandelt, S., Möller, R., Wessel, M.: Towards scalable instance retrieval over ontologies. Journal of Software and Informatics (2010)
16. Wessel, M.: Flexible und konfigurierbare Software-Architekturen fr datenintensive ontologiebasierte Informationssysteme. PhD thesis, Technische Universität Hamburg-Harburg, Hamburg, Germany (2009) ISBN 978-3-8325-2312-1

Estimating the Driver's Workload

Using Smartphone Data to Adapt In-Vehicle Information Systems

Christina Ohm and Bernd Ludwig

Chair of Information Science, Universität Regensburg, 93040 Regensburg, Germany
{christina.ohm,bernd.ludwig}@ur.de

Abstract. The use of in-vehicle information systems has increased in the past years. These systems assist the user but can as well cause additional cognitive load. The study presented in this paper was carried out to enable workload estimation in order to adapt information and entertainment systems so that an optimal driver performance and user experience is ensured. For this purpose smartphone sensor data, situational factors and basic user characteristics are taken into account. The study revealed that the driving situation, the gender of the user and the frequency of driving significantly influence the user's workload. Using only this information and smartphone sensor data the current workload of the driver can be estimated with 86% accuracy.

Keywords: Driver's Workload, Workload Estimation, In-Vehicle Information Systems.

1 Motivation

Currently, many in-vehicle information systems provide assistance and entertainment to the driver but still can be a source of distraction and cognitive load since they require an input action or at least the attention of the user. For this reason it is necessary to determine the driver's mental state in order to prevent dangerous situations and optimize her driving performance. The primary driving task itself is cognitive demanding since the motorist has to develop different levels of skills [20]:

- Control level skills: handling of the car
- Maneuvering level skills: reaction behavior to the traffic situation and other road users
- Strategic level skills: planning the trip and defining goals

In addition to these basic activities, the operator has to fulfill secondary tasks which are not directly related to the actual transportation goal but are required to ensure safety. This could be e.g. turning on the windscreen wiper or the upper beam head-lights. Using in-vehicle information systems belongs to the tertiary driving task as they are mainly used for information, communication

I.J. Timm and M. Thimm (Eds.): KI 2013, LNAI 8077, pp. 130–139, 2013.

or entertainment purposes [3]. Thus, driving is a particularly difficult situation for human computer interaction because the operator is supposed to master primary and secondary tasks before she can actually pay attention to any kind of in-vehicle information system. If the user's current workload is not optimal, she should not be bothered with even more output of an assistance or entertainment system.

In this paper a study is presented that examines which factors significantly influence the driver's workload. Furthermore, the aim was to estimate the workload using sensor data collected by a smartphone. In addition, basic characteristics of the driver are taken into account. Being able to forecast the mental load of the user in a specific situation can be used to adapt a system's output to facilitate an optimal driving performance and therefore enhance the driver's safety. In contrast to existing approaches [8, 19, 32] the concept of using just a smartphone does not depend on sensor data of the car. Consequently, this technique provides a low-cost and simple possibility to integrate the prediction into smartphone services which could be for instance phone calls that can be blocked for a short period of time if the workload is high at the moment. This is also the intent of other systems which try to predict workload [8, 19]. The following section describes the concept of workload generally as well as in the context of driving. Afterwards measurement and estimation methods are depicted. Subsequently, we present our workload self-assessment tool, the study design and our results. Finally, we draw conclusions considering the implications of our findings.

2   Workload

Basically workload can be defined as a "demand placed upon humans" [29]. However, this task-oriented definition does not mind all aspects of the concept. Especially user-centered features such as her cognitive abilities or knowledge base are not minded. This is taken into account by different definitions [4, 7, 12, 15, 16, 29], and can be summed up as follows: An operator has to fulfill a task under given situational circumstances which demands information-processing capabilities. Therefore, the task causes cognitive load. Workload is the required capability to accomplish the task satisfactorily and achieve a certain level of performance. Meanwhile, the operator has a subjective experience which results from situational factors, the requirements of the task and the user's characteristics [24]. The latter includes criteria like her cognitive, sensory or motor skills, knowledge base, behavior, personality, age, sex etc. [14, 29]. Considering the context of driving this may also include driving experience [10]. [28] identifies several important factors that influence the driver's workload which are the age of the driver, the driving context (e.g. driving on a rural road) or the traveling daytime.

In the context of driving [21] distinguish three states which derive from the relation of the situational demands and the driver's condition. If the requirements of the task exceed the skills of the user, she has to endure an Overload experience which is a suboptimal cognitive state and can lead to loss of control or at least the feeling to do so. Contrary to this is the Underload state, which can be understood as a feeling of boredom or distraction. In this case the situational demands do not challenge the driver because she has sufficient skills. Thus, if the factors are in balance, the driver achieves optimal performance. This approach to classify driver experience is quite similar to the flow theory discussed in [6]. [9] develops a Task-Capability Interface Model which also examines the connection of the task demands and the capability of the driver. The task demands include the traffic situation, the behavior of other road users or the actual traveling speed. If the skills of the driver exceed the demands, the user is in a state of control. If this is not the case, most of all situations result in a lucky escape because other road users react to an error of the operator. Otherwise, a collision impends which indicates the importance of knowing the current driver state.

A more detailed categorization can be found in [29]. Once again, in this model workload is the consequence of the relation of the driver's performance and the task demands. The author distinguishes six different states which include one state where the workload is high and the performance is low because the driving demands are not challenging. Moreover, three states can be grouped as situations where the driver is in control but either is at the edge to Under- or Overload. In the remaining two states the driver has an experience of high workload or even loss of control as the task demands are received as too high. Both Under- and Overload can lead to cognitive load which affects the health of the user and his ability to drive safely and therefore has to be avoided.

3   Workload Measurement and Estimation

At first cognitive load has to be measured in order to enable an estimation and consequently avoid a suboptimal workload level. This can be achieved using a diverse range of available tools. It is possible to measure the operator's physiological state using for instance an electroencephalogram to determine cerebral activity or an electrocardiogram to measure myocardial contraction. An overview of physiological measurements is given in [29]. However, data collected with biosensors is considered to be arguable, since it is sometimes ambiguous and hard to analyze for someone who is not an expert in medicine. Moreover, external factors, which do not indicate workload, can influence the measurement [5].

Another possibility is to use tools that relay on user self-reports which can be one- or multidimensional. An example for an one-dimensional measurement is the Rating Scale Mental Effort (RSME) [33]. The test person is asked to indicate on a 0 to 150 cm line how much effort it took to fulfill the task. Several statements like "rather much effort" are located along the scale, which are supposed to clarify the level of current effort.

One of the most established multidimensional method in this context is the NASA-Task Load Index (TLX) [4] which takes different sources of workload into account. These are in particular mental, physical and temporal demand as well as the subjectively experienced performance, effort and frustration level of the user. The test person has to rate these dimensions pairwise referring to their impact on the task's workload which leads to overall 15 comparisons. Subsequently, a weight is calculated for every dimension. Afterwards, every dimension is additionally rated on a 0 to 20 scale. The Overall Workload Index (OWI) is calculated as follows with w_i as the weight and x_i as the rate multiplied by 5 [14]:

$$\text{OWI} = \frac{1}{15} \sum_{i=1}^{6} w_i x_i$$

An overview of other multidimensional scales is for example given in [4]. In order to adapt in-vehicle information systems to the current workload of the driver, her state has not only to be measured but also estimated. Different approaches use car sensor data like the steering wheel angle or acceleration gauging to forecast the operator's load [8, 31, 32].[32] additionally use eye tracking techniques and reach up to a 65% correct driver-independent workload estimation with test data collected in a simulator. [8] take biosensors like the heart rate and environmental factors like traffic density into account.

4   Study

The overall goal of the study is to adapt in-vehicle information systems to the current workload of the driver. At first, several hypotheses were tested for validity in order to identify situational factors and user characteristics which significantly influence the driver's workload. [11, 13] show that every driving situation acquires diverse driving skills, so that it can be assumed that the level of workload differs according to this factor. Furthermore, [25] claim that women experience higher workload levels than men while driving. Accordingly, the following hypotheses were proposed:

- H_1: The workload during the driving situations "freeway", "rural road" and "city" differs.
- H_2: Women and men experience different workload while driving.

Since the test persons do not differ significantly in driving style (see Section 4.1), which is an important influencing factor on workload according to [30], other user characteristics were taken into account. [1, 30] distinguish young drivers (<25 years) from older ones and identify that these persons are likely to experience higher workload levels. This leads to the third hypothesis:

- H_3: The workload level differs considering the user's age.

[21] assume that persons who drive regularly usually experience lower workload levels so that the following hypothesis is as well tested for validity:

- H_4: The workload level differs considering the user's driving frequency.

Additionally, smartphone sensor data was collected to estimate the driver's workload.

4.1 Participants and Test Route

Eight female and twelve male students participated in the study. A detailed overview of the user characteristics is showed in Table 1.

Table 1. Overview of user characteristics separated by gender and driving frequency (DF)

	Age			Driving Experience (in years)		
	Mean	Standard deviation	Range	Mean	Standard deviation	Range
Total	24.9	2.1	21-28	6.9	2.4	1-10
Females	24.3	2.3	21-28	5.9	3.0	1-10
Males	25.3	1.9	22-28	7.5	1.8	5-10
DF "often"	25.7	2.3	21-28	7.8	2.2	5-10
DF "rarely"	24.0	1.4	22-26	5.3	2.5	1-8

All in all, the entire test group consisted of young and rather inexperienced but no complete novice drivers. Their driving style was additionally assessed by means of the Multidimensional Driving Style Inventory [26]. Most of the participants named to have a patient or careful driving style so that the test group can be considered as homogeneous concerning this factor.

None of the participants drove with the test car before. The test route consisted of three sections. After a familiarization with the test automobile (6.3 km) users drove on a rural road for 6.3 km. Afterwards they drove on a freeway section for 12 km and finally in the city of Regensburg (4.9 km). It took about 15 minutes to complete one section of the test route. None in-vehicle information systems were used as the main aim was to detect cognitive load of the primary and secondary driving task to adapt the output of assistance and entertainment systems. Moreover, there are several studies which prove that in-vehicle information systems and especially the usage of cell phones cause cognitive load [16–18, 22, 23, 27].

4.2 Measurements

The subjective workload level after accomplishing every route section was measured using a smartphone-based representation of the NASA-TLX (Fig.1). The form was filled in while parking. In addition, a self-assessment tool was implemented which enables users to rate their current workload during the driving process (Fig.1). The tool is based on the RSME. The Underload state adapted from [29] was added and the scale was simplified due to space limitations of the smartphone screen. Several potential designs could be used to visualize the workload levels. Four prototypes with different layouts were evaluated in a usability test with 10 participants. They were instructed that the application was intended to be used while driving. Qualitative as well as quantitative data was collected to determine the best design. Participants were observed by the test supervisor and asked to "think aloud". In addition they filled in the System Usability Scale (SUS) [2]. Most of the test persons agreed in one best design. This was also shown using a single factor variance analysis with repeated measurement adjusted according to Bonferroni for the SUS (p < 0.05). This resulted in the design showed in Fig.1. Colors and a scale are used to visualize the workload level and the whole screen can be clicked. During the actual test, participants were asked to indicate their current workload level every time it had changed. The smartphone was adjusted to the front screen so that only one short look and click was enough to indicate the workload level.

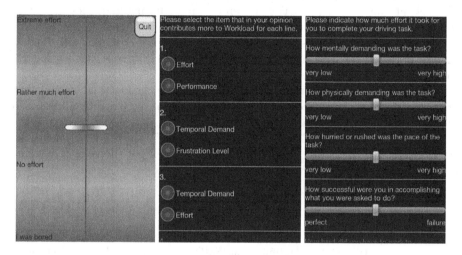

Fig. 1. Screenshots of the Android application which was used to rate the participants' workload while driving (left) and representation of the NASA-TLX (middle and right).

In addition to this, smartphone sensor data was collected to estimate the user's workload with data mining approaches. The lateral and longitudinal acceleration as well as the current speed is detected ten times per second, whereas the current workload level is assigned to this data. In a pre-test highly significant correlations with the equivalent car sensor data were measured (r > 0.85; p = 0.000). In addition, the lateral acceleration correlates highly significantly with the angle of lock (r = 0.95; p = 0.000). The sensor data described above is considered to have a significant influence on driver workload [8, 32]. Moreover, user data like gender and frequency of driving was assessed.

4.3   Results

H_1 could be confirmed considering the OWI for the different driving situations "rural road", "city" and "freeway" using a single factor variance analysis with repeated measurement. Since no sphericity could be assumed (p < 0.1), Greenhouse-Geisser results were consulted (F = 6.178; p = 0.009). Conducting a Bonferroni post-hoc test, more detailed findings could be gained: The OWI is significantly higher for "freeway" (p = 0.039) and "city" (p = 0.013) compared to the "rural road" situation.

After confirming normality using a Kolmogorov-Smirnov-Test (p < 0.05) and analyzing the histograms H_2-H_4 were tested.

H_2 could be confirmed using a T-test (T = 2.314; p = 0.024). Generally women experience slightly higher workload levels than men so that gender can be considered as an influencing factor on workload.

Age significantly correlates with driving experience in years (r = 0.913; p = 0.000), so that older test persons had higher experience levels. However, no significant difference could be detected for this factor.

No significant correlation between "gender" and "driving frequency" could be confirmed using Fisher's exact test.

The OWI of participants who named to drive rarely is significantly higher than of those who at least drive once a week (T = 2.173; p = 0.037) so that H_4 could be confirmed.

According to these findings, the driving situation, gender and driving frequency were taken into account for the estimation of workload in addition to the smartphone sensor data. On the one hand workload was categorized in the three states "Underload", "Optimal" and "Overload". On the other hand the workload levels were as well classified similar to [29] except the level of extreme Overload which results in five different states.

Table 2. Estimation accuracy in % for different classifications of workload

	Decision Tree (C4.5)	Sequential Minimal Optimization (SMO)	AdaBoost	Naive Bayes	Neural Network
Three states	85.70	63.3	62.30	63.92	70.51
Five states	72.92	46.27	46.13	46.13	54.81

Different classification algorithms were taken into account using an 80/20 split of the sample data (Table 2). The results show that the decision tree performs significantly better than the other techniques (p < 0.05).

The study revealed that the current cognitive load can be estimated with an accuracy about 86% using a decision tree. Operator-specific forecasts reach up to 96% correct predictions. If only sensor data is used, the estimation shows up to 76% accuracy. Moreover, the ROC-values of the decision tree method exceed 0.9 so that a good diagnostic accurateness can be assumed.

For a more detailed classification of the current workload level the estimation accuracy decreases to 73% with a ROC-value of 0.749.

5 Conclusion

All in all, there are many factors which influence the driver's workload since the driving situation and the characteristics of the user are very multifaceted.

However, the study presented in this paper shows that it is possible to estimate the driver's workload with very simple methods. Even if only smartphone-based data is used, cognitive load can be calculated with 76% accuracy. Moreover, if user data is taken into account, the prediction accuracy increases to 86%. Consequently, it would be very advantageous to shortly collect user characteristics, i.e. gender, driving frequency and age. In this study the latter could not be examined due to the rather homogeneous age of the participants. This should be a topic of future research.

Another improvement could be achieved through detecting the current driving situation like weather conditions or road type using e.g. data of the navigation system or the car sensors. Furthermore, taking into account whether in-vehicle information systems are used in the specific driving situation could improve the detection of the current workload level since several studies show that using this systems increases the cognitive load of the user (see above). User-dependent predictions can reach up to 96% accuracy so that a system which uses driver feedback to improve the estimation could minimize estimation errors.

The study also showed that it is important to determine the driver's workload several times per second since even if the OWI of some participants was rather low nearly everyone experienced very high or low workload for a short period of time while actually driving. Yet, it is just these moments which require workload detection to avoid dangerous situations.

Knowing the driver state can improve the user experience and safety if in-vehicle information systems are involved. As mentioned at the beginning phone calls or an output of a navigation system can be blocked for instance. If the workload level is too low music could be recommended to the user. Other application areas will surely follow.

References

1. Biermann, A., Eick, E.M., Brünken, R., Debus, G., Leutner, D.: Development and first evaluation of a prediction model for risk of offences and accident involvement among young drivers. Driver Behaviour and Training 2, 169–178 (2005)
2. Brooke, J.: SUS - A quick and dirty usability scale. Redhatch Consulting, United Kingdom (2011)
3. Bubb, H.: Fahrerassistenz primär ein beitrag zum komfort oder für die sicherheit? VDI-Berichte, pp. 25–44 (2003)
4. Cain, B.: A review of the mental workload literature. Tech. rep., DTIC Document (2007)
5. Cherri, C., Nodari, E., Toffetti, A.: Review of existing tools and methods. Tech. rep., AIDE Deliverable D2.1.1 (2004)
6. Csikszentmihalyi, M.: FLOW. Das Geheimnis des Glücks. Klett-Cotta, Stuttgart (2008)
7. Eggemeier, F., Wilson, G., Kramer, A., Damos, D.: Workload assessment in multi-task environments. In: Damos, D. (ed.) Multiple Task Performance, pp. 207–216. Taylor & Francis, London (1991)
8. Ford,
   https://media.ford.com/content/fordmedia/fna/us/en/news/2012/06/27/
   ford-research-developing-intelligent-system-to-help-drivers-mana.html

9. Fuller, R.: The task-capability interface model of the driving process. Recherche-Transports-Sécurité 66, 47–57 (2000)
10. Fuller, R.: Towards a general theory of driver behaviour. Accident Analysis & Prevention 37(3), 461–472 (2005)
11. Gaczek, D.: Entwurf und Regelung eines Verbrauchsassistenten. GRIN Verlag (2009)
12. Gopher, D., Donchin, E.: Workload - an examination of the concept. In: Boff, K., Kaufman, L., Thomas, J. (eds.) Handbook of Perception and Human Performance. Cognitive Processes and Performance, vol. 2, pp. . 41:1–41:49. Wiley, New York (1986)
13. Hale, A., Stoop, J., Hommels, J.: Human error models as predictors of accident scenarios for designers in road transport systems. Ergonomics 33(10-11), 1377–1387 (1990)
14. Hart, S.G., Staveland, L.E.: Development of nasa-tlx (task load index): Results of empirical and theoretical research. Human Mental Workload 1(3), 139–183 (1988)
15. Jex, H.R.: Measuring mental workload: Problems, progress, and promises. Advances in Psychology 52, 5–39 (1988)
16. Lysaght, R.J., Hill, S.G., Dick, A., Plamondon, B.D., Linton, P.M.: Operator workload: Comprehensive review and evaluation of operator workload methodologies. Tech. rep., DTIC Document (1989)
17. Ma, R., Kaber, D.B.: Situation awareness and workload in driving while using adaptive cruise control and a cell phone. International Journal of Industrial Ergonomics 35(10), 939–953 (2005)
18. Matthews, R., Legg, S., Charlton, S.: The effect of cell phone type on drivers subjective workload during concurrent driving and conversing. Accident Analysis & Prevention 35(4), 451–457 (2003)
19. Mayser, C., Ebersbach, D., Dietze, M., Lippold, C.: Fahrerassistenzsysteme zur unterstützung der längsregelung im ungebundenen verkehr. In: Conference Aktive Sicherheit durch Fahrerassistenz (2004)
20. Michon, J.A.: A critical view of driver behavior models: what do we know, what should we do? Springer (1986)
21. Oron-Gilad, T., Ronen, A., Shinar, D.: Alertness maintaining tasks (amts) while driving. Accident Analysis & Prevention 40(3), 851–860 (2008)
22. Pauzié, A.: Evaluating driver mental workload using the driving activity load index (dali). In: Proc. of European Conference on Human Interface Design for Intelligent Transport Systems, pp. 67–77 (2008)
23. Pauzié, A., Manzano, J.: Evaluation of driver mental workload facing new in-vehicle information and communication technology. In: Proceedings of the 20th Enhanced Safety of Vehicles Conference (ESV20), Lyon, France, vol. 10 (2007)
24. Recarte, M.A., Nunes, L.M.: Mental workload while driving: Effects on visual search, discrimination, and decision making. Journal of Experimental Psychology Applied 9(2), 119–133 (2003)
25. Schweitzer, J., Green, P.: Task acceptability and workload of driving city streets, rural roads, and expressways: Ratings from video clips (2007)
26. Taubman-Ben-Ari, O., Mikulincer, M., Gillath, O.: The multidimensional driving style inventory scale construct and validation. Accident Analysis & Prevention 36(3), 323–332 (2004)
27. Tsimhoni, O., Green, P.: Visual demand of driving and the execution of display-intensive in-vehicle tasks. In: Proceedings of the Human Factors and Ergonomics Society Annual Meeting, vol. 45, pp. 1586–1590. SAGE Publications (2001)

28. Verwey, W.B.: On-line driver workload estimation. effects of road situation and age on secondary task measures. Ergonomics 43(2), 187–209 (2000)
29. de Waard, D.: The measurement of drivers' mental workload. Groningen University, Traffic Research Center (1996)
30. Wundersitz, L., Burns, N.: Identifying young driver subtypes: relationship to risky driving and crash involvement. Driver Behaviour And Training 2, 155 (2005)
31. Zeitlin, L.R.: Micromodel for objective estimation of driver mental workload from task data. Transportation Research Record: Journal of the Transportation Research Board 1631(1), 28–34 (1998)
32. Zhang, Y., Owechko, Y., Zhang, J.: Learning-based driver workload estimation. In: Prokhorov, D. (ed.) Computational Intelligence in Automotive Applications. SCI, vol. 132, pp. 1–17. Springer, Heidelberg (2008)
33. Zijstra, C., Doorn, R.V.: The construction of a scale to measure perceived effort. Tech. rep., Department of Philosophy and Social Sciences, Delft University of Technology (1985)

Pattern-Database Heuristics for Partially Observable Nondeterministic Planning

Manuela Ortlieb and Robert Mattmüller

Research Group Foundations of AI, University of Freiburg, Germany
{ortlieb,mattmuel}@informatik.uni-freiburg.de

Abstract. Heuristic search is the dominant approach to classical planning. However, many realistic problems violate classical assumptions such as determinism of action outcomes or full observability. In this paper, we investigate how – and how successfully – a particular classical technique, namely informed search using an abstraction heuristic, can be transferred to nondeterministic planning under partial observability. Specifically, we explore pattern-database heuristics with automatically generated patterns in the context of informed progression search for strong cyclic planning under partial observability. To that end, we discuss projections and how belief states can be heuristically assessed either directly or by going back to the contained world states, and empirically evaluate the resulting heuristics internally and compared to a delete-relaxation and a blind approach. From our experiments we can conclude that in terms of guidance, it is preferable to represent both nondeterminism and partial observability in the abstraction (instead of relaxing them), and that the resulting abstraction heuristics significantly outperform both blind search and a delete-relaxation approach where nondeterminism and partial observability are also relaxed.

Keywords: AI planning, nondeterministic planning, partial observability, heuristic search, pattern databases.

1 Introduction

Classical planning is a well-understood problem that has been successfully approached over the past decades. Both for satisficing and for optimal planning, there are algorithms in the recent literature that scale well beyond simple toy problems [18,11]. Although lately the focus of research in classical planning has shifted towards algorithmic enhancements and pruning techniques orthogonal to planning heuristics, accurate domain-independent heuristics were the main driving factor in the progress of classical planning for many years. However, not all planning tasks fit into the framework of classical planning. Often, action outcomes are nondeterministic and the environment is only partially observable. We would still like to capitalize on the advances made in classical planning when solving such problems. In previous work [1,2,16], we already handled nondeterminism, but only full observability. As part of our efforts to get closer to real-world problems with the approach developed before, in this work, we consider

I.J. Timm and M. Thimm (Eds.): KI 2013, LNAI 8077, pp. 140–151, 2013.

the problem of finding so called strong cyclic plans [6] for partially observable nondeterministic planning tasks, i.e., policies that are guaranteed to never lead into states where they are undefined, and always maintain the possibility to reach a goal state. There exist various approaches to finding strong cyclic plans (for fully observable problems, but in principle adaptable to partially observable problems), including a symbolic nested fixpoint algorithm [6,13], repeated invocations of a classical planner in the all-outcomes determinization of the given nondeterministic planning task until no unsolved leaf nodes remain in the generated subgraph of the transition system [14,8], and (informed) forward search in the nondeterministic transition system induced by the planning task guided by an appropriate heuristic function [4,16]. In this paper, we study the latter approach, more specifically, LAO* search [9]. Whereas a similar study has been performed by Bryce et al. [4] before, that study only considers delete-relaxation heuristics to guide the search. Here, we want to complement that study with an investigation of domain-independent *abstraction* heuristics, more specifically, pattern-database (PDB) heuristics [7]. When Bryce et al. [4] studied relaxation heuristics, they investigated how to evaluate a belief state by either (a) sampling world states from that belief state, evaluating them using a relaxation heuristic assuming full observability, and aggregating the estimates across samples, or (b) directly evaluating the belief state by extending the relaxed planning graph from the fully observable setting to a so-called labeled uncertainty graph (LUG) for the partially observable setting. In this work, we perform a similar comparison between a sampling-based approach and a more direct evaluation of belief states for pattern-database heuristics. Our main research question is whether there is a significant difference in how well approaches (a) and (b) perform empirically, and if so, which performs better.

2   Preliminaries

2.1   Nondeterministic Planning under Partial Observability

We formalize nondeterministic planning tasks under partial observability using a *finite-domain representation* for the state variables and separate *causative and sensing actions*, extending our previous formalization for fully observable nondeterministic planning tasks [16]. A *partially observable nondeterministic planning task* is a tuple $\Pi = \langle \mathcal{V}, s_0, s_\star, \mathcal{O} \rangle$ consisting of the following components: $\mathcal{V}$ is a finite set of *state variables* v, each with a finite *domain* $\mathcal{D}_v$ and an *extended domain* $\mathcal{D}_v^+ = \mathcal{D}_v \uplus \{\bot\}$, where $\bot$ denotes the *undefined* or *don't-care* value. A *partial state* is a function s with $s(v) \in \mathcal{D}_v^+$ for all $v \in \mathcal{V}$. We say that s is *defined* for $v \in \mathcal{V}$ if $s(v) \neq \bot$. A *state* is a partial state s such that its *scope* $\text{scope}(s) = \{v \in \mathcal{V} \mid s(v) \neq \bot\}$ is $\mathcal{V}$. The set of all states s over $\mathcal{V}$ is denoted as $\mathcal{S}$, and the set of all *belief states* B over $\mathcal{V}$ is denoted as $\mathcal{B} = 2^{\mathcal{S}}$. Depending on the context, a partial state s_p can be interpreted either as a *condition*, which is *satisfied* in a state s iff s agrees with s_p on all variables for which s_p is defined, or as an *update* on a state s, resulting in a new state s' that agrees with s_p on all variables for which s_p is defined, and with s on all other variables. The *initial state* s_0 of a problem is a partial state (i.e., a compact encoding of a compactly encodable belief state), and the *goal description* $s_\star$ is a partial state. A state s is a *goal state* iff $s_\star$ is satisfied in s, and a belief state B is a goal belief state iff each state $s \in B$ is a goal state. $\mathcal{O}$ is a finite set of *actions* partitioned into *causative actions* $\mathcal{O}_c$ and *sensing actions* $\mathcal{O}_s$. Causative actions are of the form $a_c = \langle Pre, Eff \rangle$, where the *precondition Pre* is a partial state, and the *effect Eff* is a finite set of partial states *eff*, the *nondeterministic outcomes* of a. The *application* of a nondeterministic outcome *eff* to a state s is the state $app(eff, s)$ that results from updating s with *eff*. The application of an effect *Eff* to s is the set of states $app(Eff, s) = \{ app(eff, s) \mid eff \in Eff \}$ that might be reached by applying a nondeterministic outcome from *Eff* to s. Sensing actions are of the form $a_s = \langle Pre, Obs \rangle$, where the *precondition Pre* is a partial state, and the *observed variables Obs* are a subset of $\mathcal{V}$. An action is *applicable* in a state s iff its precondition is satisfied in s, and it is applicable in a belief state B if it is applicable in all $s \in B$. Actions are applied in belief states and result in *sets* of belief states. The application of an action in a belief state B is undefined if the action is inapplicable in B. Otherwise, the application of a causative action $a_c = \langle Pre, Eff \rangle$ to B is the singleton set $app(a_c, B) = \{ \{ app(eff, s) \mid eff \in Eff, s \in B \} \}$, and the application of a sensing action $a_s = \langle Pre, Obs \rangle$ to B is the set of nonempty belief states that result from splitting B according to possible observations, i.e., $app(a_s, B) = \{ \{ s \in B \mid s' \subseteq s \} \mid s' \text{ partial state with scope}(s') = Obs \} \setminus \{ \emptyset \}$. All actions have unit cost. Partially observable nondeterministic planning tasks as defined above induce nondeterministic transition systems where the nodes are the (reachable) belief states and where there is an arc from a belief state B to a belief state B' labeled with an action a iff a is applicable in B and $B' \in app(a, B)$. Given a partially observable nondeterministic planning task, we seek a strong cyclic plan solving the task, i.e., a partial mapping π from belief states to applicable actions such that for all belief states B reachable from the initial belief state $B_0 = \{ s \in \mathcal{S} \mid s \text{ satisfies } s_0 \}$ following π, B is either a goal belief state, or π is defined for B and at least one goal belief state is reachable from B following π. Later, we will occasionally simplify a partially observable problem by *assuming full observability*. In that case, the induced transition system will be defined slightly differently: First, all nodes will be world states instead of belief states, second, sensing actions will be ignored (since sensing occurs implicitly), and third, applying a causative action $a_c = \langle Pre, Eff \rangle$ to a node representing a state s will no longer lead to a unique successor node, but rather to one successor node for each successor state in $\{ app(eff, s) \mid eff \in Eff \}$ (i.e., AND nodes in the transition system are caused by nondeterministic actions instead of splitting of belief states). Also, we will sometimes simplify partially observable nondeterministic problems by *determinizing* them. In that case, we replace each causative action $a_c = \langle Pre, Eff \rangle$, $Eff = \{ eff_1, \ldots, eff_n \}$, by n causative actions $a_c^i = \langle Pre, \{ eff_i \} \rangle$ for $i = 1, \ldots, n$. Together with a unique initial state, this essentially leads to a classical planning problem.

2.2   Pattern-Database Heuristics

In classical planning, pattern-database heuristics work by projecting the planning task to a set of variables $P \subseteq \mathcal{V}$, the pattern, solving the resulting simplified planning task optimally, storing the optimal goal distances of all abstract states in a pattern database, and eventually using these abstract distances as heuristic values during search [7]. In addition, one often uses more than one pattern and maximizes over non-additive patterns and adds heuristic values from provably additive patterns. The most accurate admissible heuristic obtainable from a set of patterns is the so-called canonical heuristic function [10], which we will also use in this work. Formally, the projection of a partially observable nondeterministic planning task $\Pi = \langle \mathcal{V}, s_0, s_\star, \mathcal{O} \rangle$ to a pattern $P \subseteq \mathcal{V}$ is defined component- and element-wise: $\Pi|_P = \langle P, s_0|_P, s_\star|_P, \mathcal{O}|_P \rangle$, where $s|_P(v) = s(v)$ for all $v \in \mathrm{scope}(s) \cap P$, and $s|_P(v) = \bot$, otherwise; where $\mathcal{O}|_P = \{a|_P \mid a \in \mathcal{O}\}$, $a_c|_P = \langle Pre|_P, \{eff|_P \mid eff \in Eff\} \rangle$ for each causative action $a_c = \langle Pre, Eff \rangle$, and $a_s|_P = \langle Pre|_P, Obs \cap P \rangle$ for each sensing action $a_s = \langle Pre, Obs \rangle$. To ensure that projections preserve action applications and goal states, we require that for each pattern P to which we project, all variables in P are either observable by some sensing action, or do not occur in any precondition or goal condition, or their value is known initially and never becomes uncertain through any action application.

3   Simplifying a Partially Observable Nondeterministic Planning Task

The only problem simplification that occurs in pattern-database heuristics for classical planning is the projection to the pattern. Our partially observable nondeterministic problems differ from classical problems in two respects: nondeterministic actions and partial observability. Our main research question is to investigate the best way how to deal with these two aspects when computing pattern databases. Both nondeterminism and partial observability can easily be retained in the abstraction: If an action a leads from state s to one of two different states s_1' and s_2' in the original problem, and s_1' and s_2' can still be distinguished in the abstraction under consideration, then a will still be nondeterministic in the abstract problem, leading from the abstraction of s to either the abstraction of s_1' or the abstraction of s_2'. Similarly, if two states s_1 and s_2 cannot be distinguished in the original problem and belong to some common belief state B, their abstract versions cannot be distinguished in the abstract problem and the abstraction of B will contain the abstractions of s_1 and of s_2. Thus, besides abstracting to a pattern, we have four possibilities how to further simplify the abstract problem, namely all combinations of determinizing or not determinizing the problem and assuming or not assuming full observability in the abstraction. The resulting abstract problem will fall into one of the four categories in the following table:

	determinization	
	yes	*no*
observability *full*	**(A)** FO-Det PSPACE-complete [5]	**(B)** FO-NDet EXPTIME-complete [15]
partial	**(C)** PO-Det EXPSPACE-complete [19]	**(D)** PO-NDet 2-EXPTIME-complete [19]

This suggests that the abstract problem will be easier to solve the more sources of complexity (partial observability, nondeterminism) we abstract away. On the other hand, we expect better-informed heuristics and better guidance the fewer of these sources we abstract away:

(A) *Full observability, determinization (FO-Det):* This leads to a classical abstract problem that we can solve with classical regression search as it is usually done when computing PDB heuristics for classical problems. Information about nondeterministic outcomes belonging to the same original nondeterministic action is lost. Therefore, we implicitly minimize over possible action outcomes and thus underestimate true worst case or expected case costs. The resulting optimistic goal distances are stored in PDBs for all patterns in the pattern collection under consideration. During LAO* search, when PDB values are retrieved, since the PDBs contain (projected) world states as keys, we cannot directly look up a heuristic value for the (projection of the) belief state B we want to evaluate. Rather, we have to consider the (projections of the) world states s contained in B individually. This poses two challenges: The practical challenge lies in the fact that B can contain exponentially many world states in the number of state variables, which leads to prohibitively many PDB lookups for a single heuristic evaluation of a belief state. We resolve this by experimenting with different numbers of world state samples from B (sampling 1, 5, 10, 15, or all states). The conceptual challenge is the question how to aggregate heuristic values for individual states $s \in B$. Summing costs corresponds to assuming that all $s \in B$ have to be solved independently without positive interactions of the individual plans for each, whereas maximizing corresponds to assuming maximal positive interaction, where an optimal plan for the most expensive state $s \in B$ happens to solve all other states in B along the way. We experimented with both possible aggregation rules.

(B) *Full observability, no determinization (FO-NDet):* In this case, we end up with an AND/OR graph (a nondeterministic transition system) in the abstraction with splitting over causative action outcomes instead of over sensing action outcomes. This leads to the question of which cost measure to use in the abstract transition system. If we used weak (*optimistic*) goal distances, this would be the same as the FO-Det case above. We cannot use strong (*pessimistic*) goal distances, since this would assign cost values of ∞ to belief states that actually admit a strong cyclic solution. Instead, we perform value iteration on the resulting abstract AND/OR graph to label the abstract states with *expected* costs, i.e., expected numbers of steps to the nearest goal state. Lacking information about probabilities of different action outcomes, we assign them uniform probabilities. Moreover, the remarks about sampling of world states from the belief state under consideration from the FO-Det case still apply.

(C) *Partial observability, determinization (PO-Det):* In this case, the only uncertainty in any reachable belief state comes from initial state uncertainty. We end up with an AND/OR graph with splitting over sensing action outcomes. If the initial state happens to be unique (fully observable), PO-Det amounts to FO-Det, and the complexity reduces from EXPSPACE-complete to PSPACE-complete.

(D) *Partial observability, no determinization (PO-NDet):* In this case, states in the abstract transition system – and therefore the keys in the PDBs – are still belief states (not world states). As in the other cases where AND nodes in the abstract transition systems are involved, we have to choose an aggregation rule for interior nodes (optimistic, pessimistic, or expected costs). Again, we use expected costs under the assumption that each successor of an AND node has the same weight. We leave the idea of weighing successor nodes (belief states) by cardinality for future work.

In the experiments below we compare three of these four approaches among each other and to (a) a delete-relaxation approach with additional determinization and assumption of full observability and (b) the blind heuristic.

4   Implementation Details

We implemented a tool in Java that computes strong cyclic plans for partially observable nondeterministic planning tasks using LAO* search [9] guided by FO-Det, FO-NDet and PO-NDet PDB heuristics.[1] In all cases, we use the canonical heuristic function induced by a pattern collection computed using Haslum et al.'s local search in the space of pattern collections [10]. In the case where we preserve partial observability in the abstraction (PO-NDet), we consider two different ways of computing a pattern collection: the one where we also assume partial observability during pattern search, and the one where we avoid searching for a suitable pattern collection in the *belief* space by assuming *full* observability during pattern search. After that local search terminates, we use the resulting pattern collection to create pattern databases under *partial* observability. Within LAO*, we use a nonstandard expansion strategy in the case when there is no unexpanded non-goal leaf node in the most promising partial solution graph: We alternate between expanding an unexpanded non-goal leaf node with *minimal h value* outside the most promising partial solution graph and expanding

---

[1] We disregard PO-Det for the following reasons: (a) The additional simplification over PO-NDet appears minor and in PO-Det we would still have to deal with an AND/OR graph (instead of simply an OR graph) in the abstraction, and (b) two of the three benchmarks domains we consider (FR and BLOCKS, see below) have fully observable initial states, i.e., in these benchmarks PO-Det and FO-Det would collapse anyway.

an unexpanded non-goal leaf node outside the most promising partial solution graph which was *created earliest* among all such nodes. Moreover, our LAO* implementation uses maximization and discounting to aggregate cost estimates at interior nodes. Belief states and transitions between them are represented symbolically using Binary Decision Diagrams (BDDs) [3]. Sampling of world states from belief states represented as BDDs is done uniformly with replacement.

5   Experiments

We ran our planner on a compute server equipped with AMD Opteron 2.3 GHz CPUs. For each single planner run, we imposed a 4GB memory limit and a 30 minute time limit on the JRE. The time for the search for a pattern collection was limited to 10 minutes. When that limit was reached, the best pattern collection found so far was used. If the pattern collection search terminated in less than 10 minutes, the main LAO* search was allowed to use up the remainder of the original 30 minutes.

5.1   Benchmark Domains

We adapted the FIRSTRESPONDERS (FR) and BLOCKSWORLD (BLOCKS) domains from the fully observable nondeterministic track of the International Planning Competition 2008 by requiring active sensing for certain state variables:

- FR: The task is to plan a rescue operation where fires have to be extinguished and victims have to be treated on-scene or at a hospital. We required active sensing for victims' health statuses and for whether fires are still burning or already extinguished.
- BLOCKS: Unlike in the classical BLOCKS domain, where towers of blocks have to be reconfigured using deterministic block movement actions, in our formalization there are actions that can fail, like transferring a block from one tower to another. We require active sensing for block positions.

In addition, we experimented with a variant of the Canadian Traveler Problem:

- CTP: The Canadian Traveler Problem [17] is originally a probabilistic planning problem which we transformed into a partially observable nondeterministic one. It consists of a road map where an agent has to travel from a start to a goal location. In the original formalism, each road is passable with a specific probability and driving roads has different costs. In our transformation, driving a road has unit costs and there are roads which are definitively passable, definitively not passable or for which it is unknown if they are passable. Sensing actions are used to determine if an incident road is passable or not.

5.2   Belief State Sampling

When we assume full observability in the abstractions, in order to evaluate a belief state B during LAO* search, we need to sample world states from B, evaluate them individually, and aggregate the resulting heuristic values into a heuristic value for B. Before comparing FO-Det, FO-NDet, and PO-NDet, we first want to find suitable parameters for the numbers of belief state samples (we experimented with 1, 5, 10, 15, all) and aggregation methods (we experimented with maximizing and adding) used in FO-Det and FO-NDet. The results are summarized in Table 1. For all sampling methods except for "all", sampling is with replacements. Sampling "all" considers each state from B exactly once. In this experiment, for each problem instance, we use the same pattern collection for all configurations of sample numbers and aggregation methods to improve comparability of the results. Therefore, preprocessing times (pattern collection computation times) are the same for all configurations and hence omitted from the table. In the FR domain with summation, coverage and guidance tend to increase with the number of samples with the exception of sampling all states. With summation, it is not a good idea to sum over *all* world states, because this introduces an unjustified bias of the search towards low-cardinality belief states. With maximization, we get mixed guidance, time and coverage results for different numbers of samples, with a small advantage of maximizing over *all* world states. Overall, in FR FO-NDet has a higher coverage than FO-Det. In the BLOCKS domain, it turns out that it is often cheaper to sample *all* world states (without replacement) than to use a fixed number of samples (with replacement), since the cardinalities of the encountered belief states are very small (typically less than 10). When sampling is used, guidance and search time tend to improve with the number of samples. That means that time spent for sampling is compensated by better guidance, and in terms of coverage, FO-Det slightly outperforms FO-NDet. Overall, in BLOCKS FO-Det tends to outperform FO-NDet. In the CTP domain, it was not possible to enumerate all world states of the belief states encountered during search because of their exponential cardinality. There is no significant difference between FO-Det and FO-NDet or between maximizing and summing in the CTP domain. In conclusion, except for a few BLOCKS instances, coverage is slightly higher with FO-NDet than with FO-Det, and in both cases, the sweet spot of the sample number seems to be around 10 or 15. Summing over samples appears a bit more promising than maximizing over them.

5.3   Pattern Selection

When we assume partial observability in the abstraction, we are faced with different ways of performing the search for suitable pattern collections. In Table 2, we report on an experiment for the PO-NDet case with the following three configurations: In configuration "steps 0", we perform no pattern collection search at all, but rather use a collection of singleton patterns with one pattern for each goal variable. In configuration "pop mip0.5", we assume partial observability also

Table 1. Coverage (cov) and guidance (number of node expansions, exp) and search times (time, in seconds) on commonly solved problems 30 (FO-Det) and 28 (FO-Ndet) in FR, 10 in BLOCKS, 26 in CTP) for different numbers of samples (1, 5, 10, 15, all) and different aggregation methods (maximizing and adding)

Domain	n	FO-Det max cov	exp	time	FO-Det sum cov	exp	time	FO-NDet max cov	exp	time	FO-NDet sum cov	exp	time
FR	1	42	13835	995	41	13835	1357	40	11084	1125	40	11084	1077
(75 tasks)	5	54	6161	291	58	3644	156	58	6599	855	60	4868	206
	10	56	12194	755	62	2716	162	55	11097	494	64	3338	117
	15	51	11267	579	62	4481	320	56	11420	631	65	4998	341
	all	54	11085	395	32	27048	1900	59	9810	309	31	12751	665
BLOCKS	1	12	3573	24	12	3573	46	14	4024	49	14	4024	76
(30 tasks)	5	14	2766	50	12	2214	34	13	2647	52	13	3261	89
	10	13	2509	34	14	1863	37	12	1699	25	12	3532	77
	15	14	1922	31	14	1796	33	12	1271	25	13	2495	60
	all	13	2392	22	14	1618	16	14	2731	61	12	3007	49
CTP	1	26	751	28	26	751	31	26	728	29	26	728	32
(46 tasks)	5	26	494	76	26	460	79	26	507	74	26	488	86
	10	26	560	154	26	428	143	26	561	147	26	391	121
	15	26	518	196	26	401	195	26	523	202	26	408	198
	all	0	—	—	0	—	—	0	—	—	0	—	—

during pattern collection search and use a minimal improvement threshold [10] of 0.5 (i.e., we only perform a local search step in the pattern collection search if the fraction of samples for which the canonical heuristic value is improved is at least 0.5). Similarly, in configuration "fop mip0.5", we assume *full* observability during pattern collection search and use a minimal improvement threshold of 0.5 as well. From the data in Table 2, we conclude that it is typically preferable to search for better pattern collections than the trivial singleton pattern collections, and that assuming full observability during that search tends to improve total time because the preprocessing time is significantly decreased, whereas assuming partial observability generates better patterns at a higher preprocessing cost, but leads to faster (better informed) LAO* search.

5.4 Internal Comparison of FO-Det, FO-NDet, and PO-NDet

To determine the overall best PDB configuration, we compare the best configurations of FO-Det, FO-NDet, and PO-NDet side by side in Table 3. For FO-Det and FO-NDet, we use the configurations with summation over 15 belief state samples, and for all three configurations, we use a minimal improvement threshold of 0.5. We observe that the additional informedness of PO-NDet over the more simplistic FO-Det and FO-NDet configurations translates into fewer node expansions as well as lower search and overall times. Although there is no significant resulting increase in coverage, altogether PO-NDet appears dominant.

Table 2. Coverage (cov) and guidance (number of node expansions, exp), search times (stm, in seconds), and total times (ttm, in seconds, including pattern collection search) on commonly solved problems (39 in FR, 11 in BLOCKS, 23 in CTP) for different configurations of the pattern collection search for PO-NDet

Domain	PO-NDet											
	steps 0				pop mip0.5				fop mip0.5			
	cov	exp	stm	ttm	cov	exp	stm	ttm	cov	exp	stm	ttm
FR	40	25278	3079	3111	70	5887	*218*	1058	*73*	*5819*	262	*588*
BLOCKS	*13*	6560	630	*644*	12	*5343*	*423*	673	12	6902	779	866
CTP	*26*	526	9	*15*	23	*461*	*4*	862	*26*	480	5	314
OVERALL	79	32364	3718	3770	105	*11691*	*645*	2593	*111*	13201	1046	*1768*

Table 3. Coverage (cov) and guidance (number of node expansions, exp), search times (stm, in seconds), and total times (ttm, in seconds, including pattern collection search) on commonly solved problems (69 in FR, 10 in BLOCKS, 26 in CTP) for LAO* search with best FO-Det, FO-NDet, and PO-NDet configuration

Domain	FO-Det sum15 mip0.5				FO-NDet sum15 mip0.5				PO-NDet fop mip0.5			
	cov	exp	stm	ttm	cov	exp	stm	ttm	cov	exp	stm	ttm
FR	70	40159	9330	10320	72	28938	9140	11327	*73*	*26414*	*3851*	*6095*
BLOCKS	*14*	1796	33	85	13	2558	59	113	12	*1670*	*19*	*78*
CTP	*26*	*607*	281	*849*	*26*	*607*	270	1004	*26*	630	*7*	923
OVERALL	110	42562	9644	11254	*111*	32103	9469	12444	*111*	*28714*	*3877*	*7096*

5.5 Comparison to Delete Relaxation and Baseline

In order to assess how well our best PDB configuration (PO-NDet fop mip0.5) does in comparison to an established technique (FF heuristic [12] under assumption of full observability and determinization) and a trivial baseline (blind heuristic), we provide a direct comparison in Table 4. We can conclude that PDBs outperform FF and blind heuristic in the FR and CTP domains in terms of coverage, guidance and runtime, whereas they perform slightly worse than FF in the BLOCKS domain. A comparison to a cleverer delete-relaxation approach like LUGs [4] that could shift the picture in favor of delete relaxation again, is left for future work. We remark that we do not expect a completely reversed picture with LUGs, since the PDB approach that is most comparable to the FF approach under full observability and with determinization, namely FO-Det, still leads to a higher coverage than FF (110 vs. 78 solved problems).

Table 4. Coverage (cov) and guidance (number of node expansions, exp), search times (stm, in seconds), and total times (ttm, in seconds, including pattern collection search) on commonly solved problems (16 in FR, 6 in BLOCKS, 13 in CTP) for LAO* search with blind heuristic, FF heuristic under assumption of full observability and determinization, and the best PDB configuration

Domain	blind			FF			PO-NDet fop mip0.5			
	cov	exp	stm=ttm	cov	exp	stm=ttm	cov	exp	stm	ttm
FR	16	18716	1337	47	4381	239	*73*	*662*	*12*	*95*
BLOCKS	6	15937	488	*15*	*241*	*20*	12	276	2	37
CTP	13	36124	2128	16	13714	735	*26*	*152*	*1*	*88*
OVERALL	35	70777	3954	78	18336	993	*111*	*1090*	*16*	*219*

6   Conclusion and Future Work

We have demonstrated that abstraction heuristics can successfully guide LAO* search for strong cyclic plans for partially observable nondeterministic planning problems towards goal belief states, and that the guidance is at least competitive with the guidance provided by a delete-relaxation heuristic. We argued experimentally that preserving partial observability and nondeterminism in the abstraction leads to more informative heuristics at the cost of more expensive preprocessing. From a global perspective, the better accuracy of such heuristics pays off with better overall planner performance.

Future work includes a comparison of our results to those of Bryce et al. [4] that also takes their labeled uncertainty graph (LUG) into account as an efficient data structure for the direct evaluation of belief states within a delete-relaxation approach. Moreover, we plan to investigate more realistic benchmark problems arising from robotic applications.

Acknowledgments. This work was partly supported by the German Research Foundation (DFG) as part of the Transregional Collaborative Research Center "Automatic Verification and Analysis of Complex Systems" (SFB/TR 14 AVACS, see http://www.avacs.org).

References

1. Bercher, P., Mattmüller, R.: A planning graph heuristic for forward-chaining adversarial planning. In: Proceedings of the 18th European Conference on Artificial Intelligence (ECAI 2008), pp. 921–922 (2008)
2. Bercher, P., Mattmüller, R.: Solving non-deterministic planning problems with pattern database heuristics. In: Mertsching, B., Hund, M., Aziz, Z. (eds.) KI 2009. LNCS (LNAI), vol. 5803, pp. 57–64. Springer, Heidelberg (2009)
3. Bryant, R.E.: Graph-based algorithms for boolean function manipulation. IEEE Transactions on Computers 35(8), 677–691 (1986)

4. Bryce, D., Kambhampati, S., Smith, D.E.: Planning graph heuristics for belief space search. Journal of Artificial Intelligence Research 26, 35–99 (2006)
5. Bylander, T.: The computational complexity of propositional strips planning. Artificial Intelligence 69(1-2), 165–204 (1994)
6. Cimatti, A., Pistore, M., Roveri, M., Traverso, P.: Weak, strong, and strong cyclic planning via symbolic model checking. Artificial Intelligence 147(1-2), 35–84 (2003)
7. Culberson, J.C., Schaeffer, J.: Searching with pattern databases. In: McCalla, G.I. (ed.) Canadian AI 1996. LNCS, vol. 1081, pp. 402–416. Springer, Heidelberg (1996)
8. Fu, J., Ng, V., Bastani, F.B., Yen, I.L.: Simple and fast strong cyclic planning for fully-observable nondeterministic planning problems. In: Proc. 22nd International Joint Conference on Artificial Intelligence (IJCAI 2011), pp. 1949–1954 (2011)
9. Hansen, E.A., Zilberstein, S.: LAO*: A heuristic search algorithm that finds solutions with loops. Artificial Intelligence 129(1-2), 35–62 (2001)
10. Haslum, P., Botea, A., Helmert, M., Bonet, B., Koenig, S.: Domain-independent construction of pattern database heuristics for cost-optimal planning. In: Proc. 22nd AAAI Conference on Artificial Intelligence (AAAI 2007), pp. 1007–1012 (2007)
11. Helmert, M., Röger, G., Seipp, J., Karpas, E., Hoffmann, J., Keyder, E., Nissim, R., Richter, S., Westphal, M.: Fast downward stone soup (planner abstract). In: Seventh International Planning Competition (IPC 2011), Deterministic Part, pp. 38–45 (2011)
12. Hoffmann, J., Nebel, B.: The FF planning system: Fast plan generation through heuristic search. Journal of Artificial Intelligence Research 14, 253–302 (2001)
13. Kissmann, P., Edelkamp, S.: Solving fully-observable non-deterministic planning problems via translation into a general game. In: Mertsching, B., Hund, M., Aziz, Z. (eds.) KI 2009. LNCS (LNAI), vol. 5803, pp. 1–8. Springer, Heidelberg (2009)
14. Kuter, U., Nau, D.S., Reisner, E., Goldman, R.P.: Using classical planners to solve nondeterministic planning problems. In: Proc. 18th International Conference on Automated Planning and Scheduling (ICAPS 2008), pp. 190–197 (2008)
15. Littman, M.L.: Probabilistic propositional planning: Representations and complexity. In: Proc. 14th National Conference on Artificial Intelligence (AAAI 1997), pp. 748–754. MIT Press (1997)
16. Mattmüller, R., Ortlieb, M., Helmert, M., Bercher, P.: Pattern database heuristics for fully observable nondeterministic planning. In: Proc. 20th International Conference on Automated Planning and Scheduling (ICAPS 2010), pp. 105–112 (2010)
17. Papadimitriou, C.H., Yannakakis, M.: Shortest paths without a map. Theoretical Computer Science 84, 127–150 (1991)
18. Richter, S., Westphal, M., Helmert, M.: Lama 2008 and 2011 (planner abstract). In: Seventh International Planning Competition (IPC 2011), Deterministic Part, pp. 50–54 (2011)
19. Rintanen, J.: Complexity of planning with partial observability. In: Proc. 14th International Conference on Automated Planning and Scheduling (ICAPS 2004), pp. 345–354 (2004)

Automated Theorem Proving with Web Services

Björn Pelzer

Universität Koblenz-Landau, Institut für Informatik, 56070 Koblenz, Germany
bpelzer@uni-koblenz.de

Abstract. Automated theorem provers (ATP) usually operate on finite input where all relevant axioms and conjectures are known at the start of the proof attempt. However, when a prover is embedded in a real-world knowledge representation application, it may have to draw upon data that is not immediately available in a local file, for example by accessing databases and online sources such as web services. This leads both to technical problems such as latency times as well as to formal problems regarding soundness and completeness. We have integrated external data sources into our ATP system E-KRHyper and in its underlying hyper tableaux calculus. In this paper we describe the modifications and discuss problems and solutions pertaining to the integration. We also present an application of this integration for the purpose of abductive query relaxation.

1 Introduction

Automated theorem provers (ATP) usually operate on clearly defined logic problems, where axioms and conjectures are known from the start and no new data can enter during the derivation process. Given their roots as mathematical tools this is sufficient for many applications of ATP, but when a prover is employed within the context of knowledge representation, the ability to obtain and utilize more data during the derivation may become useful. Here the formal ontologies and datasets can be too extensive for a prover to handle in the conventional manner. Instead it is preferable to have the prover identify what data it needs during the reasoning and retrieve it from appropriate sources. Examples can be found in question answering (QA), where a prover can be used for the deduction of answers. An all-encompassing knowledge base (KB) would be too large to allow effective reasoning. This is particularly so since modern ATP usually work saturation-based, deriving all consequences from all axioms - yet obviously most axioms in such a KB are irrelevant for any given question. Also, much information is temporary in nature, such as timetables, currency exchange rates or weather forecasts, and attempting to incorporate it in a massive static KB appears futile. Instead such data should remain at its original sources, for example web services, to be requisitioned only when required. An obstacle is the slow communication with web services, which could cause delays in the reasoning. This can be mitigated by decoupling the communication from the reasoning process and inserting the received data asynchronously.

This necessitates modifications both to the prover and its underlying calculus. We will describe such adaptations within the context of our German language QA system *LogAnswer*[1] [6,7,8], where we employ our theorem prover *E-KRHyper*[2] [12] as

---

[1] http://www.loganswer.de

[2] http://www.uni-koblenz.de/~bpelzer/ekrhyper

I.J. Timm and M. Thimm (Eds.): KI 2013, LNAI 8077, pp. 152–163, 2013.
© Springer-Verlag Berlin Heidelberg 2013

a reasoning component. E-KRHyper (*Knowledge Representation Hyper Tableaux with Equality*) is an ATP and a model generation system for first-order logic (FOL) with equality. It is an implementation of the *hyper tableaux calculus* [2] and its extension with a superposition-based [1] handling of equality, the *E-hyper tableaux calculus* [3].

We elaborate on our motivations and describe our modifications, including how we deal with communication delays. We also examine the issues of soundness and completeness, the latter being problematic due to complications inherent to any attempt at incorporating external knowledge sources. Finally we describe a special application of the new features for the purpose of abductive query relaxation.

We assume a basic understanding of FOL. While the paper introduces its concepts within the context of hyper tableaux, the content is largely independent of any particular FOL calculus or readily adapted if necessary.

2   Motivation and Related Work

QA systems traditionally derive their answers from a static KB derived from a document collection [9]. Even when a QA system employs the reasoning of ATP, this kind of architecture precludes answering questions which do not have permanent answers, like:

Q_1: *"What is the weather in Stockholm today?"*
Q_2: *"How much is €2.99 in US-Dollars?"*
Q_3: *"When does the next train to the CeBIT leave?"*

Answering Q_1 requires access to weather data by time and location. Q_2 needs current currency exchange rates and arithmetics. Answering Q_3 needs not only time tables, but also the location of the CeBIT trade fair and the current location of the user. Such information cannot be found in a static knowledge base, and the ability to handle questions of this type would greatly broaden the scope and thereby the appeal of a QA system.

The QA context and the slow access to web services are the reasons why we want to connect them directly into the reasoning of the ATP system, rather than handling them separately in some preprocessing stage. While in QA it is common to first use heuristics and information retrieval methods to narrow down the full KB to some hopefully answer-relevant fragments, analogous pre-emptive web service requests before the reasoning are unfeasible due to the inability to clearly identify which requests are actually relevant. For example, in the case of question Q_1 it does not make much sense to send requests for data on words like *"weather"* and *"Stockholm"* to all connected web services before the actual relation between these words is known. The multitude of pre-emptive requests would take much time to process and result in irrelevant data, like weather information about cities other than Stockholm and Stockholm-related information outside the domain of weather. Instead we wish to access the slow web services as rarely as possible, and hence the requests should be very specific in such manner that the result will close a clearly identified and proof-relevant gap in the knowledge. This is best done in the ATP, where the relations between the words and concepts of the question are available during the derivation.

For similar reasons we also restrict ourselves to "factoid" web services that provide their respective data in an almost atomic form which the prover can treat as unit clauses. Examples would be *"cloudy"* in response to Q_1, or numeric replies like *"3.74"* for Q_2.

A related system is *SPASS-XDB* [14,15], which combines the ATP *SPASS* with web services and other external knowledge sources, but which lacks a natural language interface. The publications on SPASS-XDB focus on the selection of connected services and their possible practical usage, and less on the formal grounding of the integration or the inherent problems of completeness. They introduce the expression of *external sources (of axioms)* to refer to sources such as web services in a more abstract manner. We adopt this expression in the sequel. While we are primarily interested in web services, the more general notion allows us to use the same techniques both for web services and for any other sources with comparable characteristics, like websites that are sufficiently structured for automated processing, and even sources that are not web-based, for example large local databases.

Outside of FOL we can find similarities in the *DVLHEX* solver [5] for answer set programming (ASP). However, ultimately the fundamental differences between ASP and FOL make it difficult to apply the approach of one area within the other.

3   Formal Representation of External Sources

We now provide the formal underpinning for external sources of axioms. First we assume that the systems underlying such sources are accessed by requests, and each request is answered by a response. We introduce a new binary predicate symbol $ext/2$ that is used to represent the relation between request and response in the form of an atom $ext(q, a)$, where the *request term* q is a term representing the request and the *response term* a is a term representing the response. An external source can then be represented as a possibly infinite set of positive *ext*-units which list the requests and the associated responses. The terms q and a can be formed ina way that also encodes identity and functionality of the represented source. This allows representing multiple resources with different access methods as one external source, for example:

$ext(weather\_service(weather('Stockholm', 27\text{-}06\text{-}2012)), 'cloudy') \leftarrow$
$ext(weather\_service(temperature('Stockholm', 27\text{-}06\text{-}2012)), '15\,°C') \leftarrow$
$ext(currency\_exchange\_service(eur, usd, 2.99, 27\text{-}06\text{-}2012), '\$3.74') \leftarrow$

We assume external sources to consist only of ground positive *ext*-units, as web services typically only accept fully specified requests without variables, and we want to avoid variable requests anyway, as we only want to access web services to fill clearly identified gaps in the KB.

It must be stressed that this set representation is idealized, and its purpose is to make external sources accessible within a logical calculus. In practice the full extent of the data available from a web service is not known, as we can only send requests for specific items. We also assume all *ext*-units of external sources to always be true. Where this is a problem, a time stamp encoding as in the example above may help: The ATP can use its internal time or some other temporal data to time stamp its requests, thereby ensuring that only valid responses are returned. Of course time remains a problematic issue, as external sources may gain new *ext*-units and lose old ones over time. For example, the currency exchange service will not contain the exchange rates of tomorrow before tomorrow, and it might not keep an archive of past exchange rates. This means that the same request may sometimes result in a response and sometimes not. We have to accept this, and for the formalization we simply assume any external source to be constant, as any further attempt to account for temporal changes on the formal level is likely to overcomplicate the calculus extension beyond its benefits.

In the sequel, when defining our extended calculus, we will summarize all *ext*-units from external sources in a set $\mathcal{C}^{ext}$, and refer to this set as a single external source. Other clauses that are immediately available to the reasoning in the conventional manner will be regarded as belonging to a clause set $\mathcal{C}$. As an external source $\mathcal{C}^{ext}$ is a set of positive ground *ext*-units, $\mathcal{C}^{ext}$ is always satisfiable and so are all its elements. An ordinary clause set $\mathcal{C}$ may be unsatisfiable or satisfiable. Even if $\mathcal{C}$ is satisfiable, $\mathcal{C} \cup \mathcal{C}^{ext}$ may be unsatisfiable or satisfiable. Hence we call $\mathcal{C}$ *(un)satisfiable with respect to* $\mathcal{C}^{ext}$. Our extended calculus in the upcoming section attempts to determine this notion of satisfiability for a given clause set $\mathcal{C}$ and an external source $\mathcal{C}^{ext}$.

4   External Sources in Hyper Tableaux

In order to deal with external sources in the hyper tableaux calculus [2] we modify its only inference rule, the *hyper extension step*. While we refer to the original publication for the full details, the following quick summary of hyper tableaux should provide an idea and introduce some concepts required for the detailed extension below. A hyper tableau **T** for a clause set $\mathcal{C}$ is a tree labeled with literals. Let **B** be a branch in **T**, and let $[\![\mathbf{B}]\!]$ denote the minimal Herbrand model of the literals labeling **B** when each literal is treated as a universally quantified unit clause. Let $C = \mathcal{A} \leftarrow \mathcal{B}$ be a clause from $\mathcal{C}$ with $\mathcal{A}$ being the set of positive atoms and $\mathcal{B}$ the negated atoms. The hyper extension step extends **B** with C if all its atoms $B_1, \ldots, B_n \in \mathcal{B}$ (treated as a universally quantified conjunction) unify with literals from **B**, i.e. there is a most general substitution σ such that $[\![\mathbf{B}]\!] \models \forall (B_1 \wedge \ldots \wedge B_n)\sigma$. If the atoms in $\mathcal{A}$ share any variables, these are eliminated by *purification*, which means applying some ground substitution π. The literals from $C\sigma\pi$ are attached as new leaves to **B**. Branches with leaves labeled with negative literals are *closed* from further extension. The others are *open*. If **T** has only closed branches then $\mathcal{C}$ is unsatisfiable. If an open branch cannot be extended in a non-redundant manner, then its literals form a model for $\mathcal{C}$.

The new *hyper extension step with external access* works mostly like the original, except that *ext*-atoms from negative literals in the extending clause can also unify with units from the external source, provided the request terms in these atoms are ground before their respective unification. This may be because they were already ground in the first place in the extending clause, or because their variables got instantiated during the computation of σ. It is important to not that the new calculus is not complete (see Sec. 5), and hence a saturated open branch is not guaranteed to represent a model.

Let $\mathcal{C}$ be a finite clause set and let $\mathcal{C}^{ext}$ be an external source of ground *ext*-units. Hyper tableaux for $\mathcal{C}$ with respect to $\mathcal{C}^{ext}$ are inductively defined as follows:

Initialization step: A one node literal tree is a hyper tableau for $\mathcal{C}$ with respect to $\mathcal{C}^{ext}$.
    Its single branch is labeled as open.
Hyper extension step with external access: The following conditions are required:
    1. **B** is an open branch with the leaf node **N** in the hyper tableau **T**.

2. $C = \mathcal{A} \leftarrow \mathcal{B}$ is a clause from $\mathcal{C}$ (referred to as the *extending clause*) with $\mathcal{A} = \{A_1, \ldots, A_m\}$ $(m \geq 0)$ and $\mathcal{B} = \{B_1, \ldots, B_n\}$ $(n \geq 0)$.

3. σ is a most general substitution such that $[\![\mathbf{B}]\!] \cup \mathcal{C}^{ext} \models \forall (B_1 \wedge \ldots \wedge B_n)\sigma$; in particular, with every $B_i \in \mathcal{B}$ associate the specific literal or unit clause L_i that forms this model, i.e. $L_i \models B_i\sigma$ and $L_i \in [\![\mathbf{B}]\!] \cup \mathcal{C}^{ext}$.

4. Let V be the *set of branch-instantiated variables*, which is defined as:
   (a) $x \in V$ if x occurs in some $B_i \in \mathcal{B}$ with $L_i \in [\![\mathbf{B}]\!]$ such that there is a most general substitution γ with $L_i \models B_i\gamma$ and $x\gamma$ is ground and there is a possibly empty substitution δ such that $\gamma\delta = \sigma$ (x is directly branch-instantiated).
   (b) If there is a $B_i = ext(q_i, a_i) \in \mathcal{B}$ with $L_i \in \mathcal{C}^{ext}$ and for every x occurring in q_i it holds that $x \in V$, then for every y occurring in a_i it holds that $y \in V$ (y is indirectly branch-instantiated).
   Then for every $B_i = ext(q_i, a_i) \in \mathcal{B}$ with $L_i \in \mathcal{C}^{ext}$ and for every variable x occurring in q_i it must hold that $x \in V$.

5. π is a purifying substitution for $C\sigma$.

If all the above conditions hold, then the literal tree $\mathbf{T}'$ is a hyper tableau for $\mathcal{C}$ with respect to $\mathcal{C}^{ext}$, where $\mathbf{T}'$ is obtained from $\mathbf{T}$ by attaching $m + n$ child nodes $M_1, \ldots, M_m, N_1, \ldots, N_n$ to $\mathbf{B}$ with respective labels $A_1\sigma\pi, \ldots, A_m\sigma\pi$ and $\neg B_1\sigma\pi, \ldots, \neg B_n\sigma\pi$ and labeling every new branch with positive leaf as open and every new branch with negative leaf as closed.

A *hyper tableaux derivation with external access* for $\mathcal{C}$ with respect to $\mathcal{C}^{ext}$ is a sequence of hyper tableaux that starts with the initialization step and where each hyper tableau after the initial one has been derived from its predecessor by a hyper extension step with external access. If such a derivation contains a closed hyper tableau, then $\mathcal{C}$ is unsatisfiable with respect to $\mathcal{C}^{ext}$.

As an example[3] consider the following clauses pertaining to the introductory question Q_3, consisting of :

C_1^{ext}: $ext(user\_location\_service, 'Cologne') \leftarrow$
C_2^{ext}: $ext(next\_train\_finder\_service('Cologne', 'Hanover'), '15:05') \leftarrow$
C_1: $at('CeBIT', 'Hanover') \leftarrow$
C_2: $next\_train\_to(Event, Time) \leftarrow$
$\qquad\qquad at(Event, ToCity),$
$\qquad\qquad ext(user\_location\_service, FromCity),$
$\qquad\qquad ext(next\_train\_finder\_service(FromCity, ToCity), Time)$
Q_3: $\leftarrow next\_train\_to('CeBIT', Time)$

The clauses C_1^{ext} and C_2^{ext} form $\mathcal{C}^{ext}$ while the others form $\mathcal{C}$. Clause C_3 is the FOL representation of the question Q_3 itself as a negated conjecture. The derivation (merged into a single tableau due to space reasons) is shown in Fig. 1. The unit C_1 has been added as a literal to the initial branch right away in a trivial hyper extension step. Then C_2 is selected as an extending clause. The atom of its first negative literal unifies with the branch literal $at('CeBIT', 'Hanover')$. This instantiates the variable *Event*

---

[3] We use the Prolog convention of denoting variables by unquoted capitalized identifiers.

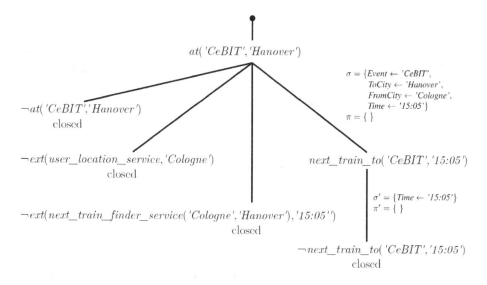

Fig. 1. Example hyper tableaux derivation

with *'CeBIT'* as well as *ToCity* with *'Hanover'*. The second negative literal of C_2, ¬*ext*(*user_location_service*, *FromCity*), has a ground request term which is used to retrieve *'Cologne'* from the external source, instantiating the variable *FromCity*.

Thus ¬*ext*(*next_train_finder_service*(*FromCity*, *ToCity*), *Time*), the third negative literal of C_2, can now be regarded as having a ground request term. This enables another request to the external source which instantiates the variable *Time* with *'15:05'*. All negative literals of C_2 have now been refuted using the common unifier σ. No purification is required, so π remains empty, and every σ-substituted literal is added as a new leaf, with the negative leaves closing their branches immediately. The branch for *next_train_to*(*'CeBIT'*, *'15:05'*) remains open, only to be closed in the next hyper extension step with C_3, thereby refuting the negated conjecture. In a QA system the answer *'15:05'* could then be extracted from the proof.

We now prove the soundness of hyper tableaux with external sources.

Theorem 1 (Soundness of Hyper Tableaux with External Sources). *Let C be a finite clause set and let C^{ext} be an external source. If the modified hyper tableaux calculus extended by the hyper extension step with external access derives a refutation for C with respect to C^{ext}, then C is unsatisfiable with respect to C^{ext}.*

Proof. We first show that the hyper extension step with external access preserves satisfiability. Let **B** be an open branch in a hyper tableau T for a finite clause set C and an external source C^{ext} of positive ground *ext*-units. Let $C = A \leftarrow B$ with $A = \{A_1, \ldots, A_m\}$ ($m \geq 0$) and $B = \{B_1, \ldots, B_n\}$ ($n \geq 0$) be a clause from C that serves as an extending clause in a hyper extension step with external access, using a most general unifier σ and a purifying substitution π. Assume C to be satisfiable with a model I. $[\![\mathbf{B}]\!] \cup C^{ext}$ consists only of positive unit clauses and is therefore satisfiable. Since

$[\![\mathbf{B}]\!] \cup \mathcal{C}^{ext} \models \forall (B_1 \wedge \ldots \wedge B_n)\sigma$, on the converse it must hold that $\neg B_1 \sigma \vee \ldots \vee \neg B_n \sigma$ is unsatisfiable. Thus $I \not\models \neg B_1 \vee \ldots \vee \neg B_n$, and instead it must hold that $I \models A_i$ for some $A_i \in \mathcal{A}$ for I to satisfy C. Then it also holds that $I \models A_i \sigma \pi$, and the new branch $\mathbf{B} \cdot M_i$ resulting from extending $\mathbf{B}$ by the node M_i labeled with $A_i \sigma \pi$ is satisfiable.

The contrapositive of the above is that if a hyper extension step with external access extends a branch $\mathbf{B}$ with no satisfiable branches, then $\mathbf{B}$ and the extending clause, the premises of this extension, are unsatisfiable with respect to $\mathcal{C}^{ext}$, too. Let therefore $\mathbf{T}$ be the closed tableau of the refutation of $\mathcal{C}$ with respect to $\mathcal{C}^{ext}$. From the contrapositive above we conclude that if a tableau $\mathbf{T}_i$ of a derivation contains only branches that are unsatisfiable , then so does the predecessor $\mathbf{T}_{i-1}$. The closed $\mathbf{T}$ contains only unsatisfiable branches. By induction on the length of the refutation we conclude that the premises of the first hyper extension step, i.e. the first extending clause and the empty initial branch, are unsatisfiable with respect to $\mathcal{C}^{ext}$, and so is $\mathcal{C}$.

5   Incompleteness

The extended calculus is not complete and thus it cannot be used for model generation, as it may end up with finite branches that are not closed, despite the input being unsatisfiable with respect to the external source. In a practical application this is unlikely to be much of a problem, but as the original hyper tableaux calculus is complete, the loss of completeness in the extension should be discussed. We believe completeness to be unattainable for external sources in general, regardless of the calculus. There are two major obstacles: Firstly, external sources typically only respond to specific requests, reflected in the need for ground request terms. If the exact term cannot be formed during the derivation, then an important response may remain inaccessible. Secondly, to form requests dynamically we must allow clauses with variables in request terms. Logically variables are more 'powerful' than ground terms, as a variable can subsume sets of terms, but it cannot access external sources. Neither problem can be circumvented due to the reality of web services, and they lead to various conflicts as shown below.

Consider the clauses $C_1^{ext} \in \mathcal{C}^{ext}$ and $C_1 \in \mathcal{C}$ with $C_1^{ext} = ext(q, a) \leftarrow$ and $C_1 = \leftarrow ext(x, y)$. Together the two clauses are unsatisfiable, but as there is no way to ground x, C_1^{ext} and the refutation remain out of reach. If we replace C_1 with its $C_2 = \leftarrow ext(q, y)$ the refutation is possible, which is unfortunate given that C_2 is an instance of C_1. Worse, now consider the clause $C_3 = p(y) \leftarrow ext(q, y)$ combined with C_1^{ext} and C_1: C_3 can access C_1^{ext} and derive $p(a)$, yet the refutation from C_1 and C_1^{ext} still fails.

The last example shows that we cannot simply disregard some web service data as unreachable and thereby irrelevant, because clearly a is retrieved, just not wherever it is needed. This can be mitigated by adding any successfully accessed unit from $\mathcal{C}^{ext}$ to $\mathcal{C}$, thereby turning it into a normal input clause that is accessible to all inferences. E-KRHyper offers this functionality, but it may have a negative effect on the performance by adding many ext-units, and it is not entirely compatible with model generation, as an ext-unit added to the input will not show up in any models derived before the addition. It also does not solve our initial problem with C_1 and C_1^{ext}.

An alternative approach is to transform $\mathcal{C}$ in a manner similar to range restriction, by adding domain clauses which enumerate the Herbrand domain in a special dom-predicate, and then to any clause C add a literal $\neg dom(x)$ for each variable x occurring in a request term of a negative *ext*-literal in C. This way request terms will always get ground-instantiated. However, a large Herbrand universe can result in a large number of irrelevant requests by exhaustively testing all possible request terms, which clearly goes against our motivations described in Sec. 2. Also, symbols exclusive to $\mathcal{C}^{ext}$ can only take part in the enumeration after having been accessed once, so important request terms may never be formed; C_1 and C_1^{ext} still cannot be refuted.

The aforementioned greater 'power' of variables leads to problems when trying to eliminate redundant clauses in an effort to keep the clause set small. Demodulation and subsumption are important tools for this, and in fact modern ATP are estimated to spend about 90% of their time on such operations rather than the normal calculus inferences [11]. Subsumption can allow non-ground clauses to eliminate ground clauses, which is problematic if only the latter could have accessed an external source. For example, together the aforementioned clauses C_1^{ext}, C_1 and C_2 are unsatisfiable with a refutation based on C_1^{ext} and C_2. But if C_1 first subsumes its instance C_2, then the refutation is prevented. Forbidding subsumption just for *ext*-literals is no solution, as any subsumption might remove symbols from the derivation that could have ended up in an important request term after a few inference steps. Demodulation in calculi with equality handling can have a similar effect, as it rewrites clauses with clauses that are equivalent yet simpler according to some term ordering. Consider the clauses $C_2^{ext} = ext(f(b), a) \leftarrow$, $C_4 = \leftarrow ext(f(b), y)$ and $C_5 = f(x) \simeq x \leftarrow$. Clearly there is a refutation between C_2^{ext} and C_4, but most modern ATP would first use C_5 to demodulate C_4 into $\leftarrow ext(b, y)$. An analogous demodulation of C_2^{ext} is not possible due to its limited accessibility, and so the one-sided simplification prevents the refutation. Similar to the subsumption problem above, demodulation would have to be outright forbidden to prevent such cases.

Clause set simplifications are so important in theorem proving that their abandonment is unacceptable, even though we are clearly losing proof confluence. Generally the problems described here appear to be inescapable consequences of the technical reality of external sources.[4] On a more positive note they may not be very likely in practical usage, as careful construction of the clauses with *ext*-literals can avoid such situations in the first place. Also, even if the access to external sources is not complete, it nevertheless allows more proofs than having no access at all.

6 Implementation

The implementation consists of the modified E-KRHyper and an interface module between the prover and the web services. The latter enables an asynchronous delivery of the responses to E-KRHyper, allowing the prover to reason concurrently while the interface carries out the slow web service communication, collecting the responses in a cache. The interface module accepts request terms from E-KRHyper over a socket. Each such request is immediately compared against the response cache and then answered synchronously[5] with one of the following three reply types:

---

[4] Indeed, we found the problems can be reproduced on SPASS-XDB, too.

[5] Note that the communication between prover and interface is synchronous, but the delivery of a web service response is asynchronous to the initial request.

wait: There is no response to this request in the cache yet, either because it is the first time E-KRHyper has made this request, in which case the interface forwards it in the proper form to the appropriate external source, or because the request has already been made at some earlier point, but the external source has not replied yet. Either way E-KRHyper continues its derivation with other inferences, and it will check again later on whether a response has been received in the meantime.

failed: The interface has already concluded the external communication regarding this particular request, but there was no successful response (the external source may be offline or simply have no data for this request). From a FOL point of view this is treated as C^{ext} not containing any unit matching this request.

<response>: The interface has already concluded the external communication regarding this particular request. It has received a proper response, converted it into a FOL response term and stored it in the cache. This is now sent to E-KRHyper as a reply. Depending on the web service it may be possible to have multiple responses to a given request; these are then treated as individual units by the prover.

In accordance with our assumption of temporally constant external sources the cache is maintained for the duration of the derivation, though optionally longer caching is possible. The prover also keeps track of pending requests that are still waiting for a response in the interface module. If an open branch cannot be extended and there are pending requests, then depending on the configuration E-KRHyper either waits until a response is received, or it postpones the branch and continues the derivation elsewhere.

Currently E-KRHyper and the interface can access the following external sources: *ECB Currency Exchange Rates*;[6] *Yahoo! GeoPlanet*,[7], which provides geographical information about cities and countries; *System Q&A TPTP*,[8] which is the intermediate interface that provides data to SPASS-XDB; and the *LogAnswer Ontology Browser*,[9] which is part of our LogAnswer project and which links ontological data from sources such as *OpenCyc* [10] and *DBpedia* [4]. Overall the integration of web services in E-KRHyper is still an experimental proof of concept with a limited range of sources.

7 Abductive Relaxation

When our LogAnswer QA system fails to find a perfect proof that answers a question, it uses *relaxation*: Heuristics remove one literal of the FOL question representation, thereby making the question less specific, and the proof attempt is restarted. This can be risky. For example, asking LogAnswer the question *"What is the weight of the 'Maus' ('Mouse') tank?"* will result in the gram weights of various species of mice, rather than the 188 tons of the German tank prototype from World War II [13]. Obviously *"tank"* is a critical piece of information here that should not have been skipped. As an alternative to relaxation by removal we have experimented with using the aforementioned Log-Answer Ontology Browser as an external source for *abductive relaxation*, where literals

---

[6] http://www.ecb.int/stats/eurofxref/eurofxref-daily.xml
[7] http://developer.yahoo.com/geo/geoplanet
[8] http://www.cs.miami.edu/~tptp/cgi-bin/SystemQATPTP
[9] http://www.loganswer.de/hop/loganswer-cyc

are replaced by semantically more general literals taken from the ontology concept hierarchy. If concept c is a subclass of concept d, then any entity of c can be deduced to also belong to d. Abduction takes the opposite direction: An entity of d might also belong to c. Abduction is not sound, its result is a hypothesis, an assumption. However, we may see now how it can help in relaxing a query. Consider the question from above together with the sentence S that was retrieved from the KB as possibly relevant:

Q: *"What is the weight of the 'Maus' ('Mouse') tank?"*
S: *"At 188 tons the 'Maus' is the heaviest armoured fighting vehicle ever built."*

While S does not mention any tank, tanks are a subclass of vehicles, and given S we could use abduction to form the hypothesis that the vehicle *'Maus'* is a tank and then answer the question.

Implemented in E-KRHyper is the following clause set transformation which aims at using an external source of axioms expressing a concept hierarchy for the purpose of query relaxation guided by abduction. Due to the inherent uncertainty of abduction, the user should receive not only answers, but also hints as to what abductive assumptions were made, so that the user can judge whether the answer is applicable.

Let C be a set of clauses with a negative query clause $Q = \leftarrow Q_1, \ldots, Q_n$ with $n \geq 0$. Let C^{ext} be an external source containing positive ground *ext*-units of the form $ext(subclass\_of(c), d) \leftarrow$, which is the external source conforming representation of the subclass relationship $subclass\_of(c, d)$ between two concept identifiers c and d. We obtain the abductive relaxation supporting clause set C^{ar} from C by adding two clauses as follows. First, add Q^{ar} with

Q^{ar}: $relaxed\_answer(rlx(c_1, x_1), \ldots, rlx(c_m, x_m)) \leftarrow$
$\qquad\qquad Q'_1, \ldots, Q'_n,$
$\qquad\qquad ext(subclass\_of(c_1), x_1), \ldots, ext(subclass\_of(c_m), x_m)$

where $c_1, \ldots, c_m$ ($m \geq 0$) are the occurrences of constants in $Q_1, \ldots, Q_n$, and where $Q'_1, \ldots, Q'_n$ are obtained from $Q_1, \ldots, Q_n$ by replacing each c_i ($0 \leq i \leq m$) with a fresh variable x_i. *relaxed_answer* is a new predicate symbol of arity m, and *rlx* is a new binary function symbol. Secondly, add a unit clause C^{rs} expressing the trivial reflexive subclass relationship of a concept with itself:

C^{rs}: $ext(subclass\_of(x), x) \leftarrow$

As $C \subset C^{ar}$, any refutational proof and answer derivable for C can also be derived for C^{ar}. The intention behind Q^{ar} is as follows. By moving the concept identifiers $c_1, \ldots, c_m$ out of the original query literals $Q_1, \ldots, Q_n$ into the new *ext*-literals and replacing their original occurrences with the response variables, it becomes possible to request more general superclass concepts from the external source and to insert these into the query. As only constants are treated this way, all the new *ext*-literals have ground request terms, making them valid for accessing the external source. The trivial reflexive subclass unit ensures that concepts do not have to be relaxed if they can already be proven without external access. Finally, once all negative literals of Q^{ar} have been refuted with an overall substitution σ, information about the specific concept relaxations can be found in the derived unit $relaxed\_answer(rlx(c_1, x_1), \ldots, rlx(c_m, x_m))\sigma \leftarrow$. If

E-KRHyper does not find a refutational proof for Q within some time limit, it can return the *relaxed_answer* units found in the branch instead, leaving it to the main LogAnswer system or the user to decide whether the generalizations are acceptable. An example will illustrate the principle:

C_1^{ext}: $ext(subclass\_of(tank), vehicle) \leftarrow$
Q: $\leftarrow is\_a('Maus', tank), has\_weight('Maus', x)$
C_1: $is\_a('Maus', vehicle) \leftarrow$
C_2: $has\_weight('Maus', '188t') \leftarrow$
Q^{ar}: $relaxed\_answer(rlx('Maus', x_1), rlx(tank, x_2), rlx('Maus', x_3)) \leftarrow$
$\qquad is\_a(x_1, x_2), has\_weight(x_3, x), ext(subclass\_of('Maus'), x_1),$
$\qquad ext(subclass\_of(tank), x_2), ext(subclass\_of('Maus'), x_3)$
C^{rs}: $ext(subclass\_of(x), x) \leftarrow$

The original query Q, specifically its first literal, cannot be proven in this set of clauses. However, the relaxation query Q^{ar} can: Its first body literal atom $is\_a(x_1, x_2)$ unifies with C_1, instantiating x_1 with *'Maus'* and x_2 with *vehicle*. The second body literal atom $has\_weight(x_3, x)$ unifies with C_2, instantiating x_3 with *'Maus'* and x with *'188t'*. While the external source contains no subclass information for *'Maus'*, the first and the third *ext*-atom unify with the trivial subclass unit C^{rs}. The second *ext*-atom on the other hand has been instantiated to $ext(subclass\_of(tank), vehicle)$, which does not unify with C^{rs}. It is a valid request to the external source, though, and the response term *vehicle* from C_1^{ext} matches the already instantiated response term in Q^{ar}, thus proving the final body literal. We derive a positive literal or unit clause C_3:

$C_3 : relaxed\_answer(rlx('Maus', 'Maus'), rlx(tank, vehicle), rlx('Maus', 'Maus')) \leftarrow$

This indicates that a proof is possible if we accept generalizing *tank* to *vehicle*. The other two "generalizations" are trivial, and we ignore them. In a QA system like Log-Answer this information could be used to answer the question *"What is the weight of the 'Maus' tank?"* with *"188t, if by 'tank' you mean 'vehicle'"*.

8 Conclusions and Future Work

External sources of axioms can enhance automated reasoning by giving ATP access to data that is normally unavailable. This is of particular interest in the context of knowledge representation applications. We have provided a formal framework for such an integration with our modifications to the hyper tableaux calculus. The basic principles can be applied to most FOL calculi, though. Unfortunately the limitations of external sources also carry over, but in practice knowledge engineers should be able to avoid many problematic situations. Regarding our implementation, at this time our integration of external sources is limited to E-KRHyper and not yet utilized within LogAnswer, for which the knowledge base would have to be augmented with *ext*-literals. As such the implementation is a proof of concept, intended to explore the possibilities and limitations of external sources. For the future we intend to experiment with using the mechanisms described here to access and combine multiple large external ontologies, evaluating whether this can serve as an alternative to heuristic axiom selection algorithms. We also want to expand the use of abduction with external knowledge bases in an effort to use ATP for a more human-like reasoning.

Acknowledgements. We would like to thank Markus Bender for implementing the web service interface module described in Sec. 6.

References

1. Bachmair, L., Ganzinger, H.: Equational Reasoning in Saturation-based Theorem Proving. In: Bibel, W., Schmidt, P.H. (eds.) Automated Deduction: A Basis for Applications. Volume I, Foundations: Calculi and Methods. Kluwer Academic Publishers, Dordrecht (1998)
2. Baumgartner, P., Furbach, U., Niemelä, I.: Hyper Tableaux. In: Orłowska, E., Alferes, J.J., Moniz Pereira, L. (eds.) JELIA 1996. LNCS, vol. 1126, pp. 1–17. Springer, Heidelberg (1996)
3. Baumgartner, P., Furbach, U., Pelzer, B.: Hyper Tableaux with Equality. In: Pfenning, F. (ed.) CADE 2007. LNCS (LNAI), vol. 4603, pp. 492–507. Springer, Heidelberg (2007)
4. Bizer, C., Lehmann, J., Kobilarov, G., Auer, S., Becker, C., Cyganiak, R., Hellmann, S.: DBpedia - A Crystallization Point for the Web of Data. Journal of Web Semantics 7(3), 154–165 (2009)
5. Eiter, T., Fink, M., Krennwallner, T., Redl, C.: Conflict-Driven ASP Solving with External Sources. TPLP 12(4-5), 659–679 (2012)
6. Furbach, U., Glöckner, I., Helbig, H., Pelzer, B.: LogAnswer - A Deduction-Based Question Answering System (System Description). In: Armando, A., Baumgartner, P., Dowek, G. (eds.) IJCAR 2008. LNCS (LNAI), vol. 5195, pp. 139–146. Springer, Heidelberg (2008)
7. Furbach, U., Glöckner, I., Helbig, H., Pelzer, B.: Logic-Based Question Answering. KI 24(1), 51–55 (2010)
8. Furbach, U., Glöckner, I., Pelzer, B.: An Application of Automated Reasoning in Natural Language Question Answering. AI Communications 23(2-3), 241–265 (2010) (PAAR Special Issue)
9. Hirschman, L., Gaizauskas, R.: Natural Language Question Answering: The View from Here. Journal of Natural Language Engineering 7(4), 275–300 (2001)
10. Lenat, D.B.: CYC: A Large-Scale Investment in Knowledge Infrastructure. Communications of the ACM 38(11), 33–38 (1995)
11. Nieuwenhuis, R.: Invited talk: Rewrite-based deduction and symbolic constraints. In: Ganzinger, H. (ed.) CADE 1999. LNCS (LNAI), vol. 1632, pp. 302–313. Springer, Heidelberg (1999)
12. Pelzer, B., Wernhard, C.: System description: E- kRHyper. In: Pfenning, F. (ed.) CADE 2007. LNCS (LNAI), vol. 4603, pp. 508–513. Springer, Heidelberg (2007)
13. Spielberger, W.J.: Spezial-Panzerfahrzeuge des deutschen Heeres. Motorbuch Verlag, Stuttgart (1993)
14. Suda, M., Sutcliffe, G., Wischnewski, P., Lamotte-Schubert, M., de Melo, G.: External Sources of Axioms in Automated Theorem Proving. In: Mertsching, B., Hund, M., Aziz, Z. (eds.) KI 2009. LNCS (LNAI), vol. 5803, pp. 281–288. Springer, Heidelberg (2009)
15. Sutcliffe, G., Suda, M., Teyssandier, A., Dellis, N., de Melo, G.: Progress Towards Effective Automated Reasoning with World Knowledge. In: Guesgen, H.W., Charles Murray, R. (eds.) FLAIRS Conference. AAAI Press (2010)

Local SVM Constraint Surrogate Models for Self-adaptive Evolution Strategies

Jendrik Poloczek and Oliver Kramer

Computational Intelligence Group
Carl von Ossietzky University
26111 Oldenburg, Germany

Abstract. In many applications of constrained continuous black box optimization, the evaluation of fitness and feasibility is expensive. Hence, the objective of reducing the constraint function calls remains a challenging research topic. In the past, various surrogate models have been proposed to solve this issue. In this paper, a local surrogate model of feasibility for a self-adaptive evolution strategy is proposed, which is based on support vector classification and a pre-selection surrogate model management strategy. Negative side effects suchs as a decceleration of evolutionary convergence or feasibility stagnation are prevented with a control parameter. Additionally, self-adaptive mutation is extended by a surrogate-assisted alignment to support the evolutionary convergence. The experimental results show a significant reduction of constraint function calls and show a positive effect on the convergence.

Keywords: black box optimization, constraint handling, evolution strategies, surrogate model, support vector classification.

1 Introduction

In many applications in the field of engineering, evolution strategies (ES) are used to approximate the global optimum in constrained continuous black box optimization problems [4]. This category includes problems, in which the fitness and constraint function and their mathematical characteristics are not explicitly given. Due to the design of ES, a relatively large amount of fitness function calls and constraint function calls (CFC) is required. In practice, both evaluation types are expensive, and it is desireable to reduce the amount of evaluations, c.f. [4]. In the past, several surrogate models (SMs) have been proposed to solve this issue for fitness and constraint evaluations. The latter is by now relatively unexplored [6], but for practical applications worth to investigate. The objective of this paper is to decrease the amount of required CFC for self-adaptive ES with a local SVM constraint SM. In the first section, a brief overview of related work is given. In Section 3, the constrained continuous optimization problem is formulated, furthermore constraint handling approaches are introduced. In Section 5, a description of the proposed SM is given. Section 6 presents the description of the testbed and a summary of important results. Last, a conclusion and an outlook is offered. In the appendix, the chosen test problems are formulated.

I.J. Timm and M. Thimm (Eds.): KI 2013, LNAI 8077, pp. 164–175, 2013.
© Springer-Verlag Berlin Heidelberg 2013

2   Related Work

In the last decade, various approaches for fitness and constraint SMs have been proposed to decrease the amount of fitness function calls and CFC. An overview of the recent developments is given in [6] and [10]. As stated in [6], the computationally most efficient way for estimating fitness is the use of machine learning models. A lot of different machine learning methodologies have been used so far: polynomials (response surface methodologies), Krigin [6], neural networks (e.g. multi-layer perceptrons), radial-basis function networks, Gaussian processes and support vector machines [10]. Furthermore, different data sampling techniques such as design of experiments, active learning and boosting have been examined [6]. Besides the actual machine learning model and sampling methodology, the SM management is responsible for the quality of the SM. Different model management strategies have been proposed: population-based, individual-based, generation-based and pre-selection management. Overall, the model management remains a challenging research topic.

3   Constrained Continuous Optimization

In literature, a constrained continuous optimization problem is given by the following formulation: In the N-dimensional search space $\mathcal{X} \subseteq \mathbb{R}^N$ the task is to find the global optimum $\mathbf{x}^* \in \mathcal{X}$, which minimizes the fitness function $f(\mathbf{x})$ with subject to inequalities $g_i(\mathbf{x}) \geq 0, i = 1, \ldots, n_1$ and equalities $h_j(\mathbf{x}) = 0, j = 1, \ldots, n_2$. The constraints g_i and h_i divide the search space $\mathcal{X}$ into a feasible subspace $\mathcal{F}$ and an infeasible subspace $\mathcal{I}$. Whenever the search space is restricted due to additional constraints, a constraint handling methodology is required. In [5], different approaches are discussed. Further, a list[1] of references on constraint handling techniques for evolutionary algorithms is maintained by Coello Coello. In this paper, we propose a surrogate-assisted constraint handling mechanism, which is based on the death penalty (DP) constraint handling approach. The DP methodology discards any infeasible solution, while generating the new offspring. The important drawback of DP is premature stagnation, because of infeasible regions, c.f. [5]. Hence, it should only be used, when most of the search space is feasible. In the following section, we motivate the use of the self-adaptive death penalty step control ES (DSES), orginally proposed in [7].

4   Premature Step-Size Reduction and DSES

An original self-adaptive approach with log-normal uncorrelated mutation and DP or penalty function suffers from premature step size reduction near the constraint boundary, if certain assumptions are true [7]. An examplary test problem is the unimodal Tangent Problem (TR). The boundary of the TR problem is by definition not orthogonal to the coordinate axis. In this case, the uncorrelated

---

[1] http://www.cs.cinvestav.mx/~constraint, last visit on August 14, 2013.

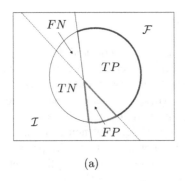 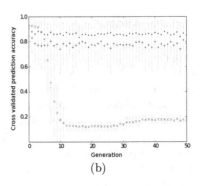

(a)   (b)

Fig. 1. (a) Cases of a binary classifier as SM, positive cases correspond to feasibility and negative cases correspond to infeasibility (b) Cross validated empirical risk with different scaling types: without any scaling (green rotated crosses), standardization (blue points) and normalization to $[0, 1]$ (black crosses) on problem S1

mutation fails to align to the boundary. Because of this characteristic, big step sizes decrease and small step sizes increase the probability of success. The latter implies that small step sizes are passed to posterior populations more often. In the end, the inheritance of too small step sizes leads to a premature step size reduction. The DSES uses a minimum step size modification to solve this issue. If a new step-size is smaller than the minimum step-size ϵ, the new step size is explicitly set to ϵ. Every ϖ infeasible trials, the minimum step size ϵ is reduced by a factor ϑ with $\epsilon' = \epsilon \cdot \vartheta$, where $0 < \vartheta < 1$, to allow convergence. The self-adaptive DSES significantly improves the EC on the TR problem [7]. Hence, it is used as a test ES for the proposed SM.

5   Local SVC Surrogate Model

In the following, we propose a local SVC SM with a pre-selection-based model management. First, the model management is described. Then, the underlying SVC configuration is explained. Last, the surrogate-assisted alignment of the self-adaptive mutation is proposed.

5.1   Model Management

The model is local in relation to the population and only already evaluated feasible and infeasible solutions are added to the training set. Algorithm 1 shows the proposed management strategy. In generation g, a balanced training set of already evaluated solutions is trained. Solutions with a better fitness are prefered, because these solutions lie in the direction of samples in the next generation $g + 1$. The fitness of infeasible solutions is not evaluated. Therefore, a ranking between those solutions without any further heuristic is impossible and not intended. In generation $g + 1$, a Bernoulli trial is executed. With probability β, the SM predicts feasibility before the actual constraint evaluation. Otherwise, the

Algorithm 1. Model Management

```
 1  initialize population P;
 2  while |f(b) − f(x*)| < ε do
 3  │   P'_F, P'_I ← ∅, ∅;
 4  │   while |P'_F| < λ do
 5  │   │   v₁, v₂ ← select_parents(P);
 6  │   │   r ← recombine (v₁, v₂);
 7  │   │   x ← mutate (r);
 8  │   │   M ← M ~ B(1, β);
 9  │   │   if M = 1 then
10  │   │   │   if feasible_with_surrogate (x) then
11  │   │   │   │   f ← feasible (x);
12  │   │   │   │   if f then  P'_F ← P'_F ∪ {x};
13  │   │   │   │   else P'_I ← P'_I ∪ {x};
14  │   │   │   end
15  │   │   else
16  │   │   │   f ← feasible (x);
17  │   │   │   if f then  P'_F ← P'_F ∪ {x};
18  │   │   │   else P'_I ← P'_I ∪ {x};
19  │   │   end
20  │   │   P ← select (P'_F);
21  │   │   train_surrogate (P, P'_I);
22  │   end
23  end
```

solution is directly evaluated on the actual constraint function. The parameter β, that we call influence coefficient, is introduced to prevent feasibility stagnation due to a SM of low quality. To guarantee true feasible-predicted classifications in the offspring, the feasible-predicted solutions are verified by the actual constraint function. The amount of saved CFC in one generation only depend on the influence coefficient β and the positive predictive value of the binary classifier. The positive predictive value is the probability of true feasible-predicted solutions in the set of true and false feasible-predicted solutions. If the positive predictive value is higher than the probability of a feasible solution without SM, it is more likely to save CFC in one generation. However, if it is lower than the probability for a feasible solution without SM, we require additional CFC in one generation. The binary classification cases are illustrated in Figure 1(a). Positive classification corresponds to feasibility and negative classification corresponds to infeasibility. The formulated strategy benefits from its simplicity and does not need additional samples to train the local SM of the constraint boundary. Unfortunately, the generation of offspring might stagnate assuming that the quality of the SM is low and β is chosen too high. In the following experiments, the DSES with this surrogate-assisted constraint handling mechanism is refered to as DSES-SVC.

5.2   SVC Surrogate Model

SVC, originally proposed in [13], is a machine learning methodology, which is widely used in pattern recognition [14]. SVC belongs to the category of supervised learning approaches. The objective of supervised learning is, given a training set, to assign unknown patterns from a feature space $\mathcal{X}$ to an appropriate label from the label space $\mathcal{Y}$. In the following, the feature space equals the search space. The label space of the original SVC is $\mathcal{Y} = \{+1, -1\}$. We define the label of feasible solutions as $+1$ and the label of infeasible solutions as -1. This implies the pattern-label pairs $\{(\mathbf{x}_i, y_i)\} \subset \mathcal{X} \times \{+1, -1\}$. The principle of SVC in general is a linear or non-linear separation of two classes by a hyperplane w.r.t. the maximization of a geometric margin to the nearest patterns on both sides. The proposed SM employs a linear kernel and the soft-margin variant. Hence, patterns lying in the geometric margin are allowed, but are penalized with a user-defined penalization factor C in the search of an optimal hyperplane and decision function, respectively. The optimal hyperplane is found by optimizing a quadratic-convex optimization problem. The factor C is chosen, such that it minimizes the empirical risk of the given training set. In [3], the sequence of possible values $2^{-5}, 2^{-3}, \ldots, 2^{15}$ is recommended. The actually used values for C remain unknown, but a parameter study is conducted in Section 6 that analyzes the limits of C on the chosen test problems. To avoid overfitting, the empirical risk is based on k-fold cross validation.

5.3   DSES with Surrogate-Assisted Alignment

A further approach to reduce CFC is to accelerate the EC. An acceleration implies a reduction of required generations and CFC, respectively. The original DSES uses log-normal uncorrelated mutation and is, as already stated, not able to align to certain constraint boundaries. In [8], a self-adaptive correlated mutation is analyzed, but it is found that self-adaption is too slow. In the following, we propose a self-adaptive correlated mutation variant, which is based on the local SM. Originally, the position of the mutated child is given by $\mathbf{c} = \mathbf{x} + \mathbf{X} \sim \mathcal{N}(0, \sigma)$, where $\mathbf{x}$ is the recombinated position of the parents and $\mathbf{X}$ is a $\mathcal{N}(0, \sigma)$-distributed random variable. In case of the proposed SM, the optimal hyperplane estimates the local linear constraint boundary. Therefore, the normal vector of the hyperplane corresponds to the orientation of the linear constraint boundary. In order to incorportate correlated mutation into the self-adaptive process, the first axis is rotated into the direction of the normal vector. The resulting mutated child is given by $\mathbf{c} = \mathbf{x} + \mathbf{M} \cdot \mathbf{X} \sim \mathcal{N}(0, \sigma)$, where $\mathbf{M}$ is a rotation matrix, which rotates the first axis into the direction of the normal vector. The rotation matrix is updated in each generation. In the following experiments, the DSES with the surrogate-assisted constraint handling mechanism and this surrogate-assisted correlated mutation is refered to as DSES-SVC-A.

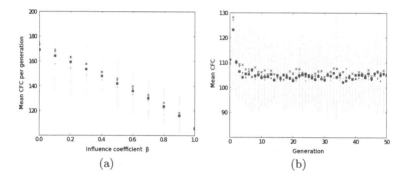

Fig. 2. (a) CFC per generation subject to the influence factor β: S1 (black rotated crosses), S2 (green crosses), TR2 (blue points) and S26C (green squares). (b) Mean CFC with DSES-SVC on all chosen test problems.

6   Experimental Analysis

In the following experimental analysis, the original DSES is compared to the DSES-SVC and the DSES-SVC-A. At first, the test problems and the used constants are formulated. Afterwards, parameter studies regarding scaling operators, the penalization coefficient C and the influence coefficient β are conducted. Last, we compare the amount of CFC per generation and the evolutionary convergence in terms of fitness precision.

6.1   Test Problems and Constants

As the interdependencies between ES, the SM and our chosen test problems are presumably complex, the following four unimodal two-dimensional test problems with linear constraints are used in the experimental analysis: the sphere function with a constraint in the origin (S1), the sphere function with an orthogonal constraint in the origin (S2), the Tangent Problem (TR2) and Schwefel's Problem 2.6 with a constraint (S26C), see Appendix A. The DSES and its underlying (λ, μ)-ES are based on various parameters. Because we want to analyze the behaviour of the SM, its implications on the CFC per generation and the evolutionary convergence, general ES and DSES parameters are kept constant. The (λ, μ)-ES constants are $\lambda = 100$, $\mu = 15$, $\sigma_i = |(s_i - x_i^*)|/N$, where the latter is a recommendation for the initial step size and is based on the start position $\mathbf{s}$ and the position of the optimum $\mathbf{x}^*$, c.f. [11]. Start positions and initial step sizes are stated in the appendix. For the self-adaptive log-normal mutation, the recommendation of τ_0, τ_1 in [2] is used, i.e., $\tau_0 = 0.5$ and $\tau_1 = 0.6$ for each problem. In [7], the $[\varpi, \vartheta]$-DSES algorithm is experimentally analyzed on various test problems. The best values for ϖ and ϑ with regard to fitness accuracy found for the TR2 problem are $\varpi = 70$ and $\vartheta = 0.3$. The test problems, which are examined in this work, are similiar to the TR2 problem, so these values are treated as constants.

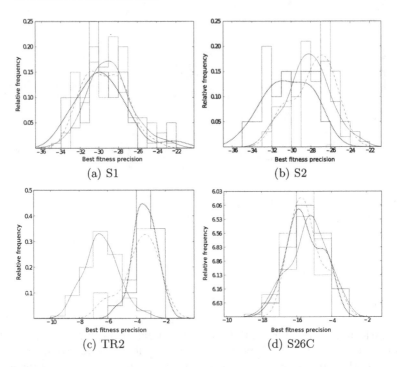

Fig. 3. Histograms of fitness precision after 50 generations with 100 repetitions visualized with kernel densitiy estimation: DSES (black dotted), DSES-SVC (green dashed) and DSES-SVC-A (blue solid) in $log_{10}(f(\mathbf{b}) - f(\mathbf{x}^*))$, where $\mathbf{b}$ is the best solution and $\mathbf{x}^*$ the optimum

6.2 Parameter Studies

Four parameter studies were conducted w.r.t. all test problems. In the following, the DSES-SVC and the constants for ES and DSES in the previous paragraph are used. In the experiments, the termination condition is set to a maximum of 50 generations, because afterwards the premature step size reduction reappears. To guarantee robust results, 100 runs per test problem are simulated. The sequence of possible penalization coefficients is set to $2^{-5}, 2^{-3}, \ldots, 2^{15}$ and the influence coefficient is chosen as $\beta = 0.5$. The balanced training set consists of 20 patterns and 5-fold cross validation is used. First, we analyzed different approaches to scale the input features of the SVC. The scaling operators *no-scaling*, standardization and normalization are tested. The results are quite similiar on all test problems. An examplary plot, which shows the cross validated prediction accuracy dependend on the scaling operator and generation, is shown in Figure 1(b). Without any scaling, the cross validated prediction accuracy drops in the first generations due to presumptive numerical problems: As the evolutionary process proceeds, the step size reduces and the differences between solutions and input patterns, respectively, converge to small numerical values. However, the standardization is significantly the most appropriate scaling on all

Table 1. Best fitness precision in 100 simulations in $log_{10}(f(\mathbf{b}) - f(\mathbf{x}^*))$

problem	algorithm	min	mean	maximum	variance
S1	DSES	-33.47	-29.67	-22.25	6.51
	DSES-SVC	-32.79	-29.46	-24.87	4.11
	DSES-SVC-A	-34.69	-28.94	-22.16	5.30
S2	DSES	-34.90	-30.28	-26.43	5.17
	DSES-SVC	-31.55	-27.80	-24.59	3.86
	DSES-SVC-A	-32.96	**-28.16**	-22.82	4.40
TR2	DSES	-5.32	-3.44	-2.01	0.58
	DSES-SVC	-6.41	-3.75	-2.05	1.35
	DSES-SVC-A	-9.19	**-6.45**	-3.22	1.40
S26C	DSES	-11.41	-9.53	-8.09	0.85
	DSES-SVC	-10.61	-9.39	-7.65	0.76
	DSES-SVC-A	-12.13	-9.34	-7.13	1.21

examined problems. In a second parameter study, we analyzed the selection of the best penalization coefficients to limit the search space of possible coefficients. It turns out that only values between $2^{-3}, 2^{-1}, \ldots, 2^{13}$ are chosen. In the following experiments, this smaller sequence is used. In the third parameter study, we analyzed the correlation between the influence coefficient β and the CFC per generation. Beside the question, whether a linear interdependency exists or not, it is worth knowing, which value for β is possible with a maximal reduction of CFC per generation and without a stagnation of feasible (predicted) solutions. The results are shown in Figure 2(a). On the basis of this figure, a linear interdependency can be assumed. Furthermore, $\beta = 1.0$ is obviously the best choice to reduce the CFC per generation. In the simulations, no feasible (predicted) stagnation appeared, so $\beta = 1.0$ is used in the comparison. The fourth parameter study examines, whether the amount of CFC per generation is constant in mean over all generations with $\beta = 1.0$ w.r.t. all chosen test problems. In Figure 2(b), the mean CFC per generation of 100 simulations is shown. With the help of this figure, a constant mean can be assumed. Hence, it is possible to compare the CFC per generation.

6.3   Comparison

The comparison is based on the test problems and constants introduced in Section 6.1. Furthermore, the results of the previous parameter studies are employed. The scaling type of input features is set to standardization. Possible values for C are $2^{-3}, 2^{-1}, \ldots, 2^{13}$ and the influence coefficient β is set to 1.0. The balanced training set consists of 20 patterns and 5-fold cross validation is used. The reduction of CFC with the proposed SM can result in a decceleration of the EC and a requirement of more generations for a certain fitness precision respectively. Hence, the algorithms are compared depending on the amount of CFC per generation and their EC. Both, the amount of CFC per generation and the EC, are measured on a fixed generation limit. The generation limit is based on

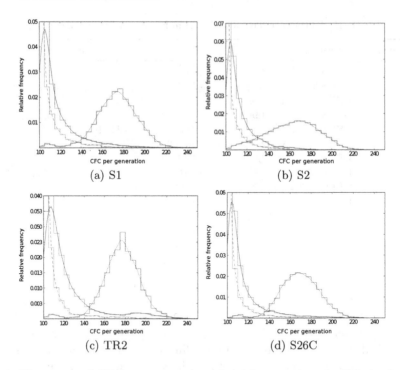

Fig. 4. Histograms of CFC per generation after 50 generations in 100 simulations with according densities: DSES (black dotted), DSES-SVC (green dashed density) and DSES-SVC-A (blue solid)

the reappearance of premature step size reduction and is set to 50 generations. First, the EC is compared in terms of best fitness precision after 50 generations in 100 simulations per test problem. In [7], it is stated that the fitness precision is not normally distributed. Therefore, the Wilcoxon signed-rank test is used for statistical hypothesis testing. The level of significance is set to $\alpha = 0.5$.

The results are shown in Figure 3 and the statistical characteristics are given in Table 1. The probability distribution of each algorithm is estimated by the Parzen-window density estimation [9]. The bandwith is chosen according to the Silverman rule [12]. When comparing the fitness precision of the DSES and the DSES-SVC, the DSES-SVC presumably degrades the fitness precision of the DSES in case of problem S1, S2 and S26C. The fitness precision of DSES-SVC on TR2 is presumably the same as the fitness precision of the DSES. On S1, S2 and S26C the distributions are significantly different. Therefore, the DSES-SVC significantly degrades the DSES in terms of fitness precision. Further, on TR2 the distributions are not significantly different. Hence, there is no empirical evidence of improvement or degradation. If the DSES is compared to the DSES-SVC-A with the help of Figure 3, presumably the DSES-SVC-A does not improve or degrades the fitness precision of the DSES on S1, S2 and S26C. On the contrary, the fitness precision on TR2 seems to be improved. When comparing the

Table 2. Experimental analysis of CFC per generation in 100 simulations

problem	algorithm	min	mean	max	variance
S1	DSES	100	173.36	243	402.82
	DSES-SVC	100	**106.57**	221	164.98
	DSES-SVC-A	100	**116.39**	635	554.53
S2	DSES	100	162.13	238	591.73
	DSES-SVC	100	**104.95**	203	103.74
	DSES-SVC-A	100	**113.17**	252	223.70
TR2	DSES	101	175.55	238	352.38
	DSES-SVC	100	**105.79**	341	185.73
	DSES-SVC-A	100	**122.39**	626	761.99
S26C	DSES	103	168.91	240	354.94
	DSES-SVC	100	**105.15**	219	117.73
	DSES-SVC-A	100	**114.54**	277	358.74

fitness precision between DSES and DSES-SVC-A based on the Wilcoxon signed-rank test, only the distributions on the problems S2 and TR2 are significantly different. This implies that the DSES-SVC-A signficantly improves the fitness precision of the DSES on TR2, but degrades the fitness precision of the DSES on S2. The distributions on the problems S1 and S26C are not significantly different, hence there is no empirical evidence of improvement or degradation. The results of the comparison regarding the fitness precision have to be considered in the following analysis of the CFC. In the comparison regarding the CFC, the previous experimental setup is used. The results are shown in Figure 4 and the statistical characteristics are stated in Table 2. When comparing the amount of CFC per generation of the DSES and the DSES-SVC in Figure 4, presumably the DSES-SVC-A reduces the amount of CFC per generation significantly in each problem. This assumption is empirically confirmed, because the distributions of each problem are significantly different. When comparing the DSES and the DSES-SVC-A, the same assumption is empirically confirmend. While both variants, i.e. DSES-SVC and DSES-SVC-A, reduce the amount of CFC per generation, only the DSES-SVC-A improves the fitness precision significantly. On the contrary the DSES-SVC degrades the fitness precision of the DSES on most test problems signficantly. Hence, the DSES-SVC-A is a successful modification to fulfill the main objective to reduce the amount of CFC on all chosen test problems.

7   Conclusion

The original objective of reducing the amount of CFC of a self-adaptive ES is achieved with the surrogate-assisted DSES-SVC and DSES-SVC-A variants. While the DSES-SVC degrades the fitness precision on most of the problems, the DSES-SVC-A achieves the same fitness precision as the DSES or signficantly improves it with surrogate-assisted alignment. Hence, it is possible to fulfill the objective with a local pre-selection SM based on SVC. The model management is simple, but it needs an additional parameter β, to avoid feasibility stagnation due to wrong predictions. Scaling of the input features is necessary to avoid numerical problems. On the test problems, the standardization seems to be an appropriate choice. In this paper, the introduced β is set manually. A future research question could be, if this coefficient could be managed adaptively and how. Furthermore, in contrast to SVC, the support vector regression could be used to approximate continuous penalty-functions. Both approaches could be integrated into the recently developed successful (1+1)-CMA-ES for constrained optimization [1].

A   Test Problems

In the following, the chosen constrained test problem are formulated.

A.1   Sphere Function with Constraint (S1)

$$\operatorname*{minimize}_{\mathbf{x}\in\mathbb{R}^2} \ f(\mathbf{x}) := \ x_1^2 + x_2^2 \quad \text{s.t.} \ x_1 + x_2 \geq 0 \tag{1}$$

$$\mathbf{s} = (10.0, 10.0)^T \text{ and } \sigma = (5.0, 5.0)^T \tag{2}$$

A.2   Sphere Function with Constraint (S2)

$$\operatorname*{minimize}_{\mathbf{x}\in\mathbb{R}^2} \ f(\mathbf{x}) := \ x_1^2 + x_2^2 \quad \text{s.t.} \ x_1 \geq 0 \tag{3}$$

$$\mathbf{s} = (10.0, 10.0)^T \text{ and } \sigma = (5.0, 5.0)^T \tag{4}$$

A.3   Tangent Problem (TR2)

$$\operatorname*{minimize}_{\mathbf{x}\in\mathbb{R}^2} \ f(\mathbf{x}) := \ \sum_{i=1}^{2} x_i^2 \quad \text{s.t.} \ \sum_{i=1}^{2} x_i - 2 \geq 0 \tag{5}$$

$$\mathbf{s} = (10.0, 10.0)^T \text{ and } \sigma = (4.5, 4.5)^T \tag{6}$$

A.4   Schwefel's Problem 2.6 with Constraint (S26C)

$$\operatorname*{minimize}_{\mathbf{x}\in\mathbb{R}^2} \ f(\mathbf{x}) \ := \ \max(t_1(\mathbf{x}), t_2(\mathbf{x})) \quad \text{s.t.} \ x_1 + x_2 - 70 \geq 0,$$
$$t_1(\mathbf{x}) \ := \ |x_1 + 2x_2 - 7| \tag{7}$$
$$t_2(\mathbf{x}) \ := \ |2x_1 + x_2 - 5|$$

$$\mathbf{s} = (100.0, 100.0)^T \text{ and } \sigma = (34.0, 36.0)^T \tag{8}$$

References

1. Arnold, D.V., Hansen, N.: A (1+1)-CMA-ES for constrained optimisation. In: Proceedings of the International Conference on Genetic and Evolutionary Computation Conference, pp. 297–304. ACM (2012)
2. Beyer, H.-G., Schwefel, H.-P.: Evolution strategies - a comprehensive introduction. Natural Computing 1(1), 3–52 (2002)
3. Chang, C.-C., Lin, C.-J.: LIBSVM: A library for support vector machines. ACM Trans. Intell. Syst. Technol. 2(3), 27:1–27:27 (2011)
4. Chiong, R., Weise, T., Michalewicz, Z. (eds.): Variants of Evolutionary Algorithms for Real-World Applications. Springer (2012)
5. Coello, C.A.C.: Constraint-handling techniques used with evolutionary algorithms. In: GECCO (Companion), pp. 849–872. ACM (2012)
6. Jin, Y.: Surrogate-assisted evolutionary computation: Recent advances and future challenges. Swarm and Evolutionary Computation 1(2), 61–70 (2011)
7. Kramer, O.: Self-Adaptive Heuristics for Evolutionary Computation. SCI, vol. 147. Springer, Heidelberg (2008)
8. Kramer, O.: A review of constraint-handling techniques for evolution strategies. In: Applied Computational Intelligence and Soft Computing, pp. 3:1–3:19 (2010)
9. Parzen, E.: On estimation of a probability density function and mode. The Annals of Mathematical Statistics 33(3), 1065–1076 (1962)
10. Santana-Quintero, L.V., Montaño, A.A., Coello, C.A.C.: A review of techniques for handling expensive functions in evolutionary multi-objective optimization. In: Computational Intelligence in Expensive Optimization Problems. Adaptation, Learning, and Optimization, vol. 2, pp. 29–59. Springer (2010)
11. Schwefel, H.-P.P.: Evolution and Optimum Seeking: The Sixth Generation. John Wiley & Sons, Inc. (1993)
12. Silverman, B.W.: Density Estimation for Statistics and Data Analysis. Chapman & Hall (1986)
13. Vapnik, V.: On structural risk minimization or overall risk in a problem of pattern recognition. Automation and Remote Control 10, 1495–1503 (1997)
14. von Luxburg, U., Schölkopf, B.: Statistical learning theory: Models, concepts, and results. In: Handbook for the History of Logic, vol. 10, pp. 751–706. Elsevier (2011)

Changes of Relational Probabilistic Belief States and Their Computation under Optimum Entropy Semantics

Nico Potyka[1], Christoph Beierle[1], and Gabriele Kern-Isberner[2]

[1] Dept. of Computer Science, FernUniversität in Hagen, 58084 Hagen, Germany
[2] Dept. of Computer Science, TU Dortmund, 44221 Dortmund, Germany

Abstract. Coping with uncertain knowledge and changing beliefs is essential for reasoning in dynamic environments. We generalize an approach to adjust probabilistic belief states by use of the relative entropy in a propositional setting to relational languages. As a second contribution of this paper, we present a method to compute such belief changes by considering a dual problem and present first application and experimental results.

1 Introduction

Agents in dynamic environments have to deal with uncertain and changing information. Over the years different approaches have been developed to deal with both problems [1, 9, 15, 8, 13]. Here, we will consider probabilistic conditional logics [16, 14].

Example 1. Suppose our agent has to watch some pets. Sometimes they attack each other and our agent has to separate them. We compare animals by their size using the binary predicate GT (greater than). Our knowledge base might contain *deterministic conditionals* like $(Bird(X) \wedge Dog(X))[0]$ expressing that a pet cannot be a bird and a dog, as well as uncertain conditionals like $(Attacks(X,Y) \mid GT(Y,X))[0.1]$ expressing that the (subjective) probability that an animal attacks a greater one is about 10%.

A conditional semantics defines which probability distributions satisfy a probabilistic conditional. Given a conditional knowledge base, we are interested in a best distribution satisfying this knowledge base. An appropriate selection criterium is the principle of maximum entropy [16]. To adapt the distribution to new knowledge, one can consider the distribution that minimizes the relative entropy to the prior distribution [10].

Following this idea, the knowledge state of our agent consists of a knowledge base $\mathcal{R}$ reflecting its explicit knowledge and a probability distribution $\mathcal{P}$ satisfying the conditionals in $\mathcal{R}$ and reflecting its implicit knowledge. According to [11], we distinguish between two belief change operations. *Revision* deals with new information in a static world. That is, old explicit knowledge remains valid, even though our epistemic state may change. For instance, in Example 1 we might learn about the pet *bully* that it is a dog. Then $\mathcal{P}(Dog(bully))$ should become 1 but the old explicit knowledge should remain valid. *Update* deals with new information in a dynamic world. That is, not only our implicit knowledge may change, but the new knowledge might be in conflict with the old explicit knowledge. For example, if we observe that small pets are getting more aggressive, e.g., due to a newly added ingredient to their food, we should increase our

I.J. Timm and M. Thimm (Eds.): KI 2013, LNAI 8077, pp. 176–187, 2013.

belief that an animal attacks a greater animal. This is in line with the distinction that is usually made in belief change theory. However, the classical AGM-theory [1] is much too weak to be able to handle such advanced change operations, as it can deal neither with probabilities nor with conditionals. In [11] it is shown how both operations can be implemented for a propositional probabilistic language by use of the relative entropy, and in [2] a corresponding conceptual agent model providing a series of powerful belief management operations is developed. The MECore system [5] implements these ideas and allows the user, e.g., to define an initial knowledge base, to apply both belief change operations, or to query the current epistemic state.

Note, however, that all approaches mentioned so far only deal with propositional logic. Thus, they do not cover conditionals with variables as in Ex. 1. In this paper, we generalize the belief change operations from [11] to relational languages. Our results hold for a full class of conditional semantics and in particular for the relational *grounding* and *aggregating* semantics [6, 12]. Basically, all belief change operations can be reduced to the core functionality of minimizing relative entropy with respect to a prior distribution. Besides providing a concept for changing relational probabilistic belief states, the second major contribution of this paper is an alternative approach to compute such belief changes. We consider the Wolfe dual of relative entropy minimization [7], which yields an unconstrained convex optimization problem and solve it with L-BFGS [18]. For entropy maximization under aggregating semantics a significant performance gain compared to a recent iterative scaling implementation [4] is obtained.

In Sec. 2 we recall the framework of conditional probabilistic logic as far as it is needed here. In Sec. 3 we generalize the belief change operations from [11] and illustrate our ideas by examples. In Sec. 4 we explain how the belief change operations can be implemented by solving the Wolfe dual of relative entropy minimization and present first evaluation results, and in Sec. 5 we conclude and point out future work.

2   Background: Probabilistic Conditionals and Semantics

The languages and semantics we consider in this section share a similar linear structure that allows to generalize the belief change approach from [11]. Note in particular that our semantics are based on probability distributions over possible worlds, whereas in the important strand of work followed in [8] all possible worlds are supposed to be equally likely and probabilities are obtained by computing asymptotic fractions of satisfied worlds over all possible worlds. Hence the corresponding results cannot be transferred immediately.

Languages: To represent knowledge, we consider logical languages $\mathcal{L}_\Sigma$ built up over *signatures* $\Sigma = (Const, Rel)$ partitioned into a finite set *Const* of *constants* and a finite set *Rel* of *relation symbols*. Relation symbols of arity zero are called *propositional variables*. We allow arbitrary logical connectives but no quantifiers. For ease of notation we abbreviate conjunction by juxtaposition, $\mathfrak{fg} := \mathfrak{f} \wedge \mathfrak{g}$, and negation by an overbar, $\bar{\mathfrak{f}} := \neg\mathfrak{f}$. We can extend $\mathcal{L}_\Sigma$ to a *probabilistic conditional language* $(\mathcal{L}_\Sigma|\mathcal{L}_\Sigma) := \{(\mathfrak{g}|\mathfrak{f})[x] \mid \mathfrak{f}, \mathfrak{g} \in \mathcal{L}_\Sigma, x \in [0,1]\}$ [15, 14]. Conditionals $(\mathfrak{g} \mid \top)[x]$ having a tautological antecedence, are abbreviated by $(\mathfrak{g})[x]$. A *knowledge base* $\mathcal{R} \subseteq (\mathcal{L}_\Sigma|\mathcal{L}_\Sigma)$ is a set of conditionals.

Example 2. In the following, for our running example in Example 1, we consider the signature $(\{bully, sylvester, tweety\}, \{Bird, Cat, Dog, Attacks, GT\})$.

Let $\mathcal{H}_\Sigma := \{p(c_1, \ldots, c_n) \mid c_1, \ldots, c_n \in Const, p \in Rel \text{ with arity } n\}$ be the set of ground atoms over a signature $\Sigma = (Const, Rel)$. A *possible world* over Σ is a function $\omega : \mathcal{H} \rightarrow \{false, true\}$ assigning a truth value to each ground atom over Σ. Let Ω_Σ be the set of all possible worlds for Σ. A ground atom $\mathfrak{a}$ is satisfied by $\omega \in \Omega_\Sigma$, $\omega \models_{\mathcal{L}_\Sigma} \mathfrak{a}$, iff $\omega(\mathfrak{a}) = true$. The definition is extended to complex formulas in $\mathcal{L}_\Sigma$ in the usual way. For a formula $\mathfrak{f} \in \mathcal{L}_\Sigma$ let $\text{Mod}(\mathfrak{f}) := \{\omega \in \Omega_\Sigma \mid \omega \models_{\mathcal{L}_\Sigma} \mathfrak{f}\}$ be the set of its classical models. Probabilistic semantics can be defined by considering probability distributions over possible worlds. Let $\mathcal{P} : \Omega_\Sigma \rightarrow [0,1]$ be a probability distribution assigning a degree of belief to each possible world. For a formula $\mathfrak{f} \in \mathcal{L}_\Sigma$ we define $\mathcal{P}(\mathfrak{f}) := \sum_{\omega \in \text{Mod}(\mathfrak{f})} \mathcal{P}(\omega)$. $\mathfrak{P}_\Sigma$ denotes the set of all such probability distributions.

Standard Semantics: A conditional semantics $\mathcal{S}$ defines which $\mathcal{P} \in \mathfrak{P}_\Sigma$ satisfy a certain conditional. For an underlying propositional language usually the definition of conditional probability is used, i.e. $\mathcal{P} \models_S (\mathfrak{g}|\mathfrak{f})[x]$ iff $\mathcal{P}(\mathfrak{f}) > 0$ and $\frac{\mathcal{P}(\mathfrak{g}\mathfrak{f})}{\mathcal{P}(\mathfrak{f})} = x$. To avoid strict inequalities, one can relax the definition by omitting the condition $\mathcal{P}(\mathfrak{f}) > 0$ and definining [16]:

$$\mathcal{P} \models_S (\mathfrak{g}|\mathfrak{f})[x] \quad \textit{iff} \quad \mathcal{P}(\mathfrak{g}\mathfrak{f}) = x \cdot \mathcal{P}(\mathfrak{f}). \tag{1}$$

We call this semantics the *standard semantics*. If both $\mathfrak{g}$ and $\mathfrak{f}$ are closed first-order formulas, the standard semantics can be applied to first-order conditionals in just the same way. To interpret open conditionals like $(Attacks(X,Y) \mid GT(Y,X))[0.1]$ in a quantifier-free language different semantics have been considered. Here, we consider only *grounding* and *aggregating* semantics, as they induce linear constraints that are beneficial from a computational point of view.

Grounding Semantics: *Grounding semantics* [6] interpret conditionals by interpreting their ground instances. Therefore, a grounding operator $\text{gr} : (\mathcal{L}_\Sigma|\mathcal{L}_\Sigma) \rightarrow 2^{(\mathcal{L}_\Sigma|\mathcal{L}_\Sigma)}$ is introduced mapping conditionals to the set of its ground instances. For instance, in our running example, the conditional $(Attacks(X,Y) \mid GT(Y,X))[0.1]$ is mapped to ground instances like $(Attacks(bully, sylvester) \mid GT(sylvester, bully))[0.1]$. In general, a distribution $\mathcal{P}$ satisfies a relational conditional $(\mathfrak{g}|\mathfrak{f})[x]$ under grounding semantics iff $\mathcal{P}$ satisfies all ground instances under standard semantics, i.e., iff [6]

$$\mathcal{P}(\mathfrak{g}_i\mathfrak{f}_i) = x \cdot \mathcal{P}(\mathfrak{f}_i) \quad \textit{for all} \quad (\mathfrak{g}_i \mid \mathfrak{f}_i)[x] \in \text{gr}((\mathfrak{g} \mid \mathfrak{f})[x]). \tag{2}$$

Grounding a knowledge base in such a way naively can easily lead to inconsistencies. For example, if we presuppose that most of our pets are birds $(Bird(X))[0.8]$ and know that *tweety* is a bird $(Bird(tweety))[1]$, the ground instance $(Bird(tweety))[0.8]$ of the former conditional is in conflict with the latter. To deal with such inconsistencies, conditionals can be associated with constraint formulas, so that gr maps a conditional with constraint formula to the set of its *admissible* ground instances. For instance, the constraint formula $X \neq tweety$ excludes the ground instance $(Bird(tweety))[0.8]$ and in this way resolves the conflict with $(Bird(tweety))[1]$.

Aggregating Semantics: The aggregating semantics [12] can deal with conflicting information without using constraint formulas. Instead of regarding a conditional containing variables as a hard template for the probability of each ground instance, their conditional probabilities just have to 'aggregate' to the stated probability. More precisely, $\mathcal{P}$ satisfies $c = (\mathfrak{g}|\mathfrak{f})[x]$ under aggregating semantics iff [12]

$$\sum_{(\mathfrak{g}_i \,|\, \mathfrak{f}_i)[x] \in \mathrm{gr}(c)} \mathcal{P}(\mathfrak{g}_i \mathfrak{f}_i) = x \cdot \left(\sum_{(\mathfrak{g}_i \,|\, \mathfrak{f}_i)[x] \in \mathrm{gr}(c)} \mathcal{P}(\mathfrak{f}_i) \right). \tag{3}$$

(3) can be regarded as a generalization of the standard semantics in (1), where the probabilities of single formulas have been replaced by sums of probabilities over all ground instances of the corresponding formulas. Note that the original definition in [12] presupposes $\sum_{(\mathfrak{g}_i \,|\, \mathfrak{f}_i)[x] \in \mathrm{gr}(c)} \mathcal{P}(\mathfrak{f}_i) > 0$.

Example 3. In our running example, the conditional $(Bird(X))[0.8]$, which abbreviates $(Bird(X) \mid \top)[0.8]$, is satisfied by $\mathcal{P}$ under aggregating semantics iff

$$\mathcal{P}(Bird(bully)) + \mathcal{P}(Bird(sylvester)) + \mathcal{P}(Bird(tweety)) = 0.8 \cdot 3 \cdot \mathcal{P}(\top).$$

If additionally $(Bird(tweety))[1]$ is satisfied by $\mathcal{P}$ the equation becomes

$$\mathcal{P}(Bird(bully)) + \mathcal{P}(Bird(sylvester)) + 1 = 2.4,$$

and is still satisfiable, e.g., if $\mathcal{P}(Bird(bully)) = \mathcal{P}(Bird(sylvester)) = 0.7$.

General Framework: As the definitions in (1), (2) and (3) indicate, a conditional is satisfied by a probability distribution under a given semantics if a certain equation over probabilities of possible worlds is satisfied. Usually these equations can be transformed into a normal form $f_c(\mathcal{P}) = 0$.

Example 4. Consider a propositional conditional $c = (\mathfrak{g}|\mathfrak{f})[x]$ under standard semantics. Subtracting $x \cdot \mathcal{P}(\mathfrak{f})$ from both sides in equation (1) yields

$$0 = \mathcal{P}(\mathfrak{g}\mathfrak{f}) - x \cdot \mathcal{P}(\mathfrak{f}) = \mathcal{P}(\mathfrak{g}\mathfrak{f}) - x \cdot (\mathcal{P}(\mathfrak{g}\mathfrak{f}) + \mathcal{P}(\overline{\mathfrak{g}}\mathfrak{f})) = (1 - x) \cdot \mathcal{P}(\mathfrak{g}\mathfrak{f}) - x \cdot \mathcal{P}(\overline{\mathfrak{g}}\mathfrak{f})$$

$$= (1 - x) \cdot \left(\sum_{w \in \mathrm{Mod}(\mathfrak{g}\mathfrak{f})} \mathcal{P}(w) \right) - x \cdot \left(\sum_{w \in \mathrm{Mod}(\overline{\mathfrak{g}}\mathfrak{f})} \mathcal{P}(w) \right)$$

$$= \sum_{w \in \Omega_\Sigma} \mathcal{P}(w) \cdot (1_{\{\mathfrak{g}\mathfrak{f}\}}(w) \cdot (1 - x) - 1_{\{\overline{\mathfrak{g}}\mathfrak{f}\}}(w) \cdot x), \tag{4}$$

where for a formula $\mathfrak{F}$ the indicator function $1_{\{\mathfrak{F}\}}(w)$ maps to 1 iff $w \models_{\mathcal{L}_\Sigma} \mathfrak{F}$ and to 0 otherwise. Let $f_c(\mathcal{P}) := \sum_{w \in \Omega_\Sigma} \mathcal{P}(w) \cdot (1_{\{\mathfrak{g}\mathfrak{f}\}}(w) \cdot (1 - x) - 1_{\{\overline{\mathfrak{g}}\mathfrak{f}\}}(w) \cdot x)$ then $\mathcal{P} \models_S (\mathfrak{g}|\mathfrak{f})[x]$ under standard semantics iff $f_c(\mathcal{P}) = 0$.

For other semantics similar transformations can be applied, see [17] for details. Whereas standard (1) and aggregating semantics (3) induce a single constraint function for a conditional c, for grounding semantics (2) we obtain one function for each admissible ground instance of c. We combine these functions in a single vector of size k_c. Thus for grounding semantics $k_c = |\mathrm{gr}(c)|$, while for standard and aggregating semantics $k_c = 1$. Now let $(\mathcal{L}_\Sigma|\mathcal{L}_\Sigma)$ be a conditional language over a signature Σ. We say a satisfaction relation $\models_S \subseteq \mathfrak{P}_\Sigma \times (\mathcal{L}_\Sigma|\mathcal{L}_\Sigma)$ defines a *conditional semantics S* iff for each conditional $c \in (\mathcal{L}_\Sigma|\mathcal{L}_\Sigma)$ there is a k_c-dimensional *constraint function* $f_c : \mathfrak{P}_\Sigma \to \mathbb{R}^{k_c}$

Table 1. Verifying and falsifying functions for $c = (\mathfrak{g}|\mathfrak{f})[x] \in (\mathcal{L}_\Sigma|\mathcal{L}_\Sigma)$ and $\omega \in \Omega_\Sigma$

Semantics	$V_c(\omega)$	$F_c(\omega)$
Standard	$1_{\{\mathfrak{g}\mathfrak{f}\}}(\omega)$	$1_{\{\overline{\mathfrak{g}}\mathfrak{f}\}}(\omega)$
Grounding	$(1_{\{\mathfrak{g}_i\mathfrak{f}_i\}}(\omega))_{(\mathfrak{g}_i\,|\,\mathfrak{f}_i)\in\mathrm{gr}((\mathfrak{g}\,|\,\mathfrak{f}))}$	$(1_{\{\overline{\mathfrak{g}_i}\mathfrak{f}_i\}}(\omega))_{(\mathfrak{g}_i\,|\,\mathfrak{f}_i)\in\mathrm{gr}((\mathfrak{g}\,|\,\mathfrak{f}))}$
Aggregating	$\sum_{(\mathfrak{g}_i\,|\,\mathfrak{f}_i)\in\mathrm{gr}((\mathfrak{g}\,|\,\mathfrak{f}))} 1_{\{\mathfrak{g}_i\mathfrak{f}_i\}}(\omega)$	$\sum_{(\mathfrak{g}_i\,|\,\mathfrak{f}_i)\in\mathrm{gr}((\mathfrak{g}\,|\,\mathfrak{f}))} 1_{\{\overline{\mathfrak{g}_i}\mathfrak{f}_i\}}(\omega)$

such that for all $\mathcal{P} \in \mathfrak{P}_\Sigma$, $c \in (\mathcal{L}_\Sigma|\mathcal{L}_\Sigma)$ it holds that $\mathcal{P} \models_\mathcal{S} c$ iff $f_c(\mathcal{P}) = 0$. By $f^{[i]}$ we denote the i-th component of a multi-dimensional function f.

Inspecting (4) more thoroughly, one notices that each world contributes a linear term to the sum. If the world *verifies* the conditional, i.e., $\omega \models_{\mathcal{L}_\Sigma} \mathfrak{g}\mathfrak{f}$, the term $\mathcal{P}(\omega) \cdot (1-x)$ is added. If it *falsifies* the conditional, i.e., $\omega \models_{\mathcal{L}_\Sigma} \overline{\mathfrak{g}}\mathfrak{f}$, the term $\mathcal{P}(\omega) \cdot x$ is subtracted. If the conditional is not applicable, i.e., $\omega \models_{\mathcal{L}_\Sigma} \overline{\mathfrak{f}}$, the term is zero. A similar observation can be made for grounding and aggregating semantics and is captured by the following definition [17].

Definition 1. *A conditional semantics $\mathcal{S}$ is called* linearly structured *iff for each conditional $c \in (\mathcal{L}_\Sigma|\mathcal{L}_\Sigma)$, there are k_c-dimensional functions $V_c : \Omega_\Sigma \to \mathbb{N}_0^{k_c}$ and $F_c : \Omega_\Sigma \to \mathbb{N}_0^{k_c}$ such that*

$$f_c(\mathcal{P}) = \sum_{\omega \in \Omega_\Sigma} \mathcal{P}(\omega) \cdot (V_c(\omega) \cdot (1-x) - F_c(\omega) \cdot x). \tag{5}$$

Equation (5) indeed generalizes (1), (2) and (3) as such functions V_c, F_c do exist. They are shown in Table 1. For grounding semantics V_c and F_c are vectors of length k_c. Whereas for standard and grounding semantics V_c and F_c indicate whether a world verifies or falsifies a (ground) conditional, for aggregating semantics the number of falsified and verified ground conditionals is counted.

For a conditional $c \in (\mathcal{L}_\Sigma|\mathcal{L}_\Sigma)$ let $\mathrm{Mod}_\mathcal{S}(c) := \{\mathcal{P} \in \mathfrak{P}_\Sigma \mid f_c(\mathcal{P}) = 0\}$ denote the set of its probabilistic models under a given conditional semantics $\mathcal{S}$. For a knowledge base $\mathcal{R} \subseteq (\mathcal{L}_\Sigma|\mathcal{L}_\Sigma)$ let $\mathrm{Mod}_\mathcal{S}(\mathcal{R}) := \bigcap_{c\in\mathcal{R}} \mathrm{Mod}_\mathcal{S}(c)$ be the set of common models of the conditionals in $\mathcal{R}$.

3   Belief Changes of Relational Probabilistic Belief States

In our framework, knowledge is represented by probabilistic conditional knowledge bases $\mathcal{R}$ in some language $(\mathcal{L}_\Sigma|\mathcal{L}_\Sigma)$ interpreted by some linearly structured semantics $\mathcal{S}$. To obtain an epistemic state that satisfies $\mathcal{R}$ and allows to evaluate arbitrary (conditional) formulas, we can select a 'best' probability distribution in $\mathrm{Mod}_\mathcal{S}(\mathcal{R})$. An appropriate selection criterion is the principle of maximum entropy [16], i.e., the epistemic state induced by $\mathcal{R}$ is a $\mathcal{P} \in \mathrm{Mod}_\mathcal{S}(\mathcal{R})$ that maximizes the entropy.

If new knowledge $\mathcal{R}^*$ becomes available, we want to adapt our current epistemic state $\mathcal{P}$ to the new knowledge. Motivated by belief change operations for logical knowledge bases [1, 9] in [10, 11] several postulates for updating probabilistic epistemic states by propositional probabilistic conditionals under standard semantics are introduced and it is shown that those can be satisfied by minimizing the relative entropy $R(\mathcal{Q}, \mathcal{P}) = \sum_{\omega \in \Omega_\Sigma} \mathcal{Q}(\omega) \cdot \log \frac{\mathcal{Q}(\omega)}{\mathcal{P}(\omega)}$. Maximizing entropy corresponds to minimizing the relative entropy with respect to the uniform distribution, therefore this approach generalizes the principle of maximum entropy. So, both for inductive reasoning and for belief change, the principles of optimum entropy provide a most powerful framework that guarantees high quality results. For a more detailed investigation with respect to postulates and properties, and for the connection to classical belief change theory, cf. [10, 11]. We will now generalize this idea to arbitrary linearly structured semantics, thus covering in particular various relational languages. We consider a belief change operator $*_S : (\mathfrak{P}_\Sigma \times 2^{(\mathcal{L}_\Sigma | \mathcal{L}_\Sigma)}) \to \mathfrak{P}_\Sigma$ defined by

$$\mathcal{P} *_S \mathcal{R}^* := \arg \min_{\mathcal{Q} \in \mathrm{Mod}_S(\mathcal{R}^*)} R(\mathcal{Q}, \mathcal{P}), \qquad (6)$$

where $0 \cdot \log(0)$ and $0 \cdot \log(\frac{0}{0})$ are defined to be 0. If $\mathcal{Q}(\omega) = 0$ whenever $\mathcal{P}(\omega) = 0$, $\mathcal{Q}$ is called *absolutely continuous with respect to* $\mathcal{P}$, written as $\mathcal{Q} \ll \mathcal{P}$. As the constraint functions for a linearly structured semantics S are linear, $\mathrm{Mod}_S(\mathcal{R}^*)$ is convex and closed. This implies that (6) has a unique solution, if there is a $\mathcal{Q} \in \mathrm{Mod}_S(\mathcal{R}^*)$ such that $\mathcal{Q} \ll \mathcal{P}$ [3]. A knowledge base satisfying the latter condition is called $\mathcal{P}$-*consistent* [10]. In particular, if $\mathcal{R}^*$ is $\mathcal{P}$-consistent and $\mathcal{Q} *_S \mathcal{R}^* = \mathcal{P}^*$, then $\mathcal{P}^* \ll \mathcal{P}$, i.e., zero probabilities remain unchanged by the belief change. Note that the propositional case considered in [10] is a special case of (6).

In [11] two belief change operations for update and revision of propositional probabilistic conditional knowledge bases are introduced.

Definition 2 ([11]). A belief base *is a pair* $(\mathcal{P}, \mathcal{R})$ *that represents the epistemic state* $\mathcal{P} *_S \mathcal{R}$. *The* revision operator $\circ_S$ *is defined by* $(\mathcal{P}, \mathcal{R}) \circ_S \mathcal{R}^* := (\mathcal{P}, \mathcal{R} \cup \mathcal{R}^*)$. *The* update operator $*_S$ *is defined by* $(\mathcal{P}, \mathcal{R}) *_S \mathcal{R}^* := (\mathcal{P} *_S \mathcal{R}, \mathcal{R}^*)$.

Note that, when performing revision, even though the corresponding epistemic state $\mathcal{P} *_S (\mathcal{R} \cup \mathcal{R}^*)$ may differ from the former, the old explicit knowledge $\mathcal{R}$ is still valid. In contrast, when applying an update, both the prior epistemic state and the prior explicit knowledge are usually changed. More precisely, the new epistemic state after revision is $\mathcal{P} *_S (\mathcal{R} \cup \mathcal{R}^*)$, whereas the new epistemic state after update is $(\mathcal{P} *_S \mathcal{R}) *_S \mathcal{R}^*$. To keep the techniques rather simple, we presuppose that all information to be processed is true, i.e., the involved agents are honest and do not fail in making correct observations. So, two pieces of information $\mathcal{R}$ and $\mathcal{R}^*$ for revision refer to the same context and must be consistent. One might deviate from this assumption and allow for inconsistent information here; in this case, a merging operator has to be applied to the different pieces of information first. Using the belief change operator $*_S$ as defined in (6), Definition 2 carries over to languages interpreted by linearly structured semantics immediately.

Example 5. We consider the signature Σ from Ex. 2 and interpret conditionals using the aggregating semantics. Our initial probability distribution is the uniform distribution $\mathcal{P}_0$ over Ω_Σ and our initial knowledge base is $\mathcal{R}_0 = \{(Attacks(X, Y) \mid GT(Y, X))[0.1],$ $(GT(X, Y) \mid Cat(x) \wedge Bird(y))[0.9], (Bird(X) \wedge Cat(X))[0], (Bird(X) \wedge Dog(X))$ $[0], (Cat(X) \wedge Dog(X))[0], (Attacks(X, X))[0], (GT(X, Y) \wedge GT(Y, X))[0]\}.$

Table 2. Queries for different epistemic states

Query	$\mathcal{B}_0 = (\mathcal{P}_0, \mathcal{R}_0)$	$\mathcal{B}_1 = \mathcal{B}_0 \circ_S \mathcal{R}_1$	$\mathcal{B}_2 = \mathcal{B}_1 \circ_S \mathcal{R}_2$	$\mathcal{B}_3 = \mathcal{B}_2 *_S \mathcal{R}_3$
$Attacks(tweety, sylvester)$	$0.3806\ldots$	$0.1395\ldots$	$0.1370\ldots$	$0.2277\ldots$
$Attacks(sylvester, tweety)$	$0.3806\ldots$	$0.4830\ldots$	$0.8005\ldots$	$0.8024\ldots$
$Attacks(tweety, bully)$	$0.3806\ldots$	$0.3832\ldots$	$0.3836\ldots$	$0.4132\ldots$

The first two conditionals state uncertain knowledge: It is unlikely that a pet attacks a greater animal and that it is likely that a cat is greater than a bird. The remaining conditionals express strict knowledge: A pet is either a bird, a cat or a dog. Furthermore, pets do not attack themselves and greater-than is an asymmetric relation. Our initial belief base is $\mathcal{B}_0 = (\mathcal{P}_0, \mathcal{R}_0)$. The first column of Table 2 shows some probabilities in the corresponding epistemic state $\mathcal{P}_0 *_S \mathcal{R}_0$. As we do not know initially about the species of the pets nor about their proportions, all probabilities are equal.

Now our agent learns that *tweety* is a bird, *sylvester* is a cat and *bully* is a dog expressed by the new knowledge $\mathcal{R}_1 = \{(Bird(tweety))[1], (Cat(sylvester)))[1], (Dog(bully)))[1]\}$. Revising $\mathcal{B}_0$ with $\mathcal{R}_1$ yields the belief base $\mathcal{B}_1 = \mathcal{B}_0 \circ_S \mathcal{R}_1 = (\mathcal{P}_0, \mathcal{R}_0 \cup \mathcal{R}_1)$. The second column of Table 2 shows the changed probabilities. As we know *tweety* is a bird and *sylvester* is a cat and we assume that birds are usually smaller than cats, the probability that *tweety* attacks *sylvester* is decreased significantly.

When the agent finds out that cats like to attack birds, $\mathcal{B}_1$ is revised with $\mathcal{R}_2 = \{(Attacks(X, Y) \mid Cat(x) \wedge Bird(y))[0.8]\}$. We obtain the belief base $\mathcal{B}_2 = \mathcal{B}_1 \circ_S \mathcal{R}_2 = (\mathcal{P}_0, \mathcal{R}_0 \cup \mathcal{R}_1 \cup \mathcal{R}_2)$. The third column of Table 2 shows the new probabilities.

Later on, it turns out that small pets get more aggressive due to a newly added ingredient to their food. Therefore, we perform an update with the new knowledge $\mathcal{R}_3 = \{(Attacks(X, Y) \mid GT(Y, X))[0.2]\}$. The new belief base is $\mathcal{B}_3 = \mathcal{B}_2 *_S \mathcal{R}_3 = (\mathcal{P}_0 \circ_S (\mathcal{R}_0 \cup \mathcal{R}_1 \cup \mathcal{R}_2), \mathcal{R}_3)$. The fourth column of Table 2 shows the changed probabilities.

4 Computing Belief Changes

In the last section, we explained how belief changes of relational probabilistic epistemic states can be realized by means of the elementary belief change $\mathcal{P} *_S \mathcal{R} = \mathcal{P}^*$ of a probability distribution. In this section, we will consider an unconstrained optimization problem, whose solution corresponds to the computation of this belief change. We first introduce a matrix notation, as it is more convenient. Using this notation we reformulate (6) in the standard form of convex optimization problems and simplify this form by removing worlds whose probability is enforced to be zero. Subsequently we consider the Wolfe dual [7] that gives rise to an equivalent unconstrained optimization problem. In particular, the special structure of the solution yields a factorization of $\mathcal{P}^*$.

Primal Problem: Let $d = |\Omega_\Sigma|$. By assuming the possible worlds are ordered in a fixed sequence $\omega_1, \ldots, \omega_d$ we can identify each $\mathcal{P} \in \mathfrak{P}_\Sigma$ with a vector $\boldsymbol{p} = (\mathcal{P}(\omega_i))_{1 \leq i \leq d} \in \mathbb{R}^d$. In the following, we will not distinguish between probability distributions $\mathcal{P}$ and the corresponding vectors $\boldsymbol{p}$. For a linearly structured semantics $\mathcal{S}$, we can write (5) more compactly as a linear equation system $f_c(\boldsymbol{p}) = \mathcal{M}_{\mathcal{S}}(c) \cdot \boldsymbol{p}$, where $\mathcal{M}_{\mathcal{S}}(c) := (V_c^{[i]}(\omega_j) \cdot (1 - x) - F_c^{[i]}(\omega_j) \cdot x)_{1 \leq i \leq k_c, 1 \leq j \leq d}$ denotes the $k_c \times d$-matrix corresponding to the coefficients in (5). For $\mathcal{R} = \{c_1, \ldots, c_m\}$ let

$$\mathcal{M}_{\mathcal{S}}(\mathcal{R}) := \begin{pmatrix} \mathcal{M}_{\mathcal{S}}(c_1) \\ \cdots \\ \mathcal{M}_{\mathcal{S}}(c_m) \\ 1 \end{pmatrix}$$

be the matrix combining all constraint functions for conditionals in $\mathcal{R}$ and the normalizing constraint assuring that all probabilities sum to 1. Let $k_{\mathcal{R}} = 1 + \sum_{c \in \mathcal{R}} k_c$ be the number of rows of $\mathcal{M}_{\mathcal{S}}(\mathcal{R})$. Then $\mathcal{P} \in \mathrm{Mod}_{\mathcal{S}}(\mathcal{R})$ iff $\boldsymbol{p} \geq 0$ and $\mathcal{M}_{\mathcal{S}}(\mathcal{R}) \cdot \boldsymbol{p} = \boldsymbol{b}$, where $\boldsymbol{b}$ is a column vector of length $k_{\mathcal{R}}$ whose last component is 1 and whose remaining components are 0.

Example 6. Consider the propositional signature $(\emptyset, \{A, B, C\})$ and the corresponding order $(\overline{A}\,\overline{B}\,\overline{C}, \overline{A}\,\overline{B}\,C, \overline{A}\,B\,\overline{C}, \overline{A}\,B\,C, A\,\overline{B}\,\overline{C}, A\,\overline{B}\,C, A\,B\,\overline{C}, A\,B\,C)$ over Ω_Σ. For standard semantics and $\mathcal{R} = \{(B \mid A)[0.9], (C \mid B)[0.7]\}$, $\mathcal{P} \in \mathrm{Mod}_{\mathcal{S}}(\mathcal{R})$ holds iff for the corresponding vector $\boldsymbol{p}$ we have $\boldsymbol{p} \geq 0$ and

$$\mathcal{M}_{\mathcal{S}}(\mathcal{R}) \cdot \boldsymbol{p} = \begin{pmatrix} 0 & 0 & 0 & 0 & -0.9 & -0.9 & 0.1 & 0.1 \\ 0 & 0 & -0.7 & 0.3 & 0 & 0 & -0.7 & 0.3 \\ 1 & 1 & 1 & 1 & 1 & 1 & 1 & 1 \end{pmatrix} \cdot \boldsymbol{p} = \begin{pmatrix} 0 \\ 0 \\ 1 \end{pmatrix}, \quad \boldsymbol{p} \in \mathbb{R}^8.$$

As we saw in Section 3, to realize update and revision, we have to compute the belief change operation $\mathcal{P} *_{\mathcal{S}} \mathcal{R}$. In matrix notation (6) becomes

$$\arg\min_{\boldsymbol{q} \in \mathbb{R}^d} \sum_{1 \leq i \leq d} \boldsymbol{q}^{[i]} \cdot \log \frac{\boldsymbol{q}^{[i]}}{\boldsymbol{p}^{[i]}}, \tag{7}$$

subject to $\mathcal{M}_{\mathcal{S}}(\mathcal{R}) \cdot \boldsymbol{q} = \boldsymbol{b}, \, \boldsymbol{q} \geq 0.$

Removing Nullworlds: Suppose we want to compute $\mathcal{P}^* = \mathcal{P} *_{\mathcal{S}} \mathcal{R}$ for a $\mathcal{P}$-consistent knowledge base $\mathcal{R}$. As we know $\mathcal{P}^* \ll \mathcal{P}$, we can ignore all worlds $\mathcal{N}_{\mathcal{P}} := \{\omega \in \Omega_\Sigma \mid \mathcal{P}(\omega) = 0\}$ as their probabilities are known to be 0. In particular *deterministic conditionals* $c = (\mathfrak{g}|\mathfrak{f})[x]$ with $x \in \{0, 1\}$ enforce zero probabilities. Let $\mathcal{R}^= := \{(\mathfrak{g}|\mathfrak{f})[x] \in \mathcal{R} \mid x \in \{0, 1\}\}$ be the set of deterministic conditionals in $\mathcal{R}$ and let $\mathcal{R}^\approx := \mathcal{R} \setminus \mathcal{R}^=$. A probability distribution satisfies $\mathcal{R}^=$ under any linearly structured semantics, if and only if it assigns probability 0 to all worlds that falsify a deterministic conditional $(\mathfrak{g}|\mathfrak{f})[x] \in \mathcal{R}^=$ with $x = 1$ or that verify one with $x = 0$ [17]. Let $\mathcal{N}_{\mathcal{R}}$ be the set of worlds that in this way are determined to have probability 0.

Let $\Omega^+_{\mathcal{P}, \mathcal{R}} = \Omega_\Sigma \setminus (\mathcal{N}_{\mathcal{P}} \cup \mathcal{N}_{\mathcal{R}})$, $d^+ = |\Omega^+_{\mathcal{P}, \mathcal{R}}|$ and consider a new sequence $\omega_1, \ldots, \omega_{d^+}$ of the worlds in $\Omega^+_{\mathcal{P}, \mathcal{R}}$. Let $\mathcal{M}^+_{\mathcal{S}}(\mathcal{R}^\approx) := (V_c^{[i]}(\omega_j) \cdot (1 - x) - F_c^{[i]}(\omega_j) \cdot x)_{1 \leq i \leq k_c, 1 \leq j \leq d^+}$ be the reduced constraint matrix of length $k_{\mathcal{R}^\approx} = 1 + \sum_{c \in \mathcal{R}^\approx} k_c$. Let $\boldsymbol{b}^+$ be the reduced column vector of length $k_{\mathcal{R}^\approx}$ whose last component is 1 and whose remaining components are 0. Then, instead of solving (7), we can solve

$$\arg \min_{q \in \mathbb{R}^{d^+}} \sum_{1 \leq i \leq d^+} q^{[i]} \cdot \log \frac{q^{[i]}}{p^{[i]}}, \tag{8}$$

$$\text{subject to } \mathcal{M}_\mathcal{S}^+(\mathcal{R}^\approx) \cdot q = b^+, \; q \geq 0.$$

Dual Problem: To guarantee that the gradient of the relative entropy R is well-defined at $\mathcal{P}^*$ with respect to $\mathcal{P}$, we presuppose that $\mathcal{P}^*$ is positive on $\Omega^+_{\mathcal{P},\mathcal{R}}$. The open-mindedness principle [16] can be generalized to show that it is sufficient that $\text{Mod}_\mathcal{S}(\mathcal{R})$ contains a single distribution that is $\mathcal{P}$-consistent and positive on $\Omega^+_{\mathcal{P},\mathcal{R}}$ for the assumption to hold. We call such a knowlede base $\mathcal{P}$-*regular*.

By applying Lagrangian techniques and introducing a multiplier λ_i for each row in $\mathcal{M}_\mathcal{S}^+(\mathcal{R}^\approx)$ one can show [7] that the solution p^* of the minimization problem (8) is positive and there is a vector λ^* of $k_{\mathcal{R}^\approx}$ Lagrange multipliers such that

$$p^* = q(\lambda^*) = (p^{[i]} \, exp((\mathcal{M}_\mathcal{S}^+(\mathcal{R}^\approx) \cdot e_i)^T \cdot \lambda^* - 1))_{1 \leq i \leq d^+}, \tag{9}$$

where $q(\lambda) = (p^{[i]} \, exp((\mathcal{M}_\mathcal{S}^+(\mathcal{R}^\approx) \cdot e_i)^T \cdot \lambda - 1))_{1 \leq i \leq d^+}$ and $e_i \in \mathbb{R}^{k_{\mathcal{R}^\approx}}$ denotes the i-th unit vector. Using this result the Wolfe dual to (8) becomes [7]

$$\arg \max_{q \in \mathbb{R}^{d^+}, \lambda \in \mathbb{R}^{k_{\mathcal{R}^\approx}}} \sum_{1 \leq i \leq d^+} q^{[i]} \cdot \log \frac{q^{[i]}}{p^{[i]}} \; - \; \lambda^T(\mathcal{M}_\mathcal{S}^+(\mathcal{R}^\approx) \cdot q - b^+), \tag{10}$$

$$\text{subject to} \qquad q(\lambda) = (p^{[i]} \, exp((\mathcal{M}_\mathcal{S}^+(\mathcal{R}^\approx) \cdot e_i)^T \cdot \lambda - 1))_{1 \leq i \leq d^+} \tag{11}$$

By putting the constraint (11) into (10), q can be eliminated from the problem [7]. In other words, q can be regarded as a function $q(\lambda)$ of the vector λ. This yields the following unconstrained optimization problem:

$$\arg \max_{\lambda \in \mathbb{R}^{k_{\mathcal{R}^\approx}}} \; - \sum_{1 \leq i \leq d^+} q(\lambda)^{[i]} + \lambda^T b^+ \tag{12}$$

Instead of maximizing, we minimize $h(\lambda) = \sum_{1 \leq i \leq d^+} q(\lambda)^{[i]} - \lambda^T b^+$, i.e.:

$$\arg \min_{\lambda \in \mathbb{R}^{k_{\mathcal{R}^\approx}}} h(\lambda) \tag{13}$$

The dual objective $h(\lambda)$ is also convex and therefore can be solved by conjugate gradient or quasi-newton methods. The gradient is $\nabla h(\lambda) = \mathcal{M}_\mathcal{S}^+(\mathcal{R}^\approx) \cdot q(\lambda) - b^+$ [7]. We summarize the essence of this section in the following proposition.

Proposition 1. *Let $\mathcal{P} \in \mathfrak{P}_\Sigma$ and let $\mathcal{R} \subseteq (\mathcal{L}_\Sigma | \mathcal{L}_\Sigma)$ be a $\mathcal{P}$-regular knowledge base interpreted by a linearly structured semantics $\mathcal{S}$. Let $\mathcal{P}^* = \mathcal{P} *_\mathcal{S} \mathcal{R}$ and let λ^* be the solution of (13). Then $\mathcal{P}^*(\omega_i) = q(\lambda^*)^{[i]}$ for $1 \leq i \leq d^+$ and $\mathcal{P}^*(\omega_0) = 0$ for $\omega_0 \in (\mathcal{N}_\mathcal{P} \cup \mathcal{N}_\mathcal{R})$.*

Using the convention $0^0 = 1$, the solution factorizes as follows.

Proposition 2. *Let $\mathcal{R}, \mathcal{P}$ and $\mathcal{P}^*$ be given as in Proposition 1. For $c \in \mathcal{R}^{\approx}$ let $\lambda_{c,i}, 1 \leq i \leq k_c$, denote the Lagrange multiplier corresponding to the i-th constraint function of conditional $c = (\mathfrak{g}|\mathfrak{f})[x_c]$. Let λ_0 denote the Lagrange multiplier corresponding to the normalizing constraint $\mathbf{1}^T x = 1$. Let $Z := exp(1 - \lambda_0)$ and for each conditional $c \in \mathcal{R}$ define k_c functions $\phi_{c,j} : \Omega_\Sigma \to \mathbb{R}$ such that for $1 \leq j \leq k_c$*

$$\phi_{c,j}(\omega) := \begin{cases} exp(\lambda_{c,j} \cdot (V_c^{[j]}(\omega) \cdot (1 - x_c) - F_c^{[j]}(\omega) \cdot x_c)) & \text{if } c \in \mathcal{R}^{\approx} \\ 0^{V_c^{[j]}(\omega) \cdot (1 - x_c) + F_c^{[j]}(\omega) \cdot x_c} & \text{if } c \in \mathcal{R}^{=} \end{cases}$$

Then for all $\omega \in \Omega_\Sigma$ it holds

$$\mathcal{P}^*(\omega) = \frac{\mathcal{P}(\omega)}{Z} \prod_{c \in \mathcal{R}} \prod_{1 \leq j \leq k_c} \phi_{c,j}(\omega). \tag{14}$$

Proof. By putting in the definition of $\mathcal{M}_S^+$ into (9) we obtain for $1 \leq i \leq d^+$

$$q(\boldsymbol{\lambda}^*)^{[i]} = \boldsymbol{p}^{[i]} exp(\lambda_0 - 1 + \sum_{c \in \mathcal{R}^{\approx}} \sum_{1 \leq j \leq k_c} \lambda_{c,j} \cdot (V_c^{[j]}(\omega_i) \cdot (1 - x_c) - F_c^{[j]}(\omega_i) \cdot x_c))$$

$$= \boldsymbol{p}^{[i]} exp(\lambda_0 - 1) \prod_{c \in \mathcal{R}^{\approx}} \prod_{1 \leq j \leq k_c} exp(\lambda_{c,j} \cdot (V_c^{[j]}(\omega_i) \cdot (1 - x_c) - F_c^{[j]}(\omega_i) \cdot x_c))$$

$$= \frac{\boldsymbol{p}^{[i]}}{Z} \prod_{c \in \mathcal{R}^{\approx}} \prod_{1 \leq j \leq k_c} \phi_{c,j}(\omega_i). \tag{15}$$

Recall that $\omega \in \mathcal{N}_\mathcal{R}$ if and only if there is a $c = (\mathfrak{g}|\mathfrak{f})[x] \in \mathcal{R}^{=}$ such that either $x = 0$ and $V_c(\omega) \neq 0$ or $x = 1$ and $F_c(\omega) \neq 0$. Hence there is a $j \in \{1, \ldots, k_c\}$ such that $\phi_{c,j}(\omega) = 0$. Conversely, if $\omega \in (\Omega_\Sigma \setminus \mathcal{N}_\mathcal{R})$, then $\phi_{c,j}(\omega) = 0^0 = 1$ for all $c \in \mathcal{R}^{=}$ and $1 \leq j \leq k_c$. Hence the product $\prod_{c \in \mathcal{R}^{=}} \prod_{1 \leq j \leq k_c} \phi_{c,j}(\omega)$ is 0 if $\omega \in \mathcal{N}_\mathcal{R}$ and 1 if $\omega \in (\Omega_\Sigma \setminus \mathcal{N}_\mathcal{R})$. Hence, if $\omega \in \mathcal{N}_\mathcal{R}$, then it holds $\frac{\mathcal{P}(\omega)}{Z} \prod_{c \in \mathcal{R}} \prod_{1 \leq j \leq k_c} \phi_{c,j}(\omega) = \frac{\mathcal{P}(\omega)}{Z} \prod_{c \in \mathcal{R}^{\approx}} \prod_{1 \leq j \leq k_c} \phi_{c,j}(\omega) \cdot 0 = 0$ and also $\mathcal{P}^*(\omega_0) = 0$ according to Prop. 1.

If $\omega \in \mathcal{N}_\mathcal{P}$, then $\mathcal{P}(\omega) = 0$. As $\mathcal{P}^* \ll \mathcal{P}$, it follows $\mathcal{P}^*(\omega) = 0$. For the factorization we also obtain $\frac{\mathcal{P}(\omega)}{Z} \prod_{c \in \mathcal{R}} \prod_{1 \leq j \leq k_c} \phi_{c,j}(\omega) = 0 \cdot \frac{1}{Z} \prod_{c \in \mathcal{R}} \prod_{1 \leq j \leq k_c} \phi_{c,j}(\omega) = 0$.

Finally, if $\omega \in \Omega_{\mathcal{P},\mathcal{R}}^+$, then $\omega = \omega_i$ for some $i, 1 \leq i \leq d^+$. The factorization yields $\frac{\mathcal{P}(\omega_i)}{Z} \prod_{c \in \mathcal{R}} \prod_{1 \leq j \leq k_c} \phi_{c,j}(\omega_i) = \frac{\mathcal{P}(\omega_i)}{Z} \prod_{c \in \mathcal{R}^{\approx}} \prod_{1 \leq j \leq k_c} \phi_{c,j}(\omega_i) \cdot 1 = q(\boldsymbol{\lambda}^*)^{[i]}$ according to (15) and also $\mathcal{P}^*(\omega_i) = q(\boldsymbol{\lambda}^*)^{[i]}$ according to Prop. 1.

Hence $\mathcal{P}^*(\omega) = \frac{\mathcal{P}(\omega)}{Z} \prod_{c \in \mathcal{R}} \prod_{1 \leq j \leq k_c} \phi_{c,j}(\omega_i)$ for all $\omega \in \Omega_\Sigma$.

Computing Iterative Belief Changes and Factorization: A sequence of update and revision operations yields a sequence of belief bases $(\mathcal{P}_0, \mathcal{R}_0), (\mathcal{P}_1, \mathcal{R}_1), (\mathcal{P}_2, \mathcal{R}_2), \ldots$, where for $k \geq 1$ either $\mathcal{P}_{k+1} = \mathcal{P}_k *_S \mathcal{R}_k$ by update or $\mathcal{P}_{k+1} = \mathcal{P}_k$ by revision. If we presuppose that $\mathcal{R}_k$ is $\mathcal{P}_k$-regular for $k \geq 0$, all corresponding epistemic states are well-defined and can be computed according to Proposition 1.

If $\mathcal{P}_0$ is any distribution that factorizes, Proposition 2 guarantees that after a sequence of revision and update operations the distribution $\mathcal{P}_k, k \geq 1$, still factorizes. Note that

Table 3. Runtime results for aggregating semantics

Knowledge base	Size of $Const$	Size of Ω_Σ	Size of $\Omega_\Sigma/\equiv_\mathcal{R}$	Iterations GIS	GIS/$\equiv_\mathcal{R}$	L-BFGS	Runtime (sec.) GIS	GIS/$\equiv_\mathcal{R}$	L-BFGS
Monkey	4	2^{20}	4,661	33,914	33,914	57	24,600	129	11
Synthetic	10	2^{20}	120	892	892	16	454	12	3
Flu	4	2^{20}	91	686	686	15	286	12	4

this in particular holds if we initialize our belief base with the uniform distribution $\mathcal{P}_0(\omega) = \frac{1}{|\Omega_\Sigma|}$, as it can be regarded as a trivial factorization.

The representation by factors is beneficial from a computational point of view, because we do not have to store each probability, but can restrict to the factors $\phi_{c,j}$. As Table 1 indicates, the internal factors V_c and F_c depend only on a subset of ground atoms from Ω_Σ that is determined by the ground instances of the conditional c. As the knowledge base grows, factors can be merged as it is explained in the theory of Markov Random Fields [13]. In particular, such factorizations induce an equivalence relation on worlds, that is referred to as conditional structure of worlds [10]. As explained in [4] for the aggregating semantics, the conditional structure can be exploited to shrink the number of worlds that have to be regarded in optimization problems. Transferred to equation (12), instead of computing $q(\lambda)^{[i]}$ for all d^+ worlds, it is sufficient to compute the value for representatives of equivalence classes, as each element of this class yields the same value.

Experiments: To evaluate the advantage of the dual problem (13), we compare runtime results for three relational conditional test sets with $|\Omega_\Sigma| = 2^{20} = 1,048,576$ and no deterministic conditionals proposed for the aggregating semantics in [4]. As a baseline we use the naive Generalized Iterative Scaling (GIS) implementation and its optimized version (GIS/$\equiv_\mathcal{R}$) that exploits equivalences of worlds from [4]. To solve the unconstrained dual problem, we apply the L-BFGS implementation of the RISO-project[1]. Table 3 shows the number of constants and the corresponding number of worlds that have to be regarded by the algorithms, the number of iterations needed to converge, and runtime results in seconds. Whereas GIS and L-BFGS use the whole set Ω_Σ, GIS/$\equiv_\mathcal{R}$ regards only the worlds in $\Omega_\Sigma/\equiv_\mathcal{R}$ and therefore is significantly faster than GIS, even though it needs the same number of iterations. The results are not fully comparable, as GIS and L-BFGS use different termination criteria. GIS terminates when the relative change of scaling factors goes below a threshold, whereas L-BFGS converges when the constraints are satisfied with respect to a certain accuracy threshold. We used a termination threshold of 10^{-3} for both GIS implementations. Then constraints were satisfied with an accuracy of approximately 10^{-4}. To avoid overoptimistic results we used an accuracy threshold of 10^{-6} for L-BFGS. L-BFGS performs remarkably better than GIS and is at least three times faster than the optimized version GIS/$\equiv_\mathcal{R}$, which primarily differs from the naive GIS implementation by significantly reduced iteration costs. As explained before, the same optimization can be applied to L-BFGS additionally.

---

[1] http://sourceforge.net/projects/riso/

5   Conclusion and Future Work

By extending the belief change operations revision and update from [11] to relational languages, we obtained a framework to deal with uncertain and changing information in a relational domain. Transforming the corresponding computational problem into its Wolfe dual allows to employ algorithms for unconstrained problems like L-BFGS [18]. For model computation for the relational aggregating semantics a significant performance gain compared to recent algorithms from [4] is obtained. In future work we will investigate to which extent the factorization in (14) can be used to apply techniques for Markov random fields [13] to further speed up the computation.

References

[1] Alchourrón, C., Gärdenfors, P., Makinson, D.: On the logic of theory change: Partial meet contraction and revision functions. Journal of Symbolic Logic 50(2), 510–530 (1985)

[2] Beierle, C., Kern-Isberner, G.: A conceptual agent model based on a uniform approach to various belief operations. In: Mertsching, B., Hund, M., Aziz, Z. (eds.) KI 2009. LNCS (LNAI), vol. 5803, pp. 273–280. Springer, Heidelberg (2009)

[3] Csiszar, I.: I-Divergence Geometry of Probability Distributions and Minimization Problems. The Annals of Probability 3(1), 146–158 (1975)

[4] Finthammer, M., Beierle, C.: Using equivalences of worlds for aggregation semantics of relational conditionals. In: Glimm, B., Krüger, A. (eds.) KI 2012. LNCS (LNAI), vol. 7526, pp. 49–60. Springer, Heidelberg (2012)

[5] Finthammer, M., Beierle, C., Berger, B., Kern-Isberner, G.: Probabilistic reasoning at optimum entropy with the MECORE system. In: Lane, H.C., Guesgen, H.W. (eds.) Proc. FLAIRS-2009. AAAI Press, Menlo Park (2009)

[6] Fisseler, J.: First-order probabilistic conditional logic and maximum entropy. Logic Journal of the IGPL 20(5), 796–830 (2012)

[7] Fletcher, R.: Practical methods of optimization, 2nd edn. Wiley-Interscience, New York (1987)

[8] Grove, A., Halpern, J., Koller, D.: Random worlds and maximum entropy. J. of Artificial Intelligence Research 2, 33–88 (1994)

[9] Katsuno, H., Mendelzon, A.: Propositional knowledge base revision and minimal change. Artificial Intelligence 52, 263–294 (1991)

[10] Kern-Isberner, G.: Conditionals in Nonmonotonic Reasoning and Belief Revision. LNCS (LNAI), vol. 2087. Springer, Heidelberg (2001)

[11] Kern-Isberner, G.: Linking iterated belief change operations to nonmonotonic reasoning. In: Proc. KR 2008, pp. 166–176. AAAI Press, Menlo Park (2008)

[12] Kern-Isberner, G., Thimm, M.: Novel semantical approaches to relational probabilistic conditionals. In: Proc. KR 2010, pp. 382–391. AAAI Press, Menlo Park (2010)

[13] Koller, D., Friedman, N.: Probabilistic Graphical Models: Principles and Techniques. MIT Press (2009)

[14] Lukasiewicz, T.: Probabilistic deduction with conditional constraints over basic events. J. Artif. Intell. Res. 10, 380–391 (1999)

[15] Nilsson, N.J.: Probabilistic logic. Artif. Intell. 28, 71–88 (1986)

[16] Paris, J.: The uncertain reasoner's companion – A mathematical perspective. Cambridge University Press (1994)

[17] Potyka, N.: Towards a general framework for maximum entropy reasoning. In: Proc. FLAIRS 2012, pp. 555–560. AAAI Press, Menlo Park (2012)

[18] Zhu, C., Byrd, R.H., Lu, P., Nocedal, J.: Algorithm 778: L-BFGS-B: Fortran subroutines for large-scale bound-constrained optimization. ACM Trans. Math. Softw. 23(4), 550–560 (1997)

Translating Single-Player GDL into PDDL

Thorsten Rauber, Peter Kissmann, and Jörg Hoffmann

Saarland University
Saarbrücken, Germany
s9thraub@stud.uni-saarland.de,
{kissmann,hoffmann}@cs.uni-saarland.de

Abstract. In the single-agent case general game playing and action planning are two related topics, so that one might hope to use the established planners to improve the handling of general single-player games. However, both come with their own description language, GDL and PDDL, respectively. In this paper we propose a way to translate single-player games described in GDL to PDDL planning tasks and provide an evaluation on a wide range of single-player games, comparing the efficiency of grounding and solving the games in the translated and in the original format.

1 Introduction

The current form of general game playing (GGP) was developed around 2005, when the first international GGP competition was held [3]. It aims at developing game playing agents that can handle and efficiently play any game that is describable using the game description language GDL [9]. In its basic form a wide range of games can be modeled, though there are severe restrictions, namely to deterministic games of full information, which immediately rule out most dice and card games. In recent years the most successful GGP agents such as CadiaPlayer [1] or Ary [11] made use of the UCT algorithm [8], which often delivers good results in multi-player games but lacks in single-player settings.

That is where action planning comes in. Similar to GGP, action planning aims at developing agents that can handle any planning task that is describable by the input language, which, since 1998, is the planning domain definition language PDDL [10]. There is a close connection between general single-player games and planning. In both cases the agent will be confronted with problems for which it has to find a solution (i.e., a sequence of moves or actions) leading from a specified initial state to a state satisfying a goal condition. While in planning the solution length is often relevant, in GGP each goal state is assigned some reward and the aim is to maximize the achieved reward. Finding an optimal solution reduces to finding a solution that results in a state satisfying a goal achieving the highest possible reward. As the programmer does not know in advance the problems that the agent will be confronted with, in both settings domain-independent approaches are required.

Even though the setting is similar, there are severe differences in the input languages. If we want to make use of the existing efficient planners (e.g., Fast-Forward [6], Fast-Downward [5], or LAMA [13]) to improve the handling of single-player games we need to provide a translation from GDL to PDDL, which is the topic of this paper.

I.J. Timm and M. Thimm (Eds.): KI 2013, LNAI 8077, pp. 188–199, 2013.

The remainder of this paper is structured as follows. We begin with a description of the two input languages PDDL and GDL (Section 2), then turn to the translation from GDL to PDDL (Section 3) and show some empirical results illustrating that the translation works well and that planners can handle the generated input, sometimes even outperforming the GGP agent we took as reference (Section 4). Finally, we discuss related work and draw some conclusions (Section 5).

2   Background

2.1   Action Planning

A planning task is a tuple $\Pi = \langle V, A, I, G \rangle$, where V are the state variables (we do not handle finite domains here, so we assume all variables to be binary), A is a finite set of actions a each of which is a pair $\langle \text{pre}_a, \text{eff}_a \rangle$ of partial assignments to V with pre_a being the precondition and eff_a the effect of action a, the initial state I is a complete assignment to V, and the goal is a partial assignment to V.

In our translation we also make use of conditional effects, which are nested effects with their own precondition cpre and effect ceff. The effect of a conditional effect is only evaluated if its precondition holds in the current state. Note that nesting conditional effects is not possible.

Derived predicates as introduced in [2] are another important feature that we will use. The idea is to infer their truth from the truth of the state variables. So derived predicates are computed from scratch in every state. A derived predicate is of the form (:derived (h ?v1 ... ?vn) b1 ... bm) and can be inferred if and only if its body b1 ... bm is true in the current state. In contrast to state variables derived predicates can only be used in preconditions and effect conditions as well as in goal descriptions. Hence they cannot be set in effects of actions [16].

We can define the semantics of a planning task in the following way by assuming that effect literals are not conflicting.

Definition 1 (PDDL Semantics). *The semantics of a planning task* $\Pi = \langle V, A, I, G \rangle$ *is given by the following state transition system* (S_0, L, u, g), *with* $S \subseteq V$ *being a state:*

- $S_0 = \{p \mid p \in I\}$ *(the initial state)*
- $L = \{(a, S) \mid a \in A \land \text{pre}_a \subseteq S\}$ *(a set of pairs* (a, S) *where action* a *can be performed in state* S)
- $u(a, S) = S \setminus \{p \mid (\text{not } p) \in \text{eff}_a\} \cup \{p \mid p \in \text{eff}_a\}$

$$\setminus \{p \mid (\textit{when } (\text{cpre})(\text{ceff})) \in \text{eff}_a \land \text{cpre} \subseteq S \land (\text{not } p) \in \text{ceff}\}$$

$$\cup \{p \mid (\textit{when } (\text{cpre})(\text{ceff})) \in \text{eff}_a \land \text{cpre} \subseteq S \land p \in \text{ceff}\}$$

   (update function giving the successor state for a chosen action a *in state* S)
- $g = \{S \mid G \subseteq S\}$ *(the set of goal states).*

Example. Figure 1 shows a PDDL example of blocksworld. It contains two actions. The stack action (lines 5–12) takes some block ?x, which is currently on the table and clear (i.e., no other block is stacked on top of it), and places it on top of another block

?y, which must be clear as well. The unstack action (lines 13–17) removes a block from another block if they are currently stacked and the upper one is clear. In addition there are two derived predicates. The first one denotes that a block is clear if no block is placed on top of it (lines 18–19), the second one denotes that a block is on the table if it is not currently stacked on some block (lines 20–21).

```
 1  (define (domain blocksworld)
 2      (:predicates (clear ?x)
 3                   (table ?x)
 4                   (on ?x ?y) )
 5      (:action stack
 6          :parameters (?x ?y)
 7          :precondition (and
 8              (clear ?x)
 9              (clear ?y)
10              (table ?x)
11              (not (= ?x ?y)) )
12          :effect (on ?x ?y) )
13      (:action unstack
14          :parameters (?x ?y)
15          :precondition (and (clear ?x)
16                             (on ?x ?y) )
17          :effect (not (on ?x ?y)) )

18      (:derived (clear ?x)
19          (forall (?y) (not (on ?y ?x))) )
20      (:derived (table ?x)
21          (forall (?y) (not (on ?x ?y))) ) )
22
23  (define (problem blocksworld3)
24      (:domain blocksworld)
25      (:objects A B C)
26      (:init
27          (on C A) )
28      (:goal
29          (and
30              (on A B)
31              (on B C) ) ) )
```

Fig. 1. PDDL example for Blocksworld

In this instance we have three blocks, A, B, and C (line 25), where initially block C is on top of block A (lines 26–27). Following the derived predicates, blocks A and B thus reside on the table and blocks B and C are clear. The goal is to reach a state where block A is on top of block B and block B is on top of block C (lines 28–31).

2.2   General Game Playing

General games are modeled by use of the game description language GDL. This language is similar to logic programs, so that a game is modeled by a set of rules. In order to derive any meaning, some fixed keywords are used:

role(p) p is a player of the game.
init(f) f holds in the initial state.
true(f) f holds in the current state.
next(f) f holds in the successor state.
legal(p,m) Player p may perform move m.
does(p,m) Player p chooses to perform move m.
terminal Whenever terminal becomes true the game ends.
goal(p,rw) Player p achieves reward rw (an integer value in [0,100]).
distinct(x,y) x and y are semantically different.

All rules are of the form $(<= h\ b_1 \ldots b_n)$ with the meaning that head h will hold if all literals $b_1, \ldots, b_n$ of the body hold. Note that in GDL all operands are given in prefix form, and that the conjunction of the bodies' literals is implicit. Rules with a head different from the keywords are called axioms, which in principle are very similar to derived predicates in PDDL: Their truth value must be derived based on the current state and with help of the other axioms.

The semantics of a general game modeled in GDL can be found in [4]. We give only the basic definition:

Definition 2 (GDL Semantics [4]). *The semantics of a valid GDL specification G of a general game is given by the following state transition system $\langle R, S_0, T, L, u, g \rangle$:*

- $R = \{r \mid G \vdash role(r)\}$ *(the players in the game)*
- $S_0 = \{p \mid G \vdash init(p)\}$ *(the initial state)*
- $T = \{S \mid G \cup S^{true} \vdash terminal\}$ *(the set of terminal states)*
- $L = \{(role, a, S) \mid G \cup S^{true} \vdash legal(role, a)\}$ *(relation specifying legal moves)*
- $u(A, S) = \{p \mid G \cup A^{does} \cup S^{true} \vdash next(p)\}$ *(state update function)*
- $g = \{(role, rw, S) \mid G \cup S^{true} \vdash goal(role, rw)\}$ *(relation specifying rewards)*

where A^{does} describes the moves that the players have chosen and S^{true} describes the state variables that are currently true in state S.

An important observation is that negation-as-failure is assumed, i.e., anything that cannot be derived is assumed to be false. That means especially that the successor state is fully specified by evaluating the next rules: Everything that can be derived by rules with head next will be true in the successor state, everything else will be false. In other words, in GDL the frame is modeled explicitly, while in PDDL only the state changes are modeled and the rest is assumed to remain unchanged.

Example. Figure 2 shows a GDL example for the same blocksworld instance as the PDDL example. The initial state (lines 3–8) is extended by a step counter, which is needed as in GGP games are supposed to terminate after a finite number of steps [9]. In order to achieve the highest possible reward of 100, the robot must find a way to reach a state where block a is on top of block b and block b is on top of block c (lines 56–58). The moves for stacking (lines 10–14) and unstacking (lines 16–18) have the same preconditions as in the PDDL example. To determine the successor state the next rules must be evaluated. While those in lines 20–28 are responsible for the actual state update, those in lines 30–50 model the frame. The constant axioms (lines 52–54) are needed to model the step counter. The terminal rules (lines 64–68) indicate that the game ends after three steps or if block a is on top of block b and block b is on top of block c.

3   Translation

The basic idea of our translation is to use derived predicates to handle most of the GDL rules, and to perform the state update in three steps in order to translate GDL's explicit modeling of the frame to PDDL. First, we set the player's action. Then we evaluate the next rules in order to get a full description of the successor state. In this step we remove the current state variables and store the successor state in temporary variables. Finally we set the successor state to the temporarily stored one.

```
 1 (role robot)
 2
 3 (init (clear b))
 4 (init (clear c))
 5 (init (on c a))
 6 (init (table a))
 7 (init (table b))
 8 (init (step 0))
 9
10 (<= (legal robot (stack ?x ?y))
11     (true (clear ?x))
12     (true (table ?x))
13     (true (clear ?y))
14     (distinct ?x ?y))
15
16 (<= (legal robot (unstack ?x ?y))
17     (true (clear ?x))
18     (true (on ?x ?y)))
19
20 (<= (next (on ?x ?y))
21     (does robot (stack ?x ?y)))
22 (<= (next (table ?x))
23     (does robot (unstack ?x ?y)))
24 (<= (next (clear ?y))
25     (does robot (unstack ?x ?y)))
26 (<= (next (step ?y))
27     (true (step ?x))
28     (succ ?x ?y))
29
30 (<= (next (clear ?x))
31     (does robot (unstack ?u ?v))
32     (true (clear ?x)))
33 (<= (next (on ?x ?y))
34     (does robot (stack ?u ?v))
35     (true (on ?x ?y)))
```

```
36 (<= (next (clear ?y))
37     (does robot (stack ?u ?v))
38     (true (clear ?y))
39     (distinct ?v ?y))
40 (<= (next (on ?x ?y))
41     (does robot (unstack ?u ?v))
42     (true (on ?x ?y))
43     (distinct ?u ?x))
44 (<= (next (table ?x))
45     (does robot (stack ?u ?v))
46     (true (table ?x))
47     (distinct ?u ?x))
48 (<= (next (table ?x))
49     (does robot (unstack ?u ?v))
50     (true (table ?x)))
51
52 (succ 0 1)
53 (succ 1 2)
54 (succ 2 3)
55
56 (<= (goal robot 100)
57     (true (on a b))
58     (true (on b c)))
59 (<= (goal robot 0)
60     (not (true (on a b))))
61 (<= (goal robot 0)
62     (not (true (on b c))))
63
64 (<= terminal
65     (true (step 3)))
66 (<= terminal
67     (true (on a b))
68     (true (on b c)))
```

Fig. 2. GDL example for blocksworld

3.1   Basic Translation

Apart from `init` and `goal` (see Section 3.3) all GDL rules are translated as derived predicates. Each rule of the form `(<= (h ?v1 ... ?vn) b1 ... bm)` is translated into a derived predicate of the form

```
(:derived (h ?v1 ... ?vn)
  (exists (?f1 ... ?fk)
    (and b1 ... bm ) ) )
```

where `?f1 ... ?fk` are the free variables appearing in the body.

Currently, we cannot handle functions in general. However, in order to store the current/next state as well as the legal/chosen moves, we translate a predicate of the form `(next (p ?v1 ... ?vn))` as `(next-p ?v1 ... ?vn)`, `(true (p ?v1 ... ?vn))` as `(current-p ?v1 ... ?vn)`, `(legal ?p (move ?v1 ... ?vn))` as `(legal-move ?p ?v1 ... ?vn)`, and `(does ?p (move ?v1 ... ?vn))` as `(does-move ?p ?v1 ... ?vn)`. Furthermore, `(distinct ?v1 ?v2)` is translated as `(not (= ?v1 ?v2))`. Any constants are translated with prefix `obj-`, as GDL allows constants starting with numbers while PDDL does not.

In case some variable ?v appears more than once in the head we must replace all but one instance of it by new variables ?vi and add (= ?vi ?v) to the body's conjunction for all of the replaced variables. If there is any constant c in the head we must replace it by a new variable ?cvar and add (= ?cvar c) to the conjunction.

Constant axioms, i.e., axiom rules with empty body, can either be placed unchanged into the initial state description or translated into derived predicates as the other rules. If for some axiom constant and non-constant rules are present we must opt for the latter.

3.2 State Update

For any move the player may perform we create an action as depicted in Figure 3. This takes the same n parameters as the original GDL move. The precondition states that the game is not yet ended, the play predicate is true, which expresses that the player can choose a move in the current state, and that the player is allowed to actually perform the move in the current state, i.e., that the corresponding derived legal predicate can be evaluated to true. When applying the action we set the corresponding move and the eval predicate to true, which brings us to perform the first of the two additional actions that simulate the state update.

```
(:action move
  :parameters (?v1 ... ?vn)
  :precondition (and
    (not (terminal))
    (play)
    (legal-move player ?v1 ... ?vn) )
  :effect (and
    (does-move player ?v1 ... ?vn)
    (not (play))
    (eval) ) )
```

Fig. 3. Move action in the translation from GDL to PDDL

The basic idea of the eval action (cf. Figure 4, top; we need only one that takes care of all predicates and moves) is to determine the successor state based on the current state and the chosen move and to store it in temporary variables. It evaluates all derived next predicates and sets the temporary variables corresponding to the satisfied ones. In addition it removes all current state variables as well as the chosen move and changes from eval to switch, which brings us to the second additional action.

The resume-play action is depicted in the bottom of Figure 4. It sets the new state's current state variables and removes the temporary ones. Then it changes back to the play predicate so that the player's next move can be chosen. Similar to the eval action, we use only one resume-play action that handles all predicates.

A state update with only a single additional action would be possible as well by creating two sets of conditional effects: One as before, setting a state variable to true

```
(:action eval
  :precondition (eval)
  :effect (and
    (forall (?vp1 ... ?vpn)
      (when (next-p ?vp1 ... ?vpn) (temp-p ?vp1 ... ?vpn) )
    (forall (?vp1 ... ?vpn)
      (not (current-p ?vp1 ... ?vpn)) )
    (forall (?vm1 ... ?vmn)
      (not (does-move player ?vm1 ... ?vmn)) )
    (not (eval))
    (switch) ) )

(:action resume-play
  :precondition (switch)
  :effect (and
    (forall (?vp1 ... ?vpn)
      (when
        (temp-p ?vp1 ... ?vpn)
        (and
          (current-p ?vp1 ... ?vpn)
          (not (temp-p ?vp1 ... ?vpn)) ) ) )
    (not (switch))
    (play) ) )
```

Fig. 4. The `eval` and `resume-play` actions

if at least one of the corresponding `next` predicates can be evaluated to true, the other setting it to false if all corresponding `next` predicates are evaluated as false. However, this often results in formulas in CNF, which most planners cannot handle efficiently.

3.3   Initial State, Rewards, and Termination

The initial state of the PDDL translation captures all state variables that are initially true. Thus, each rule (`init` (`f v1 ... vn`)) in the GDL description is translated as (`current-f v1 ... vn`) and added to the initial state. In addition, we must add the predicate `play`.

In our current setting we are only interested in finding an optimal solution, i.e., one that leads us to a goal state that achieves a reward of 100. Due to the GDL specification of a well-formed game [9] the possibility to reach a goal state with reward 100 must exist. Presuming that we have a set of goal rules:

```
(<= (goal ?p 100)
  b11 ... b1n)
...
(<= (goal ?p 100)
  bm1 ... bmn)
```

we build up the following goal description in PDDL:

```
(:goal
  (and
    (terminal)
    (or
      (exists (?v1_1 ... ?v1_n) (and b11 ... b1n))
      ...
      (exists (?vm_1 ... ?vm_n) (and bm1 ... bmn)) ) ) )
```

where `?vi_1 ... ?vi_n` are the free variables in the body of the i-th goal rule. The `terminal` predicate is necessary because we want to reach a terminal state with reward 100; the reward of the non-terminal states is irrelevant for our purposes.

3.4 Restrictions of the Translation

As pointed out earlier, currently we can only translate functions in a very limited form, namely the functions representing the state variables, as well as those representing moves. Any other form of functions is not yet supported. Replacement of any of the functions by a variable is unsupported as well. It remains future work to find efficient ways to handle these cases.

The current form of our translation cannot handle GDL descriptions that use the `goal` predicate in the body of other rules. A straight-forward fix is to translate all `goal` rules into derived predicates as well.

Concerning the rewards, we are currently only translating the maximum reward 100. By making use of plan cost minimization it is possible to also handle different rewards. We can define a new action `reach-goal` that has `terminal` and `(goal role rw)` in the precondition (where `rw` corresponds to a natural number) and sets a unique variable `goal-reached` to true. This new action has a cost of $100 - rw$, while all other actions have a cost of 0. Then the goal description reduces to the variable `goal-reached` being true. Overall, this means that if we reach a terminal state that has reward 100 in GDL we can use the action `reach-goal` with cost 0 to reach the goal in PDDL. As planners try to minimize the total cost they will thus try to reach a terminal state that has the highest possible reward.

3.5 Correctness of the Translation

In order to prove the correctness of our translation we must define the semantical equivalence of a PDDL and GDL state w.r.t. our translation.

Definition 3 (Semantical equivalence of a PDDL state and a GDL state). *A PDDL state S^{PDDL} of a state transition system $(S_0^{PDDL}, L^{PDDL}, u^{PDDL}, g^{PDDL})$ and a GDL state S^{GDL} of a state transition system $(R, S_0^{GDL}, T, L^{GDL}, u^{GDL}, g^{GDL})$ are semantically equivalent if all of the following holds:*

1. $\forall x : x \in S^{true, GDL} \Leftrightarrow (current\text{-}x) \in S^{PDDL}$
2. $\forall x : x \in R \Leftrightarrow (role\ obj\text{-}x) \in S^{PDDL}$

3. $\forall a : (role, a, S^{GDL}) \in L^{GDL} \Leftrightarrow \exists a \in A : (a, S^{PDDL}) \in L^{PDDL}$

4. $S^{GDL} \in T \Leftrightarrow \exists \text{ terminal } \in \text{ derived\_predicates} : S^{PDDL} \vdash \text{ terminal}$

5. the axiom rule ax can be fired in $S^{GDL} \Leftrightarrow$ the derived predicate of ax can be derived in S^{PDDL}

where A is the set of actions and derived_predicates is the set of derived predicates that occur in the PDDL task.

We are allowed to use Definition 1 (PDDL Semantics) in the definition of semantical equivalence above because the assumption of Definition 1 is fulfilled: The translation from GDL to PDDL does not create conflicting literals in effects per definition.

Due to space restrictions we can only outline the proof ideas; a longer version can be found in [12].

The basic idea is to prove the correctness by means of induction. First we can show that the initial states in both settings are semantically equivalent, which is apparent due to the translation of the initial state and the other rules in form of derived predicates.

Next we can prove that, for semantically equivalent states, the application of a move in GDL and the three steps for the state update in PDDL result in semantically equivalent states again. This follows immediately from the actions in our PDDL translation: The move action sets the player's chosen move, the `eval` action evaluates the `next` predicates based on the chosen move and the current state and stores only the positive `next` predicates in temporary variables while removing all instances of the `current` state variables. Finally, the `resume-play` action sets the `current` state variables according to the temporary ones.

The last thing to prove is that PDDL's goal states secure the highest possible reward of 100, which again follows immediately from the construction – we translate the conditions of the `goal` rules that award 100 points as the goal condition.

4   Empirical Evaluation

In the following we present empirical results of the proposed translation and a comparison in terms of coverage and runtime between two planners (Fast-Forward (FF) [6] and FastDownward (FD) [5]) and a GGP agent (the symbolic solver and explicit UCT player in Gamer [7]) taking the original input. All tests were performed on a machine with an Intel Core i7-2600k CPU with 3.4 GHz and 8 GB RAM. We tried to translate 55 single-player games from the ggpserver[1] with our implementation of the translation. Nine games cannot be translated by our approach due to the restrictions we posted earlier in Section 3.4. For the remaining 46 games the second column of Table 1 shows the required time of the translation. These times range between 0.15s and 0.35s, mainly dependent on the size of the game description.

The first numbers of the third and fourth column show the preprocessing (esp. grounding) and solving time of FF, the first numbers of columns 5 and 6 indicate the necessary time of the translate and search process of FD (among other things the translate process is responsible for grounding the input), and the last three columns detail

---

[1] http://ggpserver.general-game-playing.de

Table 1. Empirical results of 46 GDL games. Games where we could remove the step-counter are denoted with an asterisk (*). For FF and FD the numbers in parantheses are the times for the games with removed step-counter. All times in seconds.

Game	Trans	FF pre	FF	FD trans	FD search	G. inst	G. solv	G. play
8puzzle(*)	0.17	– (–)		9.06 (2.33)	535.54 (0.38)	0.63	22.67	err
asteroids(*)	0.2	0.7 (0.06)	5.82 (1.76)	0.51 (0.38)	0.34 (0.53)	0.16	1.69	2.85
asteroidsparallel(*)	0.21	10.47 (1.23)	– (–)	4.36 (1)	16.2 (27.85)	0.03	–	err
asteroidsserial(*)	0.23	2.41 (0.31)	– (–)	10.11 (5.8)	– (472.92)	0.41	–	–
blocks(*)	0.16	0.01 (0.01)	0.01 (0.01)	0.07 (0.08)	0 (0.02)	0.06	0.33	0.05
blocksworldparallel	0.18	–		17.57	0.24	0.31	0.77	0.06
blocksworldserial	0.18	0.04	–	0.24	0	0.1	0.57	0.06
brain_teaser_extended(*)	0.19	5.56 (0.1)	– (–)	NAI (NAI)		0.17	1.56	8.22
buttons(*)	0.17	0 (0)	0 (0.01)	0.05 (0.06)	0 (0.02)	0.05	0.3	0.05
circlesolitaire	0.16	0.02	–	NAI		0.06	0.5	0.06
cube_2x2x2(*)	0.2	– (–)		798.83 (78.24)	0.1 (0.09)	0.16	–	0.8
duplicatestatesmall	0.19	0.01	–	0.96	0.2	0.06	0.46	0.05
duplicatestatemedium	0.26	0.17	–	–		0.18	1.17	0.23
duplicatestatelarge	0.35	1.55	–	–		0.64	6.16	1.54
firefighter	0.18	–		0.34	0	0.21	–	err
frogs_and_toads(*)	0.24	– (–)		– (–)		32.94	–	–
god(*)	0.19	– (–)		67.73 (38.16)	0.38 (0.23)	–		9.67
hanoi	0.16	0.73	88.26	0.46	0.24	0.14	0.67	2.83
hanoi_6_disks(*)	0.17	232.22 (0.09)	– (–)	NAI (NAI)		0.67	1.93	13.74
hitori	0.21	–		–		–		0.38
incredible(*)	0.18	– (0.64)	– (–)	1.28 (1.25)	0.08 (0.11)	0.33	4.55	57.73
kitten_escapes_from_fire	0.18	234.36	–	NAI		0.5	0.8	0.09
knightmove	0.19	–		NAI		1.4	–	250.93
knightstour	0.18	–		–		0.24	316.2	3.07
lightsout(*)	0.18	– (–)		NAI (NAI)		0.1	183.8	err
lightsout2(*)	0.16	– (0.14)	– (–)	NAI (NAI)		0.1	185.12	err
max_knights	0.2	–		NAI		69.46	–	err
maze(*)	0.15	0.01 (0)	– (0)	0.07 (0.07)	0 (0.02)	0.05	0.35	0.06
mimikry(*)	0.2	– (–)		NAI (NAI)		11.3	4.23	12.44
oisters_farm(*)	0.18	0.06 (0.01)	0.06 (0.01)	0.32 (0.15)	0 (0.03)	0.08	0.63	0.61
pancakes	0.16	–		–		1.0	1.26	12.19
pancakes6	0.16	–		–		0.99	1.23	32.87
pancakes88	0.17	–		–		–		err
peg_bugfixed	0.18	–		–		1.63	–	err
queens	0.19	–		NAI		–		–
ruledepthlinear	0.27	–		9.05	0	0.25	0.61	0.08
ruledepthquadratic	0.34			–		–		–
statespacesmall	0.15	0.02	–	0.04	0	0.06	0.48	0.08
statespacemedium	0.22	0.03	0.03	0.09	0	0.15	1.46	err
statespacelarge	0.32	0.07	0.17	0.19	0.02	0.39	0.29	err
tpeg	0.18	–		–		1.77	–	err
troublemaker01	0.15	0.03	–	0.02	0	0.05	0.29	0.04
troublemaker02	0.15	0.01	–	0.02	0	0.05	0.29	0.05
twisty-passages	0.18	–		46.95	0.84	50.31	3.84	13.9
walkingman(*)	0.2	– (–)		28.58 (30.23)	0.18 (0.13)	878.13	3.91	0.06
wargame01(*)	0.23	– (–)		NAI (–)		–		0.26
Coverage	46	21/46 (11/19)	7/46 (5/19)	24/46 (12/19)	23/46 (12/19)	40/46	31/46	31/46

(from left to right) the results of Gamer's instantiator, solver, and Prolog-based UCT player. The value "–" indicates that the process did not terminate within the time limit of 900 seconds. In case of FD note that it cannot handle nested negated axioms (i.e., negated axioms dependent on other negated axioms) and throws an error, here denoted by "NAI" (Negated Axioms Impossible). The settings we used for the FD search process are: --heuristic "hff=ff()" --search "lazy_greedy(hff, preferred=hff)".

For FF we can see that it can ground 21 out of the 46 translatable games and solve only 7 of those within 900 seconds. With FD we can solve 23 games within this time limit. In most cases FD's translate process takes either too long (11 cases) or has trouble with nested negated axioms (11 cases). In a single case (asteroidsserial) FD's translate process finishes but no solution can be found in time. Gamer is able to solve 31 games within 900 seconds. The comparison of the runtimes between FD and Gamer delivers a mixed result. FD is faster than Gamer in 19 games whereas Gamer is faster in 17 games, but these include 7 games where FD throws the NAI exception. The UCT player can also find solutions for 31 of the games. Unfortunately, it crashes with some Prolog-related errors in ten cases. In the cases it runs fine it is able to solve four games that the solver can not. In the other games often the player is much slower than the solver and only in few cases clearly faster.

At first it seems surprising that, on the one hand, there are games like asteroidsparallel that can be solved very fast by FD while Gamer cannot find a solution within 900 seconds. On the other hand there are games like 8puzzle where the pure solving time is clearly in favor of Gamer. One explanation for this behavior becomes apparent when considering step-counters, which 19 of the games contain to ensure termination after a finite number of steps. While Gamer requires games to be finite, the planners do not mind if some paths exist where the game does not terminate. For these games we manually removed the step-counters and ran the planners again (the number in parantheses in the table). In this case we can see that in several games the time and memory-overhead for both grounding and solving decreases. FF can ground two additional games and FD can solve one additional game. The biggest decrease in solving time comes with the 8puzzle, where FD's time reduces from 536s to 0.4s, clearly below that of Gamer. However, if the step-counter is removed and we want to use the found plan in the original game we have to somehow make sure that the plan does not exceed the allowed length.

When only looking at the grounding times we can see that Gamer nearly never is slower than FF and FD if we consider only games where grounding takes more than 1s. The only domain that causes big problems for Gamer in contrast to FD is walking-man. However, the instantiator of Gamer handles the GDL input directly while FD and FF have to cope with the translated files, which bring some overhead. Thus, it is not surprising that Gamer is much faster in grounding the games.

5   Discussion and Conclusion

So far we are not aware of any refereed publications of a translation from GDL to PDDL. The only works we found are two students' theses providing translations as well. One [14] tries to find add- and delete effects, so that the state update is much easier, as the frame effects can be removed. Also, it is able to find types for different constants, which should speed up the grounding and reduce the memory consumption. However, this comes at quite an overhead as the axioms containing does terms must be rolled out so that in several cases the translator ran out of memory. Furthermore, the generated output seems to be quite troublesome for FD; of the tested games not a single one could be handled by that planner. The other thesis [15] tries to perform the state update in a single step using conditional effects. Here, several things remain unclear in the description (e.g., the handling of axioms in general and especially that of does terms appearing in the bodies of axioms) and no experimental results are presented.

We have proposed a new way to translate single-player games. From the results we have seen that the translation works fine, with some restrictions in the use of functions. The resulting PDDL files can be handled by state-of-the-art planners, though especially the grounding in those planners seems to be a bottleneck, especially in games containing a step-counter. There are several cases where a planner is faster than both, the GGP solver and player we compared against, so that it might indeed make sense to run this kind of translation and solve the games by means of a planner. Nevertheless, classical GGP agents should be run in parallel as well, as we cannot predict whether the planner or the GGP player will be more efficient. This way we can get the best of both worlds.

References

1. Björnsson, Y., Finnsson, H.: Cadiaplayer: A simulation-based general game player. IEEE Transactions on Computational Intelligence and AI in Games 1(1), 4–15 (2009)
2. Edelkamp, S., Hoffmann, J.: PDDL2.2: The language for the classical part of the 4th international planning competition. Tech. Rep. 195, Albert-Ludwigs-Universität, Institut für Informatik, Freiburg, Germany (2004)
3. Genesereth, M.R., Love, N., Pell, B.: General game playing: Overview of the AAAI competition. AI Magazine 26(2), 62–72 (2005)
4. Haufe, S., Schiffel, S., Thielscher, M.: Automated verification of state sequence invariants in general game playing. Artificial Intelligence 187, 1–30 (2012)
5. Helmert, M.: The Fast Downward planning system. Journal of Artificial Intelligence Research 26, 191–246 (2006)
6. Hoffmann, J.: FF: The fast-forward planning system. The AI Magazine 22(3), 57–62 (2001)
7. Kissmann, P., Edelkamp, S.: Gamer, a general game playing agent. KI 25(1), 49–52 (2011)
8. Kocsis, L., Szepesvári, C.: Bandit based Monte-Carlo planning. In: Fürnkranz, J., Scheffer, T., Spiliopoulou, M. (eds.) ECML 2006. LNCS (LNAI), vol. 4212, pp. 282–293. Springer, Heidelberg (2006)
9. Love, N.C., Hinrichs, T.L., Genesereth, M.R.: General game playing: Game description language specification. Tech. Rep. LG-2006-01, Stanford Logic Group (2008)
10. McDermott, D., et al.: The PDDL Planning Domain Definition Language. The AIPS 1998 Planning Competition Comitee (1998)
11. Méhat, J., Cazenave, T.: A parallel general game player. KI 25(1), 43–47 (2011)
12. Rauber, T.: Translating Single-Player GDL into PDDL. Bachelor's thesis, Department of Computer Science, Faculty of Natural Sciences and Technology I, Saarland University (2013)
13. Richter, S., Westphal, M.: The LAMA planner: Guiding cost-based anytime planning with landmarks. Journal of Artificial Intelligence Research 39, 127–177 (2010)
14. Rüdiger, C.: Use of existing planners to solve single-player games. Großer Beleg, Fakultät Informatik, Technische Universität Dresden (2009)
15. Sievers, S.: Erweiterung eines Planungssystems zum Lösen von Ein-Personen-Spielen. Bachelor's thesis, Arbeitsgruppe Grundlagen der künstlichen Intelligenz, Institut für Informatik, Albert-Ludwigs Universität Freiburg (2009)
16. Thiebaux, S., Hoffmann, J., Nebel, B.: In defense of PDDL axioms. Artificial Intelligence 168(1-2), 38–69 (2005)

Comparison of Sensor-Feedback Prediction Methods for Robust Behavior Execution

Christian Rauch[1], Elmar Berghöfer[2], Tim Köhler[2], and Frank Kirchner[1,2]

[1] University of Bremen, Robotics Research Group
[2] DFKI GmbH, Robotics Innovation Center
Robert-Hooke-Straße 5, 28359 Bremen, Germany

Abstract. Robotic applications in inaccessible environments like in space strongly depend on detailed planning in advance as there are only short communication windows, a high latency in communication, and as there is often no way of recovering the system when it gets into a fault state. Furthermore, unknown terrain requires continuous monitoring of behavior execution by a human operator. The effort on detailed planning and especially the delay through remote monitoring can be decreased by supporting the autonomy of the robot by predicting and self-monitoring behavior consequences.

Presented are three approaches for creating prediction models. The models are used to generate expectations on sensor feedback caused by given actions. The expected sensor feedback is compared with the actual sensor feedback through a monitoring stage that will trigger a change of the robot behavior in case of unexpected sensor output. Two function fitting approaches (analytic model and generic function approximation) and a vector quantization method are compared with each other. The evaluation of the triggering mechanism in real scenarios will show that the execution of emergency actions in unexpected situations is possible.

1 Introduction

A hierarchical behavior architecture was proposed earlier [8] to enable a robot to carry out high-level plans and to supervise the behavior execution by sensor state prediction and monitoring. By learning the correlation of actions (respectively desired states) executed by the robot and the sensor feedback perceived through the state change (thus, the motor-to-sensor relation), it is possible to estimate future state changes that are expected when executing an action again. Comparing predicted sensor values (i.e., expected sensor feedback resulting from a desired action) and actual sensor feedback continuously enables the behavior architecture to do a general fault analysis based on the prediction error or to trigger an emergency reaction for that particular situation. Typical disruptions that might occur in such situations are circumstances that were not considered while planning, like small obstacles or unknown terrain properties. One application could be the identification of sensor or actuator faults to trigger an appropriate reaction (e.g., changing a motion behavior, see [16]).

I.J. Timm and M. Thimm (Eds.): KI 2013, LNAI 8077, pp. 200–211, 2013.
© Springer-Verlag Berlin Heidelberg 2013

Presented are three methods from the categories analytic models, generic function approximation, and vector quantization, to generate prediction models for typical situations of a robot in a lunar environment. As analytic model a PT_3 element was chosen based on assumptions of the system's characteristics and initial measurements of the correlation of action and sensor-feedback. For general function approximation a classic Multilayer Perceptron (MLP) and a Neural Gas (NG) approach are applied without the need to know the system's characteristics. The purpose of these methods is to model the correlation of actions given to the robot and the expected sensor feedback. We therefore examine a so called *normal case* to learn expected sensor feedback for a given action (desired state). In the so called *fault case* the prediction will be evaluated on typical situations where disruptions are present, like obstacles occurring in lunar missions.

The paper is structured as follows: In the next section different applications of prediction in robotics and other areas are given. Afterwards, the prediction models and learning methods are described. Sections 4 and 5 present the robotic system, the test scenario for our experiments, and the results of the three prediction methods. The paper finishes with a conclusion and an outlook.

2   Related Work

Pure time series prediction (TSP) tasks are successfully solved by Neural Networks (NN) [3] and Auto Regressive Integrated Moving Average (ARIMA) based approaches [7]. For this kind of tasks, the prediction does not take into account the causes that have an effect on these values. Prediction in robotics is applied to fault detection by pure sensor readings. E.g., Lishuang *et al.* [9] applied least square Support Vector Machines for predicting sensor values to detect sensor faults; and Plagemann *et al.* [13] used Gaussian processes for collision detection.

The work of Wolpert *et al.* [17] suggests that there exists an inverse and a forward model in human motion planning like for grasping or when reacting to unexpected situations like slipping objects. Thus, both the actuator input and the sensor feedback need to be considered when designing prediction models. Also the work of von Holst *et al.* [5] gives empirical evidence of a reactive control within biological systems by generating deviations – so called exafferences.

Behnke *et al.* [1] for example used actions and recent sensor data in conjunction, to predict the next position of a robot to overcome control latency. The robot of Bongard *et al.* [2] is capable of applying new motion behaviors in case an actuator is broken by predicting the result of alternative behaviors. Fujarewicz [4] showed that creating a prediction model based on physical relations of sensor data can be used for prediction tasks for upto 1 s. Pastor *et al.* [12] apply prediction of action outcomes to recognize failures and eventually react on it. In their setup just the average and variance of the expected sensor feedback per action is predicted.

3   Prediction Models

As implied in Section 1 the application of the prediction method depends on whether the system that correlates the action and sensor feedback is known or not. If action and sensor feedback are correlated by a known relation, e.g., by a physical process that correlates desired velocity and measured velocity of a mass-damper system, the prediction can be modeled based on this process. In this case, the system's parameters (e.g., mass distribution and dimension of the robot, engine characteristics) must be determined by experiments and measurements or by fitting the optimal function to a data set. If the underlying process is unknown, a generic function needs to be fitted onto the measured sensor feedback or the probability distribution needs to be modeled, e.g. by a vector quantization method. Besides measured sensor feedback, the data basis for such learning can be sampled in simulation frameworks like the one presented in [15]. In the following, different kinds of approaches will be presented to determine the prediction model by different initial assumptions about the correlation of actions and sensor feedback.

The PT_3 element as an example of an analytic model is motivated by initial observations of the robot in certain situations. The initial parameters of this model are determined by a measurement and further optimized through fitting the model onto the whole data set in the *normal case*. A classical *Multilayer Perceptron* (MLP) is applied to the same data set to investigate if its ability of generic function approximation leads to a model that a) performs like the PT_3 element, and b) is able to approximate even closer to the real sensor feedback. As an alternative to function fitting by the analytic model and the MLP, the vector quantization method *Neural Gas* (NG) is used to represent the distribution of the correlation. The MLP and NG use a history of n last motion commands for predicting the sensor feedback whereas the PT_3 stores its state internally.

3.1   Analytic Model (PT_3)

Given the typical mobile robot setup, it is expected that the sensor response to changes of the desired robot velocity is delayed through several elements. The delay of each element is unknown in advance and so is the friction of the ground. Figure 1 shows the measurement of the desired velocity and the true velocity on ground for a translational motion. From this time elapse of the robot's true velocity the characteristic transient overshoot can be seen which is caused by the robot's control system and further delay elements. Given this measurement, it is expected that the sensor response can be modeled by a transfer function with the characteristic of a proportional element with n delay elements (PT_n element).

Starting from a PT_2 element that is often found in mechanical systems like mass-damper systems, we found that adding a further delay element improves the ability to fit the data onto the transfer function. The step response of this PT_3 element is given in the frequency domain by

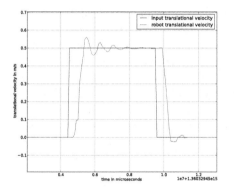 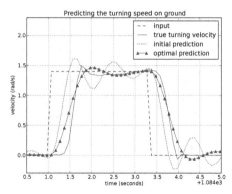

Fig. 1. Acceleration and deceleration step function and response for translational motion on planar ground

Fig. 2. Prediction of the turning speed on planar ground with initial and optimized parameters for the PT_3 element

$$X_{out}(s) = \frac{K}{(1 + 2DT_1 \cdot s + T_1^2 \cdot s^2) \cdot (1 + T_2 \cdot s) \cdot s} \tag{1}$$

where D is the damping factor and T_1 the time constant of the first PT_2 element and T_2 is the time constant of the additional delay element. The proportional factor of the PT_3 element is set to 1 and the step function is therefore $\frac{K}{s}$ with K as the relative change. The application of the PT_3 model is valid for all cases where the effect of the input is delayed due to several elements. This is exemplarily the case for movements on ground with friction and inertia.

To find the optimal system parameters D, T_1, and T_2 for Equation 1, we apply least squares fitting with initial parameters to the whole training data set. The optimization is applied on a data set where the robot is turning on ground with different velocities. Figure 2 shows the predicted response of the robot for a target velocity of 1.4 rad/s on ground alongside the step response with initial and optimized parameters (see Section 5.1 for parameter values).

3.2 Multilayer Perceptron

The *Multilayer Perceptron* (MLP) is a method from the field of neural networks. An MLP is capable of learning functional correlations between input and output values. The flexibility of the network comes from its hidden layers. Basically an MLP consists of an input layer, one or more hidden layers, and an output layer.

For the prediction task, the dimension of the MLP input layer is determined by the size of the history, specifically the n last motion commands that are used to predict the sensor feedback. The dimension of the output layer depends on the dimension of the sensor value that is to be predicted. As sigmoid activation function for the hidden layer the $tanh(\cdot)$ is used. The output layer uses a linear activation function. In future work we might optimize the topology of the MLP, e.g., by using model selection methods such as Evolutionary Acquisition of Neural Topologies (EANT, [11]) using Common Genetic Encoding (CGE) described in [6].

During the training phase of the MLP the parameters have to be optimized so that the error function is minimal on a given training data set. To minimize the error we used a variation of the well known gradient decent approach *Backprop-agation* for the experiments in this paper, which is the so called *RPROP* which is proposed by Riedmiller *et al.* in [14]. Once an MLP is trained on example data like described in Section 4, it can be used to predict a time series of sensor values of the nearby future.

3.3   Neural Gas

The Neural Gas (NG) algorithm is a vector quantization method proposed by Martinetz *et al.* [10]. Like the MLP, no assumptions on the motor-sensor correlation are needed. In contrast to the MLP and the PT_3 method, a vector quantization method like NG can cover non-gaussian distributions and ambiguities in the motor-to-sensor relation of the training set.

In this application, the NG algorithm is used as follows: The training data is a multi-dimensional space consisting of n input dimensions (motor commands) and m output dimensions (sensor values to be predicted). In learning, so-called center vectors (CV) are aligned to the training data. After learning, to generate predictions for the sensor values, the current (and p previous) motor commands are taken as input to search for the winning CV. The winner CV, in turn, gives the expected sensor values for the prediction.

4   Experimental Setup

4.1   Robot Setup and Environment

For all experiments, the skid-steering robot *Seekur Jr.* (by Adept MobileRobots) was used. The robot, shown in Figure 3, is equipped with an odometer and with an inertial measurement unit (IMU) including a gyroscope.

The experiments were carried out in two different environments: on flat ground and on a crater model, which can be seen in the background of Figure 3. The crater model consists of a rigid basis with the ability to mount stones of the same material. It is 9.5 m in width and has a height of 4 m with inclinations from 25° to 45°. Optionally, it can be partly covered with fine sand comparable to the lunar regolith.

4.2   Scenarios and Data Collection

The skid-steered robot is controlled by motion commands consisting of the desired translational and rotational velocity. For both of these input dimensions and for the sensor modality to be predicted, data is collected in an environment where no obstacles are present – the *normal case*. Based on the collected

(a) Small hill, translational velocity

(b) Stone, rotational velocity

Fig. 3. The robot Seekur Jr. equipped with a couple of sensors

Fig. 4. Scenarios to evaluate correlation of translational and rotational velocity

training data the sensor feedback for linear and the sensor feedback for rotational motion is learned. This learned sensor feedback is finally used as prediction, i.e., as expectations on sensor feedback for that motor input. To evaluate the prediction for each input dimension, two scenarios as seen in Figure 4 are created with obstacles that might cause dangerous situations for the robot. In this so called *fault case* (i.e., the disturbance of the motion by the obstacle) the discrepancy between learned and actual perceived sensor feedback should trigger an emergency action to prevent the robot from moving on.

For both input dimensions (translation, rotation) the sensor data was collected in the *normal case* for three discrete velocities with 10 trials per velocity and direction on planar ground (60 trials in total) and with two discrete velocities with 5 trials per velocity and direction on the crater (20 trials in total). The collected data was then separated into a training and a test set. In the following sections the turning case is considered on a planar ground and in the crater environment. In both environments, the IMU turning rate for the *normal case* is predicted based on the given rotation velocity. In the corresponding *fault case* a 80 kg weight is used on planar ground and a stone-shaped model as shown in Figure 4(b) is used in the crater environment. In both *fault cases* a discrepancy of predicted and actual sensor feedback is to be recognized.

5   Results

5.1   Configuration of Prediction Models

To evaluate the prediction models for turning, they are learned on a training set of the *normal case* and tested on separate test sets of, first, the *normal case* and, second, the scenarios of the *fault case*, both for planar ground and for the crater environment. Alongside the prediction and the true sensor feedback, the mean absolute error (MAE) over the last 10 prediction errors is plotted and compared for the *normal case* and the *fault case*. The sampling time in all plots is 100 ms. The prediction and action triggering is integrated into the hierarchical behavior architecture proposed in [8] to analyze the execution of emergency actions.

To fit the PT_3 response by least square onto the training set of 120 step responses, we used the initial parameters $D = 0.12800$, $T_1 = 0.14206$, and $T_2 = 0.3$, where D and T_1 are analytically determined by the step response in time domain and T_2 is set by an initial guess. After optimization we obtained the optimal step response with the PT_3 parameters $D = 0.3490451$, $T_1 = 0.2049906$, $T_2 = 0.36166818$ for Equation 1. The MLP used the last 15 motion commands as input to predict the next turning rate of the gyroscope. Hence, the input layer consists of 15 neurons and the output layer consists of one single neuron. There is one hidden layer used with 12 neurons. The application of the NG vector quantization to the test scenario uses 300 center vectors with 15×2 input and one output dimension. The NG-parameters learning rate ϵ and neighborhood constant λ decay during learning (see [10]). The initial values are $\epsilon = 1.0$ and $\lambda = 150$. The final values after 1,000,000 iterations are $\epsilon = 0.001$ and $\lambda = 0.01$.

5.2   Normal Case

After learning the sensor feedback of the training set in the *normal case* for each environment – ground and crater – separately, the prediction models are applied to the test set in the same environment. The prediction of all three approaches for the test set alongside the prediction error is shown in Figure 5 for planar ground and in Figure 6 for the crater environment. In general all three methods show similar results. For turning on planar ground (Figure 5) the rotation of the IMU is well predicted disregarding the small errors at the rising and falling edges when the robot is accelerating and decelerating. Turning within the crater environment results in much noisier IMU data (Figure 6) compared to turning on planar ground. The overshooting at rising edges caused by acceleration phases is much better fitted when learned on planar ground than on the crater. The noisy gyroscope values on the crater result in a higher prediction error in the *normal case* especially for the PT_3.

The MLP and the NG both with 15 last input samples have the ability to fit the rising and falling edges in the crater environment much better than the PT_3 (comparing Figure 5(b) and Figure 6(b)). All methods have in common that they are not able to predict the high dynamic of the IMU gyroscope values in the crater environment.

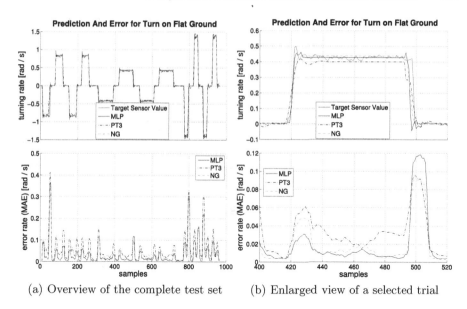

(a) Overview of the complete test set   (b) Enlarged view of a selected trial

Fig. 5. Prediction of three different turning rates and the prediction error (MAE) on flat ground. Spikes in the error correspond to rising and falling edges of step functions, where the prediction does not fit to the correct motor-sensor delay. The mean absolute errors for (a) are: MLP: 0.033703, PT$_3$: 0.055123, NG: 0.033021.

5.3   Fault Case

In both environments an obstacle is placed to which the robot is moving against. The prediction compared to the true gyroscope turning rate can be seen in Figure 7(a) for turning against the 80 kg weights on ground and in Figure 7(b) for turning on the crater against a mounted stone. At the beginning of each trial the robot is blocked for a short period which causes higher prediction errors than in the period after, when the blockade is dissolved. By finding a threshold that distinguishes this blocking by an obstacle and in normal operation, an emergency reaction is able to recover the robot from such dangerous situations.

5.4   Comparison

As one can see in Figure 5, the MLP and NG methods are capable of finding a solution which is at least comparable to the analytic solution by using the last 15 input samples. The analytic model, once learned, is applicable without the need for recent input samples as the state of the system is stored internally. Another advantage of the analytic model over the MLP and the NG is the generic application on different input values (i.e., different velocities). The modeled transfer function of the PT$_3$ is independent from the input velocity, whereas MLP and NG need to be learned at least for maximum and distributed intermediate input values. However, the application of the PT$_3$ is only possible where a linear

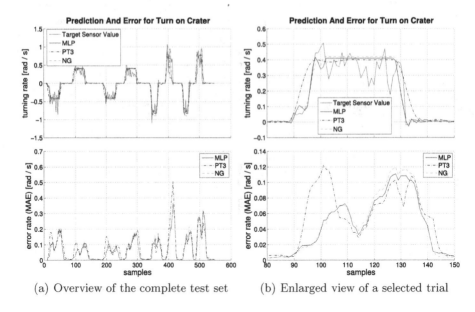

Fig. 6. Prediction of three different turning rates and the prediction error (MAE) on the crater. Due to noisy sensor data, the error is persistently higher while moving. The mean absolute errors for (a) are: MLP: 0.068910, PT$_3$: 0.080817, NG: 0.071745.

relation is to be modeled. Especially, NG can be used to model non-linear relations with non-gaussian data distributions. All three methods provide a similar prediction performance and have the common problem to accurately predict the values at rising and falling edges, which leads to spikes in the prediction error. This error becomes particular obvious for higher turning rates. Comparing the prediction error in the *fault case* (Figure 7), one can conclude that applying all tested prediction methods on the crater results in a much more fluctuating prediction error. To recognize obstacles in case of such noisy sensor data, the obstacle needs to cause a much higher prediction error, compared to turning in the *normal case*.

5.5   Implementation: Prediction, Monitoring and Triggering

To evaluate the trigger concept as proposed in the hierarchical behavior architecture, the PT$_3$ prediction method is implemented within our framework and connected to monitoring and a trigger. The monitoring averages over the last 5 prediction errors computed by the mean-absolute error (MAE) of the expected and true sensor feedback. The monitor is connected to a trigger. The trigger is configured that way, that it proposes to turn into the opposite direction when a certain fixed threshold is exceeded. This behavior is chosen as an example of an emergency reaction to avoid a potentially dangerous state like turning onto the obstacle and getting stuck. The threshold value t can be chosen based on mean μ and standard deviation σ of the error of collected data, e.g., $t = \mu + n\sigma$.

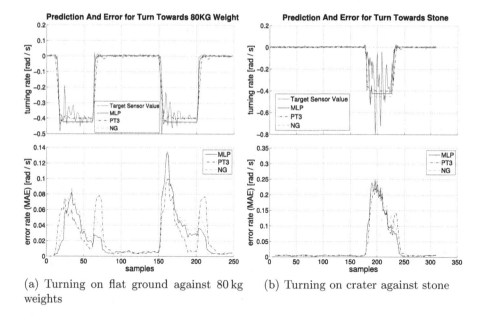

(a) Turning on flat ground against 80 kg weights

(b) Turning on crater against stone

Fig. 7. Prediction and error for predicting turning rates on flat ground and on crater when turning against obstacles. The mean absolute errors for (a) are: MLP: 0.024518, PT_3: 0.025323, NG: 0.028150 and for (b) MLP: 0.031844, PT_3: 0.031884, NG: 0.034148.

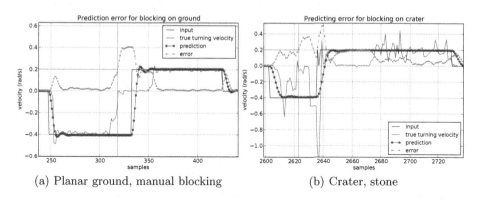

(a) Planar ground, manual blocking

(b) Crater, stone

Fig. 8. Applying the predictor component to turning against obstacles. Turning against obstacles with -0.4 rad/s and turning away with 0.2 rad/s. The triggering is visible through the change of the desired turning rate into opposite direction. The trigger threshold and the time it is exceeded is marked with a solid red line.

Depending on application and terrain, n or t can be constant. The error is shown in Figure 8 for blocking the robot on flat ground (a) and crater (b).

The parameters for both predictions were learned for their corresponding *normal case*. For the *fault case* on flat ground, the robot was blocked manually while turning which led to an error exceeding the trigger threshold

$(0.2, \approx \mu + 2\sigma)$. For turning on crater against a stone the same trigger settings, i.e., threshold $(0.2, \approx \mu + 1\sigma)$ and emergency action (turning in opposite direction), were chosen. In both environments the desired action (turning in opposite direction) was successfully proposed before the robot reached a dangerous state.

6   Conclusion and Outlook

The work evaluated the ability of an analytic model compared to more generic function approximations to predict sensor data time series for a given motion input. Besides comparing the prediction methods, the work showed the application of prediction for behavior execution monitoring and emergency triggering.

In general, the presented methods can be extended to input data of higher dimension, e.g. using translational and rotational velocity concurrently. Further experiments need to be carried out that take that and other sensor modalities like acceleration into account. So far we also did not use past sensor feedback as additional input to improve the prediction performance by measurement updates, e.g. with a Kalman filter. This can be used additionally to the possibility to inhibit the prediction error at the beginning of each step function, to minimize the error spikes caused by the rising and falling edges (Section 5.4).

For the monitoring, the MAE averaged over the last 5 samples was initially chosen as error metric. This is adequate to trigger the complementary action as shown in the blocking on planar ground and on the crater. For higher dimensional data (e.g. preprocessed image data), it is not clear yet if the MAE is satisfying to identify misbehavior. To inhibit high prediction errors at acceleration and deceleration phases and therefore to prevent wrong triggering, the application of dynamic trigger thresholds is proposed. Besides learning the mean of the expected sensor feedback, the expected standard deviation could be additionally learned and used as basis for dynamic thresholds.

In addition to improving the prediction, future work will cover the question when to use which kind of emergency action (trigger) and when to propagate the prediction error to higher instances of the hierarchical behavior architecture.

Acknowledgment. Supported by the Federal Ministry of Economics and Technology on the basis of a decision by the German Bundestag, grant no. 50RA1113 and 50RA1114.

References

1. Behnke, S., Egorova, A., Gloye, A., Rojas, R., Simon, M.: Predicting away robot control latency. In: Polani, D., Browning, B., Bonarini, A., Yoshida, K. (eds.) RoboCup 2003. LNCS (LNAI), vol. 3020, pp. 712–719. Springer, Heidelberg (2004)
2. Bongard, J., Zykov, V., Lipson, H.: Resilient machines through continuous self-modeling. Science 314(5802), 1118–1121 (2006)
3. Frank, R.J., Davey, N., Hunt, S.P.: Time series prediction and neural networks. Journal of Intelligent and Robotic Systems 31(1-3), 91–103 (2001)

4. Fujarewicz, K.: Predictive model of sensor readings for a mobile robot. In: Proc. of World Academy of Science, Engineering and Technology, vol. 20 (2007)
5. von Holst, E., Mittelstaedt, H.: The reafference principle. Interaction between the central nervous system and the periphery. The behavioural physiology of animals and man. Selected papers of Erich von Holst, Teil, Methuen, London, vol. 1, pp. 39–73 (1973)
6. Kassahun, Y., Edgington, M., Metzen, J.H., Sommer, G., Kirchner, F.: A common genetic encoding for both direct and indirect encodings of networks. In: Proc. of the 9th Annual Conference on Genetic and Evolutionary Computation, GECCO 2007, pp. 1029–1036. ACM, New York (2007)
7. Khashei, M., Bijari, M.: An artificial neural network (p, d, q) model for timeseries forecasting. Expert Systems with Applications 37(1), 479–489 (2010)
8. Köhler, T., Rauch, C., Schröer, M., Berghöfer, E., Kirchner, F.: Concept of a biologically inspired robust behaviour control system. In: Su, C.-Y., Rakheja, S., Liu, H. (eds.) ICIRA 2012, Part II. LNCS, vol. 7507, pp. 486–495. Springer, Heidelberg (2012)
9. Lishuang, X., Tao, C., Fang, D.: Sensor fault diagnosis based on least squares support vector machine online prediction. In: 2011 IEEE Conference on Robotics, Automation and Mechatronics (RAM), pp. 275–279 (2011)
10. Martinetz, T.M., Berkovich, S.G., Schulten, K.J.: 'Neural-gas' network for vector quantization and its application to time-series prediction. IEEE Transactions on Neural Networks 4(4), 558–569 (1993)
11. Metzen, J.H., Edgington, M., Kassahun, Y., Kirchner, F.: Performance evaluation of EANT in the robocup keepaway benchmark. In: Sixth International Conference on Machine Learning and Applications, ICMLA 2007, pp. 342–347 (2007)
12. Pastor, P., Kalakrishnan, M., Chitta, S., Theodorou, E., Schaal, S.: Skill learning and task outcome prediction for manipulation. In: 2011 IEEE International Conference on Robotics and Automation (ICRA), pp. 3828–3834 (2011)
13. Plagemann, C., Fox, D., Burgard, W.: Efficient failure detection on mobile robots using particle filters with gaussian process proposals. In: Proc. of the 20th International Joint Conference on Artifical Intelligence, IJCAI 2007, pp. 2185–2190. Morgan Kaufmann Publishers Inc., San Francisco (2007)
14. Riedmiller, M., Braun, H.: A direct adaptive method for faster backpropagation learning: The RPROP algorithm. In: IEEE International Conference on Neural Networks, pp. 586–591. IEEE Press (1993)
15. Römmerman, M., Kühn, D., Kirchner, F.: Robot design for space missions using evolutionary computation. In: IEEE Congress on Evolutionary Computation, CEC 2009, pp. 2098–2105. IEEE (2009)
16. Spenneberg, D., McCullough, K., Kirchner, F.: Stability of walking in a multilegged robot suffering leg loss. In: Proceedings of the 2004 IEEE International Conference on Robotics and Automation, ICRA 2004, vol. 3, pp. 2159–2164. IEEE (2004)
17. Wolpert, D.M., Kawato, M.: Multiple paired forward and inverse models for motor control. Neural Networks 11(78), 1317–1329 (1998)

Ingredients and Recipe for a Robust Mobile Speech-Enabled Cooking Assistant for German

Ulrich Schäfer[1], Frederik Arnold[2], Simon Ostermann[2], and Saskia Reifers[2,*]

[1] German Research Center for Artificial Intelligence (DFKI), Language Technology Lab, Campus D 3 1, D-66123 Saarbrücken, Germany
ulrich.schaefer@dfki.de
[2] Saarland University, Computational Linguistics Department, D-66041 Saarbrücken, Germany
{arnold,ostermann,reifers}@kochbot.de

Abstract. We describe the concept and implementation of *Kochbot*, a cooking assistant application for smartphones and tablet devices that robustly processes speech I/O and supports German recipes. Its main functions are (1) helping searching in a large recipe collection, (2) reading out loud the cooking instructions step-by-step, and (3) answering questions during cooking. Our goal was to investigate and demonstrate the use of speech assistance in a task-oriented, hands-free scenario. Furthermore, we investigate rapid domain adaptation by utilizing shallow natural language processing techniques such as part-of-speech tagging, morphological analysis and sentence boundary detection on the domain text corpus of 32,000 recipes. The system is fully implemented and scales up well with respect to the number of users and recipes.

Keywords: natural language processing, speech, mobile application, cooking assistant.

1   Introduction and Motivation

With the advent of mobile devices such as smart phones and tablets, as well as robust, speaker-independent, cloud-based speech recognition in the last few years, new applications become feasible and marketable that researchers and end users a decade ago could only dream of. In this paper, we describe the components (ingredients) and methods (the recipe) of a mobile cooking assistant application that runs with out-of-the box hardware, assuming a speech recognition in the cloud such as the Google Speech API that comes with the Android mobile operating system[1].

Moreover, the cooking assistant application itself runs on the mobile phone as an "app". Only the rather large recipe collection (32,000 recipes) currently resides on a standard PC that can serve thousands of mobile clients with recipe

---

* We thank Ulrike Schweitzer for permitting us to use her collection of more than 32,000 recipes at http://ulrikesrezeptesammlung.de, and our pioneer users for testing earlier versions of the app. A beta is available at http://www.kochbot.de
[1] http://dev.android.com/reference/android/speech/SpeechRecognizer.html

search via Internet, given that each recipe's text only needs a few kilobytes. Considering the memory reserve in current mobile devices, this recipe collection could in principle also easily be moved to the clients. In other words, the current system already now scales up with respect to the number of users and recipes.

The main tasks of the app are (1) helping searching in a large recipe collection, (2) reading out loud the cooking instructions step-by-step, and (3) answering questions during cooking. The purpose of our project was to investigate and demonstrate the feasibility and use of speech assistance in a task-oriented, hands-free scenario with state-of-art hardware. Furthermore, we investigate rapid, corpus-based domain adaptation by utilizing shallow natural language processing (NLP) techniques such as part-of-speech tagging, morphological analysis and sentence boundary detection on the domain text corpus (the recipes). By pre-processing the corpus of German recipes with these NLP tools, we can quickly access and utilize domain knowledge instead of modeling everything by hand (which some of the earlier approaches to cooking assistants did through domain ontologies).

This paper is organized as follows. In Section 2, we discuss previous and related work. Section 3 deals with the (networked) architecture of the overall system. Section 4 presents the offline pre-processing stages. Section 5 explains the mobile cooking assistant app itself: the user interface and different stages of speech interaction in search and recipe reading out mode. We conclude in Section 6 and give an outlook to future work.

2 Previous and Related Work

Various approaches to home cooking assistants and cooking tutoring dialog systems have been described in the literature. One of the earliest studies is Home Cooking Assistant [8]. Its author conducted a small usability study. According to this, over 80% of the testers thought that speech recognition is beneficial although 50% also observed that the program had difficulties in understanding them—it certainly suffered from the limited speech recognition capabilities on a Laptop PC in the kitchen scenario in 2001. The Cooking Navi [4] was meant to become a multimedia assistant and cooking teacher for beginners and experienced users. Instead of speech, it used video material and added speech balloons to explain cooking instructions. Cooking Navi also found a simplified commercial descendant as Nintendo "Shaberu! DS Oryōri Navi" that reads out loud 200 recipes in Japanese, and features instructional video clips, a cooking timer, ingredients calculator and a very simple speech recognition to turn pages. English versions with the names "Cooking Guide: Can't Decide What to Eat?", "Personal Trainer: Cooking" and "Let's Get Cooking" with 200-300 recipes each appeared in 2008 and 2010, a few more similar sequels appeared in the US, Japan and Europe. They all have in common editorially processed recipes, read out loud by (famous) professionals, and only very limited interaction. However, the commercial success of the Nintendo cooking guide series shows that there is market potential.

More intelligent dialog-based approaches have been investigated in various research projects. CookCoach [5] is a cooking tutoring assistant that supports speech interaction and read out recipes. Its authors observed the necessity to use a domain ontology, which they developed in OntoChef [7]. OntoChef contains very general concepts such as recipe classes, food, part of food, ingredient, unit, action, compound action, task and so on. However, it does not contain an elaborate list of ingredients and their classification. Except the fact that he uses a local speech recognizer, the scenario we have implemented is similar to the one described by [2] for a cooking robot. Although the study work is written in German, its author has implemented a cooking assistant for English speech I/O.

3   Architecture

The architecture of our cooking assistant is depicted in Fig. 1. The cooking assistant code, the app, resides on the mobile device, indicated by the Android logo at the top of the diagram. It contains all the program logic for user interface, speech interaction, and natural language processing to split cooking instructions into sentences, recognized quantities and units of ingredients, etc.

The app requires access to the Internet only for two purposes: (1) **recipe text server**: the recipe collection is hosted on an Apache Solr[2] structured fulltext search server at our premises. Using standard Lucene/Solr queries, it provides fulltext search to find recipes with specific ingredients or categories such as country; (2) **speech recognition**: as mentioned in the introduction, we use the Google Speech API to perform ASR (automatic speech recognition) remotely.

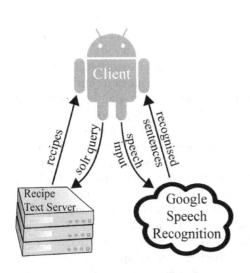

Fig. 1. Architecture overview

Fig. 2. Main view with recognized speech; identified ingredients are shown in brackets

---

[2] http://lucene.apache.org/solr/

4   Offline Pre-processing

In this section, we describe how we pre-process the recipe corpus. Pre-processing serves (1) as input for a static text analysis that e.g. computes what ingredients, quantities, units etc. are, both globally for the complete recipe collection and locally at runtime when a specific recipe is being cooked (Sect. 5.2), (2) as input for filling the recipe text search index.

4.1   Recipe Markup Format

The purpose of our cooking app is to provide assistance that guides the user in the cooking process step-by-step. Therefore, some minimal structuring of recipes is required. We call it lightly stuctured recipe markup. Basically, it contains the recipe title, ingredient lists, and cooking instructions, and optionally some categories such as the country the recipe originates from, or vegetarian, for children, etc. Finer-grained structure such as instruction steps (sentences), units and quantities of ingredients will be 'parsed' by our system on the fly.

Several recipe markup languages based on XML have been proposed, for example RecipeML[3], formerly known as DESSERT, RecipeBook XML[4], CookML[5] and REML[6]. Compared to these partly very rich markup formats, our light markup can be considered as least common denominator to which all other markups could easily be transformed. This also means that we could incorporate other recipe resources with little effort. Of course, parsing of units and quantities as we do it is not necessary in case markup already provides this information in separate fields. Figure 3 contains an example for the target markup of a single recipe. We do not provide the full specification here, as its structure is simple and shallow. The same markup is used to store recipes in the Apache Solr server (Sect. 5.4), which returns found recipes in the same way, plus some additional markup for query-processing related information.

4.2   Creating a Corpus with Recipe Markup

Originally, the recipes texts we used came in HTML format, structured in categories and in German. We downloaded all recipes and transformed the HTML into our light recipe XML format using XPath, extracting the information we needed. We then applied morphological analysis on the recipe texts in order to normalize and abstract from morphological and spelling variants. During this process, we discovered that many recipes in the collection contain OCR (optical character recognition) or typographic errors. We use three layers to standardize and refine the recipes in this offline stage.

Step 1: Regular expressions. The first step consists in removing markup and unwanted characters using regular expressions. Furthermore, we separate the cooking instructions from the ingredients list.

---

[3] http://www.formatdata.com/recipeml/
[4] http://www.happy-monkey.net/recipebook/
[5] http://www.kalorio.de/cml/cookml.html
[6] http://reml.sourceforge.net/

```
<doc>
    <field name="category">Teigwaren</field>
    <field name="subcategory">Lasagne, Canneloni und Maultaschen</field>
    <field name="title">Cannelloni al forno</field>
    <field name="ingredients">50 g geräucherter durchwachsener Speck
        100 g gekochter Schinken
        2 mittelgroße Zwiebeln
        1 Zucchini (ca. 200 g)
        1 Möhre (ca. 150g)
        200 g gemischtes Hackfleisch
        125 g Mozzarella-Käse
        250 g Cannelloni (dicke Nudelröhren zum Füllen)
        [...]
    </field>
    <field name="preparation">
        1. Speck und Schinken würfeln. Zwiebeln schälen, Gemüse putzen,
            waschen. Alles fein würfeln. Speck und Hack in 1 EL Öl anbraten.
            Schinken, Gemüse und Hälfte Zwiebeln mitdünsten.  3 gehackte
            Tomaten, 1 EL Mark und Wein zufügen, würzen.</str>
    </field>
    <field name="preparation_time">1 Std 15 Min</field>
    <field name="degree_of_difficulty">normal</field>
    <field name="servings">vier Portionen</field>
    <field name="vegetarian">Nein</field>
</doc>
```

Fig. 3. Example of recipe markup as used in the Apache Solr index

Step 2: Morphology. We use the SProUT system[3] with its built-in MMORPH [6] lemmatizer and morphological analysis tool for German to get parts of speech, genus, etc. for every word. We extract a simplified format and suppress all analysis details not needed for our purposes. At the same time, we extract e.g. all possible ingredients along with their number of occurrences in the corpus. We describe in Sect. 5 how this information is used to answer questions on ingredients and their quantity, and in speech recognition at multiple stages to rank ambiguous ASR output. Moreover, we also extract recipe titles which we need for search index preparation.

Step 3: Part-of-speech tagging. To select the most probable morphological reading according to context, we use the trigram-based part-of-speech (PoS) tagger TnT [1]. TnT takes care of the context and delivers a probability for each possible PoS tag. We use it to filter the morphological variants in the MMORPH output by choosing the PoS tag with the highest probability for each word in a recipe which considerably reduces the number of morphological variants.

5   Online System (Cooking Assistant App)

This section describes the core of the cooking assistant app, its user interface with different views for recipe search, step-by-step cooking and reading out mode. We also discuss details such as its ingredients (quantity) parser and the cooking step parser. The app needs Internet connection for speech recognition (Sect. 5.3) and for downloading recipes. Downloading only happens once when a recipe is viewed for the first time. There is no need for downloading again as long as a recipe is stored as one of the last 20 viewed recipes (*Letzte Rezepte*) or marked as a favorite recipe by the user (*Mein Kochbuch*). Apart from speech recognition and downloading recipes, an Internet connection is not required—everything else is processed on the mobile device.

5.1 User Interface

The UI design goal was to make an easy-to-use application which can be controlled using voice commands but also through standard touch interactions. The app consists of several views of which the most important ones will be described in detail below.

Initial View. The first view, which appears upon startup, presents the user with four different buttons (Fig. 2). The topmost one gives access to the last viewed recipes (*Letzte Rezepte*). *Mein Kochbuch* is the user's personal cookbook where favorite recipes can be stored. *Rezepte A-Z* gives the user access to three lists in columns, a list of categories, a list of countries and a list of ingredients from which she or he can choose an item to start a search for that particular category, country or ingredient. The button at the bottom leads to a random recipe that changes on every reload or when shaking the device.

Menubar. Most of the views have an "Action Bar"[7], a menubar on the top of the screen (see top of Fig. 2 and 5). It shows one or more icons that give the user quick access to important functionality. The icons are: a microphone for starting speech recognition, a magnifying glass for opening a search field, and three dots for opening a menu.

Search View. Starting a search, either by using the search field, voice command or the *Rezepte A-Z* view, will take the user to the search view (Fig. 5). The search view shows a list of recipes matching the given search criteria. On top of the list is an area that can be expanded and collapsed. It shows information such a the number of recipes found, search words, the category, or ingredients to occur or not to occur in the recipe. Scrolling to the bottom of the list will load more recipes if available. Choosing one of the recipes will take the user to another view showing an overview over the recipe.

Recipe Overview. The recipe overview shows information such as general information about the recipe, a list of ingredients and a list of instructions. At the bottom of the screen, there are two buttons. They both take the user to the same screen, the step-by-step view.

Step-by-step View. The step-by-step view is different from the other views. It uses the full screen and therefore does not have a menubar (Fig. 7). There are two versions of the step-by-step view. The version accessible from the right button is meant as a 'silent preview' of the step-by-step mode, it comes without continuous speech recognition (Sect. 5.3) and the steps are not read out loud. The other version reachable from the left button is the "real" step-by-step view, each step is read out loud and the user can interact with the app by using swipe

---

[7] http://developer.android.com/guide/topics/ui/actionbar.html

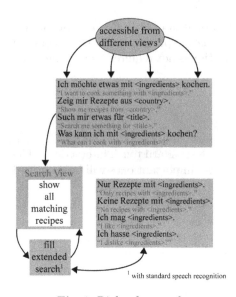

Fig. 4. Dialog for search   **Fig. 5.** Search view

gestures or voice commands (Sect. 5.3) to go to the next or previous step, or initiate question dialog.

5.2   Recipe Processing

Each recipe XML document (example in Fig. 3) has a number of fields, e.g. the recipe title, a category, a subcategory and possibly a subsubcategory, a field containing the ingredients, a field containing the instructions and some fields for other information such as calories or preparation time.

Ingredients Parser. In order to be able to answer questions such as *Wie viele Tomaten brauche ich?* 'How many tomatoes do I need?', the ingredients field needs to be parsed. Normally every line contains one ingredient, consisting of an ingredient name, an amount and a unit (example: *evtl. 2-3 Teel. Öl* 'optionally 2-3 tbs oil'). However, there are many exceptions in the actual recipes. Parsing an ingredient line is therefore divided into different steps to recognize the (partially optional) fields ingredient, quantity and unit.

Step Parser. For a hands-free interaction with the app while cooking, the steps are read out loud in the step-by-step view (Sect. 5.1). To be able to do this, sentences in the field *preparation* (Fig. 3) are separated. This is done by splitting the text after each full stop, except if the full stop belongs to a word from a list of stop words including common abbreviations. To give an example, the preparation field from Fig. 3 is divided into 22 steps/sentences (shortened here for space reasons):

```
1. Speck und Schinken würfeln
2. Zwiebeln schälen, Gemüse putzen, waschen.
```

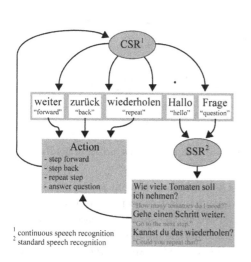

Fig. 6. Command dialog in the step-by-step view

Fig. 7. Step-by-step view

3. Alles fein würfeln.
4. Speck und Hack in 1 EL Öl anbraten.
5. Schinken, Gemüse und Hälfte Zwiebeln mitdünsten.
6. 3 gehackte Tomaten, 1 EL Mark und Wein zufügen, würzen.
[...]

5.3   Speech Input

To model user interaction with the cooking assistant, a JavaCC[8] grammar was developed. The grammar is divided into different parts that reflect the interaction stages such as searching, cooking (read out) mode, etc. (Fig. 4, 6, and 8). For speech recognition, we use the Google Speech API in the app. The API offers two different modes. Standard speech recognition (SSR) is used to process full sentences containing questions or commands (Fig. 4). After a speech input pause with a configured threshold length, the input is interpreted as a complete utterance. The second mode, continuous speech recognition (CSR), is used to recognize user interaction in the reading out mode (Fig. 6). Here, only single words are recognized, since there is no defined end of speech.

Standard Speech Recognition. Before starting speech recognition, the app checks if speech input is available. Then a speech object is created and some options are set, such as the language, the maximum number of recognized sentences to be returned, and whether partial results are to be returned or not. In the standard speech recognition mode, we do not want to receive partial results. When recognition is started, a window opens and prompts the user for speech

---

[8] https://javacc.java.net

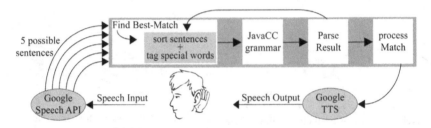

Fig. 8. Speech recognition workflow

input. After silence over threshold time, the window closes automatically and the input is sent to Google ASR.

Continuous Speech Recognition. The second mode is what we call "continuous speech recognition"[9]. It is important for a hands-free scenario in the kitchen. To initialize CSR, the speech API is initialized in the same way as for SSR, except that it is asked to return partial results. There is no guarantee to receive full sentences anymore or anything useful at all because the speech recognition does not wait for a sentence to be finished but instead just returns results when it sees fit. Everything that is returned by the speech API is split into single words and those are compared with a list of keywords to spot for. Once one of those words is found, the continuous recognition is stopped and some action such as starting the normal recognition is executed. Thus, the continuous recognition is only used to detect single command words as shown in Fig. 6.

Finding the Most Appropriate ASR Match. This applies to the SSR mode (Fig. 4, 8). As mentioned before, we chose the generic Google Speech API for the speech input part of the cooking assistant since it is easy to connect with Java code and is known to be reliable and available on all Android devices. However, the major disadvantage of this speech recognizer is the fact that it cannot be adapted to a specific domain or scenario. Therefore, we decided to establish a rating system that takes into account the current activity where the speech recognition takes place. Additionally, to make word matching more robust, we apply two different stemmers (from Apache Solr/Lucene) concurrently. They work corpus-independently and need only little space and working time.

The general idea is to give a score point for each word in a single match if the activity-specific corpus contains the word. There are three different "scanners" that correspond to three different areas that are checked: complete recipe corpus, current recipe and grammar.

Corpus Scanner. This scanner basically uses the general ingredients corpus that was extracted from *all* available recipes. It is used in all kinds of search since we assume that users often will search for ingredients. We use a bundle of four different corpus versions: (1) a stem corpus, extracted using SProUT with the MMORPH stemmer, (2) a string corpus, containing the literal ingredient entries including their morphological variants, (3) a stemmed version of the latter one,

---

[9] The "continuous speech recognition" is based on an open source project which can be found at https://github.com/gast-lib/gast-lib/blob/master/speech.md

stemmed using the 'Lucene' stemmer, (4) the same again, but stemmed using the 'Snowball' stemmer. Moreover, to support search for particular recipes, we also take into account the recipe titles. Thus, we additionally use a title corpus for scoring. The score increases as the title gets longer, i.e. *Spaghetti mit Erbsen-Rahm-Soße und Parmesan* 'Spaghetti with pea-cream-sauce and Parmesan' gets a higher rating than just *Schweinebraten* 'roast pork'.

Example: Assume we would say *Ich möchte Canneloni al forno kochen* 'I want to cook Canneloni al forno'. The corpus scanner would then start a lookup over its corpus bundle and try to find some correspondence and the best possible score. There are two possibilities:

- A rating of +1 for *Canneloni*, which is an ingredient
- A rating of +3 for *Canneloni al forno*, which is a recipe title

The match gets a rating of +3 here since we are looking for the *best* match.

Recipe Scanner. Similar to the corpus scanner, the recipe scanner checks for ingredients in a question. However, this time, it is restricted to ingredients that are used in the recipe locally in the step-by-step view. We do not want to take care of ingredients occcurring only in other recipes since questions on those ingredients are irrelevant for the current recipe. Here, the bundle contains only three corpora: (1) the already mentioned recipe text, containing ingredients, (2) a stemmed version of the latter one, stemmed by the 'Lucene' stemmer, (3) the same again, but stemmed by the 'Snowball' stemmer.

Example: Assume we are already cooking and forgot how many zucchinis we need. In this case, we could ask *Wie viele Zucchinis brauche ich?* 'How many zucchinis do I need?'. Afterwards, the scanner would start a look-up and find *Zucchini* as a relevant ingredient and thus increase the match rating by 1. We could also assume that the speech API had returned the potential match *Wie viel Zucker brauche ich?* 'How much sugar do I need?', since both words *Zucchini* and *Zucker* sound similarly in German. This match would get no point, since *Zucker* 'sugar' is an ingredient in fact, but not a relevant one for this recipe.

Grammar Scanner. This last scanner is the most important one since it uses the JavaCC grammar belonging to the current recognition for scoring. In a first step, it chooses the appropriate grammar rule that *should* match the current speech input. This matching of the current activity to a grammar rule is hard-coded. When the rule is chosen, we read in the rule and solve all JavaCC tokens that are used and mapped to "real" words. Afterwards, these words are thrown into a bag of words and serve as corpus. This scanner is very important since it simulates an input expectation which is not used in the speech recognition so far, i.e. it partially solves the problem that the Google API is domain-independent. By choosing one rule, we set a special context in which we expect the match to take place in. Tests showed that this step has the highest influence on the general scoring of matches. In contrast to the other scanners, we do not use a stemmer here, since the grammar should take care of different word forms anyway.

Example: Assume that while cooking we forgot how many zucchinis we need.

In this case, we could ask *Wie viele Zucchinis brauche ich?* 'How many zucchinis do I need?'. Afterwards, the scanner would start a look-up in the grammar and find multiple word correspondences in the bag of words for the matching grammar rule: The score should be +4 since the bag of words should contain *wie, viel, brauche* and *ich*. These three scanners look at every possible match that the ASR is returning and allocate scores to each of them. Afterwards, the matches are sorted according to their rating. The grammar then basically tries to parse the most appropriate match first; if this is not successful, it tries the next one and so on (cf. loop in Fig. 8).

Marking Phrases in a Sentence. After choosing the best match from speech input as described before, or sorting them according to their relevance, we mark special phrases such as ingredients or recipe titles. The assumption is that these are relevant for search or answering questions. Special markers in the JavaCC grammar use them as pre-terminals. To mark them, we collect all possible titles, ingredients, categories, countries and combinations of the latter that occur in the match. We afterwards choose the most appropriate one out of all possibilities and mark the appropriate parts of the string. *Example:* In *Ich will etwas mit Spaghetti und Tomaten kochen* 'I want to cook something with spaghetti and tomatoes', we would mark *Spaghetti* and *Tomaten* as ingredients: Ich will etwas mit [Spaghetti]$_I$ und [Tomaten]$_I$ kochen (Fig. 2).

5.4   Recipe Text Server

All recipes are stored on an Apache Solr server. An example document is shown in Fig. 3. The searchable fields (i.e. title, ingredients, category or country) are stored in two versions, a stemmed one and a unchanged version. The unchanged version is needed for sorting and searching for categories.

Recipe Search. A user search process is divided into different parts. The first step is generating a so called search object. In subsequent user questions (or requests), it can then be altered to fit the user's wishes, e.g. by adding ingredients that have to or must not be contained in the recipe. Each time the search object changes, a new Solr query is constructed from the given information and is sent to the Solr system.

As described earlier, the app has a view where the user can choose a category to search for. Searching for the stemmed category would in some cases lead to a problem. For example, a stemmed search for *torten mit obst* 'tortes with fruit' would match all categories containing one of the three words, except *mit* 'with' which is a stop word, and return not only recipes with the exact same category. To deal with this problem, the search object can be set to search the original fields and not the stemmed ones. Another problem that arose was that a user might want to search for a group of ingredients such as *Nudeln* 'noodles' or *Gemüse* 'vegetables' but that a search for recipes containing the actual word *Nudeln* or *Gemüse* would only return a small number of recipes. We therefore manually extended the Solr server index by a manually curated synonyms list based on the full list of ingredients and categories that was extracted initially. Now, a search for *Nudeln* also returns recipes that contain only the word *Spaghetti*.

5.5 Speech Output

For Text-to-speech (TTS), we use the Google Text-to-speech API. For obvious reasons, this has some limitations. It is for example not possible to modify pronunciation. For domain-specific expressions such as amount range, we therefore change the text string before passing it to Google TTS to pronounce it properly. Out of the box pronunciation of abbreviations (Teel. 'tbs', min.), range constructs ('1–2') and constructs like '5 x 5 cm diameter' was initially quite bad. We improved it by adding code that replaces abbreviations using regular expressions before sending them to TTS. Here, it was particularly helpful to have a list of abbreviations with their frequencies from ingredient parsing (Sect. 5.2).

6 Summary and Outlook

We have described the components and implementation of a mobile, speech-enabled cooking assistant for 32,000 German recipes. The system is fully implemented and runs stably and fluently. Due to its design with only a lean, well-scaling recipe text server in addition to cloud-based Google ASR, the app can easily be installed on thousands of mobile devices. Future work would extend the approach to utilizing linguistic parsing in both query and answer candidate sentences to further abstract from linguistic variants. Then, more complex question processing (example: "show me recipes where eggs are steamed with milk") would be possible. Furthermore, integration of sensors and devices such as barcode reader, electronic thermometers, kitchen scales, or stereo camera as further ambient assistance tools could be helpful. Due to the corpus-based approach to recognizing domain keywords, adaptation to further languages and applications such as interactive user manuals or repair guidance systems should be easy.

References

1. Brants, T.: TnT – A statistical part-of-speech tagger. In: Proc. of 6th ANLP, Seattle, Washington, pp. 224–231 (2000)
2. Chouambe, L.C.: Dynamische Vokabularerweiterung für ein grammatikbasiertes Dialogsystem durch Online-Ressourcen, Studienarbeit, University of Karlsruhe (2006)
3. Drozdzynski, W., Krieger, H.U., Piskorski, J., Schäfer, U., Xu, F.: Shallow processing with unification and typed feature structures — Foundations and applications. Künstliche Intelligenz 1, 17–23 (2004)
4. Hamada, R., Okabe, J., Ide, I.: Cooking navi: Assistant for daily cooking in kitchen. In: Proc. of 13th ACM Int. Conf. on Multimedia, Singapore, pp. 371–374 (2005)
5. Martins, F.M., Pardal, J.P., Franqueira, L., Arez, P., Mamede, N.J.: Starting to cook a tutoring dialogue system. In: SLT Workshop 2008, pp. 145–148. IEEE (2008)
6. Petitpierre, D., Russell, G.: MMORPH – the Multext morphology program. Tech. rep., ISSCO, University of Geneva (1995)
7. Ribeiro, R., Batista, F., Pardal, J.P., Mamede, N.J., Pinto, H.S.: Cooking an ontology. In: Euzenat, J., Domingue, J. (eds.) AIMSA 2006. LNCS (LNAI), vol. 4183, pp. 213–221. Springer, Heidelberg (2006)
8. Wasinger, R.: Dialog-based user interfaces featuring a home cooking assistant, University of Sydney, Australia (2001) (unpublished manuscript)

A Philosophical Foundation
for Ontology Alignments
– The Structuralistic Approach

Christian Schäufler[1], Clemens Beckstein[1,2], and Stefan Artmann[2]

[1] Artificial Intelligence Group, University of Jena, Germany
{christian.schaeufler,clemens.beckstein}@uni-jena.de
[2] Frege Centre for Structural Sciences, University of Jena, Germany
stefan.artmann@uni-jena.de

Abstract. Together with formal ontologies, ontology alignments are utilized to interconnect distributed information systems. Despite their widespread use, it is not trivial to specify a formal semantics for ontology alignments—due to the disparity of the respective domains of the involved ontologies. There are already approaches to tackle this problem, but each is relying on different presumptions. In this paper we propose an interpretation of alignments in terms of theories as they are understood in the philosophy of science following the structuralistic notion of ontological reduction. We use this framework to identify an account of the necessary presumptions of every alignment semantics. These assumptions are then used as a basis for the comparison of existing alignment semantics.

1 Introduction

Modern science incorporates huge amounts of knowledge and data, managed by a multitude of individual actors. To share knowledge between working groups and across scientific communities, the issue of exchanging knowledge becomes crucial. In the particular case of the semantic web, distributed information systems have to be accessible to each other. There is a vivid community addressing automated techniques to interconnect knowledge bases [6]. The vocabulary, the knowledge of an information system is represented in, is specified by its ontology. As knowledge bases represented w.r.t. different ontologies are not connected in a semantic manner, the involved ontologies need to be matched by alignments. With an alignment between two ontologies O and O' of two information systems IS and IS' queries of IS' expressed in the vocabulary of O' can be translated to queries to IS expressed in the vocabulary of O. Ontology alignments are widely used. As an example, the OBO foundry [12] covers more than 50 alignments between its biomedical ontologies.

For distributed knowledge in general, different kinds of formalisms have been proposed (for an overview see [4]). Because of its well understood theoretical properties and for being already the semantic foundation of description logics,

I.J. Timm and M. Thimm (Eds.): KI 2013, LNAI 8077, pp. 224–235, 2013.

we focus on the model theoretical approach. The theoretical foundation for most work in this area is *distributed first order logic (DFOL)*, a multi-theory extension to the semantics of first order logic [7]. Nevertheless there seems to be no canonical way of defining a formal semantics for ontology alignments. There are already approaches defining a model theoretical semantics for alignments, but each is relying on different presumptions.

With the concept of bridge laws, philosophy of science has also contributed to the correct interpretation of structures bridging theories and ontologies. On the one hand, bridge laws are used when theories describing distinct aspects of systems are combined to more potent theories. On the other hand, bridge laws are used to describe the relation between theories of the same domain. The most prominent inter-theory relation is theory-reduction. *Scientific structuralism* is a framework giving a set-theoretical account of the logical structure of scientific theories and reduction [2].

In this paper we try to put knowledge representation and philosophy of science research in one frame. We build upon [11], where the structuralistic concept of a theory is taken to model different meaning facets of ontologies. We now use the structuralistic framework for the interpretation of ontologies and the structuralistic concept of theory links for interpreting ontology alignments.

For this purpose we shall proceed in three steps. 1) In Section 2 we shall first recall the language for specifying alignments and the semantic problem. 2) In Section 3 the structuralistic framework will be used for a formal reconstruction of the semantics of alignments. 3) Utilizing the structuralistic framework, in Section 4 we will compare the premises of the *simple distributed semantics*, the *contextualized distributed semantics* and the structuralistic approach.

2   Syntax and Common Semantics of Ontology Alignments

2.1   Syntax

In the following we assume that ontologies are formulated in a description logic formalism as sets of axioms about ontology elements:

Definition 1. *An* ontology element *is either a term of the ontology (e.g., class name, property name, individual name) or a compound entity built out of other ontology elements and constructors from the ontology language.*

In an alignment, ontology elements of two ontologies are set into relation by inter-terminological alignment axioms where the syntax of these axioms is defined by an alignment language. A typical way to define this syntax is shown in [14]:

Definition 2. *An* ontology element relation R *is a symbol denoting a binary relation or predicate $\tilde{R}$. Given a specific alignment language, the set of usable relation symbols is written $\mathfrak{R}$.*

Frequently used relation symbols for alignments are $\sqsubseteq, \sqsupseteq, \equiv$ or $\bot$, which resemble the relation symbols used in the intra-terminological axioms of the description logics involved.

Definition 3. *A* correspondence *is a triple* $e\,R\,e'$ *where* e *and* e' *are ontology elements from the two ontologies in the alignment and* R *is the ontology element relation that the correspondence claims to hold between* e *and* e'.

Alignment axioms therefore are declarations of correspondences between ontology elements of two different ontologies. Taken together they constitute an ontology alignment:

Definition 4. *An* ontology alignment *A between ontologies* O *and* O' *is a set of correspondences coupling ontology elements belonging to* O *and* O'.

2.2   The Semantic Problem

The central difficulty in interpreting alignments is the potential domain disparity of the involved ontologies. Let, e.g., O and O' be ontologies with interpretations I and I' and $e \equiv e'$ a correspondence between two ontology elements e and e'. Because the domains D of I and D' of I' in general contain different elements, the correspondence cannot simply be interpreted extensionally in the style of

$$e^I = e'^{I'}, \text{ where } e^I \text{ is the extension of } e \text{ in interpretation } I. \tag{1}$$

Just as D and D', the extensions e^I and $e'^{I'}$ of the ontology elements e and e' in general do not share elements (see Fig. 1).

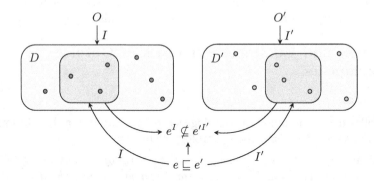

Fig. 1. A naive extensional interpretation of a correspondence

2.3   Simple Distributed Semantics

The most simple way to circumvent the problem of disparate domains is to claim that in reality they are equal – or at least that they intersect in the areas of interest. This non-logical assumption of a single domain can reasonably be made in domains consisting of physical objects as represented, e.g., by online catalogs. The commitment to the equality of domains requires the interpretation of the alignment to be done in the context of given local interpretations which indeed share one domain. As a consequence, the interpretation of the alignment A becomes the interpretation of the alignment w.r.t. given local interpretations.

A semantics of this kind is specified in [5]. For domains of this type an interpretation of alignments as attempted in equation (1) is possible:

Definition 5. *Let* O, O' *be two ontologies and* $c = e\,R\,e'$ *be a* correspondence *between* O *and* O'. c *is satisfied* by interpretations m, m' *of* O *and* O' *iff* $e^m \tilde{R} e'^{m'}$. *This is written* $m, m' \models c$.

Then, an alignment is satisfied by a pair of models iff this pair satisfies every correspondence of the alignment [14]:

Definition 6. *A* model of an alignment A between ontologies O and O' is a pair m, m' of interpretations of O, O' such that for all $c \in A : m, m' \models c$.

2.4 Common Distributed Semantics

In cases where the domains are distinct or cannot be justified to be equal in reality, the simple distributed semantics cannot be applied. In order to be able to nevertheless interpret correspondences, coherence has to be established between both domains. Two formal ways for doing that can be found in [14]:

1) In *integrated distributed semantics* a unified domain U and equalizing functions mapping every local domain to U are specified. Alignments between ontology elements of O and O' are then no longer interpreted w.r.t. D and D' but extensionally w.r.t. their common projection on U in the style of eqn. 1.

2) In *contextualized distributed semantics* a *domain relation* r is declared, relating individuals from one local domain to the other. This makes the specification of an extensional semantics in the style of eqn. 1 possible.

Definition 7. *Given two domains of interpretation* D *and* D' *, a* domain relation *is a mapping* $r : D \to D'$. [14]

Definition 8. *A* contextualized interpretation *of an alignment* A *between two ontologies* O *and* O' *is a tuple* $\langle m, m', r \rangle$ *where* m *and* m' *are interpretations of* O *and* O' *and* r *is a domain relation such that* r *relates the domain of* m *to the domain of* m'.

In contrast to interpretations of alignments in simple distributed semantics (see Def. 6) interpretations of alignments in contextualized distributed semantics additionally contain a domain relation r. As the integrated and the contextualized distributed semantic approaches share most of their properties [14], in this paper we shall focus on the contextualized approach.

Definition 9. *A contextualized interpretation* $\langle m, m', r \rangle$ *of an alignment* A *is a* contextualized model *iff* $m, m', r \models A$ *and* m, m' *are local models of* O *and* O'.

3 Structuralistic Reconstruction of Ontology Alignments

We shall now introduce a new semantics for the interpretation of ontology alignments inspired by the structuralistic conception of theories and inter-theoretical connections. Scientific structuralism is a branch of philosophy of science that attempts to reconstruct scientific theories by means of set-theoretical structures [2]. We start by introducing the structuralistic framework to interpret single ontologies. Utilizing this framework we then shall be able to formalize the assumptions of the approaches we recapitulated in Section 2 as well as the structuralistic approach. Our framework will also provide us with a formal criterion whether two ontologies can be matched.

3.1 Structuralistic Reconstruction of Models and Interpretations

First, we generalize the concept of an interpretation of an ontology. In description logic each interpretation of a theory consists of a domain and an interpretation function which maps (atomic and complex) ontology elements to (in the case of roles, pairs of) subsets of one (or sometimes more) domain(s) [1]. An interpretation which satisfies all the axioms of the ontology is called a *model* of this ontology.

As in structuralism, an interpretation of an ontology O in our approach need not consist of just one unstructured domain D, but may consist of several domains $D_1, \ldots, D_n$. The structuralists call the factors D_i of such a domain structure *(domain) terms*. All models of an ontology share the same domain terms. We may define the domain terms $D_1, \ldots, D_n$ of an ontology O by a set of disjunct concepts that, according to the ontological axioms of O, are just below the top concept $\top$ in the subsumption hierarchy induced by the ontology O. In the wine ontology [13], e.g., these domains are wine, taste, color and place of production.

3.2 Theory Elements for a Reconstruction of Ontologies

In their notion of theories, structuralists proceed from what they call the "statement view" to the "non-statement view". According to the non-statement view, a theory cannot be explicated just by a set of axioms. It is necessary to specify the set of the models of that theory. Empirical theories actually involve different kinds of statements – e.g., axioms that introduce properties, laws of first and higher order, and assertions about the intended applications. According to the non-statement view each kind of axiom is represented by its own set of models. The *theory element* T contains all sets that a theory comprises: $T = \langle M_p, M, C, L, I \rangle$.[1]

The set of *potential models* M_p denotes the possible interpretations due to the signature of the theory. The set of *actual models* M denotes those potential models

---

[1] To exclude T-theoretical concepts of a theory T from the empirical claim of T, a set M_{pp} of (non-theoretical) partial potential models can be specified. For simplicity we omit the treatment of theoretical concepts.

that satisfy the actual laws of a theory. C is a set representing intra-theory laws, also called constraints. Each element of C covers a set of potential models that are compatible under certain restrictions. C allows to express how local applications of a theory can be combined, forming a complex system. The *local link* L denotes the set of potential models which share an inter-theoretical link $\mathcal{L}$ (see next section). L represents the local part of the bridge laws between T and other theory elements. The set of *intended applications* I denotes those possible models which result from measurements performed in the intended domain (reality).

We reconstruct an ontology O in terms of a structuralistic theory element $T(O)$, in short T, where $T = \langle M_p, M, C, L, I \rangle$. The model theoretic interpretations of O – as generalized in section 3.1– correspond to the potential models M_p of T. The models of O exactly match the *actual models* M of T. The set of intended applications I involves every conceivable model, the application of the ontology O is intended for.

According to the structuralistic understanding, every model is an independent representation of an application of a theory. Each model comprises its own individuals with their model-specific property values. Domains D_x and D_y of different models x and y may overlap, allowing one and the same individual to emerge in multiple models. But from model to model, the properties of such an individual need not have the same values. Nevertheless, the constancy of an individual's properties across multiple models can be explicitly claimed resulting in a common domain with invariant properties for each individual. Formally this can be forced by a special intra-theoretical bridge law, an *identity constraint C*. C is a set of those sets of models that satisfy the desired intra-model constancy of properties ($e^x(d)$ denotes the value of property e of individual d in model x) :

$$\mathrm{C}(T) := \left\{ X \subseteq \mathrm{M}_p(T) : X \neq \emptyset \wedge \bigwedge_{x,y \in X} \bigwedge_{d \in D_x \cap D_y} e^x(d) = e^y(d) \right\} \text{ [3].}$$

3.3   Structuralistic Interpretation of Alignments

The study of types of relations between scientific theories is an important task of philosophy of science. In scientific structuralism, bridge laws between theories are denoted by sets of models. The conjunction $T_1, \ldots, T_n$ of a tuple of theory elements along with a *theory link* $\mathcal{L} \subseteq M_p(T_1) \times \ldots \times M_p(T_n)$, i.e., a distinguished subset of the cross product of the potential models $M_p(T_i)$ from each theory element, forms a so-called *theory holon*.

In contrast to contextualized distributed semantics, a link $\mathcal{L}$ in our structuralistic semantics only satisfies the bridge laws (the alignment correspondences) and takes no account of the intrinsic laws of the theory (the axioms of the involved ontologies). In order to treat a link $\mathcal{L}$ from the viewpoint of an involved theory element, it is necessary to project the link to its theory elements T_i resulting in local links $L(T_i)$:

Definition 10. *Let $\mathcal{L}$ be an n-ary link between theory elements $T_1, \ldots, T_n$. The local link $L(T_i)$ of a theory element $T_i = \langle M_p(T_i), M(T_i), C(T_i), L(T_i), I(T_i) \rangle$ is defined by:*

$$L(T_i) = \{m_i \in M_p(T_i) : \forall j \neq i \; \exists m_j \in M_p(T_j) : \langle m_1, m_2, \ldots, m_n \rangle \in \mathcal{L}\}.$$

With the help of theory links, all interesting types of inter-theoretical relations can be described by properties holding in L. Theory links that result from structuralistic classifications (e.g. reduction, equivalence and theorization [10]) always interrelate exactly two theories. In the following we will therefore only look at binary inter-theoretical links.

Ontological Theory Reduction. The most important inter-theoretical relation is theory reduction. The aim of reduction is to substitute a weak *reduced* theory by a more general *reducing* theory. The question whether an intended model is a model of the reduced theory can be answered using the reducing theory: if a potential model of the reducing theory is not an actual model of the reducing theory then there is no corresponding potential model of the reduced theory that is an actual model of the reduced theory. Reduction links are also called *entailment links*. An example of a reduction is given in [2, p. 255], where the theory of collision mechanics is reduced to classical particle mechanics. This general notion of reduction is not meant to relate the properties of the involved theories. Only *ontological reductions* as a special kind of reduction require the individuals of the domains of two theories to be relatable. This relation of domains usually is not specified for pairs of individuals but for entire classes by the domains $\langle D_1, \ldots, D_n \rangle$ of a theory element. This choice of domains, separated into different ontological kinds over a comprehensive aggregate domain, is a prerequisite for ontological reduction. In classical particle mechanics, e.g., separate domains are particles, coordinates, and points of time. Structuralists call such a partition of domains along with the relations the theory is built upon, the *ontology of the theory*. A reduction is called *ontological* iff certain domains of the reduced theory are constructible from the domains of the reducing theory in the form of echelon sets:

Definition 11. *S is called an* echelon set *on sets* $D_1, \ldots, D_n$ *(the base sets of the echelon set) iff either 1)* $S = D_i$ *for some i, or, 2)* $S_1, \ldots, S_k$ *are echelon sets on* $D_1, \ldots, D_n$ *and* $S = S_1 \times \ldots \times S_k$, *or, 3)* S' *is an echelon set on* $D_1, \ldots, D_n$ *and* $S = P(S')$, *where* $P(S')$ *is the power set of* S'.

Definition 12. *Let T and T' be theory elements with domains* $\langle D_1, \ldots, D_n; \ldots \rangle$ *and* $\langle D'_1, \ldots D'_m; \ldots \rangle$ *respectively and let a theory link ρ be a reduction $\mathcal{L}$ of T to T'. ρ is called* ontological *iff there are D_i which are elements (or subsets) of an echelon set with base sets* $D'_1, \ldots, D'_m$. *In this case D_i is called to be* reconstructible from *the domains of T'* [8, p. 320].

Two theories T and T' where at least one domain of T is reconstructible from the domains of T' are called *ontologically compatible* [9, p. 4]. Ontological compatibility is a necessary precondition for ontological reduction.

Structuralistic Interpretation of Alignments. In our approach alignments do not have a semantics per se but only w.r.t. the way they are used. The application of an alignment in our view always assumes a specific flow of information

— from a *foreign* information system w.r.t. O to the initial inquirer with a commitment to O'. In analogy to the distinction between reduced and reducing theory we distinguish between the *queried* ontology O and *querying* ontology O' involved in the application of an alignment.

A precondition of the structuralistic interpretation of alignments is a term-by-term relation between the domains of the involved ontologies.

Definition 13. *Let $D_1, \ldots, D_n$ and $D'_1, \ldots, D'_m$ be domains of ontologies O and O'. Echelon-set relationships of the form $D_i \subseteq S$, where S is an echelon-set on the sets $D'_1, \ldots, D'_m$, or of the form $D'_j \subseteq S'$, where S' is an echelon-set on the sets $D_1, \ldots, D_n$, are then called* domain inclusions *of O and O'.*

As an example, a simple domain inclusion holds between the domain of wine and the domain of alcoholic drinks. An example of a more complex domain inclusion is the one between the domain of addresses D_1 of one ontology and the domains D'_1 of streets, D'_2 of places and D'_3 of postal codes of another, because $D_1 \subseteq D'_1 \times D'_2 \times D'_3$. Here, elements of D_1 cannot be expressed as elements of a single set D'_i, but only as a combination of elements from $D'_1, \ldots, D'_3$.

With a set of domain inclusions we are able to define when two ontologies are compatible w.r.t. an alignment.

Definition 14. *Two ontologies are said to be* ontologically compatible *iff the set of domain inclusions is non-empty.*

Hence, ontological compatibility is exactly that property that distinguishes a general reduction from an ontological one (cf. Def. 12).

For the interpretation of an alignment A let us now assume that we have two ontologies O and O' with domains $D_1, \ldots, D_n$ and $D'_1, \ldots, D'_m$ and certain domain inclusions that hold between them (Fig. 2). Let us further assume that O is the queried and O' the querying ontology of the alignment.

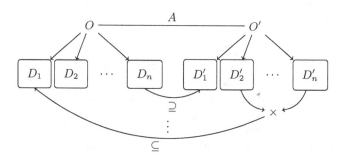

Fig. 2. Context of a structuralistic interpretation of an alignment A

Given the domain inclusions, we are able to define when two models m and m' satisfy a correspondence $e \, R \, e'$. Because the domain terms $D_1, \ldots, D_n$ match the top-level primitive concepts of ontology O, the extension of an ontology element e in O is a subset of exactly one domain D_i (or a pair of domains if e is a role) and

e' is a subset of exactly one D'_j. For an interpretation of the correspondence, both involved ontology elements have to be interpreted in the same domain. Which one of D_i and D'_j is going to be that shared domain can now be answered relative to the roles that the involved ontologies play in the alignment process: since O' is the querying ontology the interpretation of both e and e' should take place w.r.t. D'_j: Individuals of both domains are then related in the direction of the flow of information between the involved information systems. The general idea of substituting foreign domains by local ones is shown in Figure 3.

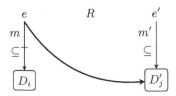

Fig. 3. The interpretation of a correspondence $e\,R\,e'$

If the domain inclusion depicts a domain that covers the extensions of both ontology elements, the interpretation of that correspondence can be done in the simple distributed semantics w.r.t. the chosen domain.

An Example. The following example shows the difficulties one may encounter with interpreting alignments in distributed domains. Let O and O' be ontologies specifying meteorological concepts. In O a concept HighPressureArea may be defined as a specific system, in O' a concept Anticyclone may be defined as a specific phenomenon. Let A be an alignment between O and O', containing a correspondence HighPressureArea $\equiv$ Anticyclone. How can the interpretation be achieved without a strange mix-up of categories, as required by the assumption of a global domain as made in simple distributed semantics? The one-to-one relation between individuals of the domains of O and O' that has to be established for contextualized distributed semantics is problematic as well: 1) An individual can only be considered as element of a domain in the context of a conceptualization. Ontologies in this sense create the individuals they are talking about. It is therefore unreasonable to assume that different ontologies, even about the same reality, always respect certain relationships between 'their' individuals. 2) There are no individuals that can be related by a domain relation if the domains of the respective models talk about different parts of reality. The domains of a weather information system for Europe and an information system for the USA, e.g., must be disjoint by their very definition.

In structuralistic semantics, 1) the domain terms of O and O' are analyzed, e.g. *System, Phenomenon, Coordinate, Height, Time, Pressure*. 2) The domain terms of the involved ontology elements are determined, e.g. HighPressureArea being a *System* and Anticyclone being *Phenomenon*. 3) The set of domain inclusions is searched for the relation of both domains, e.g. *System* × *Observation* ⊆

Phenomenon. 4) Because the domain *Phenomenon* is more comprehensive from the perspective of the querying information system IS', it is safe to interpret the extension of Anticyclone in the local domain *Phenomenon*. The correspondence can thus be interpreted in simple distributed semantics w.r.t. the domain *Phenomenon* and w.r.t. to the specific flow of information.

4 Properties of Model Theoretic Alignment Semantics

Armed with the structuralistic explication of the semantics of alignments, we analyze their premises in this section. We show under which practical conditions those premises are justified.

4.1 Simple Distributed Semantics

Simple distributed semantics can only be applied if the local models of the aligned ontologies O and O' share a common domain. In the structuralistic framework this is the case iff two conditions are fulfilled. 1) The potential models M_p of $T(O)$ and M_p' of $T(O')$ each consist of exactly one domain D and D' respectively. 2) The domain inclusions between both ontologies $D \subseteq D'$ and $D' \subseteq D$ hold. This is a quite strong restriction that is justified only if it simplifies the interpretation of an alignment very much.

4.2 Contextualized Distributed Semantics

In contextualized distributed semantics there is no explicit precondition on the involved domains. Defining a domain relation r for ontologies O and O' is a very flexible way of correlating two ontologies. The downside of this kind of semantics is that it depends on a specific pair of domains D and D' ($r \subseteq D \times D'$). All models m of O have to share domain D, all models m' of O' have to share domain D'.

Under which conditions is this assumption justified? There is a fundamental objection to this assumption: What does it mean to identify one object in different models if its properties are variant? The structuralistic answer to this question is: identity of objects in different models makes no sense if it is not guaranteed that they share at least one property. With *constraints* the structuralistic framework provides an algebraic structure enforcing this requirement. Models of matching properties are aggregated in sets $c \in C$ of identity constraints. By each c, one possible domain D of O is modeled. Structuralists have observed that a model m can be element of different constraints $c \in C$ that can nevertheless be incommensurable. To commit to a domain D for an ontology O requires to commit to a set $c \in C$ of models. The empirical claim of a theory entails that a $c \in C$ is the set I of intended applications. Therefore, by I a domain is modeled which satisfies all proposition of the theory. So the answer to the question, when the presuppositions of a contextualized distributed interpretation are justified, is: We can commit to a single empirical domain as long as there is an agreement about the individuals of this domain, e.g., because they can be measured by a certain method.

4.3   Structuralistic Semantics

In order to interpret an alignment A between two ontologies O and O' in terms of theory-elements $T(O)$, $T(O')$ and a global link $\mathcal{L}$, two presumptions have to be met.

1) The potential models of $T(O)$ and $T(O')$ are relatable by echelon-set inclusions. These inclusions define $\mathcal{L}$ by the models fitting the alignment A w.r.t. the domain inclusions. The components of $T(O)$ (and $T(O')$, respectively) are defined as follows: M are the models fitting the axioms of O (and O', respectively), L is the local link of $\mathcal{L}$ (modulo ontology O), the set of sets of models rising from identity constraints is C and the intended applications of the ontology are I.

2) A special property between these sets holds:

$$I \in \mathcal{P}(M) \cap \mathcal{P}(L) \cap C. \tag{2}$$

This property is called the *claim* of the theory. With the help of this structualistic meta-property of a theory holon we can decide whether an ontology and – even more – whether a distributed information system on the basis of O, O' and A is valid.

5   Conclusion

In this paper we applied the structuralistic conception of theories as a framework for the analysis of approaches to the semantics of ontologies and ontology alignments. By applying the concept of ontological theory reduction to ontologies, we furthermore gave an introduction to a novel kind of semantics of ontology alignments.

With the help of the structuralistic framework, the presuppositions of simple distributed semantics and contextualized distributed semantics were explicated. Both semantics depend on distinguished and fixed domains for single or pairs of ontologies. Structuralism shows that it is possible to define a semantics for alignments without relying on predetermined domains. Still one has to make assumptions, but they are weaker than in contextualized distributed semantics: Each formal ontology has to commit to a differentiation w.r.t. certain ontological kinds (domain terms), and at least some of the domain terms need to be relatable by certain domain inclusion. The structuralistic perspective on ontology alignments is a pragmatic one in the sense that the flow of information from a queried to a querying ontology shapes the interpretation of the alignment between both ontologies.

Acknowledgement. This work is part of the Computer Supported Research (CoSRe) initiative funded by Thüringer Ministerium für Bildung, Wissenschaft und Kultur under grant 12038-514.

References

1. Baader, F., Calvanese, D., McGuinness, D., Nardi, D., Patel-Schneider, P. (eds.): The Description Logic Handbook: Theory, Implementation, and Applications. Cambridge University Press, New York (2003)
2. Balzer, W., Moulines, C.U., Sneed, J.D.: An Architectonic for Science - the Structuralist Program. Reidel, Dordrecht (1987)
3. Bartelborth, T.: Begründungsstrategien – ein Weg durch die analytische Erkenntnistheorie. Akademie Verlag, Berlin (1996)
4. Brockmans, S., Haase, P., Serafini, L., Stuckenschmidt, H.: Formal and conceptual comparison of ontology mapping languages. In: Mizoguchi, R., Shi, Z.-Z., Giunchiglia, F. (eds.) ASWC 2006. LNCS, vol. 4185, pp. 616–631. Springer, Heidelberg (2006)
5. Calvanese, D., De Giacomo, G., Lenzerini, M.: Description logics for information integration. In: Kakas, A.C., Sadri, F. (eds.) Computat. Logic (Kowalski Festschrift). LNCS (LNAI), vol. 2408, pp. 41–60. Springer, Heidelberg (2002)
6. Euzenat, J., Ferrara, A., van Hage, W.R., Hollink, L., Meilicke, C., Nikolov, A., Ritze, D., Scharffe, F., Shvaiko, P., Stuckenschmidt, H., Šváb Zamazal, O., Trojahn, C.: Results of the ontology alignment evaluation initiative 2011. In: Shvaiko, P., et al. (eds.) Proceedings of the 6th International Workshop on Ontology Matching. CEUR Workshop Proceedings, vol. 814 (2011)
7. Ghidini, C., Ghidini, C., Serafini, L., Serafini, L.: Distributed first order logics. In: Frontiers of Combining Systems 2, Studies in Logic and Computation, pp. 121–140. Research Studies Press (1998)
8. Moulines, C.: Ontology, reduction, emergence: A general frame. Synthese 151, 313–323 (2006)
9. Moulines, C.U.: Ontology, reduction, and the unity of science. In: Cao, T. (ed.) The Proceedings of the Twentieth World Congress of Philosophy, pp. 19–27. Philosophy Documentation Center, Bowling Green (US-OH) (2001)
10. Moulines, C.U., Polanski, M.: Bridges, constraints, and links. In: Balzer, W., Moulines, C.U. (eds.) Structuralist Theory of Science. de Gruyter, Berlin (1996)
11. Schäufler, C., Artmann, S., Beckstein, C.: A structuralistic approach to ontologies. In: Mertsching, B., Hund, M., Aziz, Z. (eds.) KI 2009. LNCS, vol. 5803, pp. 363–370. Springer, Heidelberg (2009)
12. Smith, B., Ashburner, M., Rosse, C., Bard, J., Bug, W., Ceusters, W., Goldberg, L.J., Eilbeck, K., Ireland, A., Mungall, C.J., Leontis, N., Rocca-Serra, P., Ruttenberg, A., Sansone, S.A., Scheuermann, R.H., Shah, N., Whetzel, P.L., Lewis, S.: The OBO foundry: coordinated evolution of ontologies to support biomedical data integration. Nat. Biotech. 25(11), 1251–1255 (2007)
13. Smith, M.K., Welty, C., McGuinness, D.L.: Wine ontology – an example owl ontology (2004), http://www.w3.org/TR/2004/REC-owl-guide-20040210/wine.rdf
14. Zimmermann, A., Euzenat, J.: Three semantics for distributed systems and their relations with alignment composition. In: Cruz, I., Decker, S., Allemang, D., Preist, C., Schwabe, D., Mika, P., Uschold, M., Aroyo, L.M. (eds.) ISWC 2006. LNCS, vol. 4273, pp. 16–29. Springer, Heidelberg (2006)

Contraction Hierarchies on Grid Graphs

Sabine Storandt

Albert-Ludwigs-Universität Freiburg
79110 Freiburg, Germany
storandt@informatik.uni-freiburg.de

Abstract. Many speed-up techniques developed for accelerating the computation of shortest paths in road networks, like reach or contraction hierarchies, are based on the property that some streets are 'more important' than others, e.g. on long routes the usage of an interstate is almost inevitable. In grids there is no obvious hierarchy among the edges, especially if the costs are uniform. Nevertheless we will show that contraction hierarchies can be applied to grid graphs as well. We will point out interesting connections to speed-up techniques shaped for routing on grids, like swamp hierarchies and jump points, and provide experimental results for game maps, mazes, random grids and rooms.

1 Introduction

Efficient route planning in grid graphs is important in a wide range of application domains, e.g. robot path planning and in-game navigation. While many search algorithms like A^* provide relatively fast solutions on the fly, it might be worthwhile to allow some preprocessing to speed up query answering if the same grid map is used multiple times. For road networks state-of-the-art preprocessing techniques like *contraction hierarchies* [1] and *transit nodes* [2] enable shortest path computation in a few milliseconds or even microseconds on graphs with millions of nodes and edges. But the structure of street graphs differs clearly from grids: Shortest paths are almost always unique and some edges (e.g. corresponding to highways and interstates) occur in significantly more optimal paths than others. Therefore it is not obvious that such speed-up techniques carry over to grid graphs. Nevertheless, it was shown that the idea of transit node routing can be adapted to grid graphs [3], leading to a significantly improved performance on video game maps. Contraction hierarchies were also tested on grid graphs [4], but these grids had non-uniform costs and moreover the construction algorithm for road networks was applied without any adaption. In this paper, we will show how to modify contraction hierarchies to take care of the special structure of grid graphs.

1.1 Contribution

We will first describe in detail how contraction hierarchies can be modified to work on grid graphs, introducing some simple rules to speed up the preprocessing phase. Moreover, we especially focus on how to be able to compute canonical

I.J. Timm and M. Thimm (Eds.): KI 2013, LNAI 8077, pp. 236–247, 2013.
© Springer-Verlag Berlin Heidelberg 2013

optimal paths, i.e. paths with a minimal number of direction changes which are desirable in many applications. In our experimental evaluation, we give empirical evidence for the small amount of auxiliary data created by constructing a contraction hierarchy upon a grid. We compare query answering with our approach to the A*-baseline for several input categories, like random graphs and mazes. Finally, we also point out connections to other speed-up techniques developed for path planning on grids.

1.2 Related Work

Because of its significance in many applications, speed-up techniques for routing on grids are described in numerous papers. We distinguish between online approaches, where no preprocessing is applied – like the standard $A*$ algorithm (and variants thereof) or *jump points* [5] – and offline algorithms, which allow a preprocessing phase, like *swamps* [6]. Moreover, there are optimal and suboptimal search algorithms, with *HPA** [7] being an example for the latter. Finally, some speed-up techniques are very specific for certain instance classes (like only for 4-connected grids [8], or preferably for game maps as described e.g. by Bj önsson et al. [9]), while others are beneficial in several application domains. In this paper, we describe an offline, optimal and unspecific technique to efficiently retrieve shortest paths in grid graphs. We will come back to similarities and compatibility with other methods towards the end of the paper.

2   Contraction Hierarchies (CH) on Grids

In this section, we want to review the standard contraction hierarchy approach [1] and give some intuition why this method will work on grids (with uniform costs) besides no obvious hierarchy among the edges. Subsequently, we will describe how to use CH-search to retrieve canonical paths via an edge classifier approach.

2.1 Conventional Contraction Hierarchy

Given a (di)graph $G(V, E)$, the basic idea behind CH is augmenting the graph with shortcuts that allow to save a lot of edge relaxations at query time. To that end, in a preprocessing phase nodes are sorted according to some notion of importance. Afterwards the nodes get contracted one by one in that order while preserving all shortest path distances in the remaining graph by inserting additional edges (so called shortcuts). More precisely, after removing a node v the distance between any pair of neighbours u, w of v has to stay unchanged. Therefore an edge (u, w) with proper costs is inserted if the only shortest path from u to w is uvw. Hence if there exists a so called *witness path* with lower cost than u, v, w or with equal cost but not visiting v (typically found via a Dijkstra run from u) the shortcut can be omitted. If the graph is undirected, we assume for clarity of definitions that an edge is represented by its two directed versions. Note, that it is not necessary to use this transformation in the actual implementation. After all nodes have been removed, a new graph G' is created by adding all shortcuts to the original graph. An edge (v, w) in G' is called upward if the importance l of v is smaller than that of w ($l(v) < l(w)$) and downward otherwise. A path is called upward/downward, if it consists of upward/downward edges only. By construction, for every pair of vertices $s, t \in V$ it exists a shortest path in G', which can be subdivided into an upward and a downward path. Therefore s-t-queries can be answered bidirectionally, with the forward run (starting at s) considering only upward edges and the backward run (starting at t) considering exclusively downward edges. We call the respective subgraphs containing all upward paths starting at s or all downward paths ending in t respectively as $G^{\uparrow}(s)/G^{\downarrow}(t)$ and the highest node wrt to l on an s-t-path the peak.

To get the path in the original graph and not in G', we have to expand contained shortcuts back to paths. For that purpose, we store during the CH-construction the IDs of the two skipped edges for every shortcut. A recursive unpacking procedure allows then to retrieve the original edges.

On the first sight, the construction of a CH upon a grid seems to be a bad idea. Consider a 4-connected grid, the contraction of a node would remove four edges; but any two of these edges might form a shortest path, hence up to six shortcuts must be inserted. Contracting the neighbouring nodes this effect amplifies, giving the impression that we might end up with a quadratic number of edges in G' (see Figure 1, left). But there are two characteristics of grids preventing this: Optimal paths in grids with uniform costs are ambiguous, but only one optimal solution needs to be preserved. In fact, contracting the first node in a complete 4-connected grid, only two shortcuts instead of six have to be inserted because of ambiguity, see Figure 1 (right) for an illustration. Unfortunately, the sparser the grid, the more the ambiguity of shortest paths subsides. But if a grid is far from being complete, the holes introduce a certain kind of hierarchy as well because now shortest paths tend to use their borders. Hence CH construction upon a grid might work even if it seems counter-intuitive at the first glance.

2.2   Accelerating the CH Construction

There are actually no modifications necessary to run CH on a grid as the basic framework at least in theory works on any graph. But we can speed up the preprocessing using the characteristics of a grid with uniform costs.

Knowing the positions of the nodes in the grid, we do not have to start a witness search for u, v, w if the nodes are all on a straight line and the summed

Fig. 1. Illustration of two contraction steps (removal of the red node): On the left without considering ambiguity (or assuming non-uniform costs), on the right with inserting only shortcuts between neighboring nodes if the shortest path via the red node is unique

costs of (u, v) and (v, w) comply with the interval between u and w. Also if $c(u, v) + c(v, w)$ equals the absolute positional difference between u and w, we can restrict the witness search to the rectangle spanned by u and w. Moreover we can plug-in A* or any other search algorithm to accelerate the witness search in any case. Note, that even a suboptimal algorithm would be alright because not detecting an existing witness might lead to the insertion of a superfluous shortcut, but this will not compromise optimality. In fact, we could insert all shortcuts right away and the quality of the queries would be unaffected. But as additional shortcuts increase the graph size and therefore the runtime of the preprocessing as well as the query answering, we aim for keeping G' sparse.

2.3 Maintaining Canonical Paths

To save energy (especially concerning robot navigation) and to enable a natural way of moving, we aim for an optimal path with a minimal number of turns, i.e. a canonical path. But neither Dijkstra nor plain A* can guarantee to find such a solution if the optimal path is ambiguous.

To gain this ability in G' we proceed for a 4-connected grid as follows: We assign to an edge/shortcut $e = (u, v)$ in the graph a classifier $[a(u), t, a(v)]$, with $a(u), a(v)$ implicating with which kind of an edge the path $p(e)$ spanned by e starts/ends. Here, we use h if it is a horizontal edge and v if it is a vertical one. Moreover we assign the number of turns t on $p(e)$ to e as well. So every vertical edge in the original graph G has the classifier $[v, 0, v]$ in the beginning, every horizontal one $[h, 0, h]$. Bridging two edges via a new shortcut, the classifier can easily be determined: Let the node skipped by the shortcut be v and the two bridged edges $e_1 = (u, v)$ and $e_2 = (v, w)$ with classifiers $[a(u), t_1, a(v)]$ and $[a'(v), t_2, a'(w)]$. If $a(v) = a'(v)$ the shortcut (u, w) receives the classifier $[a(u), t_1 + t_2, a'(w)]$, otherwise $[a(u), t_1 + t_2 + 1, a'(w)]$. To maintain canonical solutions – without inserting too many shortcuts – we adapt the CH-construction slightly: Whenever the resulting classifier for a potential shortcut reveals $t = 0$ or $t = 1$, we insert the shortcut right away (despite the possible existence of a witness), because the spanned paths are trivially canonical (at most one turn) and therefore optimal for sure. But as soon as $t \geq 2$, we have to apply witness search again. If a witness is found with lower cost or equal cost and fewer turns, we omit the shortcut, otherwise we insert it. If at some point a potential shortcut (u, w) exhibits the same costs but fewer turns than an already existing edge (u, w), we update the respective classifier (and do not need to start a witness search).

We will now prove by induction over the number of turns that this approach maintains for every pair of vertices $s, t \in V$ a canonical shortest path between them in the CH. For the base clause, we first verify the claim for paths with at most one turn.

Lemma 1. *Every optimal trivially canonical-s-t-path (i.e. exhibiting at most one turn) can be reconstructed considering only $G^{\uparrow}(s) \cup G^{\downarrow}(t)$.*

Proof. If the shortest path between s and t is a straight line, the optimal path is unique and therefore contained in $G^{\uparrow}(s) \cup G^{\downarrow}(t)$ for sure. So let now z be the

Fig. 2. Illustration of the proof for Lemma 1: Blue numbers imply the contraction order of the nodes, original edges are black, shortcuts are coloured blue. The red background colour marks an upwards path, the green colour indicates a downward path, showing that the canonical path from s to t via z is contained in $G^{\uparrow}(s) \cup G^{\downarrow}(t)$.

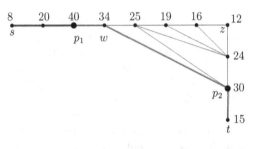

turning point on the path as depicted in Figure 2. As s-z and t-z are unique optimal paths, they can be given in CH-description. So let p_1, p_2 be the peak nodes on those subpaths, w.l.o.g. $l(p_1) > l(p_2)$ and w the lowest node on the path p_1-z with $l(w) > l(p_2)$. As w-z goes downwards and z-p_2 upwards, the shortcut (w, p_2) will be considered and inserted because it represents a trivial canonical path. Hence s-p_1 is in $G^{\uparrow}(s)$ and p_1-w-p_2-t in $G^{\downarrow}(t)$.   ∎

Theorem 1. *For every pair of vertices $s, t \in V$ all optimal canonical shortest paths between them are contained in $G^{\uparrow}(s) \cup G^{\downarrow}(t)$.*

Proof. Our induction hypothesis is, that for every pair of vertices s, t with an optimal canonical path between them exhibiting $\leq k$ turns, the path can be found in $G^{\uparrow}(s) \cup G^{\downarrow}(t)$. For $k \leq 1$ we proved correctness in Lemma 1. Now, for the induction step, let z be the last turning point on a canonical s-t-path. By induction hypothesis the path from s to z is contained in $G^{\uparrow}(s) \cup G^{\downarrow}(z)$. Also let z' be the last turning point on the path s-z (if s-z is a straight line, set $z' = s$), p'' the peak node on this path, and further p' the peak node on z'-z and p the peak node on z-t (which both must be well defined as the respective paths are unique shortest paths). Following the argumentation in the proof of Lemma 1, the shortcut (p', p) will be inserted for sure. If $l(p') > l(p)$, we are done, because s-$p'' \in G^{\uparrow}(s)$ and p''-p'-p-$t \in G^{\downarrow}(t)$. Otherwise assume $l(p'') > l(p)$. Then let w be the node on the path p''-p with the smallest label exceeding $l(p)$. Hence at some point, we have to decide whether to insert the shortcut (w, p). As there can not exist a witness with lower costs or one with equal costs and fewer turns (otherwise the considered s-t-path would not be canonical), the (w, p) will be inserted. Therefore s-$p'' \in G^{\uparrow}(s)$ and p''-w-p-$t \in G^{\downarrow}(t)$. If $l(p'') < l(p)$ the argumentation works exactly the same, now choosing w to be the node on p'-p with the smallest label exceeding $l(p'')$, resulting in s-p''-w-$p \in G^{\uparrow}(s)$ and p-$t \in G^{\downarrow}(t)$.   ∎

On the basis of Theorem 1, we now want to describe how to extract a respective canonical path for given s, t, considering only nodes and edges in $G^{\uparrow}(s) \cup G^{\downarrow}(t)$. We still use two Dijkstra runs, one in $G^{\uparrow}(s)$ and the other one in $G^{\downarrow}(t)$. The crucial difference is now that during edge relaxation we do not only update the tail node v of the edge if we can reduce the costs, but also if the costs stay the same and the number of turns can be decreased. This number can be easily computed along, as the summed number of turns of the classifiers along the path from s/t to v plus the number of nodes on the path at which we change from horizontal to vertical or vice versa (with the information being contained in the classifiers as well). But now we have to be careful, because it makes a difference with which kind of edge (h or v) a path ends as it influences the number of turns on superpaths. Therefore we allow now the assignment of two labels per node if both exhibit the same costs and number of turns, but the first one corresponds to a path ending with a vertical edge and the other one to a path with the final edge being horizontal. After termination of the two Dijkstra computations, we iterate over all expanded nodes in both runs and keep track of the node which minimizes the summed costs and also the summed turns (incremented by one if a turn occurs at this node, too). For the resulting node, we backtrack the two subpaths and unpack them to get the final path in the original graph.

The whole argumentation carries over to 8-connected grids with uniform costs (i.e. diagonal edges cost $\sqrt{2}$). Here, we introduce two new direction parameters in the edge classifier, d_1 and d_2, indicating diagonal movement (from the lower left corner to the upper right or from the lower right corner to the upper left). Turning points are now also nodes where movement is changed from straight to diagonal or vice versa. One could argue, that the change of direction is less significant here, as the turning angle is now only $45°$ and not $90°$. Hence we could also increase our turn counter by only 0.5 instead of 1 for each such direction change. In the extraction phase the Dijkstra algorithm can now assign four different labels to each node, but as with the edge classifiers this only results in a constant overhead.

3   Experimental Results

Now we want to evaluate the impact of our approach on real-world and synthetic instances[1]. We implemented CH-search in C++ and performed experiments on an Intel i5-3360M CPU with 2.80GHz and 16GB RAM. We start by providing some implementation details for the CH-construction and measure the amount of auxiliary data created in the preprocessing phase. Upon that, we analyse the number of expanded nodes for our approach in comparison to A*. We also describe, how to combine CH- and A*-search and provide experimental results for this scenario as well. Then, for several input categories, we will individually give some intuition why CH-search accelerates the query answering. Finally, we will draw some connections to other speed-up techniques.

3.1   Preprocessing

To construct a CH, we have to define the order in which the nodes should be contracted. As one goal is to keep the resulting graph as sparse as possible, the classical indicator for road networks is the so called edge-difference (ED) [1].

---

[1] Extracted from `http://movingai.com/`

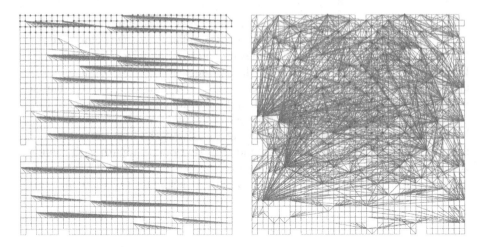

Fig. 3. Two different CH-construction schemes tested on a 40x40 grid graph with 5% randomly deleted vertices and uniform costs, exhibiting 2867 edges. The 10% of the nodes which were contracted last are coloured red. Left: Contraction order is the enumeration order of the nodes, resulting in a CH-graph with only 3490 edges but no measurable speed-up. Right: Contraction order based on weighted edge-difference and consecutively chosen independent set of nodes. The number of edges here is 6771, in a random query in this graph the number of expanded nodes is only halve the number of expanded nodes for plain A*.

The ED is the number of edges we have to insert when removing the node minus the number of adjacent edges. So normally the lower the ED the better. Therefore one always contracts the node with the current lowest ED next. In our application this could lead to an undesired effect: We might add no shortcuts at all. Consider a complete 4-connected finite grid with uniform costs; we could just enumerate the nodes row-by-row from left to right and use these numbers as the importance l. Contracting the nodes in this order, a node has at most two adjacent edges (removing nodes with less than two edges does not lead to shortcut insertion anyway). For nodes with two edges, the path over these two is indeed optimal, but also ambiguous at the moment of contraction, so no shortcut has to be inserted. Of course, as an artefact of our canonical path maintenance strategy, we would insert shortcuts here as well, but even this would be superfluous as also all canonical paths are preserved automatically by the contraction order. What seems to be a nice feature at the first glance – the CH-construction not increasing the graph size at all – is unfortunately not an advantage, because using this contraction order the search space does not diminish at all as the subgraph of G in the spanned rectangle of source and target is completely contained in $G^{\uparrow}(s) \cup G^{\downarrow}(t)$. So to force shortcut insertion, we have to make sure that not always nodes at the border of the actual graph are contracted. One way to achieve this, is to use a weighted version of the ED where removing edges from the graph gets more rewarded. A second approach is to contract always an independent set of nodes in the graph, which is found in a greedily manner considering the nodes sorted increasingly by their actual ED. As independent nodes do not influence the shortcut insertion of each other, this approach does not compromise optimality but induces the contraction of 'inner' nodes as an early stage of the CH-construction process. In Figure 3 the resulting CH-graph for this construction scheme is compared to the one for the enumeration approach.

For the witness search we used A* with the straightforward distance estimation for 4- and 8-connected grids. Of course, for certain instance classes better heuristics are at hand, and using them might speed up the CH-construction. But here we want to emphasize that CH can be used without prior knowledge of the kind of input.

For road networks, the number of shortcuts in G' equals approximately the number of original edges, i.e. the CH doubles the graph size. In Table 1 (left) we collected the main parameters describing the CH-construction for a 512x512 4-connected grid with uniform costs and varying percentage of randomly deleted nodes. We observe that the augmentation factor (AF) of the CH-graph depends strongly on the number of deleted vertices, but even for a complete grid (0% deletion) the graph size increases only by a factor of seven, which is a tolerable space overhead. In the right table, the CH-construction is summarized for several input categories, all being based on 8-connected grids. here, the augmentation factor is always below three and for mazes and rooms even below the typical value of two for street graphs. The preprocessing time is about 10 seconds for all inputs, corresponding to the time to answer approximately 1700 queries on average over all instances. Hence constructing the CH-graph on the fly does only make sense if the number of queries exceeds this bound. But for many applications, like in-game navigation, the preprocessing time does not play a major role as the CH-graph can simple be provided as the map itself.

3.2   Query Answering

In the augmented graphs, we applied CH-search as described in Section 2.3 between randomly chosen source-target pairs $s, t \in V$. Our baseline is the number of expanded nodes using A* (with Manhattan-metric for 4-connected grids and the obvious octile metric for 8-connected ones). Hence we evaluated the performance

Table 1. CH-construction: Number of original edges and edges in the CH-graph (original + shortcuts) for several input categories. The augmentation factor (AF) describes the ratio between those two. 'p' in the left table described the percentage of randomly deleted nodes in a 512x512 grid. The column 'time' in the right table gives the preprocessing time in seconds.

p	# edges	# CH-edges	AF
0	523,264	3,590,007	6.8
10	423,229	1,387,549	3.2
25	293,081	604,939	2.0
50	130,664	137,388	1.0

input type	# edges	# CH-edges	AF	time (secs)
mazes	682,922	1,064,079	1.6	10
rooms	847,871	1,242,509	1.5	9
game maps	271,532	768,002	2.8	10
random	492,857	1,319,287	2.7	12

of our approach as the ratio of this value and the number of expanded nodes by CH-search (i.e. the higher the better). Moreover the CH-approach reveals the advantage of being easily combinable with other speed-up techniques as it allows to extract a small subgraph $(G^\uparrow(s) \cup G^\downarrow(t))$ in which optimal query answering is guaranteed. Therefore we also implemented a combination of CH-search and A*-search. Because A* is known to work better embedded in an unidirectional computation, we modified the approach by marking first all edges in $G^\downarrow(t)$ and then run CH-A*-search from s using edges in $G^\uparrow(s)$ and marked ones. This unidirectional variation of CH-search was used before on street graphs, e.g. for one-to-many queries [10] or when edge costs were given as functions complicating the backward search (see e.g. Batz et al. [11]). The results for our two search approaches are collected in Table 2, subdivided by input category. We observe a reduction for all inputs, but the speed-up is most significant for mazes and rooms. For these two, the number of expanded nodes by CH-A* is even below the optimal path size on average. This means that any Dijkstra-based path finding approach, which does not use a compressed path description, cannot expand fewer nodes than our method. For game maps we observed mixed results, some inputs responded very well (speed-up by two orders of magnitude) while the structure of other maps led to a large set of long disjoint optimal paths which is not beneficial for our approach. In Figure 5 positive and negative examples are shown. We expect better improvements for game maps when the CH-search is combined with other techniques developed for road networks, like e.g. partitioning [12]. For random maps, the speed-up increases with the sparseness of the grid as the A* baseline gets worse but our approach expands almost the same number of nodes for varying deletion ratios. The reduction of expanded nodes does not fully transfer into run time decrease, as we have some static overhead introduced by marking the edges in $G^\downarrow(t)$ and also path unpacking is included here. Nevertheless averaged over all instances we achieve a speed-up over 50.

3.3   Connections to other Speed-Up Techniques

Pochter et al. [6] introduced the concept of *swamp hierarchies* with a swamp being a set of nodes that can be excluded a priori from the search space for

Table 2. Experimental results for finding optimal paths in 8-connected grids with the basic map size being 512x512. The speed-up describes the ratio of expanded nodes by A* and CH-A*, the value in brackets equals the ratio of the respective runtimes. All values are averaged of 1000 random queries (10 maps for every category with 100 queries on each).

input type	avg. path size	# of expanded nodes			speed-up
		A*	CH-Dijkstra	CH-A* (uni)	
mazes	1,240	104,949	630	499	210 (198)
rooms	282	35,739	625	275	130 (67)
game maps	196	18,477	4,614	937	20 (7)
random	234	16,121	5,158	531	30 (10)

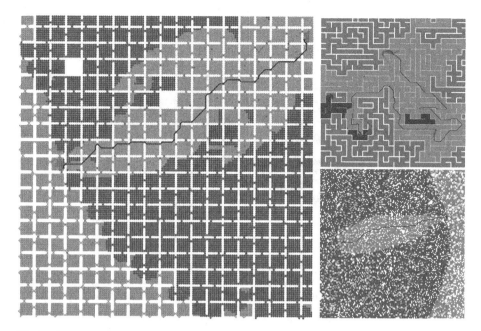

Fig. 4. Examples for rooms, mazes and random graphs. Nodes expanded by Dijkstra blue, by A* green and by the CH-Dijkstra red.

given s, t. In a CH-graph also the nodes $\notin G^{\uparrow}(s) \cup G^{\downarrow}(t)$ are pruned directly. So both approaches allow for the extraction of a smaller subgraph in which the optimal path must be contained. Nevertheless the kind of blocked nodes differ significantly, hence a combination of both approaches promises further improvement.

Other techniques based on map decomposition (and therefore requiring a preprocessing phase as well) were described by Björnsson et al. [9], in particular the *dead-end heuristic* and the *gateway approach*. In the latter, the graph is divided into subareas with a preferably small number of connections between adjacent ones. For these connections – the gateways – pairwise distances are precomputed. Looking at our results for the rooms instances, we observe that door nodes are naturally considered important in our CH-construction and direct shortcuts exist between almost any two of them. So in some way the *gateway heuristic* is automatically embedded in our approach.

The idea of jump points was presented by Harabor et al. [5]. Here no preprocessing is necessary, but sets of nodes between on the fly computed jump points are removed from the search space. The pruning rules applied there have similar effects as a CH-search, namely that many nodes on shortest subpaths can be ignored – because they lie between two consecutive jump points or on the shortest path between two nodes in the CH which are directly connected via a shortcut. Moreover the jump points approach also computes canonical paths, hence it appeals that CH can be seen as kind of an offline jump points approach.

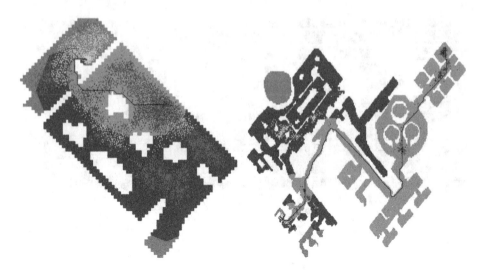

Fig. 5. CH-search on game maps, expanded nodes by Dijkstra (blue), A* (green), CH-Dijkstra (red), bidirectional CH-A* (yellow) and unidirectional CH-A* (black).

But in contrast to their method we are not bound to uniform grid costs. Instead any kind of costs assigned to the edges are allowed, and also directed arcs can be taken into account.

4   Concluding Remarks

In this paper we presented modifications for the speed-up technique contraction hierarchies to work on grid graphs. Despite being developed for road networks, we showed that with minor changes an acceleration of shortest path queries by up to two orders of magnitude can be achieved when applying contraction hierarchies to instances of e.g. rooms or mazes. Moreover we developed an approach based on edge classifiers, which allows to retrieve optimal canonical paths, using only a constant time and space overhead.

Future work includes further reduction of the preprocessing time and evaluating with which other methods contraction hierarchy based search can be combined to accelerate query answering.

References

1. Geisberger, R., Sanders, P., Schultes, D., Delling, D.: Contraction hierarchies: Faster and simpler hierarchical routing in road networks. In: McGeoch, C.C. (ed.) WEA 2008. LNCS, vol. 5038, pp. 319–333. Springer, Heidelberg (2008)
2. Bast, H., Funke, S., Matijevic, D., Sanders, P., Schultes, D.: In transit to constant time shortest-path queries in road networks. In: ALENEX (2007)
3. Antsfeld, L., Harabor, D.D., Kilby, P., Walsh, T.: Transit routing on video game maps. In: AIIDE (2012)

4. Bauer, R., Delling, D., Sanders, P., Schieferdecker, D., Schultes, D., Wagner, D.: Combining hierarchical and goal-directed speed-up techniques for Dijkstra's algorithm. ACM Journal of Experimental Algorithmics 15 (2010)
5. Harabor, D.D., Grastien, A.: Online graph pruning for pathfinding on grid maps. In: AAAI (2011)
6. Pochter, N., Zohar, A., Rosenschein, J.S., Felner, A.: Search space reduction using swamp hierarchies. In: AAAI (2010)
7. Botea, A., Müller, M., Schaeffer, J.: Near optimal hierarchical path-finding. Journal of Game Development 1(1), 7–28 (2004)
8. Harabor, D., Botea, A.: Breaking path symmetries on 4-connected grid maps. In: AIIDE (2010)
9. Björnsson, Y., Halldórsson, K.: Improved heuristics for optimal path-finding on game maps. In: AIIDE, pp. 9–14 (2006)
10. Eisner, J., Funke, S., Herbst, A., Spillner, A., Storandt, S.: Algorithms for matching and predicting trajectories. In: Proc. of the 13th Workshop on Algorithm Engineering and Experiments (ALENEX), Citeseer, pp. 84–95 (2011)
11. Batz, G.V., Delling, D., Sanders, P., Vetter, C.: Time-dependent contraction hierarchies. In: Proceedings of the 11th Workshop on Algorithm Engineering and Experiments (ALENEX 2009), pp. 97–105 (2009)
12. Delling, D., Goldberg, A.V., Pajor, T., Werneck, R.F.: Customizable route planning. In: Pardalos, P.M., Rebennack, S. (eds.) SEA 2011. LNCS, vol. 6630, pp. 376–387. Springer, Heidelberg (2011)

– Mastering *Left* and *Right* –
Different Approaches to a Problem That Is Not Straight Forward

André van Delden[1] and Till Mossakowski[1,2]

[1] Research Center on Spatial Cognition (SFB/TR 8), University of Bremen, Germany
[2] DFKI GmbH Bremen, Germany

Abstract. Reasoning over spatial descriptions involving relations that can be described as *left*, *right* and *inline* has been studied extensively during the last two decades. While the fundamental nature of these relations makes reasoning about them applicable to a number of interesting problems, it also makes reasoning about them computationally hard. The key question of whether a given description using these relations can be realized is as hard as deciding satisfiability in the existential theory of the reals. In this paper we summarize the semi-decision procedures proposed so far and present the results of a random benchmark illustrating the relative effectiveness and efficiency of these procedures.

Keywords: Left-Right Distinction, Qualitative Spatial Reasoning, Oriented Matroid, Consistency, Realizability, Semi-Decision Procedure, Benchmark.

1 Introduction

When describing a spatial scene using relative directions, the relations *left* and *right* are the most primitive, yet unavoidable, notions. These relations are contained in almost any spatial language that is able to express relative directions. They naturally occur in indoor and outdoor navigation as well as in architectural and mechanical layout design, and they are almost ubiquitous in verbal human-robot interaction. Much research has been done by different scientific communities to investigate the properties of these relations. It turns out that the fundamental nature of these relations makes reasoning about them computationally hard. The key question of whether a given spatial description using *left* and *right* can be realized is as hard as deciding satisfiability in the existential theory of the reals [15,20]. Furthermore, the prevailing reasoning technique in qualitative spatial reasoning (QSR), deploying path consistency through a qualitative calculus, totally fails on the so called $\mathcal{LR}$ calculus when only using the relations *left* and *right* [10].

The $\mathcal{LR}$ calculus is a spatial calculus that is considerably simpler than most other relative directional calculi that have been proposed [17,18,11,12]. Although it is a ternary calculus, its simplicity allows it to be embedded into many binary relative directional calculi by describing line segments by their endpoints and by describing oriented points as line segments of appropriate size. Its close relation to the theory of order types [17] even makes its properties relevant to more advanced calculi like the qualitative trajectory calculus [6].

In order to overcome the shortcomings of the path consistency algorithm regarding the $\mathcal{LR}$ calculus, [9] developed a polynomial time consistency semi-decision procedure

I.J. Timm and M. Thimm (Eds.): KI 2013, LNAI 8077, pp. 248–259, 2013.

for the $\mathcal{LR}$ calculus based on the angles of triangles in the Euclidean plane. They refer to this method as *triangle consistency* (TC). Another domain specific reasoning method applicable to $\mathcal{LR}$ is the algebraic geometric approach included in the qualitative spatial reasoning toolbox SparQ [21]. This method is often referred to as *algebraic reasoning* (AR). Furthermore, there is a close connection between the $\mathcal{LR}$ calculus and oriented matroid (OM) theory [2]. Most interestingly, this connection has been pointed out very early by [17] but its use and implications for QSR have been pointed out only recently by [20]. Oriented matroid theory is an active research area with specialized semi-decision procedures for realizability. All of the methods mentioned above have polynomial runtime and while some of them are able to decide consistency for small networks, in general all of them only approximate consistency.

We present the results of a benchmark using random constraint networks of suitable density. Since a feasible proper decision procedure for $\mathcal{LR}$ is not known, the results are presented in a relative manner, illustrating the effectiveness and efficiency of the tested procedures relative to each other. Our benchmark of these procedures not only provides an overview of when and how to choose one of these very different reasoning procedures; more importantly it serves as a general indicator for which kind of reasoning might be more promising to yield good results for more complex relation sets.

In the following we give a short description of the $\mathcal{LR}$ calculus, followed by concise descriptions of composition table based reasoning, algebraic reasoning, a triangle consistency procedure and oriented matroids. Then we explain the benchmark procedure and give a detailed analysis of the results of this benchmark applied to these procedures.

2   The $\mathcal{LR}$ Calculus

The $\mathcal{LR}$ calculus [18] is a relative orientation calculus in which three points are related, two of which determine a vector serving as frame of reference. The third point can then be either to the left (l) or right (r) of this vector or in front (f), in the back (b) or inside (between the points) (i) of it. It can also coincide with the start point (s) or the end point (e) of the vector. Additionally, there are two relations which describe that the first two points are the same but distinct from the third one (dou) resp. that all points are the same (tri).

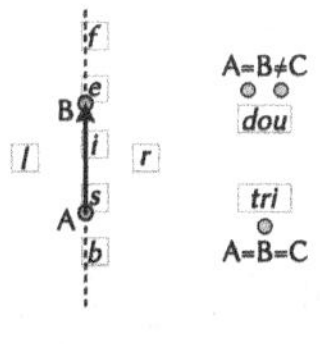

Qualitative calculi like this are employed for representing knowledge about an infinite domain using only a finite set of relations. In order to ensure that any constellation of domain objects is captured by exactly one relation, the calculi are based upon so called *base relations* which are defined such that they partition the given domain. Indeed, the nine ternary base relations l, r, f, b, i, s, e, dou and tri of the $\mathcal{LR}$ calculus partition the $\mathbb{R}^2$.

Fig. 1. The $\mathcal{LR}$ base relations

In the $\mathcal{LR}$ calculus, if for three points A, B and C the triple (A, B, C) is in the relation l, then obviously (B, A, C) must be in the relation r. For ternary calculi there are five different permutation operators. Qualitative reasoning concerned with solving constraint satisfaction problems over relations of a calculus like this, borrows definitions from the field of CSP [5].

Definition 1. *Let $\mathcal{R}$ be a set of general relations over a set of n-ary base relations over the domain $\mathcal{D}$, and let $\mathcal{V}$ be a set of variables taking values from $\mathcal{D}$.*

A qualitative constraint *over $(\mathcal{R}, \mathcal{V})$ is a formula $R(x)$ with $x \in \mathcal{V}^n$ and $R \in \mathcal{R}$. A* constraint network *is a set of constraints. A constraint network is called* atomic *if it relates all n-tuples of variables by a base relation or the universal relation, such that it complies with the permutation operations. An atomic network is called a* scenario *if it relates all n-tuples of variables by a base relation.*

A constraint network is called consistent *if a valuation of all variables exists, such that all constraints are fulfilled.*

The key problem, to decide whether a given constraint network is consistent or not, can be very hard to solve. Infinity of the domain underlying qualitative constraint satisfaction problems inhibits searching for an agreeable valuation of the variables.

3   The Decision Procedures

3.1   Algebraic Closure

This approach strongly influenced the way research on qualitative spatial reasoning has been done until today. The algebraic closure algorithm is essentially the common path consistency algorithm modified to be based on the composition operation. While for binary relations, composition is well-known, for ternary relations, one can define both a binary and a ternary composition operation.

Definition 2   ([22], [4]). *Let $R_1, R_2, R_3 \in \mathcal{R}_B$ be a sequence of three general relations in a ternary qualitative calculus over the domain $\mathcal{D}$. Then the operation*

$$R_1 \circ R_2 := \{\, (x, y, z) \in \mathcal{D}^3 \mid \exists u \in \mathcal{D}, (x, y, u) \in R_1, (y, u, z) \in R_2 \,\}$$

is called binary composition *and the operation*

$$\circ\, (R_1, R_2, R_3) := \{\, (x, y, z) \in \mathcal{D}^3$$
$$\mid \exists u \in \mathcal{D}, (x, y, u) \in R_1, (x, u, z) \in R_2, (u, y, z) \in R_3 \,\}$$

is called ternary composition.

With this information of permutations and compositions of spatial relations given, it is possible to propagate local information in a constraint network through the network in order to make implicit information explicit.

Definition 3. *A constraint network over ternary relations is called* algebraically closed for binary composition *if for all variables x, y, z, u and all relations R_1, R_2, R_3 the constraint relations*

$$R_1(x, y, u), \quad R_2(y, u, z), \quad R_3(x, y, z)$$

satisfy $R_3 \subseteq R_1 \circ R_2$. To enforce algebraic closure, the operation $R_3 := R_3 \cap (R_1 \circ R_2)$ (as well as a similar operation for converses) is applied for all such variables until a fixed-point is reached.

Ternary algebraic closure is defined analogously. Several polynomial time algorithms computing this fixed-point are discussed in [7].

Enforcing algebraic closure preserves consistency, i.e., if the empty relation is obtained during refinement, then the constraint network is inconsistent. The converse is not necessarily true. The SparQ toolbox [19] implements algebraic closure for a variety of calculi, including $\mathcal{LR}$. While binary algebraic closure is often faster, the ternary variant provides a better approximation due to less loss of information.

3.2 The Algebraic Geometric Approach

In the algebraic geometric reasoning approach integrated into the SparQ toolbox an n-ary qualitative relation R over a domain $\mathcal{D}$ is modeled as the zero set of a set of multivariate polynomials F_R over real-valued variables $y_1, \ldots, y_k$:

$$\forall x_1, \ldots, x_n \in \mathcal{D} : R(x_1, \ldots, x_n) \Leftrightarrow$$
$$\exists y_1, \ldots, y_k \in \mathcal{R} : \forall f \in F_R : f(y_1, \ldots, y_k) = 0 \, .$$

Thus basic objects of the qualitative relations are expressed by means of real-valued variables. For example, a point A positioned in the plane can be represented by a pair (x_A, y_A), a circle by its center and radius and so forth. A qualitative spatial reasoning problem can then be modeled by a set of polynomials.

The relations of the $\mathcal{LR}$ calculus, are modeled by conjunctions of the following geometric primitives:

$$\text{equal}(A, B) \equiv \begin{pmatrix} x_A \\ y_A \end{pmatrix} = \begin{pmatrix} x_B \\ y_B \end{pmatrix}$$

$$\text{notEqual}(A, B) \equiv \left\| \begin{pmatrix} x_B - x_A \\ y_B - y_A \end{pmatrix} \right\|^2 > 0$$

$$\text{inline}(A, B, C) \equiv \begin{pmatrix} x_C \\ y_C \end{pmatrix} = \begin{pmatrix} x_A \\ y_A \end{pmatrix} + \lambda \begin{pmatrix} x_B - x_A \\ y_B - y_A \end{pmatrix}$$

$$\text{between} \equiv \text{inline} \wedge 0 < \lambda < 1$$
$$\text{inFront} \equiv \text{inline} \wedge 1 < \lambda$$

$$\text{left}(A, B, C) \equiv \begin{pmatrix} x_B - x_A \\ y_B - y_A \end{pmatrix}^\top \begin{pmatrix} x_C - x_A \\ y_C - y_A \end{pmatrix} > 0$$

Using these primitives it is straight forward to describe the $\mathcal{LR}$ base relations. The way how the actual reasoning is performed is relatively elaborate. It is based on Gröbner reasoning and involves a set of polynomial transformation rules. At a first stage SparQ searches half-randomly for a solution for the inequalities. If no solution is found in this stage, SparQ tries to prove insatisfiability of the inequalities.

For detailed information about this and the SparQ toolbox in general we refer to [21]. This approach is often referred to as *algebraic reasoning*, which is not to be confused with algebraic closure.

3.3 The Triangulation Approach

Any n point solution of an $\mathcal{LR}$ constraint network induces $n \cdot (n-1)/2$ undirected lines connecting all the points. The connecting lines between three arbitrary points form a (possibly degenerated) triangle. The triangulation approach of [9] uses simple properties of the angles of these triangles, like the sum of the three angles always adding up to π. Moreover, the relations l and r lead to positive and negative angles of the corresponding triangles, while the other relations lead to angles 0 or π.

Any $\mathcal{LR}$ constraint network can thus be translated into a system of equalities and inequalities over angles of triangles. Obviously, this system has a solution if the original $\mathcal{LR}$ constraint network has one: just read off the angles from the solution in the Euclidean plane. The converse does not necessarily hold, which means that the triangulation approach can detect inconsistencies but not demonstrate consistency. Triangle consistency can be verified in polynomial time by using an algorithm for solving systems of linear inequalities [3].

3.4 Oriented Matroids

The theory of oriented matroids is broadly connected to many mathematical areas, such as combinatorial geometry, optimization, dimension theory and many branches in physics [13]. Many seemingly distinct mathematical objects have a representation in oriented matroid theory, such as point and vector configurations, pseudoline arrangements, arrangements of hyperplanes, convex polytopes, directed graphs and linear programs, which can be generalized to matroid programs [2]. In general, oriented matroids provide an abstraction that makes it possible to model and analyze combinatorial properties of geometric configurations, often qualifying the quantitative information just enough to allow for efficient reasoning about an otherwise intractable problem.

In the context of $\mathcal{LR}$ constraint networks oriented matroids are best introduced in their appearance as *chirotopes*.

Definition 4 (Chirotope). *Let $E = \{1, \ldots, n\}$ and let $r \in \mathbb{N}$ with $1 \leq r \leq n$. A chirotope of rank r is an alternating sign map $\chi \colon E^r \to \{-, 0, +\}$, not identically zero, such that for all $x_1, x_2, \ldots, x_r, y_1, y_2, \ldots, y_r \in E$ with*

$$\chi(x_1, x_2, \ldots, x_r) \cdot \chi(y_1, y_2, \ldots, y_r) \neq 0$$

there exists an $i \in \{1, 2, \ldots, r\}$ such that

$$\chi(y_i, x_2, \ldots, x_r) \cdot \chi(y_1, y_2, \ldots, y_{i-1}, x_1, y_{i+1}, \ldots, y_r)$$
$$= \chi(x_1, x_2, \ldots, x_r) \cdot \chi(y_1, y_2, \ldots, y_r).$$

Interpreting the nodes of $\mathcal{LR}$ networks as vectors in $\mathbb{R}^3$ any consistent $\mathcal{LR}$ scenario is necessarily an acyclic chirotope of rank 3, where *acyclic* means that all vectors lie in an open half-space [20]. This alone gives a feasible semi-decision procedure for the consistency of $\mathcal{LR}$ constraint networks. Furthermore an $\mathcal{LR}$ scenario is consistent iff its associated acyclic chirotope is realizable. Since every rank 3 chirotope with up to 8 points is realizable [8,15], only verifing the axioms of an acyclic chirotope provides a polynomial time decision procedure for $\mathcal{LR}$ constraint networks with up to 8 points.

However, there exists a distinct polynomial time semi-decision procedure for the realizability of chirotopes of arbitrary rank based on a concept called *biquadratic final polynomials* [1,14]. This procedure has been used [16] to prove some famous incidence theorems like Pascal's theorem and Desargues's theorem.

If a given $\mathcal{LR}$ network is consistent, its relations can be understood as the signs of the determinants of the vectors $v_1, \ldots, v_n \in \mathbb{R}^3$ that correspond to the nodes in the network. The determinants of the $(r \times r)$ submatrices of a $(r \times n)$-matrix M are not independent since most of the entries in M occur in several of them. These dependencies are known as the *Grassmann-Plücker relations*. Here we are interested in the 3-term Grassmann-Plücker relation, which states that for every set of distinct vectors $u_1, \ldots, u_{r-2}, v_1, \ldots, v_4$ in an r-dimensional vector space the following equation holds.

$$\det(u_1, \ldots, u_{r-2}, v_1, v_2) \cdot \det(u_1, \ldots, u_{r-2}, v_3, v_4)$$
$$- \det(u_1, \ldots, u_{r-2}, v_1, v_3) \cdot \det(u_1, \ldots, u_{r-2}, v_2, v_4)$$
$$+ \det(u_1, \ldots, u_{r-2}, v_1, v_4) \cdot \det(u_1, \ldots, u_{r-2}, v_2, v_3) = 0$$

Though the following holds for every rank, we will stick to the case of rank 3 from now on. Writing determinants as brackets and sorting the vectors if necessary, such that all determinants are positive, we can write this equation in the form

$$[u, v_1, v_2][u, v_3, v_4] + [u, v_1, v_4][u, v_2, v_3] = [u, v_1, v_3][u, v_2, v_4]$$

where all six brackets are positive. This equation implies the following inequalities.

$$[u, v_1, v_2][u, v_3, v_4] < [u, v_1, v_3][u, v_2, v_4]$$
$$[u, v_1, v_4][u, v_2, v_3] < [u, v_1, v_3][u, v_2, v_4]$$

Treating the brackets as symbolic variables, we can take the logarithm on both sides and, ranging over all nodes, we obtain a linear system of inequalities,

$$(u, v_1, v_2) + (u, v_3, v_4) < (u, v_1, v_3) + (u, v_2, v_4)$$
$$(u, v_1, v_4) + (u, v_2, v_3) < (u, v_1, v_3) + (u, v_2, v_4),$$

where the tuples again are treated as variables. Using linear programming we can test the feasibility of this system of inequalities. If it is infeasible then we obtain – as the dual solution of the linear program – a positive integer linear combination of the left hand sides which equals the same linear combination of the right hand sides, resulting in the contradiction $0 < 0$. This linear combination can be propagated back in order to learn more about the nature of the inconsistency. However, if the intention is only to prove inconsistency, then this step is not necessary.

4   The Benchmarking Procedure

We wrote a library for qualitative constraint networks in Haskell and implemented the triangle consistency and oriented matroid procedures describe above. The inequality systems arising in these procedures are handled using interfaces to the SMT solver

Yices and the linear programming solver *lp_solve*. In order to compute the algebraic closure we used the qualitative spatial reasoning toolbox *SparQ*.

Due to the huge yet generally unknown number of possible $\mathcal{LR}$ constraint networks of a given size and the lack of a big database of real world constraint networks, the only way to benchmark the given methods is by random networks. A straightforward approach is to generate random scenarios, but this approach is only feasible for small scenarios for which the set of relations is restricted to $\{l, r\}$, otherwise the ratio of trivially inconsistent networks would be too high. One way to overcome this restriction, and to allow for networks also containing the relations in $\{b, i, f\}$, is to adjust network parameters that are independent from the calculus and methods at hand. A simple yet interesting parameter is the network density. It is especially suited for this problem, since it imposes as little structure on the generated networks as possible and is very likely to have a phase transition, i.e. a small range of densities in which the transition from mostly consistent to mostly inconsistent networks happens.

Our program takes the arguments $rels$, d, t, n, m, M, $methods$ and generates n networks for each size between m and M allowing only relations from $rels$ and giving each method in $methods$ a time of t seconds to decide the consistency of a network. Starting with the smallest size m and the initial density d it generates one random connected atomic network at a time, collects the results of the methods and adjusts the density of the next network according to the following rule: Let d and s be the density and size of the latest generated network and let d' and s' be the density and size of the network to be generated next. If $s' = s + 1$ then d' is set to the multiple of $\binom{s'}{3}^{-1}$ that is closest to d, $\binom{s'}{3}$ being the number of possible triples of s' nodes. If $s' = s$ then the new density is calculated depending on the results collected so far: Let Δ be the difference between the networks of size s and density d generated so far that have been shown to be inconsistent – by any method in $methods$ – and those that have not been detected as inconsistent. Then the new density is set to

$$d' := \min\left(1, \ \max\left(\frac{6}{s(s-1)}, \ d - \operatorname{sgn}(\Delta)\binom{s}{3}^{-1}\right)\right).$$

The lower bound is due to the restriction that the networks have to be connected. Although not mentioned above, these bounds are also applied to the first case. We noticed that after a few steps into the wild, the density converges very fast towards a small range. So we indeed find the common phase transition of the combined methods regarding the density of the networks and can be sure to generate mostly non-trivial networks.

We compared the following six methods: binary and ternary algebraic closure (BAC and TAC), algebraic reasoning (AR), triangle consistency (TC) and the axioms for acyclic chirotopes with and without search for a biquadratic final polynomial (denoted by BFP and OM, resp.).

All of the tested methods can handle atomic networks directly with the exception of the oriented matroid approach, which takes a scenario as input, so that we have to use backtracking pruned by ensuring the axioms for acyclic chirotopes. This means that, contrary to the other methods, the runtime of the OM procedure grows with growing sparseness of the networks. Our results show however that this dependency is strongly superseded by the steepness of the phase transition.

In addition to 1000 $\{l, r\}$-scenarios for each size from 5 to 8 nodes using a timeout of 2 minutes, we compared these methods on 1000 connected atomic networks for each size from 5 to 20 in the six different combinations of using a timeout of 3, 20 and 120 seconds and using the relations in $\{l, r, b, i, f\}$ and using only the relations l and r, using an initial density of $\frac{1}{2}$ and adjusting it as described. The three different timeouts represent strongly, moderately and non-time critical use cases.

4.1 Results

Since the number of isomorphism classes of all possible $\mathcal{LR}$ scenarios is unknown, an absolute statistical analysis of this benchmark cannot be achieved. However, we can compare the individual methods against each other and look at the ratio of the number of inconsistent networks found by each individual method to the number of inconsistent networks found by all methods together thus comparing the exactness of the methods. Figures 2a, 3, 4, 5, 12, 13 and 14 depict this comparison for each of the seven test cases. The respective next diagrams compare the average runtime of each method. The third and last diagram of each test case shows for each network size the ratio of networks detected as inconsistent to tested networks per network density.

There is evidence that our results are not purely random: The given background knowledge of the compared methods and the fact that the graphs are highly structured and nearly identical in the last two timescales strongly support that the results are highly statistically significant.

The first obvious result of this benchmark is that limited time is a critical factor. The impact of the timeout can be observed by relating the diagrams depicting the average runtime with those depicting the percentage of inconsistent networks identified by each method. Without a timeout all time curves would show cubic or higher growth, a decline of this growth indicates that a method reaches the timeout more often. Naturally this concurs with a decline of the percentage of inconsistencies found. This can especially be observed in Fig. 4 at a size of 16 where the graph of the ternary algebraic closure suddenly drops. In Fig. 13 the effect of the timeout can be observed by the decline of the oriented matroid test accompanied by a rise of the graph of the triangle consistency method. The swap of these methods that happens between the sizes 9 and 10 indicates that, given enough time, the oriented matroid test supersedes the triangle consistency. This is supported by the fact that using longer timeouts the swap happens at higher network sizes with the low point of triangle consistency reaching ever smaller percentages down to 60%.

However, in Figs. 2a and 2b, which depict the scenario test case, the oriented matroid test equals triangle consistency regarding the percentage of inconsistent networks found and with growing network size strongly supersedes it regarding runtime. Here the influence of the pruned backtracking in the oriented matroid test becomes clearly visible. But also note that in this setting the average runtime of the algebraic reasoning method strongly declines with growing network size. This indicates that the inconsistencies get more and more trivial. Indeed, from a size of 5 to 8, the ratio of the number of inconsistent networks to the number of tested networks grows as this: #5 $\mapsto$ 75.8%,

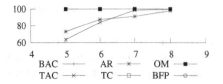
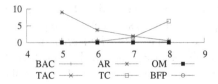

(a) Percentage of inconsistent networks iden-   (b) Average time in seconds that each method
tified by each method; per network size.   needed; per network size.

Fig. 2. 1000 $\{l, r\}$-scenarios using a timeout of 2 minutes

#6 $\mapsto$ 98.5%, #7 $\mapsto$ 100%, #8 $\mapsto$ 100%. Our benchmarking procedure addresses exactly this problem, by replacing scenarios with atomic networks, i.e. by lowering the chances of trivial inconsistencies but still allowing for complex ones.

The timeout of the 3 seconds benchmark setting is short enough so that the graphs for runtime and thus also those for detection-percentage actually cross each other. In Fig. 3 we observe a rapid decline of the binary algebraic closure shortly after its average runtime exceeds half the timeout, naturally accompanied by a rise of most other methods. Due to the missing reasoning power at higher network sizes the densities of the generated networks also rise relatively to those in the other test cases. In Fig. 6 we can see the effect this has on the runtime of the oriented matroid test and on triangle consistency. Note that the additional search for a biquadratic final polynomial almost never improved on the oriented matroid test. The difference it makes is so small that the graphs actually coincide in the diagrams.

An unexpected result of this benchmark is the reverse behaviour of algebraic closure versus triangle consistency regarding inline relations. While [10] already showed that any scenario only containing the relations l and r already is algebraically closed, the triangle consistency performs very well in this case. However, when allowing for inline relations, i.e. allowing for the relations l, r, b, i, f, the binary and ternary algebraic closure outperform the other methods by large, with triangle consistency, while being very fast, performing unexpectedly poor.

The runtime of the algebraic geometric approach integrated in the SparQ toolbox is so high that we decided to take it out of the comparison for network sizes bigger than 10. Interestingly, despite it reaching the timeout very often, it performs about as good as ternary algebraic closure in the $\{l, r\}$-only test cases, while in the test case of 2 minutes and allowing inline relations its performance is about on par with triangle consistency but likely to decline faster for higher network sizes.

The respective third figures clearly show how our benchmark approach finds the phase transition of the density from where the combined methods mostly found inconsistent networks to where they mostly found no inconsistencies. In order to improve readability some network sizes are left out. A comparison of the three timescales shows how algebraic closure and triangle consistency dominate the benchmark. The only big difference in the phase transitions between the different timescales happens in the 3 seconds test case, where these reasoning methods hit the timeout and thus rapidly decline in their reasoning power for higher network sizes.

Results of the benchmark using $rels = \{l, r, b, i, f\}$

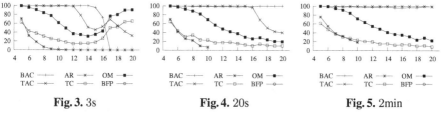

Fig. 3. 3s   **Fig. 4.** 20s   **Fig. 5.** 2min

Percentage of inconsistent networks identified by each method; per network size.

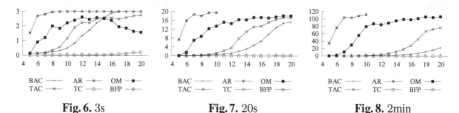

Fig. 6. 3s   **Fig. 7.** 20s   **Fig. 8.** 2min

Average time in seconds that each method needed; per network size.

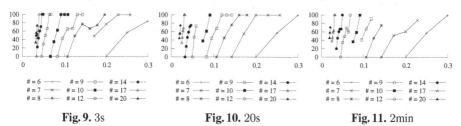

Fig. 9. 3s   **Fig. 10.** 20s   **Fig. 11.** 2min

Ratio of networks detected as inconsistent to tested networks for each network size in percent; per density.

5 Summary and Outlook

We implemented a way to benchmark qualitative spatial reasoning methods and used it to compare several semi-decision procedures for the consistency of $\mathcal{LR}$ networks regarding their time and decision performance in seven different settings. The results show that, although a proper statistical analysis is impossible when deployed on the $\mathcal{LR}$ calculus, the benchmarking procedure yields relevant information.

Concerning the $\mathcal{LR}$ calculus our results show that, depending on the set of relations, overall algebraic closure and triangle consistency outperform the other methods in all three timescales, while given smaller $\{l, r\}$-networks up to a size of 10 the oriented matroid test yields better results at the cost of a relatively long runtime. The results of the 3 seconds benchmark suggest that searching for inconsistencies in networks of sizes bigger than 16 is impractical using the methods given today.

The benchmark library we developed is not restricted to a specific calculus and is able to automatically detect phase transitions of the tested procedures regarding relevant

Results of the benchmark using $rels = \{l, r\}$

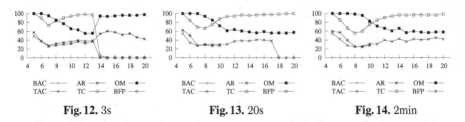

Fig. 12. 3s   **Fig. 13.** 20s   **Fig. 14.** 2min

Percentage of inconsistent networks identified by each method; per network size.

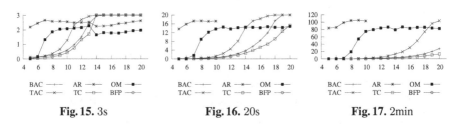

Fig. 15. 3s   **Fig. 16.** 20s   **Fig. 17.** 2min

Average time in seconds that each method needed; per network size.

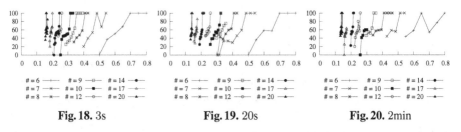

Fig. 18. 3s   **Fig. 19.** 20s   **Fig. 20.** 2min

Ratio of networks detected as inconsistent to tested networks for each network size in percent; per density.

parameters, such as density, timeouts and size of relations. Future work will consist of deploying this benchmark to momentarily arising decision procedures for oriented point calculi.

Specific to the $\mathcal{LR}$ calculus it would be relevant to implement a working version of the rubber band algorithm for pseudolines into our library. This algorithm positively semi-decides the stretchability problem for pseudolines, which are another representation of matroids, by simulating pseudolines as rubber bands.

Acknowledgements. Work on this article has been supported by the DFG-funded collaborative research center SFB/TR 8 Spatial Cognition as well as the DFKI GmbH Bremen. We thank Diedrich Wolter, Jae Hee Lee and Dominik Lücke for their helpful discussions on this topic.   ●

References

1. Altshuler, A., Bokowski, J., Steinberg, L.: The classification of simplicial 3-spheres with nine vertices into polytopes and nonpolytopes. Discrete Mathematics 31(2), 115–124 (1980)
2. Björner, A.: Oriented matroids. Encyclopedia of mathematics and its applications. Cambridge University Press (1999)
3. Bradley, A.R., Manna, Z.: The calculus of computation - decision procedures with applications to verification. Springer (2007)
4. Condotta, J.F., Saade, M., Ligozat, G.: A Generic Toolkit for n-ary Qualitative Temporal and Spatial Calculi. In: TIME 2006: Proceedings of the Thirteenth International Symposium on Temporal Representation and Reasoning, pp. 78–86. IEEE Computer Society (2006)
5. Dechter, R.: From Local to Global Consistency. Artificial Intelligence 55, 87–108 (1992)
6. Delafontaine, M., Cohn, A.G., Van de Weghe, N.: Implementing a qualitative calculus to analyse moving point objects. Expert Systems with Applications 38(5), 5187–5196 (2011)
7. Dylla, F., Moratz, R.: Empirical complexity issues of practical qualitative spatial reasoning about relative position. In: Proceedings of the Workshop on Spatial and Temporal Reasoning at ECAI 2004 (2004)
8. Goodman, J.E., Pollack, R.: Proof of Grünbaum's conjecture on the stretchability of certain arrangements of pseudolines. Journal of Combinatorial Theory, Series A 29(3), 385–390 (1980)
9. Lücke, D., Mossakowski, T.: A much better polynomial time approximation of consistency in the lr calculus. In: Proceedings of the 5th Starting AI Researchers' Symposium, pp. 175–185. IOS Press, Amsterdam (2010)
10. Lücke, D., Mossakowski, T., Wolter, D.: Qualitative reasoning about convex relations. In: Freksa, C., Newcombe, N.S., Gärdenfors, P., Wölfl, S. (eds.) Spatial Cognition VI. LNCS (LNAI), vol. 5248, pp. 426–440. Springer, Heidelberg (2008)
11. Moratz, R., Lücke, D., Mossakowski, T.: A condensed semantics for qualitative spatial reasoning about oriented straight line segments. Artificial Intelligence 175(16-17), 2099–2127 (2011)
12. Mossakowski, T., Moratz, R.: Qualitative reasoning about relative direction on adjustable levels of granularity. CoRR (2010)
13. Nieto, J.A.: Chirotope concept in various scenarios of physics. Revista Mexicana de Fisica 51, 5 (2005)
14. Richter-Gebert, J.: On the realizability problem of combinatorial geometries–decision methods. TH Darmstadt (1992)
15. Richter-Gebert, J., Ziegler, G.: Oriented Matroids, ch. 6, 2nd edn. Discrete Mathematics and Its Applications, pp. 129–151. Chapman and Hall/CRC (2004)
16. Richter-Gebert, J.: Mechanical theorem proving in projective geometry (1993)
17. Schlieder, C.: Reasoning about ordering. In: Kuhn, W., Frank, A.U. (eds.) COSIT 1995. LNCS, vol. 988, pp. 341–349. Springer, Heidelberg (1995)
18. Scivos, A., Nebel, B.: The Finest of its Class: The Natural, Point-Based Ternary Calculus $\mathcal{LR}$ for Qualitative Spatial Reasoning. In: Freksa, C., Knauff, M., Krieg-Brückner, B., Nebel, B., Barkowsky, T. (eds.) Spatial Cognition IV. LNCS (LNAI), vol. 3343, pp. 283–303. Springer, Heidelberg (2005)
19. Wallgrün, J.O., Frommberger, L., Wolter, D., Dylla, F., Freksa, C.: Qualitative Spatial Representation and Reasoning in the SparQ-Toolbox. In: Barkowsky, T., Knauff, M., Ligozat, G., Montello, D.R. (eds.) Spatial Cognition 2007. LNCS (LNAI), vol. 4387, pp. 39–58. Springer, Heidelberg (2007)
20. Wolter, D., Lee, J.: Qualitative reasoning with directional relations. Artificial Intelligence 174(18), 1498–1507 (2010)
21. Wolter, D.: Analyzing qualitative spatio-temporal calculi using algebraic geometry. Spatial Cognition & Computation 12(1), 23–52 (2011)
22. Zimmermann, K., Freksa, C.: Qualitative spatial reasoning using orientation, distance, and path knowledge. Applied Intelligence 6(1), 49–58 (1996)

Move Prediction in Go – Modelling Feature Interactions Using Latent Factors

Martin Wistuba and Lars Schmidt-Thieme

University of Hildesheim
Information Systems & Machine Learning Lab
{wistuba,schmidt-thieme}@ismll.de

Abstract. Move prediction systems have always been part of strong Go programs. Recent research has revealed that taking interactions between features into account improves the performance of move predictions. In this paper, a factorization model is applied and a supervised learning algorithm, Latent Factor Ranking (LFR), which enables to consider these interactions, is introduced. Its superiority will be demonstrated in comparison to other state-of-the-art Go move predictors. LFR improves accuracy by 3% over current state-of-the-art Go move predictors on average and by 5% in the middle- and endgame of a game. Depending on the dimensionality of the shared, latent factor vector, an overall accuracy of over 41% is achieved.

Keywords: go, move prediction, feature interaction, latent factors.

1 Introduction

Since the early days in research of Computer Go, move prediction is an essential part of strong Go programs. With the application of Upper Confidence bounds applied to Trees (UCT) in 2006 [1,2], which improved the strength of Go programs a lot, it became even more important. Go programs using UCT infer from semi-random game simulations which move is a good candidate. The policies for choosing the next move during the simulations are implied by predicting a human expert's move. Due to the fact that an average Go game has 250 turns with 150 possible move choices on average, the move position evaluation does not only need to be accurate but also fast to compute to achieve a positive impact on the strength of the Go program.

State-of-the-art move predictors are ranking moves on the board by the use of different features. Upfront, the strength of each feature is learned with various supervised learning algorithms. The prediction can be improved by using additional features, but as seen in [3,4] it can also be improved by considering the impact of feature interactions.

The contribution of this paper are fourfold.

- A supervised move ranking algorithm for Go is presented which is by now the most accurate. Additionally, it is easy to implement and fast to compute.

I.J. Timm and M. Thimm (Eds.): KI 2013, LNAI 8077, pp. 260–271, 2013.

- The model of Factorization Machines [5] is transfered from the domain of recommender systems to move prediction in Go.
- A new update rule for ranking with Factorization Machines is presented.
- Deeper insights into Go move features and its interactions are given and in detail investigated.

2   Related Work

Most move predictors for Go are either using Neural Networks [6,7] or are estimating ratings for moves using the Bradley Terry (BT) model or related models [3,4,8]. Latter mentioned approaches model each move decision as a competition between players, the move chosen by the human expert player is then the winning player and its value is updated accordingly.

Another possibility to divide the Go move predictors into two classes is how they consider interactions between features. There are two variants, one models the full-interaction of all features [3,9] and the others do not consider them at all [4,6,8].

The first mentioned approach which is modelling all interactions has the advantage that more information is taken into account. The disadvantage is that this approach does not scale because the amount of training data needed increases exponentially with the number of features. The latter approach does not have this disadvantage but therefore also has no information about the feature interactions. In practice, approaches not considering feature interactions at all proved to be more accurate. Stern's [3] full-interaction model used a learning set of 181,000 games with 4 feature groups but only predicted 34% of the moves correctly. Using the same approach with no interaction, Wistuba et al. [4] has shown that easily 9 feature groups can be used and, using a learning set of only 10,000 games, 37% of moves were predicted correctly. Ibidem, it was tried to combine advantages of both approaches by using an approach without feature interaction and adding a special feature that represented a combination of few features. It was shown that this can improve the prediction quality significantly.

The contribution of this work is to introduce a method which cannot be sorted into the before mentioned categories. It introduces an algorithm for the move prediction problem of Go that is combining both advantages by presenting a model which learns the strength of interactions between features but still scales with the number of features.

3   Game of Go

The game of Go is one of the oldest two player board games which was probably invented around the 4th century B.C. in China. It is played on a board with $n \times n$ intersections (n is usually 9, 13 or 19). The players move alternately. At each turn the player has the option to place a stone at an intersection or to pass. Enemy stones that are surrounded by own stones will be removed from the board. The aim of the game is to capture enemy stones and territory. The game ends after both players have passed, the winner is then the one with more points which are calculated by the number of captured stones and the size of the captured territory. Further informations can be found at http://gobase.org.

3.1 Technical Terms

Finally some technical terms in Go are explained to make it possible to understand the features used in this work.

Ko. The ko rule is a restriction on the legal moves. Moves that change the board state to the same state like two moves before are forbidden.

Chain. The connected string of stones of same color.

Liberty. An empty intersection next to a chain is called liberty.

Atari. A chain is in atari if there is only one liberty left, so that the opponent can capture the chain within one move.

Capture. If you place your stone in such a way that the enemy chain has no liberties left. This chain will be removed from the board and each stone is called a prisoner and count as one point each.

Illegal Move. A move is illegal if it either breaks the ko rule, places a stone at an intersection that is already occupied or it captures an own chain.

3.2 Complexity

Go is one of the last board games not being mastered by computer programs. Actually, Go programs are still far away from beating professional players, only playing on the level of stronger amateurs on the 19×19 boards. One of the reasons is the high complexity of Go. The upper bound of possible board positions is $3^{361} \approx 10^{170}$ and still 1.2% of these are legal [10]. Comparing Go with Chess, not only the board size is bigger (19x19 vs. 8x8) but also the number of potential moves. The average number of potential moves per turn in Go is about 150, Chess has only a few dozen. Additionally, no static heuristic approximating the minimax value of a position was found so far. That is, it is not possible to apply depth limited alpha-beta search with reasonable results. Concluding, even from a perspective of complexity Go is by far more difficult than Chess. A perfect strategy for $n \times n$ Chess only requires exponential time but Go is PSPACE-hard [11] and even subproblems a player has to deal with in every turn has proven to be PSPACE-complete [12].

4   Move Prediction Using Feature Interactions

This section first introduces the terminology and a model which is capable to represent interactions between features. Then, the Latent Factor Ranking algorithm is presented in Section 4.3. Finally, Section 4.4 describes the features used for the experiments.

4.1 Terminology

This work will use the terminology introduced in [4]. A single game in Go is formalized as a tuple $G := (\mathcal{S}, \mathcal{A}, \Gamma, \delta)$ where $\mathcal{S} := \mathcal{C}^{n \times n}$ is the set of possible states and $\mathcal{C} := \{black, white, empty\}$ is the set of colors. The set of actions $\mathcal{A} := \{1, \ldots, n\}^2 \cup \{pass\}$ defines all possible moves and $\Gamma : \mathcal{S} \to \mathcal{P}(\mathcal{A})$ is the function determining the subset of legal moves $\Gamma(s)$ in state s. $\delta : \mathcal{S} \times \mathcal{A} \to \mathcal{S} \cup \{\emptyset\}$ is the transition function specifying the follow-up state for a state-action pair (s, a), where $\delta(s, a) = \emptyset$ iff $a \notin \Gamma(s)$. In the following, a state-action pair (s, a) will be abstracted by m features represented by $x \in \mathbb{R}^m$. Even though x is only the abstracted state-action pair, in the following for notational convenience it will anyways be called state-action pair.

In this work only binary features $x_i \in \{0, 1\}$ are used and so the set of active features in (s, a) is defined as $\mathcal{I}(x) := \{i : x_i = 1\}$.

Given a training set $\mathcal{D}$ of move choice examples

$$\mathcal{D}_j := \left\{ x^{(1)} = x(s_j, a_1), \ldots, x^{(|\Gamma(s_j)|)} = x(s_j, a_{|\Gamma(s_j)|}) \right\},$$

it is assumed without loss of generality that $x^{(1)}$ is always the state-action pair chosen by the expert.

4.2 Problem Description and Model

The *move prediction problem* in Go is defined given a state s, to predict the action $a \in \Gamma(s)$ that is chosen by the expert player. Due to the fact that there might be several similar good moves and the application of move prediction in the UCT algorithm, a ranking of the legal moves is searched such that the expert move is ranked as high as possible. Therefore, a ranking function is sought that minimizes $\sum_{\mathcal{D}_i \in \mathcal{D}} \sum_{j=1}^{rank(a_1)} \frac{1}{j}$, where $rank(a_1)$ is the ranking of the action chosen by the human expert in the decision problem $\mathcal{D}_i$.

Like other contributions on the topic of move prediction in Go, this work also is a supervised method that estimates the strength of different features based on a set of games between strong human players. The big difference is that additionally the strength of the interaction of two features is considered. The model of Factorization Machines [5] is applied which is defined as

$$\hat{y}(x) := w_0 + \sum_{i=1}^{m} w_i x_i + \sum_{i=1}^{m} \sum_{j=i+1}^{m} v_i^T v_j x_i x_j.$$

Because in this work only binary features are used, a notation-wise simpler model is applied

$$\hat{y}(x) := w_0 + \sum_{i \in \mathcal{I}(x)} \left(w_i + \sum_{j \in \mathcal{I}(x), i \neq j} \theta_{i,j} \right),$$

with

$$\theta_{i,j} := \frac{1}{2} v_i^T v_j.$$

where w_i is the influence of the feature i independent of all other occurring features, whereas $\theta_{i,j}$ is the interaction between features i and j. The matrix $V \in \mathbb{R}^{m \times k}$ implies the matrix $\Theta \in \mathbb{R}^{m \times m}$ and is the reason why LFR does not struggle with the problem of full-interaction models i.e. the lack of examples. The dimension $k \ll m$ has to be chosen by the user. The greater k, the more potential information can be stored in the interaction vectors v_i. The k latent factors per feature will then be shared and thus scalability problems are avoided when the number of features increases while the number of feature values is kept low. As shown in Figure 5(a), already for very small k LFR seems to be optimal. Thus, k can be treated as a constant and only $\Theta(m)$ values are needed. Nevertheless, for computational reasons, which are very important for Go playing programs based on UCT, it makes sense to precompute the matrix Θ.

We want to continue the discussion from Section 2 and explain the counterintuitive fact that no-interaction models achieve better results than full-interaction models. Also, we want to show why the model for LFR is capable of achieving better results.

There are various learning techniques using these models but they have the way how state-action pairs are ranked in common. No-interaction models learn weights w_i for each feature i whereas full-interaction models learn weights $w_{\mathcal{I}(x)}$. Then, all legal state-action pairs $x^{(j)}$ are ranked in descendend order of its predicted strengths $\sum_{i \in \mathcal{I}(x^{(j)})} w_i$ respectively $w_{\mathcal{I}(x^{(j)})}$. So far, it still looks like the full-interaction model considers more information. But useful values for $w_{\mathcal{I}(x^{(j)})}$ can only be estimated if $\mathcal{I}(x^{(j)})$ was seen at least once in the learning set. Thus, in practice, both kind of models do not have the same features to predict a state-action pairs strength. Normally, the no-interaction models have access to larger shape features which are very predictive and this additional information is worth more than the interaction.

The model of LFR is capable of using the same features as no-interaction models but still can consider feature interactions so that in this case indeed more information is used.

4.3   Latent Factor Ranking

The Latent Factor Ranking (LFR) is defined as follows. Each state-action pair is labeled with

$$y(x) = \begin{cases} 1 & \text{if } x \text{ was chosen in the example} \\ 0 & \text{otherwise} \end{cases}.$$

For the estimation of vector w and matrix Θ a stochastic gradient descent with $l2$ regularization is applied. The gradients are given as

$$\frac{\delta}{\delta\phi}\hat{y}(x) = \begin{cases} 1 & \text{if } \phi = w_0 \\ 1 & \text{if } \phi = w_i \text{ and } i \in \mathcal{I}(x) \\ \sum_{j \in \mathcal{I}(x) \setminus \{i\}} v_{j,f} & \text{if } \phi = v_{i,f} \text{ and } i \in \mathcal{I}(x) \\ 0 & \text{otherwise} \end{cases}$$

Instead of taking every state-action pair x into account, only those pairs with rank at least as high as the pair chosen by the expert i.e. $\hat{y}(x) \geq \hat{y}(x^{(1)})$ are used. The idea behind this is that an implicit transitive relation between features is achieved, and moves that are not responsible for wrong rankings do not need to be touched.

Vector w is initialized with 0, V is initialized with values randomly drawn from the normal distribution with mean 0 and standard deviation 0.1. Learning rate α and regularization parameters λ_w and λ_v need to be estimated upfront as well as the dimension k. Algorithm 1 describes LFR in detail. In the following LFR with a specific dimension k is called LFRk. During the experiments, convergence was assumed when the prediction accuracy did not improve within the last three iterations.

Algorithm 1. Latent Factor Ranking

Input: Training set $\mathcal{D}$ with move decisions $\mathcal{D}_j = \left\{ x^{(1)}, x^{(2)}, \ldots, x^{(|\Gamma(s_j)|)} \right\}$ in state s_j where $x^{(1)}$ was chosen by the expert.
Output: V and w necessary to predict future moves.
  $w \leftarrow 0$, $v_{if} \sim \mathcal{N}(0, 0.1)$
  while not converged **do**
    for all $\mathcal{D}_j \in \mathcal{D}$ **do**
      for all $x \in \mathcal{D}_j$ **do**
        if $\hat{y}(x) \geq \hat{y}(x^{(1)})$ **then**
          $\Delta y \leftarrow \hat{y}(x) - y(x)$
          $w_0 \leftarrow w_0 - \alpha \cdot \Delta y$
          for all $i \in \mathcal{I}(x)$ **do**
            $w_i \leftarrow w_i - \alpha (\Delta y + \lambda_w w_i)$
            for $f = 1$ to k **do**
              $v_{i,f} \leftarrow v_{i,f} - \alpha \left(\Delta y \frac{\delta}{\delta v_{i,f}} \hat{y}(x) + \lambda_v v_{i,f} \right)$

4.4   Features

In Go two different kinds of features are distinguished, shape features and non-shape features. Shape features take the shape around a specific intersection on the board into account, non-shape features are every other kind of features in a move situation you can imagine. How shapes are extracted, harvested and represented is explained very well in [3].

In this work the same features are used as in [4]. That is, a feature subset of those proposed in [8] are used in order to allow a comparison to further prediction models. Since [4] does not define the features explicitly, this is caught up here. Features are divided into nine groups, from each group at most one feature is active for a given state-action pair, first mentioned features have higher priorities within the feature group. All features are binary because the approaches LFR is compared to cannot deal with other features types.

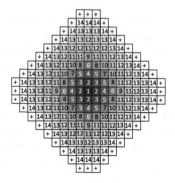

Fig. 1. The shapes are harvested as proposed in [3]: Fourteen circle shaped, nested templates are used which are regarded to be invariant to rotation, translation and mirroring. The shape template of size 14 considers the full board state.

1. **Pass** Passing in case of the last move was 1) no pass or 2) a pass.
2. **Capture** Capturing an enemy chain such that 1) an own chain is no longer in atari, 2) previous move is recaptured, 3) a connection to the previous move is prevented or 4) any other capture.
3. **Extension** Stone is placed next to an enemy chain such that it is in atari.
4. **Self-atari** Placing a stone such that your own chain is in atari.
5. **Atari** Placing a stone such that enemy chain is in atari when there is 1) a ko or 2) no ko.
6. **Distance to border** is one, two, three or four.
7. **Distance to previous move** is $2, \ldots, 16, \geq 17$ using distance measure $d(\Delta x, \Delta y) = |\Delta x| + |\Delta y| + \max\{|\Delta x|, |\Delta y|\}$
8. **Distance to move before previous move** is $2, \ldots, 16, \geq 17$ using distance measure $d(\Delta x, \Delta y) = |\Delta x| + |\Delta y| + \max\{|\Delta x|, |\Delta y|\}$
9. **Shape** Can be any shape that appeared at least ten times in the training set using the templates shown in Figure 1.

5   Experiments

In the following, at first LFR is compared to other Go move prediction algorithms and it is shown that it is significantly better for k. It will be shown that the interactions have a positive impact especially in situations where no big shapes are matched (shape sizes greater than 4) which finally results in the observed lift. Finally, the features and its interactions are discussed.

For the experiments a set of 5,000 respectively 10,000 games (i.e. approximately 750,000 respectively 1,500,000 move decisions) from the KGS Go Server[1] was used. These games are without a handicap and were played between strong human amateurs i.e. both are ranked at least 6d or at least one has a rank of 7d. As mentioned before, shapes were used if they occurred at least 10 times in the

---

[1] http://www.gokgs.com/

training set. In this way, 48,071 respectively 94,030 shapes were harvested and used for the learning process. Hyperparameters for LFR were estimated on a disjoint validation set and sought on a grid from 0 to 0.01 with step size 0.001. The learning rate $\alpha = 0.001$ was selected. For LFR1 the regularization parameters $\lambda_w = 0.001$ and $\lambda_v = 0$ were chosen, while for LFR5 $\lambda_w = 0.001$ and $\lambda_v = 0.002$ are optimal. All experiments were made on the 10k learning set otherwise explicitly stated. LFR is compared to Coulom's Minorization Maximization [8] (MM) as well as two further algorithms introduced in [4]: These are on the one hand an improvement of Stern's algorithm [3] now capable to deal with arbitrary many features, the Loopy Bayesian Ranking (LBR), and a variant of Weng's Bayesian Approximation Method [13] based on the Bradley Terry model adapted to the Go move prediction problem, the Bayesian Approximation Ranking (BAR). The experiments are made on a testing set of 1,000 games which are disjoint from the training and validation set. The accuracy is defined as the average accuracy of the first 12 game phases, where a game phase consists of 30 turns.

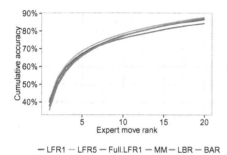 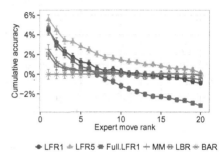

(a) Cumulative prediction accuracy in respect to the expert move rank.

(b) The move prediction accuracy given by the difference of the accuracy of an algorithm and BAR. (95% conf. intervals)

Fig. 2. The cumulative prediction accuracy in respect to the expert move rank

The resulting prediction quality of the aforementioned algorithms is depicted in Figure 2(a). Figure 2(b) shows this in detail by providing the results substracted by the results of BAR. The expert move rank is the rank assigned to the move chosen by the expert player in the actual game. Full-LFR1 is LFR1 which considers all state-action pairs for the update. Its results justify the choice of considering only state-action pairs $x^{(i)}$ where $\hat{y}\left(x^{(i)}\right) \geq \hat{y}\left(x^{(1)}\right)$ because Full-LFR performs poor for high expert move ranks. As can be seen, LFR outperforms the other algorithms significantly, especially for low expert move ranks. For FPR5 this holds even up to 18. Especially the lift for very low expert move ranks is notable.

Table 1. Probability for predicting the move chosen by the expert for different learning set sizes

Training set size	MM	LBR	BAR	LFR1	LFR5
5,000	37.00%	36.36%	34.24%	38.60%	**39.96%**
10,000	37.86%	37.35%	35.33%	39.78%	**40.90%**

Additionally, Table 1 compares the different prediction algorithms on two different sized training sets. Again, LFR outperforms every other algorithm. Finally, Figure 5(a) shows the predicting performance of LFR with growing k. The accuracy increases fast but then converges. It can be assumed that for $k > 10$ there will be no big improvements.

The intuition of learning move strengths by considering interactions between features was to achieve a higher prediction accuracy for cases where only smaller shapes are matched. Smaller shapes have less information and usually are more often matched in the later game phases. This goal is achieved by LFR as seen in Figure 3(a). The prediction accuracy in the first game phases (each game phase consists of 30 turns) is higher than the average accuracy due to the fact that there are standard opening moves. These can be learned very accurately by the shape features because most of these moves were harvested with very large shape sizes. This is also the reason why LFR is not better than the other algorithms because the shape features simply dominate all the others. Then, starting in game phase 6, when smaller shapes are matched and the other features gain more influence, the impact of the interactions becomes visible. Accuracy of LFR is then up to more than 5% better than all other approaches.

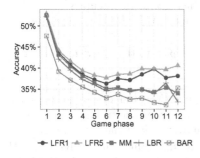

(a) Move prediction accuracy in different game phases. Each game phases consists of 30 turns.

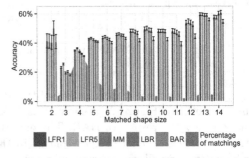

(b) Accuracy of predicting the right move depending on the shape size of the right move. The red part in the background is the percentage of shape sizes of the matched shapes in total. (95% conf. intervals)

Fig. 3. LFR is better in ranking moves where only small shapes are available

Figure 3(b) also supports the claim of successfully estimating the right move if only small shapes are matched. It shows the prediction accuracy in respect of the matched shape size of the expert move. For shape sizes 5-13 there is no significant change in comparison to the other algorithms, for full board shapes it is even worse. Matters are quite different for shapes sizes 3 and 4. The interactions seem to be responsible for the significant improvement of the accuracy. More than 40% of matched shapes for the move chosen by the expert are of sizes 3 or 4. This is the reason for the dramatic lift of the average prediction accuracy and the prediction accuracy in the later game phases. Additionally, considering that full board shapes are only matched during the first game phases and probably being part of standard opening moves, the advantage of the other algorithms for full board shapes is even more weakened. Using opening books for Go AI and that LFR has still a similar prediction accuracy in the first game phase (see Figure 3(a)) does not justify the preference of one of the other algorithms.

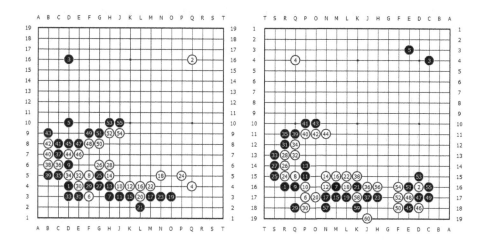

Fig. 4. On the left side are the first moves of a game played between two artificial players using the LFR1 always choosing the move with highest ranking. By means of comparison, the first moves of a game played between two of the ten strongest players on the KGS Go Server are shown on the right side.

On the left side, Figure 4 shows a game of Go between two LFR1 predictors which are always choosing the most likely action. The right side shows the first moves of a game played between two very strong players who were ranked within the top 10 of the Go GKS Server. At first glance, both games look very similar. On a closer look, the first moves are indeed almost the same. However, from move 10 on, LFR strongly prefers moves close to the moves made before and never takes the initiative by placing a stone somewhere else as seen in the game between the human players. The reason is simple: LFR is a move predictor optimized for accuracy. As one can see, in most cases a move is made close to the last moves. Thus, it would be unreasonable to do these kind of moves. Nonetheless, this is exactly the reason why a move predictor alone is not a strong Go player. Anyways, it is very surprising how similar these games are.

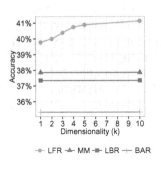

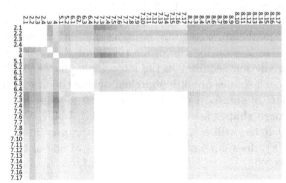

(a) Move prediction accuracy depending on the dimension k.

(b) Feature interaction heat map learned on 10,000 games with LFR1 without shapes. Each intersection shows the influence of the interaction of two features. Red values have the worst, green the best positive influence.

Fig. 5. Influence of the dimensionality and the feature interactions

The advantage of our model is that the received feature interaction weights also give an insight into Go and the importance of each feature. The main idea of combining features was that combinations of features might give more information. For instance, a feature appearing alone might indicate a bad move, but in interaction with another feature it might indicate a good move or vice versa. Unfortunately, restricting only to the non-shape features, an example of this kind of feature was not found. Nonetheless, the heat map in Figure 5(b) has exposed some interesting facts. Unsurprisingly, feature 4 (self-atari) indicates bad moves and feature group 2 (capture) indicates good moves. Feature groups 7 and 8 (distance to previous moves) has some kind of reinforcing effects. Feature values of moves close to the previous moves have a stronger impact than moves further away. So feature group 2 is a better feature for moves close to the last move. Furthermore, feature group 4 is a worse feature for these moves. A possible explanation for this observation is that a player is more aware of his actual area of interest. Additionally, if he decides not to do a move that has a positive feature but places stones in another part of the board, this could indicate that the move is probably not good.

6   Conclusion

This work has introduced a model for the move prediction problem of Go which is able to model interactions between features in an efficient way. The Latent

Factor Ranking is not only easy to implement but learning can also be done online and hence does not have memory issues like MM. Finally, experiments have demonstrated the move prediction quality of LFR and how it can be used to gain insights into used features.

For future research interactions between more than two features could be of interest as well as user-specific predictions and folding in informations gained during a game.

References

1. Kocsis, L., Szepesvári, C.: Bandit based Monte-Carlo Planning. In: Fürnkranz, J., Scheffer, T., Spiliopoulou, M. (eds.) ECML 2006. LNCS (LNAI), vol. 4212, pp. 282–293. Springer, Heidelberg (2006)
2. Gelly, S., Wang, Y.: Exploration exploitation in Go: UCT for Monte-Carlo Go. In: NIPS: Neural Information Processing Systems Conference On-line trading of Exploration and Exploitation Workshop, Canada (December 2006)
3. Stern, D., Herbrich, R., Graepel, T.: Bayesian Pattern Ranking for Move Prediction in the Game of Go. In: ICML 2006: Proceedings of the 23rd International Conference on Machine Learning, pp. 873–880. ACM Press, New York (2006)
4. Wistuba, M., Schaefers, L., Platzner, M.: Comparison of Bayesian Move Prediction Systems for Computer Go. In: CIG, pp. 91–99. IEEE (2012)
5. Rendle, S.: Factorization Machines. In: 2010 IEEE 10th International Conference on Data Mining (ICDM), pp. 995–1000 (2010)
6. van der Werf, E., Uiterwijk, J.W.H.M., Postma, E.O., van den Herik, H.J.: Local Move Prediction in Go. In: Schaeffer, J., Müller, M., Björnsson, Y. (eds.) CG 2002. LNCS, vol. 2883, pp. 393–412. Springer, Heidelberg (2003)
7. Sutskever, I., Nair, V.: Mimicking Go Experts with Convolutional Neural Networks. In: Kůrková, V., Neruda, R., Koutník, J. (eds.) ICANN 2008, Part II. LNCS, vol. 5164, pp. 101–110. Springer, Heidelberg (2008)
8. Coulom, R.: Computing Elo Ratings of Move Patterns in the Game of Go. ICGA Journal 30(4), 198–208 (2007)
9. Araki, N., Yoshida, K., Tsuruoka, Y., Tsujii, J.: Move Prediction in Go with the Maximum Entropy Method. In: IEEE Symposium on Computational Intelligence and Games, CIG 2007, pp. 189–195 (2007)
10. Müller, M.: Computer Go. Artificial Intelligence 134, 145–179 (2002)
11. Lichtenstein, D., Sipser, M.: GO Is Polynomial-Space Hard. J. ACM 27(2), 393–401 (1980)
12. Crâsmaru, M., Tromp, J.: Ladders are PSPACE-Complete. In: Marsland, T., Frank, I. (eds.) CG 2001. LNCS, vol. 2063, pp. 241–249. Springer, Heidelberg (2002)
13. Weng, R.C., Lin, C.J.: A Bayesian Approximation Method for Online Ranking. Journal of Machine Learning Research 12, 267–300 (2011)

Algorithmic Debugging for Intelligent Tutoring: How to Use Multiple Models *and* Improve Diagnosis

Claus Zinn

Department of Computer Science, University of Konstanz
Funded by the DFG (ZI 1322/2/1)
`claus.zinn@uni-konstanz.de`

Abstract. Intelligent tutoring systems (ITSs) are capable to intelligently diagnose learners' problem solving behaviour only in limited and well-defined contexts. Learners are expected to solve problems by closely following a *single* prescribed problem solving strategy, usually in a fixed-order, step by step manner. Learners failing to match expectations are often met with incorrect diagnoses even when human teachers would judge their actions admissible. To address the issue, we extend our previous work on cognitive diagnosis, which is based on logic programming and meta-level techniques. Our novel use of Shapiro's algorithmic debugging now analyses learner input independently against *multiple* models. Learners can now follow one of many possible algorithms to solve a given problem, *and* they can expect the tutoring system to respond with improved diagnostic quality, at negligible computational costs.

1 Introduction

The intelligent tutoring community aims at building computer systems that simulate effective human tutoring. A key building block is the diagnoser that analyses learner input for correctness with regard to the current problem solving context. Much of the intelligent behavior of state-of-the-art tutoring systems is due to learning interactions that highly constrain learners' scope of action. Usually, learners are expected to solve a given problem by executing the steps of a *single* prescribed procedure. User interfaces ask learners to enter their answers in a structured and often piece-meal fashion, and systems intervene after each and every problem-solving step, preventing learners to pursue their own (correct or potentially erroneous) problem-solving paths. The tight leash between tutoring system and learners has more practical than pedagogical reasons. While human tutors are capable of dealing with free discovery interactions and recognizing and accommodating alternative problem-solving strategies, most machine tutors only possess a fixed *single* problem solving strategy to diagnose anticipated input.

In [9], we propose a novel method to trace learners' problem solving behaviour using the programming technique *algorithmic debugging*. In [10], we interleave our method with program transformations to perform *deep* cognitive analyses. While our method has many benefits (*e.g.*, low authoring costs, any-time feedback), so far, it only uses a single frame of reference. In this paper, we extend

I.J. Timm and M. Thimm (Eds.): KI 2013, LNAI 8077, pp. 272–283, 2013.

our previous work by comparing learner behaviour independently against *multiple* models. Our new contribution permits learners to exhibit a wider range of problem solving strategies, while at the same time *improving* diagnostic quality, with little additional computational cost.

The paper is structured as follows. Sect. 2 introduces the cognitive task multi-column subtraction as tutoring domain. It presents the technique of algorithmic debugging, and our adaptation of the method to support reasoning about learner input. Sect. 3 is the main part of the paper, and shows how our variant of algorithmic debugging can be improved to track learner behaviour across multiple models, while at the same time improving the quality of the diagnosis. Sect. 4 discusses related work, while Sect. 5 concludes.

2   Background

2.1   Encoding Cognitive Task Models in Prolog

Cognitive task analysis (CTA) aims at giving a qualitative account of the processing steps an individual problem solver takes to solve a given task. Our research uses logic programming as vehicle for encoding cognitive task models and for tracking and diagnosing learner behaviour. Our domain of instruction is multi-column subtraction, a well-studied domain in the ITS community. Its expert model(s), resulting from CTA, can be concisely encoded in Prolog. In the *Austrian method* (AM), see Fig. 1, sums are processed column by column, from right to left. The predicate `subtract/2` determines the number of columns, and calls `mc_subtract/3`, which implements the recursion (decrementing the column counter CC at each recursive call). The clause `process_column/3` gets a partial sum, processes its right-most column and takes care of borrowing (`add_ten_to_minuend/3`) and payback (`increment/3`) actions. A column is represented as a term (M, S, R) representing minuend, subtrahend and result cell. If the subtrahend S is greater than the minuend M, then M is increased by 10 (borrowing) before the difference M-S is taken. To compensate, the S in the column left to the current one is increased by one (payback). – The introduction of the column counter CC is not an essential part of the subtraction method, but a technical requirement for mechanising the Oracle part of our diagnosis engine (see below).

We have also been implementing three other subtraction algorithms that reuse code fragments from Fig. 1. The *trade-first* variant of the Austrian method (TF) performs the same steps as the Austrian method, but in a different order; first, all payback and borrowing operations are executed, then all differences are taken. The *decomposition* method (DC) realizes the payback operation by decrementing minuends rather than incrementing subtrahends. The *left-to-right* method (LR) processes sums in the opposite direction; also, payback operations are performed on result rather than minuend or subtrahend cells.

2.2   Algorithmic Debugging for Tutoring

Shapiro's algorithmic debugging technique defines a systematic manner to identify bugs in programs [6]. In the top-down variant, the program is traversed from

```
subtract(PartialSum, Sum) :- length(PartialSum, LSum),
  mc_subtract(LSum, PartialSum, Sum).
mc_subtract(_,  [], []).
mc_subtract(CC, Sum, NewSum) :-
  process_column(CC, Sum, Sum1),
  shift_left(Sum1, Sum2, ProcessedColumn), CC1 is CC - 1,
  mc_subtract(CC1, Sum2, SumFinal),
  append(SumFinal, [ProcessedColumn], NewSum).

process_column(CC, Sum, NewSum) :-
  butlast(Sum, LastColumn),    allbutlast(Sum,RestSum),
  subtrahend(LastColumn, Sub), minuend(LastColumn, Min),
  ( Sub > Min
  -> ( add_ten_to_minuend(CC, LastColumn, LastColumn1),
       take_difference(CC, LastColumn1, LastColumn2),
       butlast(RestSum, LastColumnRestSum), allbutlast(RestSum, RestSum1),
       increment(CC, LastColumnRestSum, LastColumnRestSum1),
       append(RestSum1, [LastColumnRestSum1,LastColumn2],NewSum) )
  ; ( take_difference(CC, LastColumn, LastColumn1),
      append(RestSum, [LastColumn1], NewSum) ) ).

shift_left( SumList, RestSumList, Item ) :-
  allbutlast(SumList, RestSumList), butlast(SumList, Item).

add_ten_to_minuend(CC, (M,S,R),  (M10,S, R) ) :- irreducible, M10 is M+10.
increment(         CC, (M,S,R),  (M,  S1,R) ) :- irreducible, S1 is S+1.
take_difference(   CC, (M,S,_R), (M,  S, R1)) :- irreducible, R1 is M-S.

minuend( (M,_S,_R), M).                    subtrahend( (_M,S,_R), S).
```

Fig. 1. Multi-column subtraction (Austrian method)

the goal clause downwards. At each step during the traversal of the program's AND/OR tree, the programmer is taking the role of the *oracle*, and answers whether the currently processed goal holds or not. If the oracle and the buggy program agree on the result of a goal G, then algorithmic debugging passes to the next goal on the goal stack. Otherwise, the goal G is inspected further. Eventually an *irreducible agreement* will be encountered, hence locating the program's clause where the buggy behaviour is originating from. In [9], we turn Shapiro's algorithm on its head: instead of having the oracle specifying how the assumed incorrect program should behave, we take the expert program to take the role of the buggy program, and the role of the oracle is filled by a student's potentially erroneous answers. An irreducible disagreement between program behaviour and given answer then indicates a student's potential misconception. In [9], we have also described how to mechanise the Oracle by reconstructing learners' answers from their submitted solution. In [10], we refine the Oracle to complement irreducible disagreements with the attributes *incorrect, missing*, or *superfluous*. We then interleave algorithmic debugging with program transformation to incrementally reconstruct, from the expert program, an erroneous procedure that the learner is following, allowing deep diagnoses of learners with multiple bugs.

Example. Our algorithmic debugger, given the learner's answer to $401 - 199$:

$$
\begin{array}{c c c c}
 & 4 & {}^{1}0 & {}^{1}1 \\
- & 1 & 9\ \boxed{10}\ & 9 \\
\hline
= & 3 & 1 & 2
\end{array}
$$

and the Austrian method (see Fig. 1), yields the following (abbreviated) dialogue:

```
do you agree that the following goal holds:

  mc_subtract( 3, [(4, 1, R1), ( 0, 9, R2), ( 1, 9, R3)],
                  [(4, 2, 2), (10, 10, 0), (11, 9, 2)])    |: no.

  process_column(3, [(4,1,R1), (0,9,R2),  (1, 9,R3)],
                    [(4,1,R1), (0,10,R2), (11,9,2)])       |: no.

  add_ten_to_minuend(3, (1,9,R3), (11,9,R3 )               |: yes.

  increment(2, (0, 9, R2), (0, 10, R2))                    |: no.

=> irreducible disagreement: ID = increment(2, (0,9,R2), (0,10,R2))
```

Whenever the learner submits a solution, such a dialogue can be automatically generated, and hence, the irreducible disagreement deduced. Compared with existing methods for cognitive diagnosis, our method has a number of advantages. To locate learners' errors, it requires only an expert model, which is an executable Prolog program; no representation of buggy knowledge is required. Moreover, learners are no longer limited to providing their solution in a piecemeal fashion; algorithmic debugging easily copes with input that spans multiple, potentially erroneous, problem-solving steps. Like many other approaches, however, our method only supported a single expert model to solve a given task; it thus fails to recognise learners using algorithms different than the prescribed one. The application of our variant of Shapiro's algorithm on the Austrian method will return irreducible disagreements ("errors") for learners who *correctly* follow one of the other three subtraction algorithms. Moreover, when learners follow one of the other algorithms *incorrectly*, error diagnosis will return incorrect analyses as they are based on the assumption of the Austrian method. Clearly, tutoring systems shall be less prescriptive when asking learners to tackle problems.

3   Input Analysis across Models

The diagnostic engine of our tutoring system shall be able, *e.g.*, to cope with learners following any of the four subtraction methods, or erroneous variants thereof. The method reported in [9] must be generalized.

Step	Austrian (AM)	Trade-first (TF)	Decomposition (DC)	Left-to-right (LR)
1	$4\ 0\ {}^{1}1$ $-\ 1\ 9\ 9$ $=$	$4\ 0\ {}^{1}1$ $-\ 1\ 9\ 9$ $=$	$4\ 0\ {}^{1}1$ $-\ 1\ 9\ 9$ $=$	$4\ 0\ 1$ $-\ 1\ 9\ 9$ $=3$
2	$4\ 0\ {}^{1}1$ $-\ 1\ 9_1\ 9$ $=$	$4\ 0\ {}^{1}1$ $-\ 1\ 9_1\ 9$ $=$	$4\ {}^{1}0\ {}^{1}1$ $-\ 1\ 9\ 9$ $=$	$4\ {}^{1}0\ 1$ $-\ 1\ 9\ 9$ $=3$
3	$4\ 0\ {}^{1}1$ $-\ 1\ 9_1\ 9$ $=\quad 2$	$\boxed{\begin{array}{l} 4\ {}^{1}0\ {}^{1}1 \\ -\ 1\ 9_1\ 9 \\ = \end{array}}$	$4\ 9\ {\cancel{10}}\ {}^{1}1$ $-\ 1\ 9\quad 9$ $=$	$4\quad {}^{1}0\ 1$ $-\ 1\quad 9\ 9$ $=2\ \sout{3}$
4	$4\ {}^{1}0\ {}^{1}1$ $-\ 1\ 9_1\ 9$ $=\quad 2$	$4\ {}^{1}0\ {}^{1}1$ $-\ 1_1\ 9_1\ 9$ $=$	$3\ 4\ 9\ {\cancel{10}}\ {}^{1}1$ $-\ 1\quad 9\quad 9$ $=$	$4\quad {}^{1}0\ 1$ $-\ 1\quad 9\ 9$ $=\sout{23}\ 1$
5	$4\ {}^{1}0\ {}^{1}1$ $-\ 1_1\ 9_1\ 9$ $=\quad 2$	$4\ {}^{1}0\ {}^{1}1$ $-\ 1_1\ 9_1\ 9$ $=\quad 2$	$3\ 4\ 9\ {\cancel{10}}\ {}^{1}1$ $-\ 1\quad 9\quad 9$ $=\quad 2$	$4\quad {}^{1}0\ {}^{1}1$ $-\ 1\quad 9\ 9$ $=\sout{23}\ 1$
6	$4\ {}^{1}0\ {}^{1}1$ $-\ 1_1\ 9_1\ 9$ $=\quad 0\ 2$	$4\ {}^{1}0\ {}^{1}1$ $-\ 1_1\ 9_1\ 9$ $=\quad 0\ 2$	$3\ 4\ 9\ {\cancel{10}}\ {}^{1}1$ $-\ 1\quad 9\quad 9$ $=\quad 0\ 2$	$4\quad {}^{1}0\ {}^{1}1$ $-\ 1\quad 9\ 9$ $=\sout{23}\ \sout{01}$
7	$4\ {}^{1}0\ {}^{1}1$ $-\ 1_1\ 9_1\ 9$ $=2\ 0\ 2$	$4\ {}^{1}0\ {}^{1}1$ $-\ 1_1\ 9_1\ 9$ $=2\ 0\ 2$	$3\ 4\ 9\ {\cancel{10}}\ {}^{1}1$ $-\ 1\quad 9\quad 9$ $=2\quad 0\quad 2$	$4\quad {}^{1}0\ {}^{1}1$ $-\ 1\quad 9\ 9$ $=\sout{23}\ \sout{01}\ 2$

Fig. 2. Problem Solving States in Four Algorithms for Multi-Column Subtraction

3.1   Correct Learner Behaviour

For the time being, consider learners being perfect problem solvers. They will solve any given subtraction problem by consistently following one of the four aforementioned subtraction algorithms. At any problem solving stage, we would like to identify the algorithm that they are most likely following. Fig. 2 depicts all correct states for solving the subtraction problem $401 - 199$ in each of the four algorithms. Fig. 3 illustrates the basic idea of our approach, which we will later refine. Given some partial learner input at the root (the learner is correctly executing the trade-first variant, see boxed third step in Fig. 2), we run algorithmic debugging on each of the four subtraction methods. As a result, we obtain four different diagnoses. With regard to AM, the learner failed to take the difference in the ones column; for TF, he failed to increment the subtrahend in the hundreds column; for DC, he failed to decrement the minuend in the tens; and for LR, he failed to take the difference in the hundreds column.

This result is unsatisfactory as we cannot derive which of the algorithms the learner is following. For this, let us consider the number of *agreements before*

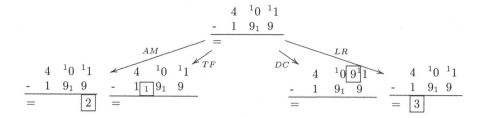

Fig. 3. Algorithmic Debugging (AD) for Four Algorithms on Identical Input

an *irreducible* disagreement between program and learner behaviour is identified. While all methods disagree on their respective top goal subtract/2, there are varying *reducible* disagreements that contain partial *agreements*. For AM, while disagreeing with the goal process_column/3 (ones column), we have **two** agreements with regard to its observable actions in the subgoals add_ten_to_minuend/3 (ones column) and increment/3 (tens column). For TF, we have an agreement with regard to process_column/3 in the ones column, but a disagreement for this clause in the tens column. However, we find an agreement with one of its subgoals, namely add_ten_to_minuend/3, yielding a total of **two** agreements. For DC, while disagreeing with the goal process_column/3 in the ones column, we find **two** agreements, one with its subgoal add_ten_to_minuend/3, and one with the partial execution of the decrement operation. And for LR, there are **zero** agreements before the irreducible disagreement is found. In summary, the number of agreements only indicates that the learner is most likely *not* following the LR method; all other methods receive two agreements.

First Refinement. To better rank the methods, we now take into account the size of the code pieces that are being agreed upon. For this, we count the number of *irreducible agreements* before the first irreducible *disagreement*. Fig. 4 depicts the relevant execution trace of AM for the task $401 - 199$. All leafs that are marked "irreducible" (see Fig. 1) have weight 1; the weights of nodes are accumulated upwards. For brevity, **borrow** represents add_ten_to_minuend/3, and **payback** represents increment/3. With this refinement, there is no change in the agreement score for AM, DC and LR – as all agreements are on leafs nodes. For TF, however, the score increases by one; our agreement on process_column/3 in the ones column now contributes a value of 2 rather than 1 (as the TF implementation of this predicate has the two leaf nodes add_ten_to_minuend/3 and increment/3). For the given example, the refinement thus yields the intended diagnosis; in fact, this holds for most problem solving steps given in Fig. 2.

Evaluation. Each of the four matrices in Fig. 5 shall be read as overlay to Fig. 2. Fig. 5(a), *e.g.*, gives the results of analysing each problem solving step – performed in each of the four subtraction methods – in the context of AM. Learners perfectly executing AM receive "full marks" when their actions are evaluated against AM; when their actions are evaluated against the other three

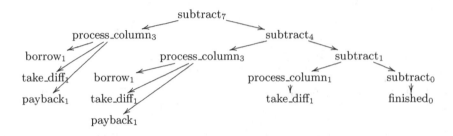

Fig. 4. Execution Trace for the Austrian Method on $401 - 199$

methods, they receive a lesser score. It shows that our first refinement weighting yields the correct diagnoses in all cases.

AM	TF	DC	LR
1	1	1	0
2	2	1	0
3	2	1	0
4	2	2	0
5	5	2	0
6	6	2	0
7	7	2	0

(a) Ref: AM

AM	TF	DC	LR
1	1	1	0
2	2	1	0
2	3	2	0
3	4	2	0
5	5	2	0
6	6	2	0
7	7	2	0

(b) Ref: TF

AM	TF	DC	LR
1	1	1	0
1	1	2	0
1	2	3	0
2	2	4	0
2	2	5	0
2	2	6	0
2	2	7	0

(c) Ref: DC

AM	TF	DC	LR
0	0	0	1
0	0	0	2
0	0	0	3
0	0	0	4
1	1	2	5
1	1	2	6
1	1	2	7

(d) Ref: LR

Fig. 5. Evaluation Matrix (Correct Learner Behaviour)

3.2 Buggy Learner Behaviour

Learner errors are rarely random but result from correctly executing a procedure that has been acquired incorrectly [7,8]. This makes it possible to analyse learner input in terms of expert models or buggy deviations thereof. We distinguish *problematic cases* that cannot be reliably associated with expert models, *standard cases* that can be associated with expert models, and *complex error patterns* that can only be matched to carefully designed buggy models, see Fig. 6.

Problematic Cases. Consider Fig. 6(a), where the student always subtracted the smaller from the larger digit. With no payback and borrowing operation observed, there cannot be sufficient evidence to link learner behaviour to any of the four algorithms. Nevertheless, algorithmic debugging returns useful diagnoses: the irreducible disagreement indicates that the learner failed to borrow in the ones (AM, TF, DC) or tens (LR) column. In Fig. 6(b), the learner forgets to payback after borrowing. Since the main differentiator between the four methods is the location of the payback operation. we cannot, in principle, differentiate between the methods. Again, our algorithmic debugger yields the same type of diagnosis: the learner forgot to payback, either by failing to increment the subtrahend in the tens column (AM, TF), or by failing to decrement the minuends in the tens (and hundreds) column (DC), or by failing to decrement the result cell

$$\begin{array}{rrr} 4 & 0 & 1 \\ - \quad 1 & 9 & 9 \\ \hline = \quad 3 & 9 & 8 \end{array}$$
(a) Smaller from larger digit

$$\begin{array}{rrr} 4 & {}^{1}0 & {}^{1}1 \\ - \quad 1 & 9 & 9 \\ \hline = \quad 3 & 1 & 2 \end{array}$$
(b) Forgot to payback

$$\begin{array}{rrr} 4 & {}^{1}0 & {}^{1}1 \\ - \quad 1_1 & 9_1 & 9 \\ \hline = \quad 2 & 0 & 3 \end{array}$$
(c) Wrong subtraction fact

$$\begin{array}{rrrr} 3\!\!\!4 & 9\!\!\!\dotdiv\!\!\!0 & {}^{1}1 & 0 \\ - \quad 1 & 9 & 9 & 9 \\ \hline = \quad 2 & 0 & 2 & 0 \end{array}$$
(d) Zero digit confusion

$$\begin{array}{rrrr} 1 & {}^{1}1 & {}^{1}2 & 3 \\ - \quad & 4 & 9_1 & 0_1 \\ \hline = \quad 1 & 7 & 2 & 2 \end{array}$$
(e) Combining LR with AM

Fig. 6. Three Groups of Frequent Errors

in the hundreds column (LR). It shows that the comparison of learner behaviour against a set of models strengthens the credibility of the diagnosis.

Standard Cases. Erroneous behaviour that is not directly related to borrowing and payback can be better associated with one of the four subtraction methods. In Fig. 6(c), the learner has followed AM or TF, but got a basic subtraction fact wrong in the ones column. In Fig. 6(d), the student has followed DC, but showed a misconception wrt. columns where the minuend is zero (ones column); in this case, the learner takes the result cell to be zero as well. Note that both errors occur – with respect to AM and DC – early in the problem solving process, and both solutions have no other errors. When we run algorithmic debugging on Fig. 6(c), we obtain wrt. AM and TF an incorrect difference in the ones column (**2** agreements). For DC, the learner failed to decrement minuends in the tens and hundreds (**2** agreements); and for LR, there is a superfluous increment of the subtrahend in the ones (**0** agreement). With each of AM, TF and DC sharing the same number of irreducible agreements, we cannot select one diagnosis over the other. Running the diagnoser on Fig. 6(d), we obtain no agreement for AM, TF, and DC (failed to borrow in the ones column), and also no agreement for LR (superfluous decrement of minuend in the thousands). Given that Fig. 6(d) is almost correct wrt. DC, we need to further refine our algorithm to better recognise the method learners are following.

Second Refinement. When errors occur early in the problem solving process, our simple algorithm for method recognition must perform poorly. Now, instead of only counting the number of irreducible agreements *before* the first irreducible disagreement, we also take into consideration irreducible agreements *after* the first and any subsequent irreducible disagreements. *I.e.*, once an irreducible disagreement between expert model and learner behaviour has been identified, our algorithmic debugger now continues to trace through and analyse the execution tree until all agreements and disagreements have been counted, see Fig. 7.

With this refinement, we now get these (dis-)agreement scores for Fig. 6(c): For AM and TF, we obtain **6** irreducible agreements (*i.e.*, correct cell modifications), and **1** irreducible disagreement (erroneous difference in the ones column). For DC, we have **4** irreducible agreements (correct borrow in the ones; initiated

```
 1: NumberAgreements ← 0, NumberDisagreements ← 0
 2: Goal ← top-clause of subtraction routine
 3: Problem ← current task to be solved, Solution ← learner input to task
 4: procedure ALGORITHMICDEBUGGING(Goal)
 5:     if Goal is conjunction of goals (Goal1, Goal2) then
 6:             ← algorithmicDebugging(Goal1)
 7:             ← algorithmicDebugging(Goal2)
 8:     end if
 9:     if Goal is system predicate then
10:             ← call(Goal)
11:     end if
12:     if Goal is not on the list of goals to be discussed with learners then
13:             Body ← getClauseSubgoals(Goal)
14:             ← algorithmicDebugging(Body)
15:     end if
16:     if Goal is on the list of goals to be discussed with learners then
17:             SystemResult ← call(Goal), given Problem
18:             OracleResult ← call(Goal), given Problem and Solution
19:             if results agree on Goal then
20:                 Weight ← computeWeight(Goal)
21:                 NumberAgreements ← NumberAgreements + Weight
22:             else
23:                 if Goal is leaf node (or marked as irreducible) then
24:                     NumberDisagreements ← NumberDisagreements + 1
25:                 else
26:                     Body ← getClauseSubgoals(Goal)
27:                         ← algorithmicDebugging(Body)
28:                 end if
29:             end if
30:     end if
31: end procedure
32: Score ← NumberAgreements − NumberDisagreements
```

Fig. 7. Pseudo-code: Top-Down traversal of model, keeping track of (dis-)agreements

payback in the tens; correct differences in the tens and hundreds), and **5** irreducible disagreements (wrong difference in the ones; two superfluous increments of the subtrahend in the tens and hundreds; incorrect minuends in the tens and hundreds as payback is not fully carried out). For LR, we yield **4** irreducible agreements (correct borrowing in the ones and tens and correct differences in the tens and hundreds), and **3** irreducible disagreements (incorrect difference in the ones, and two superfluous increments of the subtrahends in the tens and hundreds). Combining the (dis-)agreements, we get for AM/TF the highest score $(6 − 1 = 5)$, and hence correctly recognize that the learner followed this method. Our scoring for Fig. 6(d) also correctly determines that the learner followed DC.

Complex Error Patterns. Some learner input is too erroneous to be associated with any of the available expert models. Consider Fig. 6(e), where the learner is mixing-up two expert algorithms, applying the Austrian method from left to right. Running our algorithmic debugger against all four expert models will yield the following irreducible (dis-)agreements. For AM and TF, $2 - 8 = -6$; for DC, $2 - 8 = -6$; and for LR, $4 - 6 = -2$. All diagnoses acknowledge that learners performed two correct borrow operations, but missed that corresponding paybacks were performed, albeit at wrong positions. While the LR method is identified as the most likely candidate, the diagnoses are unsatisfactory; they are not sufficiently close to the compound diagnosis "combines two algorithms". Here, it is advisable to complement expert with buggy models to capture such complex erroneous behaviour. If we add the respective buggy model to the existing expert models, a run of algorithmic debugging against the resulting five models clearly associates the learners' solutions in Fig. 6(e) with the buggy model.

4 Related Work

Logic Programming Techniques in Tutoring. There is only little recent research in the ITS community that builds upon logic programming and meta-level reasoning techniques. In [1], Beller & Hoppe also encode expert knowledge for doing subtraction in Prolog. To identify student error, a fail-safe meta-interpreter executes the Prolog code by instantiating its output parameter with the student answer. While standard Prolog interpretation would fail on erroneous outputs, a fail-safe meta-interpreter can recover from execution failure, and can also return an execution trace. Beller & Hoppe then formulate *error patterns*, which they match against the execution trace; with each match indicating a plausible student bug. It is unclear, however, how Beller & Hoppe deal with learner input that cannot be properly diagnosed against some given model, as the chosen model sets the stage for all possible execution traces and the patterns that can be defined on them. Their approach would need to be extended to multiple models, including a method to rank matches of error patterns to execution traces.

In Looi's tutoring system [4], Prolog itself is the domain of instruction, and diagnosing learner input is naturally defined in terms of analysing Prolog code. Learners' programs are debugged with the help of different LP techniques such as the automatic derivation of mode specifications, dataflow and type analysis, and heuristic code matching between expert and student code. Moreover, Looi employs Shapiro's algorithmic debugging techniques [6] in a standard way to test student code with regard to termination, correctness and completeness. It is interesting that Looi also mechanised the Oracle. Expert code that most likely corresponds to given learner code is identified and executed to obtain Oracle answers. *Given* the variety and quality of the expert code, Looi's approach should be able to track learners following multiple solution paths.

In [3], Kawai et al. also represent expert knowledge as a set of Prolog clauses; Shapiro's Model Inference System (MIS) [6], following an inductive logic programming approach, is used to synthesize learners' (potentially erroneous) procedure from expert knowledge and student answers. Once the procedure to fully capture learner behaviour is constructed, Shapiro's Program Diagnosis System, based upon standard algorithmic debugging, is used to identify students' misconceptions, *i.e.*, the bugs in the MIS-constructed program. The inductive approach helps addressing the issue that learners may follow one of many possible solution paths, *given* that the expert knowledge used for synthesis is carefully designed.

Both Kawai et al. and Looi's work use algorithmic debugging in the traditional sense, thus requiring an erroneous procedure. By turning Shapiro's algorithm on its head, we are able to identify simple and common learner errors by only using expert models. For the diagnosis of more complex error patterns, our approach naturally admits the use of additional, buggy, models. Our taking into account of multiple models adds to the robustness and the quality of the diagnosis, esp. given our well-defined criteria for differentiating between models.

Model Tracing Tutors. Most intelligent tutoring systems are based on production rule systems [2]. Here, declarative knowledge is encoded as working memory elements (WMEs) of the production system, and procedural knowledge is encoded as IF-THEN rules. *Model tracing* allows the recognition of learner behaviour: whenever the learner performs an action, the rule engine tries to find a sequence of rules that can reproduce the learner's action – and update the working memory correspondingly. With the successor state identified, the system can then provide adaptive feedback. Model tracing tutors, however, have two major drawbacks; high authoring costs, and the need to keep learners close to the correct solution path to tame the combinatorial explosion in the forward-reasoning rule engine.

We focus on the authoring cost. As production rule systems are forward-chaining, goal-directness must be induced by preconditions that check whether goal-encoding WMEs hold, or postconditions that maintain goal stacks or perform sub-goaling. Moreover, as conditions are framed in terms of WMEs, there is little if any abstraction. The programmer thus has the tedious burden to give a correct and complete specification of a rule's pre- and postconditions, glueing-together declarative and procedural knowledge. This makes rules verbose, and hence less readable and maintainable. When each expert rule is associated with buggy variants, a cognitive model of multi-column subtraction can grow quickly to more than fifty rules. Their authoring becomes increasingly complicated, costly, and a process prone to error. It is thus not surprising that there is no tutoring system based on production rules that supports more than a single algorithm for solving a given task. This is in line with O'Shea et al, who argues that model tracing systems have had only limited success in modelling arithmetic skills. They only "build single-level representations, with no support for modelling multiple algorithms" [5, p. 265].

5   Conclusion

In our previous work, we presented a variant of algorithmic debugging that compares learner action against a single expert model. We have extended our approach to multiple models. Our refined method now continues past the first and any subsequent irreducible disagreements until the entire execution tree of a Prolog program has been traversed. In the process, agreements and disagreements are being counted, and the code size being agreed upon taken into account.

These numbers are used to identify, among all available models, the algorithm the learner is most likely following. For the domain of multi-column subtraction, we have illustrated the effectiveness of our approach. Perfect learners get correct diagnoses at any stage of their problem solving process. Our approach is also robust for erroneous problem solving. For this, we have distinguished three cases. For problematic cases, where the lack of a central skill prevents any discrimination between given expert models, our multi-model analysis yields, nevertheless, a consistent set of irreducible disagreements that clearly indicates the missing, central skill in question. We have also illustrated the effectiveness of our method for standard cases where the central skills are observable, but other errors are made. For complex error pattern, where learners exhibit central skills, but perform them in a seemingly untimely or chaotic manner, our method is equally applicable. By complementing expert models with buggy models, and by subsequently analysing learner input in the context of both expert and buggy models, we yield diagnoses of high accuracy. Our extension has three benefits. First, the tutoring system can be less prescriptive as learners can now follow one of many predefined algorithms to tackle a given problem. Second, the quality of the diagnosis improves despite of the wider range of input that is taken into account. Third, the improvement comes with little computational costs.

References

1. Beller, S., Hoppe, U.: Deductive error reconstruction and classification in a logic programming framework. In: Brna, P., Ohlsson, S., Pain, H. (eds.) Proc. of the World Conference on Artificial Intelligence in Education, pp. 433–440 (1993)
2. Corbett, A.T., Anderson, J.R.: Knowledge tracing: Modeling the acquisition of proc. knowledge. User Modeling and User-Adapted Interaction 4, 253–278 (1995)
3. Kawai, K., Mizoguchi, R., Kakusho, O., Toyoda, J.: A framework for ICAI systems based on inductive inference and logic programming. New Generation Computing 5, 115–129 (1987)
4. Looi, C.-K.: Automatic debugging of Prolog programs in a Prolog Intelligent Tutoring System. Instructional Science 20, 215–263 (1991)
5. O'Shea, T., Evertsz, R., Hennessy, S., Floyd, A., Fox, M., Elson-Cook, M.: Design choices for an intelligent arithmetic tutor. In: Self, J. (ed.) Artificial Intelligence and Human Learning: Intelligent Computer-Aided Instruction, pp. 257–275. Chapman and Hall Computing (1988)
6. Shapiro, E.Y.: Algorithmic Program Debugging. ACM Distinguished Dissertations. MIT Press (1983); Thesis (Ph.D.) – Yale University (1982)
7. VanLehn, K.: Mind Bugs: the origins of proc. misconceptions. MIT Press (1990)
8. Young, R.M., O'Shea, T.: Errors in children's subtraction. Cognitive Science 5(2), 153–177 (1981)
9. Zinn, C.: Algorithmic debugging to support cognitive diagnosis in tutoring systems. In: Bach, J., Edelkamp, S. (eds.) KI 2011. LNCS, vol. 7006, pp. 357–368. Springer, Heidelberg (2011)
10. Zinn, C.: Program analysis and manipulation to reproduce learner's erroneous reasoning. In: Albert, E. (ed.) LOPSTR 2012. LNCS, vol. 7844, pp. 228–243. Springer, Heidelberg (2013)

Combining Conditional Random Fields and Background Knowledge for Improved Cyber Security

Carsten Elfers[1], Stefan Edelkamp[2], and Hartmut Messerschmidt[2]

[1] Neusta Software Development GmbH, 28217 Bremen, Germany
[2] Universität Bremen, 28359 Bremen, Germany

Abstract. This paper shows that AI-methods can improve detection of malicious network traffic. A novel method based on Conditional Random Fields combined with Tolerant Pattern Matching is presented. The proposed method uses background knowledge represented in a description logic ontology, user modeled patterns build on-top of this ontology and training examples from the application domain to improve the detection accuracy of IT incidents, particularly addressing the problem of incomplete information.

1 Introduction

The cyber criminal threat against the IT infrastructure is a well-known and steadily growing problem for many organizations. A single product, such as a firewall, an anti-virus program, or an Intrusion Detection System (IDS) is not capable of fulfilling the task of recognizing complex cyber attacks [1, p.665]. Therefore, complex IT networks are monitored by several of these products. During the years, the complexity of IT infrastructures and, therefore, the amount of security events from these sources have increased. Accordingly, the need for an efficient grouping and correlation of these events has grown. Large organizations, e.g., car manufacturers or financial institutes, have deployed Security Information and Event Management (SIEM) systems [14] to manage and detect relations between those events to detect possible IT incidents.

Since events related to critical IT incidents are sparse in the large amount of event data being processed by SIEM systems, sophisticated correlation approaches are needed. In this paper, we propose a novel correlation method which is based on Conditional Random Fields (CRF) and Tolerant Pattern Matching (TPM) for recognizing those incidents. The system is able to generalize or abstract expert knowledge as well as to learn from examples given during the application of the system (by the use of the CRF).

From the intrusion detection perspective, two incident detection methods are conceivable, i.e. anomaly detection [7,10,13,16] where each deviating system behavior of a previously trained normal behavior is suggested to be an incident, or a rule-based method [11,15,19,8] that detects incidents by correlating the input events with previously specified patterns. SIEM systems like the market-leading product ArcSight or the Symantec Security Information Manager typically use predefined rules to correlate the events [14]. While some products like NitroSecurity SIEM, AlientVault Unified SIEM, RSA enVision, or the Q1 Labs correlation (used by Enterasys, Juniper and Nortel) are making use of integrated anomaly detection methods (such as detecting baseline deviations), the final decision making is almost completely rule based.

I.J. Timm and M. Thimm (Eds.): KI 2013, LNAI 8077, pp. 284–287, 2013.

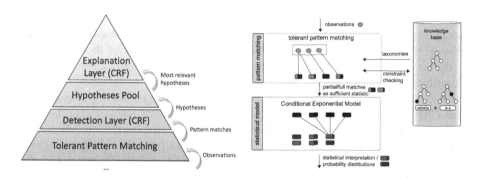

Fig. 1. Dataflow in the Proposed SIEM system and Inclusion of Background Knowledge

2   Our Approach of Combining TPM and CRFs

The application of a rule-based final decision making in the mentioned products links to the requirement of processing huge amounts of events and the problems inherent to anomaly detection such as an increased false-positive rate and the absence of an interpretation of the detected incident.However, the focus on rule-based methods leads to possibly unrecognized incidents due to a lack in the rule set. Therefore, we propose to solve this problem by combining Conditional Random Fields (CRF) [12] and Tolerant Pattern Matching (TPM) [5].

This approach can be understood as hybrid machine learning approach. Such kind of approaches have dominated the research for intrusion detection in the recent years [20]. They use different techniques to improve detection accuracy, such as preprocessing the data by clustering or by generating intermediate results for classification. Fig. 1 shows that we pre-process the data with TPM and post-process it by the exponential CRF model. The latter part takes the matching values of the TPM as input for a statistical interpretation of incident hypotheses. With this approach the partially matching patterns can be combined by a CRF to determine a probability for a serious security incident. Initially, modeled incidents can be used as a priori training data while this data can be successively refined by "real" training data from the application domain. This offers the possibility to easily adapt the combined approach by training which patterns are useful for the detection of incidents and which are less significant to improve the detection accuracy.

Beyond this, expert knowledge can still be modeled by the preprocessing of the TPM. It uses ontological representations, logical expressions and generalizations of them in the matchmaking process. The post-processing part takes the matching values of the TPM as input for a statistical interpretation of incident hypotheses by the use of CRF. We have chosen the TPM approach to fulfill the requirement of handling sparsity, to address the problem of incomplete background knowledge, and to transfer modeled background knowledge to unknown cases. Additionally, expert knowledge must be acquired by comprehensible concepts, like modeling logical expressions as in other SIEM systems. As CRFs cannot directly use or represent logical expressions, background knowledge has to be transformed.

Further, we propose to use two layers of CRFs, both sharing the same input features (the patterns) but different labels. The first layer is used to determine if a serious security incident has been occurred or not, so we use three labels for this layer to describe the threat resulting from the pattern matching values, i.e., the threat dangerous (describing that an incident occurred), suspicious (potentially an incident) or normal (no serious incident and most likely a false positive from the underlying sensor data). This CRF structure is very small and therefore most efficient for detecting the incidents out of huge amounts of sensor data. The artificial threat "suspicious" is used to keep some events for long-term correlation which might result in a dangerous threat by being combined with other events. The inference result can be presented to security officers to decide which incidents should be revisited in detail. After a security officer decides to investigate an incident, a second (more complex) CRF layer is used to find an appropriate explanation for the detected incident. Therefore, a probability distribution over all known incidents is determined. With this information, the security officer can assess which kind of incident or at least which most likely and most similar incidents have been detected to plan further investigations.

The modeling of incidents by experts often produces an artificial imbalance [4] between benign and malign incidents. This occurs since incidents are modeled without the information about how frequent incidents occur. This problem is reduced by learning from examples, but remains to be a challenge for the first deployment of the detection engine. Imbalanced data is a serious problem for several machine learning approaches [9] and a known intrusion detection problem [4]. We applied oversampling [2].

A widely applied training scheme for CRFs is Improved Iterative Scaling (IIS) [3]. However, one problem inherent in this algorithm is that it tends to overfit the data which we have found to be critical for the proposed combined approach. Therefore, we suggest to use regularization to overcome this problem. In regularization, the model parameters themselves are considered as random variables with a specified prior distribution. Smith et al. [18] discovered that different regularization priors "perform roughly equally well" if they are appropriately parameterized. With IIS, regularization and oversampling we are well-prepared to train the CRFs with examples as well as with modeled incidents.

3   Experimental Outcome

We have implemented the proposed novel method for detecting security incidents on a SIEM level of detection by the combination of CRFs and TPM. The technical report [6] provides detailed experiments for standard benchmarks and for sandnet data set consisting of recorded malware samples and their generated Snort events. These samples are a subset of the generated samples from the sandnet project [17]. One month (31 days) of traffic has been analyzed by a Snort IDS with the same rule set as used in the sandnet malware analysis. The resulting dataset has been filtered by using 24 static IP addresses to avoid that the benign dataset becomes contaminated by mobile computers with potential malware infections. The results show, that this combination can improve the true positive to false-positive ratio of current enterprise SIEM systems, and that it can be realized efficiently. Furthermore, the report shows which challenges should be considered while training the system and how they can be overcome (regularization and oversampling).

References

1. Anderson, R.J.: Security Engineering: A Guide to Building Dependable Distributed Systems, 2nd edn. Wiley Publishing, Inc. (2008)
2. Batista, G.E.A.P.A., Prati, R.C., Monard, M.C.: A study of the behavior of several methods for balancing machine learning training data. SIGKDD Explor. 6 (2004)
3. Berger, A.: The improved iterative scaling algorithm: A gentle introduction (1997)
4. Chawla, N.V., Japkowicz, N., Kotcz, A.: Editorial: special issue on learning from imbalanced data sets. SIGKDD Explor. Newsl. 6, 1–6 (2004)
5. Elfers, C., Edelkamp, S., Herzog, O.: Efficient tolerant pattern matching with constraint abstractions in description logic. In: Intern. Conf. on Agents and Artificial Intelligence (ICAART), pp. 256–261 (2012)
6. Elfers, C., Edelkamp, S., Messerschmidt, H., Sohr, K.: Advanced event correlation in security information and event management systems. Technical Report 71, TZI, Universität Bremen (2013)
7. Forrest, S., Perelson, A.S., Allen, L., Cherukuri, R.: Self-nonself discrimination in a computer. In: Symposium on Research in Security and Privacy, pp. 202–212 (1994)
8. Gonzalez, J.M., Paxson, V., Weaver, N.: Shunting: a hardware/software architecture for flexible, high-performance network intrusion prevention. In: ACM Conference on Computer and Communications Security, pp. 139–149 (2007)
9. Gu, Q., Cai, Z., Zhu, L., Huang, B.: Data mining on imbalanced data sets. In: Intern. Conf. on Advanced Computer Theory and Engineering, pp. 1020–1024 (December 2008)
10. Krügel, C., Toth, T., Kirda, E.: Service specific anomaly detection for network intrusion detection. In: ACM Symposium on Applied Computing, pp. 201–208 (2002)
11. Kumar, S., Spafford, E.H.: A Software Architecture to support Misuse Intrusion Detection. In: National Information Security Conference, pp. 194–204 (1995)
12. Lafferty, J., Zhu, X., Liu, Y.: Kernel conditional random fields: representation and clique selection. In: Intern. Conf. on Machine Learning (2004)
13. Laskov, P., Schaefer, C., Kotenko, I.: Intrusion detection in unlabeled data with quarter-sphere support vector machines. In: DIMVA, pp. 71–82 (2004)
14. Nicolett, M., Kavanagh, K.M.: Magic quadrant for security information and event management. Gartner Research document G00176034 (2010)
15. Paxson, V.: Bro: A system for detecting network intruders in real-time. In: Computer Networks, pp. 2435–2463 (1999)
16. Rieck, K., Laskov, P.: Language models for detection of unknown attacks in network traffic. Journal in Computer Virology 2, 243–256 (2007)
17. Rossow, C., Dietrich, C.J., Bos, H., Cavallaro, L., van Steen, M., Freiling, F.C., Pohlmann, N.: Sandnet: Network traffic analysis of malicious software. In: Building Analysis Datasets and Gathering Experience Returns for Security, pp. 78–88 (2011)
18. Smith, A., Osborne, M.: Regularisation techniques for conditional random fields: Parameterised versus parameter-free. In: Dale, R., Wong, K.-F., Su, J., Kwong, O.Y. (eds.) IJCNLP 2005. LNCS (LNAI), vol. 3651, pp. 896–907. Springer, Heidelberg (2005)
19. Sommer, R., Paxson, V.: Enhancing byte-level network intrusion detection signatures with context. In: 10th ACM Conference on Computer and Communications Security, CCS 2003, pp. 262–271 (2003)
20. Tsai, C.-F., Hsu, Y.-F., Lin, C.-Y., Lin, W.-Y.: Intrusion detection by machine learning: A review. Expert Systems with Applications 36(10), 11994–12000 (2009)

Adapting a Virtual Agent's Conversational Behavior by Social Strategies

Nikita Mattar and Ipke Wachsmuth

Artificial Intelligence Group, Bielefeld University
Universitätsstr. 25, 33615 Bielefeld, Germany
{nmattar,ipke}@techfak.uni-bielefeld.de

Abstract. Interpersonal encounters are a complex phenomenon in hu-
man-human interaction. As social encounters with virtual agents become
more important, these agents have to cope with problems of social perception, as well. To account for tasks concerned with the acquisition,
utilization, and recall of social information, we earlier proposed to equip
virtual agents with a Person Memory. In this paper we present how information available through a Person Memory enables the conversational
agent Max to tackle different interpersonal situations.

Keywords: conversational agents, intelligent virtual agents, human-
agent interaction, person memory, interpersonal encounters, social
information, person perception.

1 Introduction

In intelligent virtual agent research an important goal is to create agents that
are as believable as possible, motivated by the advancement of virtual agents
from tools to human-like partners. For instance, so called companion agents are
envisioned to interact over a long period of time with, or even beyond the life-
time of, their owners [8], [7]. Human-like memory systems, i.e., autobiographic
and episodic memories, are employed to improve believability of such agents [3],
[2]. However, these systems focus on the agent's own experiences. As conversational agents start to appear in everyday interaction scenarios, the question
arises if such egocentric memory systems are sufficient to handle requirements
that come up in social encounters. To be accepted as human-like conversational
partners, virtual agents may have to cope with various interpersonal situations.
For instance, in initial encounters *altruistic* behavior may seem appropriate for
a companion agent, whereas a slightly *selfish* behavior may be more adequate in
situations where a companion agent acts on the behalf of its owner.

In this paper we present how information of a model of Person Memory can
be exploited to adapt a virtual agent to its interlocutors according to different social situations. In the following, social memory tasks and social memory
strategies used in the model are described. Brief sample dialogs demonstrate how
the Person Memory can be exploited to tackle social encounters by using social
strategies: an altruistic, a balanced, and a selfish strategy. The paper concludes
with an outlook on future work.

I.J. Timm and M. Thimm (Eds.): KI 2013, LNAI 8077, pp. 288–291, 2013.
© Springer-Verlag Berlin Heidelberg 2013

2   Adapting Conversational Behavior by Social Strategies

In order to examine and grasp effects of so called *human person perception* – the acquisition, utilization, and recall of social information during human interpersonal encounters –, we proposed to equip virtual agents with a Person Memory [5]. To exploit information provided by the Person Memory in social situations, *Social Memory Tasks* and *Social Strategies* are a crucial part of our model. Social Memory Tasks define how the information is exploited. They are divided into *core* and *extended* tasks. Core tasks handle basic actions, like storage of new, or retrieval of existing, information. Extended tasks carry out more context based information retrieval and manipulation on the data, like calculating probabilities for the use of dialog sequences (*"Question/Answer"* vs. more complex sequences like *"Question/Counter/Probe/Reply"*, cf. [6]), or selecting a topic according to different categories (*"communication"*, *"immediate"*, *"external"*, cf. [1]). Furthermore, extended tasks can be exchanged dynamically at run time. This allows to define tasks including different information, for instance, when selecting a topic the agent should bring up during conversation.

Social strategies are used in this model of Person Memory to activate tasks appropriate for a situation. So far, they consist of a trigger that is sensitive to a certain social situation and a mapping of social memory tasks to keywords that are used to identify tasks within the Person Memory. When a strategy is activated by a situation, its associated tasks are registered within the Person Memory. The registered tasks are used subsequently when a task with an according keyword is scheduled for execution. Algorithm 1 depicts a sample implementation of a social memory task as used by a balanced social strategy. Here, a topic for conversation is selected according to the information of the interlocutor and the agent that is available in the Person Memory. An altruistic, or a selfish, task can be obtained from the balanced task by returning the interest of the interlocutor, or the agent, respectively.

Algorithm 1. Pseudocode for selecting a topic in a balanced strategy

---

function PERFORM_TASK
    topics_self = pmem→executeTask("getTopicsFor","self")
    topics_other = pmem→executeTask("getTopicsFor","other")

    candidate_self = getInterestWithMaxUtility(topics_self)
    candidate_other = getInterestWithMaxUtility(topics_other)
    candidate_both = getInterestWithMaxUtility(topics_self $\cap$ topics_other)

    return randomlySelect(candidate_self, candidate_other, candidate_both)
end function

This way, information contained in the Person Memory, together with strategies and accompanying tasks that influence how the information is exploited, allow for an adaptation of the agent to different social encounters.

3   Sample Dialogs

The following dialog excerpts (translated to English) demonstrate how one aspect – choice of utterances – of the conversational style of the agent Max [4] is adapted by the use of social strategies. While the current implementation allows to adapt further aspects, the capabilities of the Person Memory can be demonstrated here by adapting a single feature (yet the resulting dialogs may appear somewhat superficial).

Altruistic Strategy

Max:	Hello Paula!	
Max:	Do you like music?	[source="other"]
Paula:	Yes of course.	
Max:	Do you have a favorite music band?	[source="other"]
Paula:	I don't really have one.	
Max:	Have you seen the soccer match on television yesterday?	[source="other"]

Balanced Strategy

Max:	Hello Paula!	
Max:	Do you like music?	[source="other"]
Paula:	Yes of course.	
Max:	Looks like we have something in common!	[source="both"]
Max:	Did you know that my favorite music band is Kraftwerk?	[source="self"]
Paula:	No, I didn't know that.	
Max:	Have you seen the soccer match on television yesterday?	[source="other"]

Selfish Strategy

Max:	Hello Paula!	
Max:	Did you know that I really love chess?	[source="self"]
Paula:	Yes, I think you mentioned it before.	
Max:	Did you listen to the latest album of Kraftwerk yet?	[source="self"]
Paula:	No, I didn't.	
Max:	Did you know that my favorite music band is Kraftwerk?	[source="self"]

3.1   Discussion

The possibility to change between memory tasks based on different social strategies allows Max to adapt to different application scenarios. In the first case an altruistic strategy is used, so Max focuses on the interests of its interlocutor and avoids remarks about own interests. When using the balanced strategy, Max selects interests of the interlocutor as well as of his own as topics for conversation. In the third example, Max completely ignores his interlocutor's interests.

In contrast to the first case, interests of the agent are only selected as topics for conversation when using a selfish strategy.

4 Future Work

In this paper, we demonstrated how information contained in a model of Person Memory can be utilized to adapt a virtual agent's behavior according to social strategies. An evaluation of the model will be conducted when the Person Memory is ready to be deployed in a real-life application, like the museum setting the agent Max already operates in. More aspects of conversational behavior than touched upon in this paper will be adapted, e.g., the dialog structure and topic categories (cf. 2). By that, we expect to obtain hints on promising combinations that lead to more natural dialogs in different social settings.

References

1. Breuing, A., Wachsmuth, I.: Let's Talk Topically with Artificial Agents! Providing Agents with Humanlike Topic Awareness in Everyday Dialog Situations. In: Proceedings of the 4th International Conference on Agents and Artificial Intelligence, ICAART 2012, pp. 62–71. SciTePress (2012)
2. Brom, C., Lukavský, J., Kadlec, R.: Episodic Memory for Human-like Agents and Human-like Agents for Episodic Memory. International Journal of Machine Consciousness 2(02), 227–244 (2010)
3. Ho, W., Dautenhahn, K.: Towards a Narrative Mind: The Creation of Coherent Life Stories for Believable Virtual Agents. In: Prendinger, H., Lester, J.C., Ishizuka, M. (eds.) IVA 2008. LNCS (LNAI), vol. 5208, pp. 59–72. Springer, Heidelberg (2008)
4. Kopp, S., Gesellensetter, L., Krämer, N.C., Wachsmuth, I.: A Conversational Agent as Museum Guide – Design and Evaluation of a Real-World Application. In: Panayiotopoulos, T., Gratch, J., Aylett, R.S., Ballin, D., Olivier, P., Rist, T. (eds.) IVA 2005. LNCS (LNAI), vol. 3661, pp. 329–343. Springer, Heidelberg (2005)
5. Mattar, N., Wachsmuth, I.: A Person Memory for an Artificial Interaction Partner. In: Proceedings of the KogWis 2010, pp. 69–70 (2010)
6. Mattar, N., Wachsmuth, I.: Small Talk Is More than Chit-Chat – Exploiting Structures of Casual Conversations for a Virtual Agent. In: Glimm, B., Krüger, A. (eds.) KI 2012. LNCS, vol. 7526, pp. 119–130. Springer, Heidelberg (2012)
7. O'Hara, K.: Arius in cyberspace: Digital Companions and the limits of the person. In: Wilks, Y. (ed.) Close Engagements with Artificial Companions: Key Social, Psychological, Ethical and Design Issues, p. 68. John Benjamins Publishing Company (2010)
8. Wilks, Y.: Artificial Companions as a new kind of interface to the future Internet. Research Report 13, Oxford Internet Institute/University of Sheffield (2006)

Encoding HTN Heuristics in PDDL Planning Instances
(Extended Abstract)

Christoph Mies and Joachim Hertzberg

Osnabrück University
Albrechtstraße 28, 49076 Osnabrück, Germany
{cmies,joachim.hertzberg}@uos.de

1   Contribution and Related Work

The paper sketches a transformation process that allows *Hierarchical Task Network (HTN)* based domain-dependent planning heuristics to be encoded into *Planning Domain Definition Language (PDDL)* [1] planning instances. SHOP2 [2] is chosen as a representative of the many different HTN planning approaches in the literature, but the paper discusses modifications of the transformation applicable to other HTN based planning approaches, too. The evaluation, based on five state-of-the art PDDL planners from the public domain, shows that incorporating HTN heuristics accelerates the planning process in terms of computation time and improves the quality of the resulting plans.

Automated Planning is a well-known and powerful decision making technique. Planning systems are applied to decision problems, called planning instances, from various application areas. They exploit abstract domain independent search heuristics for problem solving. In this paper, we encode HTN based domain-dependent planning heuristics into PDDL planning instances.

PDDL was designed to be a standard language for planning instances. Its motivation was to make different planning systems comparable and planning instances re-usable to create standard benchmarks for planning systems [1]. The maxim behind the language specification was to model "physics, not advice" [1, p. 4]. Additionally, the language was designed to be neutral, i.e. "it doesn't favor any particular planning system" [1, p. 4]. These prerequisites set up barriers for planning systems exploiting domain-dependent search heuristics. In particular, PDDL does not fulfill the input requirements of HTN based planning approaches. For the first *International Planning Competition (IPC)*, McDermott noticed that "researchers with hierarchical planners lost interest rapidly as it became clear how great the distance was between PDDL and the kind of input their planners expected" [1, p. 17].

The most important advantages of considering domain-dependent planning heuristics during planning are these: Firstly, domain experts are usually able to provide heuristics that enable *fast generation* of plans with *high quality*. Additionally, the resulting plans usually *match the expectations* of the domain designer, since the plan generation can be *explained* with respect to the given HTNs, i.e. the designer can *trace* the task decomposition and adapt it if required.

I.J. Timm and M. Thimm (Eds.): KI 2013, LNAI 8077, pp. 292–295, 2013.
© Springer-Verlag Berlin Heidelberg 2013

The contribution of this paper is the sketch of a translation of a planning instance of one well-known representative of the HTN planning approaches, SHOP2, to PDDL. As a result of the introduced transformation, we encode the HTN based domain-dependent planning heuristics of SHOP2 planning instances into PDDL planning instances, which forces the PDDL planner to follow SHOP2's task decomposition strategy. Thus, we close the gap between the input needed for SHOP2 and PDDL's expressiveness. Due to lack of space, we concentrate on the management of open SHOP2 tasks in the PDDL planning instances. This management is flexible enough to support the encoding of other HTN based planning approaches, too.

The idea to transform a planning formalism incorporating control knowledge to domain-independent formalisms is not new. Fritz et al [3] provide a translation from CONGOLOG, a well-known situation calculus based planning formalism, to PDDL 2.1 [4]. The concept of threads employed in the transformation in this paper is inspired by their approach. In the definition of the transformation, we focused on the generation of efficiently solvable planning instances. Since Fritz's transformation handles CONGOLOG, a more expressive formalism, we expect their generated planning instances to be not as efficiently solvable as ours.

Alford et al [5] provide a transformation from the restricted HTN variant *Total-Order Simple Task Network Planning* [6, ch. 11.3] to PDDL. Our introduced transformation sketch can be modified to support different HTN based planning approaches, especially this one.

Another way to incorporate HTN heuristics into planning is *hybrid planning*. An exemplary approach is introduced by Schattenberg et al [7], who combine HTN based domain-dependent heuristics with partial order causal link (POCL) planning. They abstract the planning operators: As in most planning approaches, an operator has a precondition as well as an effect to model when it is executable and how the world is changed due to its execution. But in addition, it can have partial plans as operator decomposition.

2   Transformation Sketch

Due to lack of space, we only sketch the transformation of planning instances containing HTN definitions to PDDL instances roughly. We have chosen SHOP2 as an exemplary HTN planning formalism.

Each SHOP2 language entity is transformed to a PDDL construct. Basically, SHOP2 tasks and task networks are encoded by PDDL predicates; operators and methods by PDDL actions. Most importantly, the PDDL planning instance must enforce the transformed planning system to follow the SHOP2 task decomposition strategy, which is encoded into the PDDL planning instances.

The key concept of the transformation is the book-keeping of *open tasks* during planning, i.e. tasks that have not yet been accomplished in the current world state. We perform the marking with two types of technical objects that we insert into the PDDL planning instance: **thread** and **stackitem**. When several tasks have to be solved sequentially, they are bound to the same thread object. If not, the tasks are bound to several thread objects. Each thread has its own stack, which ensures the correct sequential order of its tasks. PDDL requires a finite number of objects in the domain and does not allow numerics as arguments for actions [4, p. 68]. Thus, we have to provide enough thread and stack item objects in the PDDL planning instance in advance. This restriction regards the number of open tasks that can be represented in one PDDL state. The two related approaches [3,5] face similar restrictions. Both use a finite number of objects representing a finite counter.

Now, how many thread and stack item objects are needed in a PDDL planning instance to solve the problem? Unfortunately, the answer is not simple and requires an analysis of the SHOP2 planning instance at hand. To determine the required number of thread and stack item objects, we have to investigate all possible applications of the hierarchical task networks. In terms of SHOP2, we have to determine the possible call hierarchies of the given methods. The number of available threads in a planning instance denotes the number of open tasks that can be solved in parallel and the number of stack items limits the number of open tasks that can be assigned to each thread. Note that the number of required marking objects is not proportional to the resulting plan length, since long plans can be generated by short recursive call chains of methods.

From a logical point of view, the introduction of two object types, thread and stack item, is not needed. The thread type would suffice, since parallel as well as a sequential task relations can be expressed by explicit called-by relations. The management of the thread objects is complex, since we have to ensure that whenever a new thread is chosen by the PDDL planning system, exactly one thread is chosen. The management of stack items is simple. It is possible to employ a stack data structure, since "SHOP2 generates the steps of each plan in the same order that those steps will later be executed" [2, p. 379].

To adapt the introduced transformation to other HTN planning approaches, the marking has to be modified. For example, we consider the HTN definition *Simple Task Network (STN)* [6, ch. 11.2]. The method definition is similar to that of SHOP2, but only allows one single precondition and one decomposition. STNs are used by Alford et al [5] (cf. Section 1) in combination with the planning algorithm *Total-Order STN Planning* [6, ch. 11.3]. This algorithm also generates the plan steps in their final execution order as SHOP2 does. Additionally, the considered task networks are totally ordered. When transforming planning instances of this formalism, our transformation needs exactly one thread and several stack items. Planning instances of the planning algorithm *Partial-Order STN Planning* [6, ch. 11.4] can also be transformed by our approach with minimal modifications.

3   Conclusion

We have sketched an approach to encode HTNs containing domain-dependent planning heuristics in PDDL planning instances. Of the many different variants of hierarchical task networks in the literature, we have chosen SHOP2 as representative HTN based planning formalism. Encoding domain-dependent HTNs containing planning heuristics to a PDDL is advantageous, because this encoding can speed up the planning process, it can improve the quality of the resulting plans and it may raise the acceptance of human domain experts.

We performed a first evaluation with five different PDDL planning systems (PROBE, SGPLAN, LAMA-2011, CBP and CBP2) being involved[1]. They have been applied to the transformed planning instances and, as comparison, to pure PDDL instances without HTN search heuristics. Four of five PDDL systems solve the enriched instances faster, with improved quality or even larger planning instances when solving the transformed planning instance.

The two related approaches introduced in Section 1 [3,5] suffer from the same restriction as our transformation does: PDDL requires that all available (finitely many) objects are defined in the planning instance. Our transformation is, amongst others, able to handle the HTN based planning algorithms transformed by Alford et al [5]. GOLOG, the variant handled by Fritz et al [3], is a very rich formalism. Thus, we expect our transformation to result in more efficiently solvable PDDL planning instances.

In future work, we will apply the transformation to other domains from the literature for further experiments. Then, the cooperation of pure PDDL parts and encoded domain-dependent heuristics within the same PDDL planning instance is of interest. If there are no powerful HTN heuristics for parts of the application domain, the PDDL planning system should solve these parts. Hybrid planning, e.g. [7], exploits such a co-existence of HTN and non-HTN planning and profits from the strengths of both formalisms.

References

1. McDermott, D.: The 1998 AI Planning Systems Competition. AI Magazine 21(2), 35–55 (2000)
2. Nau, D., Au, T.-C., Ilghami, O., Kuter, U., Murdock, W., Wu, D., Yaman, F.: SHOP2: An HTN Planning System. JAIR 20, 379–404 (2003)
3. Fritz, C., Baier, J.A., McIlraith, S.A.: ConGolog, Sin Trans: Compiling ConGolog into Basic Action Theories for Planning and Beyond. In: KR 2008, Sydney, Australia, September 16-19, pp. 600–610 (2008)
4. Fox, M., Long, D.: PDDL2.1: An Extension to PDDL for Expressing Temporal Planning Domains. JAIR 20, 51–124 (2003)
5. Alford, R., Kuter, U., Nau, D.: Translating HTNs to PDDL: A Small Amount of Domain Knowledge Can Go a Long Way. In: IJCAI 2009, pp. 1629–1634. Morgan Kaufmann Publishers Inc., San Francisco (2009)
6. Ghallab, M., Nau, D., Traverso, P.: Automated Planning: Theory and Praxis. Morgan Kaufmann Publishers, Boston (2004)
7. Schattenberg, B., Weigl, A., Biundo, S.: Hybrid planning using flexible strategies. In: Furbach, U. (ed.) KI 2005. LNCS (LNAI), vol. 3698, pp. 249–263. Springer, Heidelberg (2005)

---

[1] See http://www.inf.uos.de/kbs/htn2pddl.html for input files, domain description and evaluation results etc.

Towards Benchmarking Cyber-Physical Systems in Factory Automation Scenarios

Tim Niemueller[1], Daniel Ewert[2], Sebastian Reuter[2], Ulrich Karras[3],
Alexander Ferrein[4], Sabina Jeschke[2], and Gerhard Lakemeyer[1]

[1] Knowledge-based Systems Group, RWTH Aachen University, Germany
{niemueller,gerhard}@kbsg.rwth-aachen.de
[2] Institute Cluster IMA/ZLW & IfU, RWTH Aachen University, Germany
first.last@ima-zlw-ifu.rwth-aachen.de
[3] Festo Didaktik
ulrich.karras@t-online.de
[4] Electrical Engineering Department, Aachen Univ. of Appl. Sc., Germany
ferrein@fh-aachen.de

Abstract. A new trend in automation is to deploy so-called cyber-physical systems (CPS) which combine computation with physical processes. In future factory automation scenarios, mobile robots will play an important role to help customizing the production process, for instance, by transporting semi-products and raw materials to the machines. Therefore it will be important to compare the performance of mobile robots in such future logistics tasks. In this paper we sketch how the novel RoboCup Logistics League with its automated referee and overhead tracking system can be developed into a standard benchmark for logistics application in factory automation scenarios.

1 Introduction

A new trend in automation is to deploy so-called cyber-physical systems (CPS) to a larger extent. These systems combine computation with physical processes. They include embedded computers and networks which monitor and control the physical processes and have a wide range of applications in assisted living, advanced automotive systems, energy conservation, environmental and critical infrastructure control, or manufacturing [1]. In particular, mobile robots will be deployed for transportation tasks, where they have to get semi-finished products in place to be machined in time. In this new and emerging field, it will be very important to evaluate and compare the performances of robots in real-world scenarios. Hence, real-world benchmarks for logistics scenarios for CPS will be required. In [2], Dillmann mentions three essential aspects for a robot benchmark: (1) the robot needs to perform a real mission, (2) the benchmark is accepted in the field, and (3) the task has a precise definition. Furthermore, features such as repeatability, independency and unambiguity are required together with a performance metrics to measure the outcome of the task. This implies that ground-truth data are available in order to measure the performance objectively.

I.J. Timm and M. Thimm (Eds.): KI 2013, LNAI 8077, pp. 296–299, 2013.

In this paper we show that the novel RoboCup *Logistics League Sponsored By Festo* (LLSF) is well-suited for benchmarking logistics scenarios. The rest of this paper is organized as follows. In the next section we briefly overview the Logistics League and outline some interesting challenges of the league in Sect. 3. In Sect. 4 we show how the LLSF can become a benchmark test for logistic scenarios. Then we conclude.

2   The Logistics League Sponsored by Festo

In this section, we introduce the *Logistics League Sponsored by Festo* (LLSF) as a novel league under the roof of the RoboCup Federation. The objective of the LLSF is the following. Teams of robots have to transport semi-finished products from machine to machine in order to produce some final product according to some given production plan. Machines can break down, products may have inferior quality, additional important orders come in and need to be machined at a higher prior-ity. For the LLSF, a team consisting of up to three robots starts in the game area of about 5.6 m × 5.6 m. A number of semi-finished products is represented by RFID-tagged *pucks*. Each is in a particular state, from

Fig. 1. A LLSF competition during the RoboCup 2012 in Mexico City

raw material through intermediate steps to being a final product. The state can-not be read by the robot but must be tracked and communicated among the robots of a team. On the playing field are *machines*, RFID devices with a signal light indicating their processing status. When placed on a proper machine type, a puck changes its state according to the machine specification. The outcome and machine state is indicated by particular light signals. During the game a num-ber of different semi-finished products need to be produced with ten machines on the playing field. Orders are posted to the robots requesting particular final products to be delivered to specific delivery gates and in specified time slots. All teams use the same robot base, a Festo Robotino which may be equipped with additional sensor devices and computing power, but only within certain limits.

3   Challenges in the LLSF

The LLSF poses a number of very interesting AI and robotics research ques-tions to be addressed ranging from planning algorithms for flexible supply chain optimization, path planning, dealing with incomplete information and noisy per-ception to multi-robot cooperation. The robots need to be autonomous, detect the pucks, detect and identify the light signals from the machines, know where they are and where to deliver the final product to. Basic robotics problems such as localization, navigation, collision avoidance, computer vision for the pucks and the light signals needs to be solved. Of course, all these modules have to be integrated into an overall robust software architecture. On top of that, the teams need to schedule their production plan. This opens the field to various concepts from full supply chain optimization approaches to simpler job market approaches. If the robots are able to prioritize the production of certain goods they can maximize the points they can achieve. In order to avoid resource conflicts (there can only be one robot at a machine at a time), to update other robots about the current states of machines and pucks, and to delegate (partial) jobs of the production process, inter-robot communication is required. There is a variety of complex scenarios that is captured by the LLSF which are important for evaluating the performance of logistics robots. Currently, only some tasks and command variables of the production process are taken into account. In the future, further tasks can be defined for evaluating different objectives such as efficient machine usage, throughput optimization, or energy efficient production. In the next section we outline how the LLSF can be developed into a benchmark for logistics scenarios before we conclude.

4 Developing the LLSF into a Benchmark

What features are required for the LLSF to become a benchmark for logistics scenarios for mobile robots? Following [2], features for a benchmark are: (1) the robot needs to perform a real mission; (2) the benchmark must be accepted in the field; (3) the task has a precise definition; (4) repeatability, independency, unambiguity of the test; (5) collection of ground-truth data.

The key question is what are the important aspects which a standard test must include. An important dimension for logistics scenarios for CPS are *supply chain optimization* (SCO) in an uncertain domain with failing machines and varying product qualities. Here, not only a single-robot scenario can be tested but also a multi-robot scenario can be benchmarked. The important aspect that can be tested is the *performance of the robot system* as such, e.g., how good are the path planning or collision avoidance capabilities of the robot while being deployed in a real task. The tasks can vary from different command variables such as *overall output of goods* or *operating grade of a machine*. In order to evaluate these aspects, we make use of an (semi-)automated referee system [3] which keeps track of the score that is achieved by the competitor and an overhead camera tracking system [4] (which is being tested at the moment) which provides ground-truth data of the positions of the robots and products (pucks) during the game. Additionally, the referee box keeps track of the machine states, so that the whole game can be reconstructed from the logged data. This allows for an unambiguous benchmark as each (automated) decision can be retraced. As the behavior of the machines can be programmed, each team could get the same machine setup. This ensures repeatability of the test. Some quantitative result of the supply chain optimization aspects such as throughput could fairly easily be judged by the score that a team achieves during a game. Other robotics tasks such as path planning or shortest paths metrics could be tracked with the overhead tracking system. An overall score could be established in comparison to a reference algorithm. The standard tests we are aiming at are to test capabilities of supply chain optimization in single- and multi-robot scenarios and integrated robotics tasks. The former can be tested by varying the command variables of the production process in different production scenarios, the latter can be tested with the provided ground-truth data. This way, parameters as effective path planning, collision avoidance and cooperative team behavior can be evaluated.

5 Conclusion

In this paper, we proposed the novel RoboCup Logistic League Sponsored by Festo as a robot competition benchmark for the emerging research field for cyber-physical system on the backdrop that logistic robots will become ever more important in future production scenarios. The LLSF is an interesting scenario for testing supply chain optimization algorithms where the production plan is carried out by robots in a real (mock-up) assembly line, either as a single-robot or even as a multi-robot problem. An interesting aspect is that the environment is uncertain, machines can fail, products can have inferior quality. Another source of uncertainty is the robot itself. The produced goods are carried around by real robots. This requires to deal with incomplete information, address noisy sensing, and build integrated logistic robot systems.

Besides the interesting aspects of logistics scenarios that are captured by the LLSF, for the LLSF an automated referee system (referee box) [3] and an overhead tracking system has been implemented. The referee box keeps track of all important events of the game, tracking the states of the machines during the game and points scored by a team. Together with the overhead robot tracking system, which has been adopted from a tracking system from RoboCup's Small-Size League [4], the referee box is also able to track the robots' and the products' positions during the game. This allows for a complete log-file of the match. With this information automated evaluations of games can be done allowing to compare different aspects of logistics scenarios. With these systems in place the LLSF has a high potential to develop into a standard testbed for logistics tasks.

References

1. Lee, E.: Cyber Physical Systems: Design Challenges. In: 11th IEEE International Symposium on Object Oriented Real-Time Distributed Computing (ISORC 2008), pp. 363–369 (2008)
2. Dillmann, R.: Benchmarks for robotics research. Technical report, EURON (2004), http://www.cas.kth.se/euron/euron-deliverables/ka1-10-benchmarking.pdf
3. Niemueller, T., Ewert, D., Reuter, S., Ferrein, A., Jeschke, S., Lakemeyer, G.: RoboCup Logistics League Sponsored by Festo: A Competitive Factory Automation Testbed. In: RoboCup Symposium 2013 (in press, 2013)
4. Zickler, S., Laue, T., Birbach, O., Wongphati, M., Veloso, M.: SSL-Vision: The Shared Vision System for the RoboCup Small Size League. In: Baltes, J., Lagoudakis, M.G., Naruse, T., Ghidary, S.S. (eds.) RoboCup 2009. LNCS, vol. 5949, pp. 425–436. Springer, Heidelberg (2010)

Syntactic Similarity for Ranking Database Answers Obtained by Anti-Instantiation

Lena Wiese

Institute of Computer Science
University of Göttingen, Goldschmidtstrasse 7, 37077 Göttingen, Germany
lena.wiese@uni-goettingen.de

Abstract. Flexible query answering can be implemented in an intelligent database system by query generalization to obtain answers close to a user's intention although not answering his query exactly. In this paper, we focus on the generalization operator "Anti-Instantiation" and investigate how syntactic similarity measures can be used to rank generalized queries with regard to their closeness to the original query.

1 Introduction

Searching for data in a conventional database is a tedious task because a correct and exact formulation of the query conditions matching a user's query intention is often difficult to achieve. This is why users need the support of intelligent and flexible query answering mechanisms. *Cooperative* (or *flexible*) query answering systems internally revise failing user queries and return answers to the user that are more informative for the user than just an empty answer. In this paper, we devise a ranking based on similarity of conjunctive queries that are generated by a generalization procedure. With this ranking the database system has the option to only answer the queries most similar to the original query.

In this paper we focus on flexible query answering for conjunctive queries. Throughout this article we assume a logical language $\mathscr{L}$ consisting of a finite set of predicate symbols (for example denoted *Ill*, *Treat* or P), a possibly infinite set *dom* of constant symbols (for example denoted Mary or a), and an infinite set of variables (for example denoted x or y). A query formula Q is a conjunction of atoms with some variables X occurring freely (that is, not bound by variables); that is, $Q(X) = L_{i_1} \wedge \ldots \wedge L_{i_n}$. The CoopQA system [1] applies three generalization operators to a conjunctive query (which – among others – can already be found in the seminal paper of Michalski [2]). In this paper we focus only on the **Anti-Instantiation** (AI) operator that replaces a constant (or a variable occurring at least twice) in Q with a new variable y.

Example 1. As a running example, we consider a hospital information system that stores illnesses and treatments of patients as well as their personal information (like address and age) in the following three database tables:

I.J. Timm and M. Thimm (Eds.): KI 2013, LNAI 8077, pp. 300–303, 2013.

Ill	PatientID	Diagnoses
	8457	Cough
	2784	Flu
	2784	Bronchitis
	8765	Asthma

Treat	PatientID	Prescription
	8457	Inhalation
	2784	Inhalation
	8765	Inhalation

Info	PatientID	Name	Address
	8457	Pete	Main Street 5, Newtown
	2784	Mary	New Street 3, Newtown
	8765	Lisa	Main Street 20, Oldtown

The example query $Q(x_1, x_2, x_3) = Ill(x_1, Flu) \wedge Ill(x_1, Cough) \wedge Info(x_1, x_2, x_3)$ asks for all the patient IDs x_1 as well as names x_2 and addresses x_3 of patients that suffer from both flu and cough. This query fails with the given database tables as there is no patient with both flu and cough. However, the querying user might instead be interested in the patient called Mary who is ill with both flu and bronchitis. For $Q(x_1, x_2, x_3) = Ill(x_1, Flu) \wedge Ill(x_1, Cough) \wedge Info(x_1, x_2, x_3)$ an example generalization with AI is $Q^{AI}(x_1, x_2, x_3, y) = Ill(x_1, Flu) \wedge Ill(x_1, y) \wedge Info(x_1, x_2, x_3)$. It results in an non-empty (and hence informative) answer: $Ill(2748, Flu) \wedge Ill(2748, Bronchitis) \wedge Info(2748, Mary, 'New\ Street\ 3, Newtown')$.

2   Similarity Measures

Based on feature sets of two objects a and b, similarity between these two objects can be calculated by means of different similarity measures. That is, if A is a feature set of a and B is the corresponding feature set of b, then $A \cap B$ is the set of their common features, $A \setminus B$ is the set of features that are only attributed to A, and $B \setminus A$ is the set of features that are only attributed to B. We obtain the cardinalities of each set: $l = |A \cap B|$, $m = |A \setminus B|$, and $n = |B \setminus A|$ and use them as input to specific similarity measures. In this paper, we focus on the ratio model [3] (in particular, one of its special cases called Jaccard index).

Definition 1 (Tversky's Ratio Model [3], Jaccard Index). *A similarity measure sim between two objects a and b can be represented by the ratio of features common to both a and b and the joint features of a and b using a non-negative scale f and two non-negative scalars α and β. The Jaccard index is a special form of the ratio model where $\alpha = \beta = 1$ and f is the cardinality $| \cdot |$:*

$$sim_{jacc}(a, b) = \frac{|A \cap B|}{|A \cap B| + |A \setminus B| + |B \setminus A|} = \frac{|A \cap B|}{|A \cup B|} = \frac{l}{l + m + n}$$

Ferilli et al [4] introduce a novel similarity measure that is able to also differentiate formulas even if $l = 0$; this measure is parameterized by a non-negative scalar α. We call this similarity measure α-similarity and let $\alpha = 0.5$ by default.

Definition 2 (α-Similarity [4]). *The α-similarity between two objects a and b consists of the weighted sum (weighted by a non-negative scalar α, and adding*

1 to the numerators and 2 to the denominators) of the ratios of shared features divided by the features of a alone and the features of b alone whenever $a \neq b$:

$$sim_\alpha(a,b) = \alpha \cdot \frac{|A \cap B| + 1}{|B| + 2} + (1 - \alpha) \cdot \frac{|A \cap B| + 1}{|A| + 2} = \alpha \cdot \frac{l+1}{l+n+2} + (1-\alpha) \cdot \frac{l+1}{l+m+2}$$

In case $a = b$ the similarity is 1: $sim_\alpha(a,a) = 1$.

3   Similarity for Anti-Instantiation

We calculate the similarity between the original query Q and a query Q^{AI^*} obtained by the AI operator. We concentrate on the following sets of features:

Predicates in the query: The predicates of Q and Q^{AI^*} are identical: $Pred(Q) = Pred(Q^{AI^*})$ leading to similarity 1 on the predicate feature.

Constants in the query: The set of constants in Q^{AI^*} might be reduced compared to Q: $Const(Q^{AI^*}) \subseteq Const(Q)$; we have $l \leq 0$, $m \leq 0$ and $n = 0$.

Variables in the query: Because each AI step introduces a new variable, we have $Vars(Q) \subseteq Vars(Q^{AI^*})$ and hence $l \leq 0$, $m = 0$ and $n \leq 1$.

Star of a literal: For each literal L_i of Q the amount of connections to other literals is always greater or equal to the amount of connections in Q^{AI^*}. We borrow the definition of a star of a literal [4] that contains all predicate symbols of other literals that share a term with the chosen literal. We denote $Terms(L_i, Q)$ the set of terms of literal L_i in Q.

Definition 3 (Star of a literal [4])). *For a literal L_i in a given query Q we define the star of L_i to be a set of predicate symbols as follows*

$$Star(L_i, Q) = \{P \mid \text{ there is } L_j \in Q, i \neq j, \text{ such that } L_j = P(t_1, \ldots t_k) \text{ and }$$
$$Terms(L_j, Q) \cap Terms(L_i, Q) \neq \emptyset\} \subseteq Pred(Q)$$

Hence, $Star(L_i, Q^{AI^*}) \subseteq Star(L_i, Q)$ and $l \leq 0$, $m \leq 0$ and $n = 0$.

Relational positions of a term: Lastly, we borrow the notion of relational features from [4]. Such a relational feature of a term is the position of the term inside a literal $L_j = P(t_1, \ldots t_k)$: If a term t appears as the h-th attribute in literal L_i (that is, $t_h = t$ for $1 \leq h \leq k$), then $P.h$ is a relational feature of t. Let then $Rel(t, Q)$ denote the multiset of all relational features of a term t in query Q. For a term t in Q some its positions might be lost in Q^{AI^*}. Hence, $Rel(t, Q^{AI^*}) \subseteq Rel(t, Q)$ and $l \leq 0$, $m \leq 0$ and $n = 0$.

Example 2. The example query $Q(x_1, x_2, x_3) = Ill(x_1, Flu) \wedge Ill(x_1, Cough) \wedge Info(x_1, x_2, x_3)$ can be generalized (by anti-instantiating cough with a new variable y) to be $Q_1^{AI}(x_1, x_2, x_3, y) = Ill(x_1, Flu) \wedge Ill(x_1, y) \wedge Info(x_1, x_2, x_3)$. Another possibility (by anti-instantiating one occurrence of x_1 with a new variable y) is the query $Q_2^{AI}(x_1, x_2, x_3, y) = Ill(y, Flu) \wedge Ill(x_1, Cough) \wedge Info(x_1, x_2, x_3)$. Summing all features (predicates, constants, variables, stars and relational) and dividing by 5 gives us the overall average for each similarity measure and for each formula: The first query Q_1^{AI} (with an average Jaccard index of 0.81 and an average α-similarity of 0.84) is ranked very close to the second query Q_2^{AI} (with an average Jaccard index of 0.80 and an average α-similarity of 0.84) because while more constants are lost in Q_1^{AI} more joins are broken in Q_2^{AI}.

Next, we analyze the effect of multiple applications of the AI operator on the similarity values. We have the following monotonicity property: if A is a feature set of the original Q, B is the corresponding feature set of Q^{AI^*}, and C is the corresponding feature set of a query Q^{AI^+} such that Q^{AI^+} can be obtained from Q^{AI^*} by applying more AI steps, then we have that either a) more variables are added in Q^{AI^+} (that is, $B \setminus A \subseteq C \setminus A$) or b) (in case of all other feature sets) more features lost (that is, $A \setminus B \subseteq A \setminus C$). If one of these inclusions is proper, then the similarity of Q^{AI^*} to Q is higher than the similarity of Q^{AI^+}. More formally, for $n = |B \setminus A|$ and $n' = |C \setminus A|$ as well as $m = |A \setminus B|$ and $m' = |A \setminus C|$ and postulating that $n < n'$ or $m < m'$ for any feature, we have that $sim(Q, Q^{AI^*}) > sim(Q, Q^{AI^+})$. Due to this monotonicity property, queries with more anti-instantiations are ranked lower as shown in the following example.

Example 3. We consider two steps of Anti-Instantiations on our example query $Q(x_1, x_2, x_3) = Ill(x_1 \, Flu) \wedge Ill(x_1, Cough) \wedge Info(x_1, x_2, x_3)$. One such generalized query can be $Q^{AI,AI}(x_1, x_2, x_3, y, z) = Ill(y, Flu) \wedge Ill(x_1, z) \wedge Info(x_1, x_2, x_3)$ with two new variables y and z (which is a combination of the two AI steps of Q_1^{AI} and Q_2^{AI}). The query with two anti-instantiations is ranked below the queries with one anti-instantiation: 0.63 for the Jaccard index and 0.73 for α-similarity. Queries with one anti-instantiations would hence preferably answered.

4   Discussion and Conclusion

We applied two similarity measures (Jaccard index and α-similarity) to evaluate the syntactic changes that are executed on conjunctive queries during anti-instantiation and can hence support the database system to intelligently find relevant information for a user. A comprehensive similarity framework that respects all possible combinations of the operators DC, GR and AI (as introduced and analyzed in [1]) is the topic of future work as well as a comparison to related approaches and the consideration of semantic (term-based) similarity.

References

1. Inoue, K., Wiese, L.: Generalizing conjunctive queries for informative answers. In: Christiansen, H., De Tré, G., Yazici, A., Zadrozny, S., Andreasen, T., Larsen, H.L. (eds.) FQAS 2011. LNCS, vol. 7022, pp. 1–12. Springer, Heidelberg (2011)
2. Michalski, R.S.: A theory and methodology of inductive learning. Artificial Intelligence 20(2), 111–161 (1983)
3. Tversky, A.: Features of similarity. Psychological Review 84(4), 327–352 (1977)
4. Ferilli, S., Basile, T.M.A., Biba, M., Mauro, N.D., Esposito, F.: A general similarity framework for horn clause logic. Fundamenta Informaticae 90(1-2), 43–66 (2009)

Towards the Intelligent Home:
Using Reinforcement-Learning for Optimal
Heating Control

Alexander Zenger[1], Jochen Schmidt[1], and Michael Krödel[2]

[1] Fakultät für Informatik, Hochschule Rosenheim, Germany
[2] Fakultät für Angewandte Natur- und Geisteswissenschaften
Hochschule Rosenheim, Germany

Abstract. We propose a reinforcement learning approach to heating control in home automation, that can acquire a set of rules enabling an agent to heat a room to the desired temperature at a defined time while conserving as much energy as possible. Experimental results are presented that show the feasibility of our method.

1 Introduction

By far the most energy in homes is used on heating, one of the main reasons being badly insulated buildings that were constructed before there was any legal obligation to conserve energy. Using home automation technology the energy consumption of buildings can be controlled much more efficiently than by adjusting heating parameters manually. Up to now, mainly model-based methods are used for this purpose, e. g. [2] where a model of environment and building has to be parametrized. Correct modeling is complex and requires expertise on how buildings and rooms behave when heated. As the behavior can change over time due to modifications (e. g., replacing carpet by solid hardwood flooring), the model has to be adjusted accordingly each time. Therefore, adaptable machine learning techniques that do not require model building are an interesting way of dealing with these issues in home automation. Machine learning approaches have been applied in home automation to some degree. For example [4] uses a neural network to learn when inhabitants are at home in order to control residential comfort systems according to their needs. While reinforcement learning is relatively popular in control engineering for designing low-level control units (cf. [1]), to our knowledge, this is the first time reinforcement learning is used in the context described in this paper. Not only is it important that the desired temperature is reached, but also that this is achieved with low energy consumption. The goal is to heat a room, which has cooled-off to a certain temperature, to a defined temperature within a given period of time. This is a typical use-case for office buildings, where the heating is normally ramped down over night to conserve energy. In the morning, when employees arrive at their workplace, room temperature should have reached a pleasant level again. Obviously, as the room cool-off over night, the heating has to be turned on at a certain point: Done

I.J. Timm and M. Thimm (Eds.): KI 2013, LNAI 8077, pp. 304–307, 2013.

too early, this leads to waste of energy and increased heating costs. The optimal moment depends on several factors, e. g., inside and outside temperatures, construction materials, etc., and is different for each room. We propose a system for automatic heating control that acquires a set of rules automatically during normal use. A heating controller is capable of learning actively by executing defined actions. No data collection is required beforehand.

2   Environment Model and Learning

In reinforcement learning, the agent has no a priori knowledge of the environment's behavior. The system learns by trial and error how actions and states are linked. The algorithm used in this paper is SARSA(λ) [5,6], which learns state-action pairs. We reward the learning algorithm only when the final state is reached, therefore a modified version of this method is used as described in [3], where a history of actions and states is stored in each iteration. At the end of an iteration the history is traversed reversely and the utility values are propagated.

After several iterations the system has learned a set of rules that would always be used from there on, as it is the best rated one. A balance is required between exploitation of already learned actions and exploration of new ones. We apply the ϵ-greedy strategy for exploration, where the present solution is used with a probability of $1 - \epsilon$, and a randomly selected action otherwise. At the start, ϵ should be high, so that new rules can be learned quickly. It can be reduced after some solutions have been found based on the residual error.

The system's performance depends highly on the rewards r_i that the agent receives for its actions. We suggest to use the following reward function:

$$r_i = \begin{cases} (r_{i-1}/\alpha) + 0.01\,r_{i-1} & \text{if target temperature reached and end of duration} \\ -0.01 & \text{if target temperature not reached and end of duration} \\ 0.0 & \text{otherwise} \end{cases}$$

$$(1)$$

where α is the learning rate. The "duration" is a defined maximum number of actions that the agent can perform. The design of the reward function (1) is based on the observations that (a) less heating cycles must result in higher rewards and (b) when a better solution is found by the learning algorithm just once, it should result in a positive reward that is high enough for leaving the current range of rewards. To compute a reward for a given index, a suitable initial value r_0 has to be defined. It has to be sufficiently small, so that no overflows are generated, but high enough so that it can be represented by the selected floating point data type. We use a double precision type and $r_0 = 0.01$. This allows for up to 316 iterations, while a negative reward can still be balanced even in the worst case.

For evaluation we used two main setups: One setup is a pure software solution, i. e., there is no actual heating mechanism controlled. This allows for fast simulation of heating and cooling processes, which might take hours or even days in a real environment. The second setup (the *Model Room*) consists of a physical small-scale room model as well as an actual heating element and sensors connected to a home automation controller. Only the latter will be described here. As heating a real room to conduct experiments would not lead to reproducible results due to uncontrollable environment conditions, we use a small scale model room for this purpose instead. Its behavior corresponds to the situation in a real building and requires a pre-heating (or pre-cooling-off) period before experiments are conducted to reach the desired initial room temperature. The model room consist of a styrofoam box, which has insulation characteristics similar to those of a real room. The outside environment is simulated by placing the box inside a refrigerator which lets the model room cool-off over time while not heated. Temperature sensors are mounted inside the box and the refrigerator, respectively. A 15 watt light bulb located in the center of the box is used as the heating element. It can be turned off and on by a controller that also collects temperature information and is connected to a Unix server running the AI software. We use a WAGO controller [7], which is a standard component for process or building automation.

3   Experimental Results

To evaluate the presented system, we conducted different experiments; only one will be described here. Each experiment consists of a number of iterations. A single iteration corresponds to a complete run heating up the room starting at a defined initial temperature of 8.0°C to a target temperature of 15.0°C. In each iteration, the agent has a defined number of steps where actions can be taken. The number of steps is called duration further on. The set of possible actions consists of turning the heating element on or off. Every experiment begins with an empty data set, which means the agent has no previous knowledge and thus has to learn everything anew. Rewards are computed according to (1) using r_0 for initialization. The minimum heating cycles in the first iteration are initialized using the duration value of 10 steps. To accelerate and improve the learning process, the ϵ parameter is varied as follows: For the first 100 iterations we increased ϵ to a value of 0.8, thus allowing the agent to explore more. Then ϵ was decreased to 0.01, and the algorithm ran another 123 iterations, thereby letting the agent exploit the recently learned data and generate a stable outcome (100 iterations for learning, and additional 23 iterations to check the validity of the result). Figure 1 (left) shows that the target temperature was reached in about 50% of the cases. The process is depicted in Fig. 1 (right). It shows that the defined temperature is immediately reached and kept after decreasing ϵ at iteration 101. This is because a first solution was already found at iteration 24, and improved at iteration 44 during the intensive exploration phase. As a result the target temperature was reached faster and more often. Further improvement is possible by decreasing ϵ right after the first time a solution was found.

The main advantage of our approach over more traditional model building ones is that it does not require tedious manual adjustments of model parameters, which have to be performed anew for each room, as every one behaves

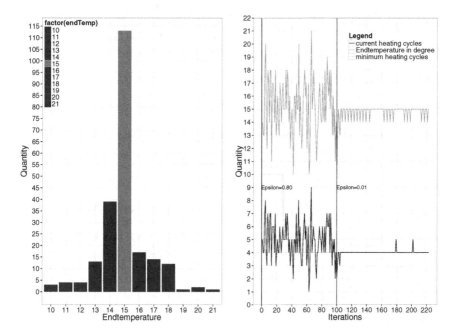

Fig. 1. Left: Reached temperatures histogram. Right: Experiment process.

differently. We have presented experimental results demonstrating that the target temperature is reached and kept over time. Future work will include dynamic adaptions of exploitation and exploration phases, as well as further experiments in real environments, in particular normal size rooms.

References

1. Anderson, C., Hittle, D., Ketchmar, R., Young, P.: Robust reinforcement learning for heating, ventilation, and air conditioning control of buildings. In: Si, J., Barto, A., Powell, W., Wunsch, D. (eds.) Learning and Approximate Dynamic Programming, ch. 20, pp. 517–534. D., John Wiley & Sons (2004)
2. Ellis, C., Hazas, M., Scott, J.: Matchstick: A room-to-room thermal model for predicting indoor temperature from wireless sensor data. In: Proc. of IPSN 2013 (2013)
3. Krödel, M.: Autonome Optimierung des Verhaltens von Fahrzeugsteuerungen auf der Basis von Verstärkungslernen. Ph.D. thesis, Universität Siegen, Germany (2006)
4. Mozer, M.C.: The neural network house: An environment that adapts to its inhabitants. In: Coen, M. (ed.) Proc. of the AAAI Spring Symposium on Intelligent Environments, pp. 110–114. AAAI Press (1998)
5. Rummery, G.A., Niranjan, M.: On-line q-learning using connectionist systems. Tech. rep., University of Cambridge, Department of Engineering (1994)
6. Sutton, R.S., Barto, A.G. (eds.): Reinforcement Learning: An Introduction (Adaptive Computation and Machine Learning). The Mit Press (1998)
7. WAGO Kontakttechnik GmbH & Co. KG., http://www.wago.us

A Prolog-Based Tutor for Multi-column Subtraction with Multiple Algorithms Support
(Software Demonstration)

Claus Zinn

Department of Computer Science, University of Konstanz
Funded by the DFG (ZI 1322/2/1)
claus.zinn@uni-konstanz.de

Abstract. We present an intelligent tutoring system capable of analysing learner input across multiple reference models. Its main component, the diagnoser, is build upon logic programming techniques. It uses a novel variant of Shapiro's algorithmic debugging method, whose scientific aspect is described in our full technical contribution to KI-13 [3]. In this poster, we show the use of the diagnoser in the overall tutoring system.

1   Introduction

Intelligent systems appear intelligent because they are designed to perform in well-defined contexts. This also holds for intelligent tutoring systems (ITSs), where the diagnosis of learner behaviour is best possible in domains that tend to be highly structured, and for which problem solving strategies can be easily represented and executed. It is clear that ITS designers must define the system's domain of instruction, and thus the amount of expertise that it requires. But all too often, the designers also expect learners to solve tasks in the chosen domain by following a single, prescribed algorithm. The actions that learners can perform are further constrained by the design of the system's graphical user interface (GUI) and the design of the interaction. Often, learners are forced to submit their solution in a piece-meal fashion, leaving little room for learners to explore, and deviate from, the solution space on their own.

All constraints have rather practical than pedagogical reasons. They reduce the cost of authoring, and keep manageable the computational complexity of the diagnosis engine. In addition, if learners were allowed to exhibit multiple problem solving strategies, then the system must be capable of identifying the strategy learners are most likely following. With learner input being often erroneous, this task is not trivial.

Our method for the cognitive diagnosis of input is based upon an innovative use of Shapiro's algorithmic debugging technique [1], whose adaptation is described in [2]. Our technical contribution to KI-2013 describes how we extended our method to take into account multiple reference models for the analysis of learner input [3]. As a result, we are able to loosen the tight leash between tutoring system and learner. In this system demonstration paper, we describe the practical use of our method in a prototypical intelligent tutoring system.

I.J. Timm and M. Thimm (Eds.): KI 2013, LNAI 8077, pp. 308–311, 2013.

2   The Domain of Instruction

Our chosen domain of instruction is multi-column subtraction, an area well studied in the intelligent tutoring community. There are several algorithms.

In the *Austrian method*, sums are processed column by column, from right to left. If the subtrahend S of the current column is greater than the column's minuend M, then M is increased by 10 (borrowing) before the difference M-S is taken. To compensate, the S in the column left to the current one is increased by one (payback). The *trade-first* variant of the Austrian method performs the same steps than the Austrian method, but in a different order. First, all payback and borrowing operations are executed, then all differences are taken. The *decomposition* method realizes the payback operation by decrementing minuends rather than incrementing subtrahends. The *left-to-right* method processes sums in the opposite direction; also, payback operations are performed on result rather than minuend or subtrahend cells. – All methods have been implemented in (SWI-)Prolog, see http://www.swi-prolog.org/.

3   The Look and Feel of the Tutoring System

Figure 1 depicts the GUI of our subtraction tutor. It has four main areas.

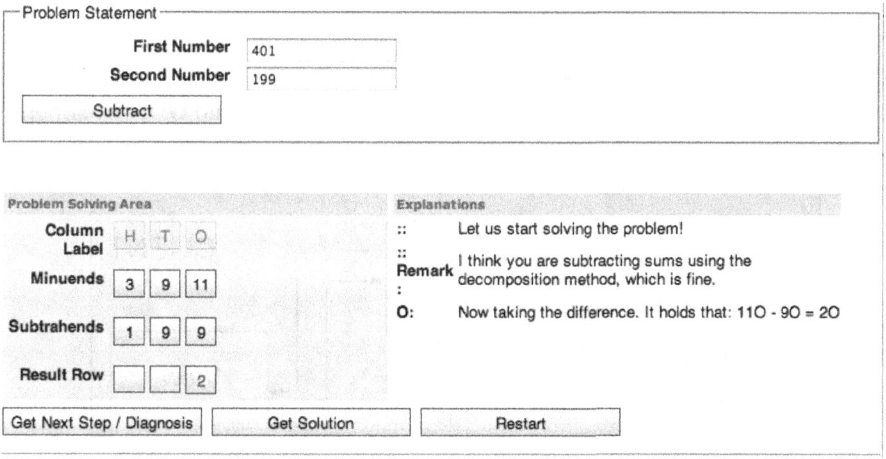

Fig. 1. The Front-End of the Tutoring System

The *problem statement area* (top) allows users to define their own subtraction problems. Unlike other systems, there are no predefined problems that learners *must* choose from. When the user enters two arbitrary integers and presses "Subtract", the problem solving area is automatically generated, with the task to subtract the smaller from the larger number.

The *problem solving area* (middle left) display the subtraction problem as a matrix of four rows. Each column has a label ("ones" (O), "tens" (T), "hundreds" (H) *etc.*) as well as a minuend, subtrahend, and result cell. Learners can interact with all but the label cells, and in arbitrary order. A click on a minuend or subtrahend cell (resp. result cell) opens a number pane with numbers ranging from 0 to 19 (resp. 0 to 9); the learner's selection is entered in the cell.

In the *explanation area* (middle right), learners receive feedback when asking for next-step help, or the diagnosis of their input. All feedback is directly derived from our algorithmic debugger, which determines the first irreducible disagreement between the tutor's expert subtraction method (the best-ranked method, which the system believes the learner is following) and observed learner behaviour [2,3]. System feedback is verbalised using template-based natural language generation. Feedback also involves filling or modifying cells in the subtraction matrix; those are marked red.

In the *command area*, learners can request – at *any time* during problem solving – help or diagnosis, the entire solution to a given problem, or a restart.

The GUI is designed not to favour any particular subtraction method. Learners can perform actions following any of the four subtraction methods, or erroneous variants thereof. Moreover, learners can click on any of the interaction elements at any time; system feedback is only given when learners request it.

4   Technical Architecture

The client-server architecture of our system follows a Model-View-Controller (MVC) design pattern, see Fig. 2. There is, thus, a clear separation of knowledge sources, which supports the division of labour among Prolog and GUI developers.

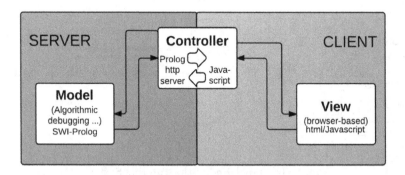

Fig. 2. The Technical Architecture of the Tutoring System

The *model*, hosted on the server, encapsulates an application's business logic or state. In our system, the model is entirely implemented in Prolog. It contains: (i) four modules, each containing one algorithm for multi-column subtraction; (ii) a domain-independent diagnosis module that encodes algorithmic debugging, including the ranking method that identifies the strategy the learner is most likely following [3]; (iii) four modules, each mechanising the Oracle for one of the subtraction algorithms; and (iv) a state handler, which stores the current subtraction task, its solution, and some other state-related information.

The *view*, on the client-side, represents an application's GUI. It displays a representation of the world state, allows users to perform actions to manipulate the state, and displays graphical and textual feedback. It is written in HTML and Javascript and makes use of the Dojo Toolkit `http://dojotoolkit.org/`.

All information flow between the model and the view is mediated by the *controller*. The controller is divided in a client-side (Javascript) and a server-side (Prolog) component. The client-side controller translates a GUI interaction into an HTTP request that is sent to the server-side controller, which translates it to an appropriate request to the model. When the model's answer is received, it is then mediated back from the server-side controller to the client-side controller, which in turn, instructs the view to update its display accordingly.

5   Conclusion and Future Work

We have presented a subtraction tutor that loosens the tight leash between system and learners. Our learners are free to follow one of four possible problem solving strategies; the tutor's GUI and interaction design restricts learners' scope of action as little as possible; and system feedback will only be delivered upon request. In [3], we show that our approach increases the diagnostic capability of the system, despite of the wider range of input that needs to be processed. The computational costs are negligible, permitting the addition of more strategies.

In the future, we would like to adapt the GUI so that school children can comfortably use it. For this, we will include teachers and learners to improve the system's usability. We also envision a system where learners can solve subtraction problems more naturally, and have started integrating a handwriting recognition engine. Ideally, we want users of touch-enabled computer devices to solve problems very close to the natural paper and pencil approach.

System Availability. The subtraction tutor is available at `http://www.inf.uni-konstanz.de/~zinn/`. We have also implemented single-model tutors for each of the subtraction methods. Feedback is highly welcome.

References

1. Shapiro, E.Y.: Algorithmic Program Debugging. ACM Distinguished Dissertations. MIT Press (1983); Thesis (Ph.D.) – Yale University (1982)
2. Zinn, C.: Algorithmic debugging to support cognitive diagnosis in tutoring systems. In: Bach, J., Edelkamp, S. (eds.) KI 2011. LNCS, vol. 7006, pp. 357–368. Springer, Heidelberg (2011)
3. Zinn, C.: Algorithmic debugging for intelligent tutoring: How to use multiple models and improve diagnosis. In: Timm, I.J., Thimm, M. (eds.) KI 2013. LNCS (LNAI), vol. 8077, pp. 272–283. Springer, Heidelberg (2013)

Author Index